School of American Research
Advanced Seminar Series

JONATHAN HAAS, GENERAL EDITOR

The Chemistry of Prehistoric Human Bone

SCHOOL OF AMERICAN RESEARCH ADVANCED SEMINAR SERIES

Published by Cambridge University Press

Dreaming Anthropological and Psychological Interpretations
BARBARA TEDLOCK

The Anasazi in a Changing Environment
GEORGE J. GUMERMAN

Regional Perspectives on the Olmec
ROBERT J. SHARER AND DAVID C. GROVE

Published by the University of New Mexico Press

Reconstructing Prehistoric Pueblo Societies
WILLIAM A. LONGACRE

New Perspectives on the Pueblos
ALFONSO ORTIZ

Structure and Process in Latin America
ARNOLD STRICKON and SIDNEY M. GREENFIELD

The Classic Maya Collapse
T. PATRICK CULBERT

Methods and Theories of Anthropological Genetics
M. H. CRAWFORD and P. L. WORKMAN

Sixteenth-Century Mexico: The Work of Sahagun
MUNRO S. EDMONSON

Ancient Civilization and Trade
JEREMY A. SABLOFF and C. C. LAMBERG-KARLOVSKY

Photography in Archaeological Research
ELMER HARP, JR

Meaning in Anthropology
KEITH H. BASSO and HENRY A. SELBY

The Valley of Mexico: Studies in Pre-Hispanic Ecology and Society
ERIC R. WOLF

Demographic Anthropology: Quantitative Approaches
EZRA B. W. ZUBROW

The Origins of Maya Civilization
RICHARD E. W. ADAMS

Explanation of Prehistoric Change
JAMES N. HILL

Explorations in Ethnoarchaeology
RICHARD A. GOULD

Entrepreneurs in Cultural Context
SIDNEY M. GREENFIELD, ARNOLD STRICKON, and ROBERT T. AUBEY

The Dying Community
ART GALLAHER, JR and HARLAND PADFIELD

Southwestern Indian Ritual Drama
CHARLOTTE J. FRISBIE

Lowland Maya Settlement Patterns
WENDY ASHMORE

Simulations in Archaeology
JEREMY A. SABLOFF

Chan Chan: Andean Desert City
MICHAEL E. MOSELEY and KENT C. DAY

Shipwreck Anthropology
RICHARD A. GOULD

Elites: Ethnographic Issues
GEORGE E. MARCUS

The Archaeology of Lower Central America
FREDERICK W. LANGE and DORIS Z. STONE

Late Lowland Maya Civilization: Classic to Postclassic
JEREMY A. SABLOFF and E. WYLLYS ANDREWS V

THE CHEMISTRY OF PREHISTORIC HUMAN BONE

EDITED BY
T. DOUGLAS PRICE
Department of Anthropology
University of Wisconsin–Madison

A SCHOOL OF AMERICAN RESEARCH BOOK

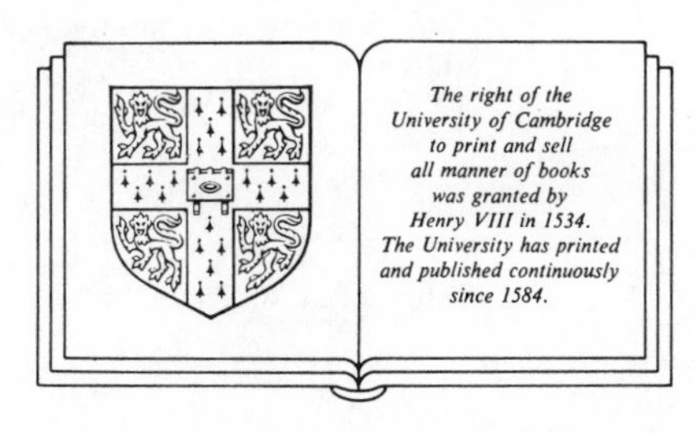
The right of the
University of Cambridge
to print and sell
all manner of books
was granted by
Henry VIII in 1534.
The University has printed
and published continuously
since 1584.

CAMBRIDGE UNIVERSITY PRESS
Cambridge
New York · New Rochelle · Melbourne · Sydney

Published by the Press Syndicate of the University of Cambridge
The Pitt Building, Trumpington Street, Cambridge CB2 1RP
32 East 57th Street, New York, NY 10022, USA
10 Stamford Road, Oakleigh, Melbourne 3166, Australia

First published 1989

Printed in Great Britain at the University Press, Cambridge

British Library cataloguing in publication data

The Chemistry of prehistoric human bone.
1. Prehistoric man. Bones. Chemical
analysis
I. Price, T. Douglas II. Series
573.3

Library of Congress cataloging in publication data

The Chemistry of prehistoric human bone / edited by T. Douglas Price.
p. cm. – (School of American Research advanced seminar series)
"A School of American research book."
Bibliography.
Includes index.
ISBN 0–521–36216–4
1. Bones – Analysis. 2. Animal remains (Archaeology)
3. Archaeological chemistry. I. Price. T. Douglas (Theron Douglas)
II. Series.
CC79.5.A5C48 1989 573.3 – dc19 88–23740 CIP

ISBN 0 521 36216 4

wv

To Glynn Isaac

The School of American Research thanks Marianne and J. Michael O'Shaughnessy for their support of its archaeological publishing program.

Contents

Illustrations

Tables

Contributors

Michael Alcorn
Hampshire College
Amherst, Massachusetts 01002

George J. Armelagos
Department of Anthropology
University of Massachusetts
Amherst, Massachusetts 01003

Barrett Brenton
University of Massachusetts
Amherst, Massachusetts 01003

Jane E. Buikstra
Department of Anthropology
University of Chicago
Chicago, Illinois 60016

M. Pamela Bumsted
Department of Anthropology
University of Auckland
Aukland, New Zealand

Brian S. Chisholm
Archaeology Department
Simon Fraser University
Burnaby, B.C. V5A 1S6, Canada

Jonathon E. Ericson
Program in Social Ecology
University of California
Irvine, California 92717

Susan Frankenberg
Department of Anthropology
Northwestern University
Evanston, Illinois 60201

Harold W. Krueger
Geochron Laboratories
Cambridge, Massachusetts 02139

Joseph B. Lambert
Department of Chemistry
Northwestern University
Evanston, Illinois 60201

Debra Martin
Hampshire College
Amherst, Massachusetts 01002

Nikolaas J. van der Merwe
Peabody Museum
Harvard University
Cambridge, Massachusetts 02138

List of contributors

T. Douglas Price
Department of Anthropology
University of Wisconsin
Madison, Wisconsin 53706

Margaret J. Schoeninger
Department of Anthropology
University of Wisconsin
Madison, Wisconsin 53706

Andrew Sillen
Department of Archaeology
University of Cape Town
Rondebosch 7700, South Africa

Charles H. Sullivan
Geochron Laboratories
Cambridge, Massachusetts 02139

Dennis P. Vangerven
University of Colorado
Boulder, Colorado 90309

Michael West
Los Angeles County Museum of Natural History
Los Angeles, California 90007

Liang Xue
Department of Chemistry
Northwestern University
Evanston, Illinois 60201

Foreword

In the 1950s, radiocarbon dating transformed the discipline of archaeology. After decades of struggling with the problem of chronology, archaeologists found a new, "hard science" technique for obtaining absolute dates on prehistoric sites. This new technique vastly increased the potential for interpreting and understanding the archaeological record.

An equally revolutionary development is maturing in the 1980s: the analysis of bone chemistry. The papers assembled here represent the forefront of the revolution in studies of bone chemistry and human behavior.

When the School of American Research was first approached about the possibility of holding an Advanced Seminar on "Bone Chemistry and Human Behavior," the idea was treated with some skepticism. After all, here was a fairly esoteric subject with a small pool of specialized practitioners. The in-crowd of bone chemistry experts would benefit from a seminar, but would there be any broader ramifications useful to archaeologists and anthropologists in general? Doug Price, Jane Buikstra, and a directed reading list quickly presented a convincing case that there would indeed be dramatic ramifications outside the boundaries of the seminar itself.

What radiocarbon dating did for chronology, bone chemistry studies do for diet. And just as the significance of radiocarbon dating has reached far beyond chronology, bone chemistry's potential stretches far beyond simple dietary reconstruction. Of course, just getting information on diet is a significant contribution alone, as the chapters by Chisholm and Schoeninger illustrate. From the skeletal remains of past populations, we can now gain insight into how much meat people were eating, the proportion of fish to mammals, and the general kinds of plant foods in the diet (see chapter 4). This basic dietary information then can be used to provide new dimensions to studies of status and rank, access to resources, the transition from hunting and gathering to horticulture, the role of domesticated animals in agricultural economies, economic relationships between pastoral nomads and settled village horticulturalists, and similarities or differences in the behavior and nutrition of males and females.

Yet bone chemistry analyses are not limited solely to issues of diet. The chemical composition of bones can also be used to help reconstruct past environments (see chapter 5), and it is at least theoretically possible to begin looking at the movement of populations over the landscape by comparing the elemental and isotopic composition of teeth with that of skeletal bone (Ericson 1981). According to the theory, the chemical composition of teeth is set during childhood and should therefore reflect the area in which a person grew up. In contrast, the chemical composition of skeletal bone continues to change throughout a person's lifetime and should therefore reflect the area where he or she lived in the years just prior to death. Thus, by comparing the chemical composition of a skeleton's teeth with that of its bones, the analyst should be able to tell whether or not a person grew up in the same area where he or she died. Such analyses, which might show patterns of postmarital residence, migration, or slavery, for example, remain at the level of theory for two major reasons. Indeed, I believe that most of the more general, anthropological applications of bone chemistry remain at the theoretical level for these same two reasons.

First, archaeologists still seem skeptical about the reliability and capability of bone chemistry studies. I think this doubt results partly from the relative newness of the field and partly from lack of understanding of its techniques. The technology of bone chemistry analysis is just developing and is, in fact, the subject of highly specialized investigation by a very few people (see chapters 6 and 7). These people argue vehemently about such recondite subjects as isotopes and elements, diagenesis and collagens. Those of us not privy to their technical expertise are often dazzled, baffled, or discouraged by the mystical lingo of the scientist and can only glimpse the potential contribution of bone chemistry to archaeology. Yet technical obscurity cannot hinder for long the incorporation of the relevant methods and techniques into archaeological research designs. Just as a non-specialist scholar can make regular use of dating techniques without necessarily understanding the physics and chemistry involved, so too can an archaeologist without a Ph.D. in biochemistry make effective use of bone chemistry.

Second, the bone chemistry specialists themselves are far from agreement about what can and cannot be learned by analysing the elemental and isotopic composition of long-buried bone from the prehistoric past (see chapter 8). One of the exciting things about this Advanced Seminar was that points of disagreement could be discussed at length by members of different schools of thought. While they could not always resolve their arguments, they reached considerable consensus about what kinds of data need to be collected and analyses conducted in order to begin answering critical questions in the vibrant new discipline of bone chemistry. The last chapter in this book reflects some of this consensus, and the book as a whole provides a background for understanding not only the debates going on within bone chemistry studies, but also the potential for new insights into patterns of past human behavior.

JONATHAN HAAS
School of American Research

Preface

As an archaeologist interested in the postglacial hunter-gatherers of northwestern Europe, several of the major questions I want to answer are related to past diet. Much of the daily activity of the members of these prehistoric societies must have revolved around the food quest. Any reasonable reconstruction of their lifeways must incorporate such information. My initial investigations of these "Mesolithic" adaptations were carried out in the Netherlands, during and immediately after graduate school. There were numerous concentrations of stone tools and charcoal in the sandy topography of the northern Netherlands. Some information was available on the size of these sites and perhaps the length of occupation, but very little could be learned about the foods that had been consumed or what these people had hunted and gathered. Sandy, acidic soils in this area have prohibited the preservation of the bone and plant remains that might have provided the direct evidence of subsistence.

I then shifted the focus of my investigations to southern Scandinavia, an area renowned for the preservation of prehistoric materials. Excavations along the shoreline of a former inlet on the island of Zealand, north of Copenhagen, uncovered bone, antler, and plant remains – the direct evidence for diet that I had been seeking. This evidence resulted in tabulations of the species that had been present and hunted in the area, but little could actually be said about the relative importance of these foodstuffs in the diet. Foolishly late I realized that even with the preserved food remains themselves, so many factors had intervened between the actual consumption of the food and the excavation of the site that we would never be able to accurately reconstruct past subsistence practices simply from the identification of materials in the ground.

I continued and fortunately remembered a bit of research from graduate school in Ann Arbor in the early 1970s. Tonie Brown, a fellow student, had begun some studies concerning the chemistry of prehistoric bone, particularly regarding the amounts of the element strontium in bone, in relation to diet. I began to read more recent studies on the subject. Investigations by Bender, van der Merwe, Schoeninger, Sillen, and others by the end of the 1970s were beginning to document the potential of such techniques of analysis. With the assistance of the Graduate School Research Committee at the University of Wisconsin, I was able to initiate a series of similar chemical analyses of human skeletal remains. This project by now includes a large number of samples from different time periods in the United States, Africa, and Europe, and we are beginning to develop a reasonable picture of diet among various groups of hunter-gatherers and early farmers.

These investigations have been rewarding and enjoyable. Archaeological data from the ground are very fragmentary and somewhat "soft." Interpretation of these remains is often highly speculative, uncertain, and somewhat frustrating. For myself, the more objective and quantitative data that derive from the chemical analyses of bone have provided a welcome complement to the more subjective character of most archaeological data. In addition, the interface between biological anthropology, archaeology, and chemistry provides a number of new avenues for research and thought. Such research has made possible an association with a wider range of colleagues in each field.

This volume has resulted from one of the more pleasant aspects of this research on bone chemistry – a research seminar on the subject at the School of American Research in Santa Fe, New Mexico. This seminar emphasized the conjunction of the fields of archaeology, biological anthropology, and chemistry, bringing together a group of specialists to consider a common issue. Discussions concerned both the practical and theoretical connections between the chemical composition of bone and past human behavior. Topics included the nature of early hominid subsistence, the evolution of human subsistence, male versus female diets, marine versus terrestrial diets, the importance of plants versus meat in the diet, and the transition to agriculture. The significance of prehistoric bone as a bearer of paleoecological signals for past climate and environment was also emphasized.

Other aspects of the discussions at the seminar focused on problem areas in this new field: the development of comparable procedures for analysis, the utilization of interlaboratory reference materials, and the determination of additional sources of variation in the chemistry of human bone, with particular emphasis on post-depositional chemical changes. Comparability in methods of analysis and in the reporting of results offers a major advance toward more productive investigations. Agreement on the use of a common reference material for all laboratories and a request for a bone tissue standard from the National Bureau of Standards emerged at the seminar.

There was consensus at the seminar that too little is known regarding the sources of variation in the composition of human bone. While it is clear that environment and diet are major contributors, other biological and natural factors are also important. Differences within a population due to metabolism, age, gender, or reproductive status need to be investigated more thoroughly. Variation within a single bone, between teeth and bone, or within the skeleton of a single individual is also an important area for investigation. Diagenetic changes (post-depositional chemical alterations) are apparent in most studies of prehistoric bone and cannot be ignored. It is clear that evidence from a variety of archaeological contexts must be considered in order to understand the effects of diagenesis on the reconstruction of past diet. Methods for the measurement of diagenetic changes, including an emphasis on a multi-element approach, were considered at the seminar. New directions for research include the examination of other elements and isotopes as potential indicators of past diet and behavior.

A number of people contributed to the success of the seminar and this subsequent volume. The School of American Research provided the funding and format for the session meeting and an ideal location for the lengthy and rewarding discussions that ensued. The research director of the School, Jonathan Haas, and his staff spent a number of days in preparation for the session and in caring for the bone composition of the participants. Jane Kepp, the editor at SAR, has helped to make this manuscript a coherent whole, both quickly and competently. Thanks are due as well to the president of the School, Doug Schwartz, for his interest and support.

It is apparent that the study of archaeological bone chemistry is at a turning point, in transition from an experimental procedure to a major research technique. The seminar at Santa Fe may well have provided the essential groundwork to ensure that such investigations move on a firm footing and in extraordinary new directions. Many of the participants arrived in Santa Fe emphasizing the problems that have arisen, but virtually everyone left the seminar with renewed optimism and excitement about the potential for such investigations. Certainly there is justification for enthusiasm for a methodology that will provide greater resolution for our view of the human past.

DOUGLAS PRICE
Department of Anthropology
University of Wisconsin–Madison

1
Bones, chemistry, and the human past

T. DOUGLAS PRICE

Department of Anthropology
University of Wisconsin–Madison

The human skeleton is much more than a structural framework for supporting our bodies. Bone tissue also contains a wide variety of information about the individual to whom it is attached. The length and thickness of bone, for example, provides an indication of the size and strength of an individual. Traces of disease or illness are often embedded in bone structure as well. The chemistry of bone contains a number of signals about the environment in which an individual lived. Bone chemistry has been used for chronological determinations (e.g. Cook and Heizer 1953, Middleton 1844, Oakley 1955), for the study of the process of fossilization (e.g. Barber 1939, Cook 1951), and of past climates and environments (e.g. Rottländer 1976, van der Merwe, this volume).

The investigation of the chemical content of bone for the reconstruction of past diet, however, is a relatively recent development. Several recent reviews (Klepinger 1984, Price *et al.* 1985b, Sillen and Kavanagh 1982) provide an overview of bone chemistry and paleonutrition. Aspects of past subsistence such as the importance of marine and terrestrial components in the diet, the contribution of plants versus animals, the presence of certain species of plants or animals, and more, can now be estimated using more rigorous, quantitative techniques involving the chemical composition of bone.

It is the purpose of the present volume to provide chemists and anthropologists – particularly archaeologists and biological anthropologists – with some indications of the basic principles and recent research directions in bone chemistry. The chapters that follow this brief introduction are the result of a seminar held at the School of American Research in Santa Fe, New Mexico, in 1986. They provide information on both the promise and the problems of research into the chemical composition of prehistoric human and animal bone. They offer case studies as examples and, more specifically, address problems and questions raised by bone chemistry research. The chapters by Chisholm and Schoeninger consider the isotopic evidence for past diet. Ericson *et al.* provide an outstanding case study of dietary reconstruction using a variety of both isotopic and elemental information. Van der Merwe documents the paleoecological significance of carbon isotopes in the reconstruction of past environments and climate. Chapters by Price and Buikstra *et al.* consider the multi-elemental composition of bone and its relationship to both diagenetic and dietary factors. Sillen considers the question of diagenesis from a physiological and chemical perspective and outlines an important procedure for the removal of diagenetic effects. Some of the biological factors affecting the elemental and isotopic composition of bone are outlined by Armelagos in the penultimate paper in this volume. A series of conclusions, questions, and directions for future research make up the final chapter, authored by the entire seminar group.

THE STUDY OF PREHISTORIC SUBSISTENCE

There is today a definite resurgence of interest in past human diet, buoyed no doubt by current concerns with health and fitness. The quest for food directed and conditioned many aspects of prehistoric human society, including group size and social organization, residence patterns and settlement location, tool manufacture and technology, and transportation. Information on past diet is essential to characterize the trophic position of prehistoric human populations, the utilization of the environment, the determinants of site placement, the nature of subsistence activities, status differentiation, and the like.

Existing evidence for diet comes from a number of lines of research: faunal analysis, paleoethnobotany, fecal studies, dental studies of wear and the frequency of caries, physical anthropology, ethnographic analogy, and quantitative modeling. Closer consideration, however, reveals serious deficiencies in each of these methods. The vast majority of archaeological sites do *not* contain preserved organic materials or any trace of food remains. Only in unusual circumstances do conditions of soil acidity and/or moisture content provide for the preservation of plant and animal remains. Even in situations of good preservation, such remains are never sufficiently well discarded or deposited to provide an accurate picture of what was actually consumed (Carbone and Keel 1985). The highly visible residues of certain foods – particularly animal bones, mollusc shells, and nutshells – bias archaeological interpretations in favor of these more durable categories. The fragile and ephemeral nature of many food remains renders them less visible and significant in reconstructions of past diet.

Studies of stature and other skeletal indicators can provide information on the quality of the diet. For example, there appears to be a significant decline in human stature from the Upper Paleolithic to the Neolithic (Frayer 1980, Meiklejohn *et al.* 1984) but little is known of the reasons for this decrease. Studies of dentition and caries have been used for a number of years as indicators of diet and nutrition (e.g. Christopherson and Pedersen 1939) but without clear resolution. Meiklejohn *et al.* (1984:87) observe that rates of dental caries suggest marked dietary differences between the Mesolithic and the Neolithic but specific causes are unknown. Dental caries are less common in the Mesolithic, perhaps as a result of greater tooth wear. Other dental attributes from this period indicate stress.

Predictive models provide intriguing patterns for possible dietary and subsistence arrangements (e.g. Jochim 1976, Winterhalder 1986). Jochim (1976), for example, utilized certain characteristics of various food sources, such as weight, density, mobility, and non-food value, to estimate their relative importance during the south German Mesolithic. Although such formulations appear precise, they are in fact based upon a variety of assumptions and missing data. These projections are dependent upon extant archaeological evidence for the list of food categories to include and they exhibit a pronounced meat bias. Further, such estimates are completely unverifiable given the present state of our knowledge. Thus, predictive models may be informative but do not provide reliable estimates of past diet.

T. DOUGLAS PRICE

BONE CHEMISTRY AND DIET

Bone is a dynamic, cellular tissue with both structural and physiological functions. These activities require a complex substance. Bone tissue is essentially a network of mineralized fibers, composed of a matrix of organic collagen filled with inorganic calcium phosphate (hydroxyapatite) crystals. Bone contains three major components: a mineral fraction (bone ash), an organic matrix (collagen), and water. By dry weight, organic materials constitute about 30% and minerals about 70% of bone. Collagen, a protein, comprises 90% of the organic portion of dry, fat-free bone. In addition to the major components – calcium, phosphate, and water – a number of minor and trace elements are incorporated during the manufacture of bone tissue. Both the *elemental* and the *isotopic* composition of bone have been considered in studies concerned with dietary reconstruction. Isotopic studies concentrate on the organic part of bone (collagen) while elemental analyses focus on the mineral portion (apatite).

Isotopic analyses

Isotopic analysis to date has concentrated on carbon and nitrogen. While the amount of these *elements* in bone is under strict metabolic control, the ratios of stable *isotopes* ($^{13}C/^{12}C$ and $^{15}N/^{14}N$) in bone collagen reflect the ratios found in the diet and in nature. A scientific instrument such as a mass spectrometer is used to measure these isotopic ratios in collagen.

The interpretation of carbon isotopic ratios in bone collagen is relatively straightforward. Diagenesis – post-depositional chemical change in bone – does not appear to alter isotopic ratios. Individual variability in isotope ratios is due largely to diet as the reservoirs of carbon isotopes in the sea and in the atmosphere are constant. Carbon isotope ratios are reported in terms of $\delta^{13}C$ values (see the chapter by Chisholm, below) that generally increase along a continuum from plants, to herbivores, to carnivores in both marine and terrestrial regimes.

Carbon isotope ratios in human bone have been used to distinguish the consumption of marine versus terrestrial organisms in the diet. The $^{13}C/^{12}C$ ratio in seawater bicarbonate is higher than in atmospheric carbon dioxide. These differences are observed in the plants that inhabit the two regimes, as well as in the bone collagen of animals that feed on these species. Tauber (1981), Chisholm *et al.* (1982), and Schoeninger *et al.* (1983) have used this phenomenon to distinguish marine and terrestrial organisms in the human diet. In addition, many tropical grasses such as sorgum, millet, amaranth, and maize (designated as C_4 species) utilize a photosynthetic pathway that efficiently metabolizes carbon dioxide by initial conversion to a four-carbon compound which incorporates more available ^{13}C. The C_3 plants, which are more common in temperate areas, produce a three-carbon compound. The carbon isotope ratios in the bone collagen of animals feeding on three- or four-carbon plants reflect the differences in the two categories. This principle has been used by Vogel and van der Merwe (1977), Bender *et al.* (1981), and others to study the introduction of corn into prehistoric North America.

Hayden *et al.* (1987) have used the carbon isotope analysis of human bone from Upper Paleolithic sites in southwestern France to examine questions regarding the importance of salmon in the diet. Various authors have suggested that intensive salmon harvesting may have been responsible in part for the complexity witnessed in the Upper Paleolithic in this area. Use of these anadromous fish would have resulted in a reflection of marine resources in the carbon isotope ratios of human bone. Carbon isotope ratios indicated that marine foods were not important in the diet in this area.

Stable isotope ratios of nitrogen ($^{15}N/^{14}N$) in animal bone reflect the ratio in diet. Three major classes of organisms can be distinguished using nitrogen isotopes (DeNiro and Schoeninger 1983, Schoeninger 1985): (1) nitrogen-fixing plants and the animals that feed on those plants, (2) terrestrial food chains not involved in nitrogen-fixation, and (3) marine foods not based on nitrogen-fixation. Freshwater systems may constitute another class but are not yet well documented. Given this information, it should be possible to examine human bone to distinguish groups whose diets are based largely on leguminous plants, marine, or terrestrial (non-leguminous) foods. To date, however, studies of nitrogen isotope ratios in archaeological materials are rare (e.g. Farnsworth *et al.* 1985, Schoeninger *et al.* 1983). Examination of both carbon and nitrogen isotopes in human bone from Tehuacan, Mexico, by Farnsworth *et al.* (1985) indicated that consumption of tropical grasses began much earlier than is evidenced in the archaeological remains.

Elemental analyses

Concern with the by-products from nuclear testing during the 1950s initiated intensive investigations of the relationship between bone chemistry and diet. Strontium^{90}, a harmful radioactive isotope produced by fission weapons testing, appeared in substantial quantities in milk and other foods and in the human skeleton. Studies of the movement of both the Sr isotopes and the whole element through the food chain indicated that the element was differentially distributed as a consequence of certain physiological and/or dietary processes. For example, the amount of strontium in vegetation varies by plant part and species. This information was used initially to distinguish browsing and grazing diets among fossil herbivores through the analysis of strontium in their bones. In animals, approximately 99% of all body strontium is deposited in bone tissue.

Clear differences in bone strontium levels also can be seen along the food chain. Marine fish and shellfish exhibit quite high levels of strontium due to the higher mineral content of ocean waters. Lower strontium levels are found in freshwater fish and shellfish. Plants concentrate strontium in roots and lower leaves but some species of nuts also contain high levels of strontium. Terrestrial herbivores incorporate only about 20–25% of the strontium they ingest in bone tissue. Carnivores both consume less strontium in their diets and also discriminate metabolically against it. Thus, the bones of herbivores and carnivores can be distinguished by strontium content. Omnivores fall between the two extremes, depending upon the amount of plant food in their diet.

Human bone strontium levels represent a contribution from various foods, with marine animals and plants contributing higher levels of strontium. Human bone is completely remodeled over a period of five to ten years so that chemical information on diet represents a composite summary. Brown (1973) first employed the principle of strontium flow in the food chain for the investigation of past *human* subsistence. Strontium analysis since has been used to examine the relative contribution of plants and animals to prehistoric diets (e.g. Price and Kavanagh 1982, Sillen 1981b), marine versus terrestrial foods in subsistence (Connor and Slaughter 1984, Nelson *et al.* 1983a), the transformation from hunting-gathering to agriculture (Schoeninger 1982, Sillen

1981b), the relationship between status and diet (Lambert *et al.* 1979, Schoeninger 1979b), and the age of weaning (Sillen and Smith 1985).

PROBLEMS

Bone chemistry appears to be a major new technique for the investigation of prehistoric human subsistence. However, the promise and potential of this research tool are as yet unfulfilled. The method is still in an experimental stage and a number of questions remain to be resolved regarding other possible sources of variation. Questions regarding the proportion of plants and animals in the diet have not been resolved as yet. Studies relating status to diet remain questionable because of uncontrolled variables. Diet and the environment are the major sources of strontium in human bone. Local environmental levels of natural strontium determine the total amount of strontium available to the food chain. Differences in strontium levels among local populations may be due to natural levels of strontium in the lithosphere. The composition of diet, i.e. the proportion of plants versus meat, determines the amount of strontium entering the blood stream and bone tissue. Two additional sources of variation, individual differences and diagenesis, must be better understood, however, before bone chemistry can begin to portray past dietary practices accurately.

Individual variability within a population is relatively high, with a coefficient of variation (c.v.) ranging between 20% and 35% (Price *et al.* 1985b, Schoeninger 1979). Sources for this variability include age, sex, and individual metabolism. Strontium levels in bone increase slightly with age (Sowden and Stitch 1957). Lambert *et al.* (1979) found that relative concentrations of strontium, sodium, and zinc decreased in childhood, increased during adolescence, remained generally stable between the ages of 20 and 50, and showed a slight increase in individuals over 50. Tanaka *et al.* (1981) have reported a gradual increase in strontium levels with age. Because of high variation in strontium levels among sub-adults, most paleodietary studies have concentrated on the bones of individuals older than eighteen years of age.

Nor are sex-related differences within a population adequately documented. Early tests on modern bone samples indicated no differences (Turekian and Kulp 1956). Tanaka *et al.* (1981) reported very little difference between modern males and females in Japan. However, Snyder *et al.* (1964) recorded significant differences in a study of U.S. males and females between the ages of 20 and 59. Lambert *et al.* (1979) observed statistically higher strontium levels in males in the Late Woodland period in Illinois than were noted among earlier Middle Woodland burials.

The effects of diagenesis are not well understood. Studies of diagenesis to date have been contradictory. Toots and Voorhies (1965), Parker and Toots (1970, 1980), and others have argued that no significant post-mortem changes in bone strontium levels occur. Sillen (1981), on the other hand, examined strontium concentrations in herbivore and carnivore bone from Aurignacian levels in Israel and observed no significant difference between the two classes of animals. The absence of an expected difference was suggested to be due to the equilibrating effects of diagenesis. Lambert *et al.* (1982, 1985a) have considered chemical differences between trabecular and cortical bone and between soil and bone to study diagenesis. The absence of difference in strontium levels between ribs and femurs, and between soil and bone, suggested that strontium was generally stable in the depositional environment.

In most studies of diagenesis, however, experimental conditions have not been well designed for the examination of changes in bone strontium during burial. Strontium levels appear unaffected in some depositional contexts and dramatically changed in others (Pate and Brown 1985, White and Hannus 1983). This question is addressed at length in subsequent chapters by Price, Buikstra *et al.*, and Sillen. In essence, diagenetic changes in bone strontium and other elements are probable in virtually all depositional contexts and must be considered in the reconstruction of past diet.

CONCLUSIONS

Isotopic and elemental analyses are in a developmental stage as means for the investigation of prehistoric diet. Nitrogen isotope analysis has only rarely been applied to date. Carbon isotope analyses have documented the importance of maize or marine resources in the diet. Elemental analyses of bone strontium have indicated the importance of terrestrial or marine resources as well as the relative contribution of meat to the diet. The importance of foods such as freshwater fish, shellfish, and plants in past human diets remains difficult to assess.

A number of other elements may become important as indicators of paleodiets as more is learned regarding their physiological behavior and depositional stability in bone. Barium, copper, and magnesium have not yet been examined in depth. Barium resembles strontium in its passage through the food chain and in distinguishing trophic levels in terrestrial and marine systems. Animals and certain seafoods are better sources of copper than are plants. Magnesium is generally found in higher concentrations in plant foods, but the effects of diagenesis on this element are not yet clear. A number of ultratrace elements have yet to be considered.

Through the investigation of these and other elements and isotopes in bone, the next decade may well provide the essential chemical keys to past human diets as well as paleoenvironmental conditions. In conjunction with the continued study of faunal assemblages, paleoethnobotany, and physical anthropology, bone chemistry brings the precise reconstruction of prehistoric subsistence and environment much closer to reality.

2

Variation in diet reconstructions based on stable carbon isotopic evidence

BRIAN S. CHISHOLM

Archaeology Department
Simon Fraser University

There are a number of questions that may be addressed, at least in part, through dietary reconstructions, including (1) what foods were available and used by prehistoric societies, (2) in what relative proportions were the various foods present in the diet, and (3) did these proportions vary through time and space or between and within populations?

The first question is qualitative in nature and is usually dealt with through examination of preserved food remains, and the tools used in their procurement and preparation. The remaining two questions are quantitative in nature and are more difficult to answer. However, such answers are essential to address questions relating to the broader arena of human behavior and its relationship to the food quest. In order to obtain useful data that may address these questions, it is clear that a degree of accuracy and precision greater than that found in presence–absence data is required. It would be desirable to determine small-scale differences, on the order of only a few percent, between adjacent sampling areas and sites. In practice such resolution may be impossible to achieve, but we should be able to see differences on the order of 5 to 10 percent.

Recently, the stable isotope analysis of carbon and nitrogen in prehistoric human bone has been applied in an attempt to address these quantitative questions. The majority of these studies have been restricted to identifying the presence or absence of certain alternatives in local diets, and thus to detect shifts in diet through time. Only a few studies have dealt with the relative proportions in which the alternatives are present, and fewer yet have dealt with, or indicated, the magnitude of any errors associated with the analysis, beyond the accuracy and precision of the actual isotopic measurements themselves.

The following discussion attempts to address the problems of proportion determinations, and of variability in the results. To date most studies done have concentrated on stable carbon isotopes and they are considered here. Nitrogen isotope studies are becoming more common and will need to be considered in the same manner since many of the same problems will exist.

THE CARBON ISOTOPE TECHNIQUE

Within the last decade the analysis of stable isotopes of carbon (and nitrogen) in preserved bone has provided a new method for studying both modern and past environments and diets. This technique has been used in both laboratory and field studies to examine the relationship between a consumer and its diet (Bender *et al.* 1981, DeNiro and Epstein 1978b, 1981, Macko *et al.* 1982a,b, Schoeninger and DeNiro 1984, Terri and Schoeller 1979, Tieszen *et al.* 1979a,b, 1983, Vogel 1978, and others), to determine herbivore foraging behavior in both recent (DeNiro and Epstein 1978a, Tieszen *et al.* 1979a,b, Vogel 1978) and archaeological or paleontological contexts (Bombin and Muehlenbachs 1985, Chisholm *et al.* n.d.), and to determine the presence of maize (or other C_4 species of plants) in prehistoric diets (Bender *et al.* 1981, Broida 1983, Bumsted 1984, Burleigh and Brothwell 1978, DeNiro and Epstein 1981, Katzenberg 1984, Lynott *et al.* 1986, Norr 1981, Schwarcz *et al.* 1985, van der Merwe and Vogel 1978, van der Merwe *et al.* 1981, and others). Marine versus terrestrial comparisons have been reported for archaeological and recent samples (Chisholm *et al.* 1982, 1983c, Hayden *et al.* 1987, Hobson and Collier 1984, Schoeninger and DeNiro 1984, Schoeninger *et al.* 1983, Sealy and van der Merwe 1985, Tauber 1979, 1981).

The theory underlying the method of stable carbon isotope analysis has been explained by DeNiro and Epstein (1978b), van der Merwe and Vogel (1978), and others for dietary maize determinations, and by

Chisholm *et al.* (1982, 1983c) for marine versus terrestrial comparisons. O'Leary (1981) has provided an overview of carbon isotope behavior in plants. The technique has been reviewed by van der Merwe (1982) and only a brief outline is provided here.

Isotope fractionation is the selection for or against one or more isotopes of an element during the course of a chemical or physical reaction. As a result there is a change in the relative concentration of the isotopes involved in the reaction. In this case we are concerned with the ratio of carbon-13 to carbon-12. Ratios for samples are compared to the ratio for a standard and the results are expressed, in parts per mil (‰), as follows:

$$\delta^{13}C(‰) = \left[\frac{(^{13}C/^{12}C)_{sample}}{(^{13}C/^{12}C)_{standard}} - 1 \right] \times 1000$$

A negative value indicates a sample that is depleted in ^{13}C relative to the standard, i.e. it is isotopically "lighter." The standard is the Pee Dee Belemnite (PDB) from South Carolina. Carbon isotope measurements are taken on carbon dioxide using a dual-beam isotope-ratio mass spectrometer. Sample preparation involves cleaning, separation of the required carbon-containing components, and combustion to obtain the required CO_2.

Carbon, found in the atmosphere as CO_2 with a virtually constant $^{13}C/^{12}C$ ratio of about 1:99, is incorporated into plant tissues via photosynthesis. Isotopic fractionation takes place during this process, altering the $^{13}C/^{12}C$ ratio. Most plants use the Calvin–Benson, or C_3, photosynthetic pathway, which generates a molecule containing three carbon atoms (phosphoglyceric acid) as its first intermediate product. This group includes most of the flowering plants, trees, and shrubs, and most of the temperate zone grasses. C_4, or Hatch–Slack, plants follow a pathway that incorporates the CO_2 carbon into a four-carbon molecule (oxaloacetate) as the first photosynthesis intermediate. This group is represented in about ten plant families and the majority of species are xeric environment grasses. Of particular interest are maize, some millets, some sorghums, cane sugar, some amaranths, and some chenopods. A third group, the Crassulacean Acid Metabolism (CAM) plants, is made up of tropical succulents, such as pineapple and various cacti, few of which are found in any quantity in the diet of herbivores or humans. Marine plants approximate the C_3 cycle but obtain their carbon from dissolved oceanic bicarbonates which have isotope ratio values differing from atmospheric CO_2.

Because the photosynthetic pathways differ chemically they produce different degrees of isotopic fractionation. This observation has been used to classify species as being either C_3, C_4, or CAM. Values averaging about $\delta^{13}C = -26.5‰$ characterize modern C_3 plants, while modern C_4 species values average about $-12.5‰$ (O'Leary 1981, Smith and Epstein 1971, van der Merwe 1982, Vogel 1978, and others). The separation of about 14‰ between the group averages allows for discrimination between them. Modern marine plankton have values averaging about $\delta^{13}C = -19.0‰$ (Brown *et al.* 1972, Degens *et al.* 1968, Deuser *et al.* 1968, Sackett *et al.* 1965, and others).

When either terrestrial or marine herbivores eat plants, their metabolism selects and recombines plant chemicals, resulting in further fractionation of the carbon isotopes. While the whole body average value of a consumer is displaced from its diet by only $0.8 \pm 1.1‰$ (DeNiro and Epstein 1978b), the increment between the diet and bone collagen of the consumers, called the "collagen enrichment factor," or "ΔDC," appears to be about 5‰ (Chisholm *et al.* 1982, 1983, van der Merwe 1982). This means that the bone collagen from a modern herbivore subsisting solely on C_3 grasses will give a value for $\delta^{13}C$ of $(-26.5 + 5)‰$ or $-21.5‰$. If the diet were based solely on C_4 grasses then the value would be $-7.5‰$. Thus the 14‰ spread is maintained at the consumer's level. In the case of the carnivores or omnivores, including humans, in the next trophic level, a further fractionation of about 1‰ from the diet average has been reported (Bender *et al.* 1981, DeNiro and Epstein 1978b, McConnaughey and McRoy 1979, Schoeninger 1985, Tieszen *et al.* 1983), provided the same tissue is examined (e.g. herbivore and carnivore muscle, or herbivore and carnivore collagen). However, owing to the low numbers of samples examined and the uncertainties which, when given, are larger than the increment itself, the difference between trophic levels cannot be considered adequately demonstrated yet. If the value of about 1‰ is correct then carnivores subsisting upon either of the above two herbivore types would have values for bone collagen of $-20.5‰$ and $-6.5‰$ for the C_3 and C_4 herbivore alternatives respectively. We would also expect human tissues to be displaced by 1‰ from similar tissues of their dietary species (Fig. 2.1). Using these values we may construct a table of expected values for the trophic levels of various food chains

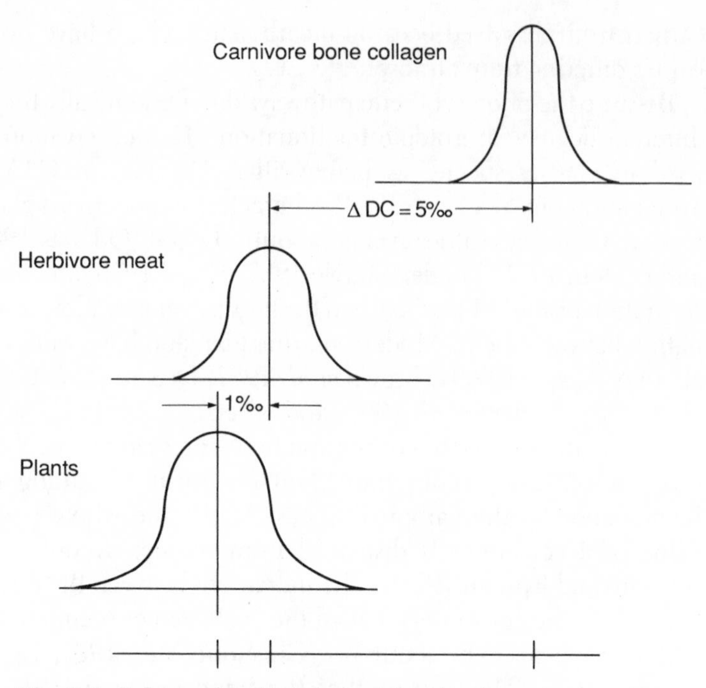

Fig. 2.1 Relationship between trophic levels

(Table 2.1) in order to illustrate their general relationship. Of course, these may be altered by changes in the values for the oceanic and atmospheric carbon reservoirs, or by dietary mixing, etc.

Based on these values, if a modern consumer samples both C_3 and C_4 species, then the $\delta^{13}C$ value for its collagen will lie somewhere between the extremes of −21.5‰ and −7.5‰. A simple linear interpolation, locating the sample value between the two extremes, will result in an estimate of the proportionate amounts of C_3 and C_4 species in that particular consumer's diet (Fig. 2.2). For example, a value of $\delta^{13}C = -11.0$‰, which is $\frac{3}{4}$ of the way toward the C_4 extreme from the C_3 extreme, will indicate a diet that is 75% C_4 for that particular consumer. A similar approach may be taken for any other pair of dietary alternatives.

In archaeological situations, bone collagen extract (commonly called gelatin) is analysed because it is the only organic tissue that is reliably preserved in sufficient quantity for analysis. Since bone collagen turnover is slow, taking at least ten years for complete replacement

Table 2.1. *Predicted collagen values for consumers of specific diets*

Diets and their $\delta^{13}C$ averages (‰)		Consumer collagen (‰)
C_3 plants only	(–26.5)	–21.5
Meat from herbivores on C_3 diets	(–25.5)	–20.5
C_4 plants only	(–12.5)	– 7.5
Meat from herbivores on C_4 diets	(–11.5)	– 6.5
Marine plankton only	(–19.5)	–14.5
Meat from marine herbivores	(–18.5)	–13.5
Meat from marine carnivores	(–17.5)	–12.5

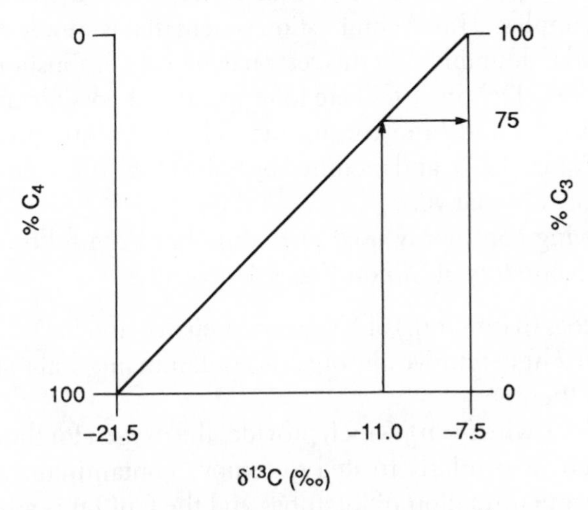

Fig. 2.2 Interpreting proportions from $\delta^{13}C$ values

(Libby *et al.* 1964, Stenhouse and Baxter 1979), seasonal and other short-term variations average out. The measurement obtained may therefore represent a lifetime average for the individual sampled.

VARIATION IN ANALYSIS

This discussion considers the stages at which variation may be introduced into stable carbon isotopic ratios, starting with the methods of analysis themselves and proceeding to the materials analysed, i.e., the actual collagen and the dietary species that contribute carbon to that collagen, and concluding with data interpretation and other theoretical problems, some relating to the $\delta^{13}C$ values given above.

The most straightforward and most easily controlled variation relating to the analysis of carbon isotope content in bone is associated with sample combustion and measurement. The major considerations in sample combustion are that (1) the combustion products include those that are desired for analysis, (2) carbon from the samples is not distributed through a number of combustion products, but that it all goes into only the desired product (in this case CO_2), and (3) the combustion is complete so that there is no chance for fractionation due to incomplete conversion of the sample.

For archaeological studies it is usually necessary to handle large numbers of samples. Thus a combustion system that is simple, inexpensive, and rapid is desirable. For this reason dynamic combustion systems (e.g. Craig 1953, DeNiro 1977) are to be avoided if possible as they are relatively complex and time consuming. The technique proposed by Stump and Fraser (1973) and modified by Sofer (1980) provides a simple and satisfactory alternative.

The following commonly used procedure has been followed in the radiocarbon laboratory at Simon Fraser University:

(1) tubes (6 mm o.d.) of Vycor are prepared and baked at 900 °C for 2 hr to remove any organic contaminants that may adhere to them;
(2) CuO (wire form), which provides the oxygen for the combustion, is similarly treated to remove contaminants (to avoid recontamination of the tubes and the CuO it is advisable to store them under vacuum and perhaps over a dessicant until use);
(3) appropriate quantities of sample (typically about 5 mg) are loaded into the Vycor tubes along with about 1 gm of the prepared CuO;
(4) the sample tubes are evacuated (*ca.* 2×10^{-3} torr) and sealed; and
(5) loaded tubes are baked at 900 °C for 2 hr in a preheated oven and then allowed to cool slowly in the oven before removal, usually overnight. The samples are then ready for analysis.

Analysis of the gases resulting from the combustion has shown that the only carbon-containing gas present is CO_2 (T. Brown, Simon Fraser

University, personal communication). We have not observed any SO_2 to be present, but have seen indications of native sulfur and $CuSO_4$ remaining in the sample tubes. Although we have not had any problems, it may be beneficial to use a small amount of pure Cu or Ag wire to catalyse N_2 formation and aid in removal of sulfur from the gases (Bombin and Muehlenbachs 1985). In some cases, particularly where water vapor is present, it is conceivable that some of the carbon could be diverted to form carbonates or carbonic acid if sample gases are left in the combustion tubes for an extended period (Stuiver *et al.* 1984). Loss of CO_2 to carbonates or other compounds could result in fractionation of the carbon. Of course, this can be tested by determining the CO_2 yields. To avoid this potential problem it is only necessary to ensure that the samples are dry before the tubes are sealed and combusted, and that the combustion and analysis occur within a short period of each other (i.e., the same day). Since most amino acids, peptides, and proteins are hygroscopic to some degree, it will be necessary to use the vacuum system to evaporate off any residual water before sealing the tubes.

In the early stages of our work at Simon Fraser University sample combustion was carried out in borosilicate glass (Pyrex) tubes at 550 °C as suggested by Sofer (1980). DeNiro (1982, personal communication) expressed concern that this temperature might be insufficient to ensure complete combustion of the samples. At that time a comparison of results for the two alternative combustion methods, i.e., in Pyrex at 550 °C and in Vycor at 900 °C was made (Chisholm *et al.* 1982, 1983a). The results of this comparison are repeated in Table 2.2.

Although our results, and those of Sofer (1980), indicate that there is no significant difference between the two methods, we adopted the higher temperature approach in the interest of consistency and to decrease any risk of error in combustion. More recently Bombin and

Table 2.2. *Comparison of combustion methods*

Sample Type	Number	Method	$\delta^{13}C$ (‰) Mean ± 1 s.d.
Collagen	6	Pyrex @ 550 °C	−12.7 ± 0.14
Collagen	6	Vycor @ 900 °C	−12.6 ± 0.12
Meat	3	Pyrex @ 550 °C	−23.8 ± 0.04
Meat	3	Vycor @ 900 °C	−24.0 ± 0.05

Source: Chisholm *et al.* 1983a.

Muehlenbachs (1985) carried out a similar comparison and also found no difference in results for samples combusted at 550 °C in Pyrex and at 700 °, 800 °, and 900 °C in Vycor. Perhaps a more important consideration is that of proper preheating of the oven before the samples are inserted, as mentioned by Sofer (1980). Failure to preheat the oven may lead to premature charring of some samples which can result in incomplete combustion and hence possible fractionation of the carbon (Sofer 1980). Heating to 900 °C seems to combust even charred materials thereby avoiding the problem, as should proper preheating of the oven.

Proper long-term storage of uncombusted samples that may be needed for further analysis is necessary to avoid the addition of contaminants via bacterial action or growth of molds. While bacteria and molds would be feeding on the carbon in the samples they may also incorporate contaminating CO_2 from the atmosphere. While it should be possible to separate the sample from any bacterial or mold growths, any carbon that had been incorporated by them would be lost from the sample, which could result in fractionation of the carbon.

Modern instrumentation allows measurement precision levels of about ±0.01 to ±0.02‰. The contribution of this error is therefore not a problem. However, a potential problem lies in the possibility of interlaboratory calibration errors in isotopic analysis. This problem was first illustrated by Mann (1982) who arranged to have a number of laboratories carry out isotopic measurements of NBS (National Bureau of Standards) radiocarbon standards. The reported results have variations of 0.5–0.6‰ (at 1σ) with the range of values being about 1 to 1.5‰ (Mann 1982). A further indication of this problem comes from analyses carried out on materials from the British Columbia coast (Chisholm *et al.* 1983). In that study 48 samples from 15 different sites were measured at three different laboratories with a variation of 0.99‰ (1σ). When only the 37 samples that were measured at McMaster University were examined the variation was reduced to 0.4‰.

Control of this variation can only be obtained when laboratories doing isotope analysis adhere closely to some conventional standard, as they generally do. The above results indicate, however, that such is not always the case. While carbon standards exist for radiocarbon dating and mass spectrometry, these are not collagen samples such as those analysed in paleodiet studies. To date the only bone standard is one prepared for trace element analysis by the I.A.E.A. in Vienna.

Such a standard should probably include a group of samples, i.e., material from a large C_3-plant consuming herbivore mammal, from a large C_4-plant consuming herbivore mammal, and from a large marine mammal. These three types would provide examples for each of the three major dietary alternative groups. In addition to carefully prepared, well-mixed, collagen extracts (gelatin), it will be necessary to include some powdered, but unextracted, material from the same bone sample in order to compare each laboratory's extraction procedures with those of others.

VARIATION INHERENT IN COLLAGEN ITSELF

The formation of bone collagen is governed by RNA, as is the formation of all proteins. Thus for a single individual all bone collagen will be structurally identical. If the sequencing of amino acid residues in collagen molecules is not correct then the collagen may not be able to assume its stable structure (Yutani *et al.* 1985) and therefore may not stabilize in the intracellular bone matrix. While some variation may occur in the end members of procollagens, such irregularities in mature collagens would be found largely at the terminal ends of the fibrils (Kuhn 1982). If they do occur, the number of variant residues will be very small, i.e. 1 or 2 residues in a thousand (Mahler and Cordes 1966), or the molecule will not function correctly. However, any variant amino acid residues will have come from the same sources as all of the others in the collagen and therefore should not introduce any isotopic variation. In addition, the procollagen non-helical end units are removed as the collagen fibrils form (Kuhn 1982, Tanzer 1982). Thus structural irregularities should not affect the isotopic character of mature collagen. In addition, when we analyse gelatin we are looking at many molecules so that minor differences in one molecule should be masked.

Different bones, and different areas of the same bones, in an individual will all contain collagen that is structurally identical and hence should not differ isotopically for an individual on a constant diet. DeNiro and Schoeninger (1983) have shown that there was less than 1.0‰ variation in results for bone samples taken from a group of three rabbits and fifteen mink. However, they did not report results for different bones from single individuals so it is unclear how little

Table 2.3. *Reproducibility of results for different extractions from the same individual.*

Sample	No. of measurements	Difference (‰) Mean ± 1 s.d.
Same bone, same individual	5 pairs	0.1 ± 0.06
Different bone, same individual	4 pairs	0.2 ± 0.14

variation should be expected. The results for samples prepared at Simon Fraser University are shown in Table 2.3. While the number of samples measured is small, they do suggest that there is less variation than found in DeNiro and Schoeninger's (1983) lumped samples.

Bumsted (1985) argues that sex, age, and metabolism may affect $\delta^{13}C$ variability. Recent evidence presented by Lovell *et al.* (1986) suggests otherwise. For a large sample of 50 prehistoric Oxbow people from the Gray site in southwestern Saskatchewan, subsisting on one food reservoir, the average $\delta^{13}C$ value was -17.5 ± 0.3‰. Between males ($n = 9$) and females ($n = 9$) the difference was ≤ 0.1‰, while specific identified age groups were within 0.3‰ of the population average (Lovell *et al.* 1986). In addition, no gender differences appear in these samples from the interior (Lovell *et al.* n.d.) or from the coast (Chisholm *et al.* 1983) of British Columbia. These results suggest that variation between humans of different age or sex that is greater than 0.3‰ and 0.1‰, respectively, must be based on dietary differences and is not metabolic.

The isotopic composition of collagen may differ from one area of bone to another because of change in an individual's diet as he/she grows and accumulates or replaces collagen. Different bones in different regions of the body mature at different times. If the diet of an individual changes during periods of active growth then we may expect to see differences between collagen formed before, and collagen formed after, the change in diet. This potential for variation has not yet been observed or tested.

The turnover rate of bone collagen is not adequately documented. Stenhouse and Baxter (1979) suggest a thirty-year period for complete replacement, Libby *et al.* (1964) suggest a period of about ten years, while Bumsted (1985) suggests from two to ten years. While turnover studies have been carried out for various other forms of collagen, few, if any, have been done for bone collagen. We do know that bone collagen turns over slowly, likely requiring at least ten years for complete replacement. While this period allows for changes in the isotopic composition of bone collagen, any sample of collagen molecules will include a mixture of old and newly formed collagen, thereby averaging and obscuring short-term changes. This phenomenon would negate the use of bone collagen for determinations of short-term seasonal or annual events. However, collagen or other stable proteins from tissues such as skin, hair, and nails may be useful for such studies since they are replaced much more rapidly.

The averaging effect of slowly changing collagen also means that the variation within a group of individuals eating a similar diet will be less than the variation within the dietary alternatives that feed them (Fig. 2.1). Consequently, a small number of individuals should be representative of a population, unless there is significant variation in the diets of the individuals of that population. The small variation, of about ±0.3‰, for groups that lived at one site or within a small local area supports this (Chisholm *et al.* 1983, Nelson *et al.*, n.d.).

PROTEIN VERSUS CARBOHYDRATES AND THE ROLE OF LIPIDS

The amino acids from which collagen is assembled are obtained from dietary materials. Seven of these amino acids (isoleucine, leucine, lysine, methionine, phenylalanine, threonine, valine) are considered essential in the human diet, meaning that they must be ingested as either the specific amino acids or their non-aminated precursors (Falconer 1969, Mahler and Cordes 1966, Meister 1965, White *et al.* 1978), since humans cannot synthesize the carbon skeletons for these particular acids. Arginine may be essential in some species, such as the rat, but is only essential in growing humans, not adults (Falconer 1969). The remaining amino acids are considered non-essential because they may be synthesized by the human body, if necessary, from metabolic materials. Some of the non-essential amino acid precursors are derivable from the carbohydrate metabolism (Mahler and Cordes 1966, Meister 1965, White *et al.* 1978). However, in normal circumstances, protein intake is sufficient to provide non-essential amino acids as well as the essential ones and no synthesis is necessary (White *et al.* 1978). In areas such as the British Columbia coast where meat is the major dietary item and where carbohydrate is not a major dietary component (Drucker 1955, Suttles 1968), it is likely that virtually all collagen-forming amino acids had their origin in dietary protein. In other areas where carbohydrate intake is higher, both protein and carbohydrates must be considered.

Lipids in the diet are a source of energy but do not contribute to amino acid synthesis (White *et al.* 1978), except perhaps in the case of serine, a minor constituent of collagen (Mahler and Cordes, 1966). Measurements by DeNiro (1977) and by Vogel (1978) show that $\delta^{13}C$ values for the protein and carbohydrate components of a single tissue are very close, within 1‰, while lipid values are removed from them by about 7‰ (Smith and Epstein 1971, Vogel 1978). Since lipids may be present in highly variable quantities (Geiger and Borgstrom 1962, McConnaughey and McRoy 1979), and since different lipids have different values (Parker 1964), they are likely to differentially bias $\delta^{13}C$ values for dietary flesh (and possibly bone samples), and to partially obscure the relationship between diet and collagen. The obvious solution to this problem is to extract lipids, from both bone and dietary samples, before analysis. However, the presence of lipids in archaeological bone samples may not be a problem that requires attention, because the depositional environment tends to remove the lipids before samples are recovered and prepared for analysis. Attempts to extract lipids from British Columbia coastal prehistoric samples yielded no measurable materials. This question is discussed further below.

VARIATION DUE TO DIAGENETIC PROCESSES

One of the advantages of working with collagen as a material for analysis is that it is an extremely stable molecule, increasingly so in older individuals (Eyre 1980, Hedges and Wallace 1978). Samples of collagen have been found in bone as old as 100,000 years (Sinex and Faris 1959) and perhaps up to 380 million years (Abelson 1956, Isaacs *et al.* 1963). While the stability of collagen makes it a reliable source of carbon for dating and stable isotope analysis, we must still consider the possibility of diagenetic change in collagen molecules. Such changes could be in the form of (1) the biased removal of portions of the collagen in such a way that isotope fractionation could occur, (2) the addition of contaminant carbon to the collagen, or (3) the replacement of some of the collagen carbon by contaminating carbon atoms.

After death and deposition, bone collagen breaks down into large peptide units which themselves eventually break into individual amino acids. At each step the degradation products become more soluble and easily removed by ground water (Ortner *et al.* 1972). Selective removal of particular collagen parts should not be a problem. Such removal would require alteration and partial breakdown of the collagen fibrils, rendering the remaining products soluble and permitting their removal from the bone. In any case, peptides and amino acid breakdown products that may remain after diagenesis should be removed during sample pretreatment, leaving the remaining intact collagen for analysis.

The addition of carbon contaminants, including collagen from other bones, and other proteins and organic compounds, to the deposited bone requires some sort of transport mechanism, such as ground water. If the contaminants are sufficiently soluble to be transported then they should be sufficiently soluble to be removed by either more ground water or laboratory pretreatment. Any other mechanism would likely involve alteration of the collagen. Addition of contaminants to the collagen itself would have to occur at a position on the molecule where a projecting group (NH_3, COOH, OH or R) was accessible and where the carbon skeleton would not be affected. Proper sample pretreatment should reverse such reactions and remove the attached contaminants as easily as they replaced the original projecting groups, leaving the carbon skeleton intact. Contaminants such as humic and fulvic acids, deposited interstitially in the bone, should also be removed by proper treatment. Replacement of the carbon atoms in the main skeleton would require cleaving of the molecule, resulting in denaturing, increased solubility, and subsequent removal, either by ground water or during pretreatment.

After carbon contaminants and lipids are removed, either in the ground or the laboratory, the only other organic materials that may be present in bone samples would be other proteins and, possibly, carbohydrates from the same individual. They are less stable than collagen and are removed more readily. The presence of other proteins in any significant quantity should be revealed by amino acid analysis, since they will have different relative proportions for amino acid residues and will lack the distinctive glycine, hydroxyproline, and proline characteristics of collagen. As their origin will have been the same as the collagen carbon, they should differ very little isotopically from the collagen, if at all.

VARIATION DUE TO COLLAGEN EXTRACTION PROCESSES

The most obvious problems leading to variation in results are the failure to remove contaminants from bone samples, and the alteration or degradation of the extracted collagen due to improper procedures. Sample extraction procedures therefore must meet a number of requirements:

(1) they must remove all contaminating carbon-bearing materials;
(2) they should not selectively remove or alter any of the collagen, but if they do then they should remove all fragments of collagen and any amino acids hydrolysed from it, leaving only intact molecules or representative large peptide fragments for analysis;
(3) they should not add any carbon containing materials to the sample;
(4) for the purposes of archaeological interpretation and economy, it is desirable that the process should be simple to follow.

The process used for sample extraction at Simon Fraser University is derived from Pieter Grootes of the University of Washington (1980, personal communication) and is a modification of Longin's (1971) technique. Bone samples are first mechanically cleaned to remove any obvious contamination such as rootlets, glue residues, inked and lacquered numbers, etc., and then are ground in a Wiley mill so as to pass through a screen of *ca.* 1 mm. Demineralization and removal of all acid-soluble and water-soluble materials is accomplished via repeated extractions, at room temperature, with 0.25N HCl until the solution pH stabilizes, usually at pH 1 or slightly below. This treatment is more gentle than Longin's (1971) method, which uses 1.0N HCl for about 20 minutes. Grootes' procedure is intended to remove all acid- and water-soluble materials, including free amino acids and soluble peptides while minimizing the loss of collagen. Further treatment of the residue from the Longin process with 0.25N HCl has revealed that removal of minerals and contaminants was not complete after 20 minutes. Comparison of sample splits indicated that extending the Longin treatment beyond about 20 minutes reduces the yield of collagen, as pointed out by Longin (1971). Because of problems with the commonly used NaOH soak (DeNiro and Epstein 1978b, Häkansson 1976, Land *et al.* 1980), discussed below, we have omitted that step. To prohibit any acid-insoluble materials (such as humic and fulvic acids) from entering the solution, an acid pH is maintained at all times. Collagen is extracted as in Longin (1971) by heating to 90 °C for about 10 hours, or overnight, while maintaining an acid pH of about 3. Collagen that is denatured via this heating comes into solution while the acid-insoluble materials remain in the residue (Häkansson 1976). As long as complete molecules of collagen, or all of the large representative peptides resulting from the hydrolysis of complete molecules, are brought into solution during this last step we do not have to worry whether the extraction of all of the collagen in the bone has been completed. Further extractions of the residue obtained through this process have yielded no more gelatin.

Amino acid analysis of the collagen extract (gelatin) has been carried out for a number of samples and the proportions of the amino acids present are as expected for human bone collagen (Table 2.4). There is no evidence for the presence of amino acids such as ornithine, cystine, or tryptophane, which are found in plant and other animal proteins. These amino acids should be found in at least small quantities if such contaminants were present. In addition, the proportions of about $\frac{1}{3}$ glycine and $\frac{1}{5}$ hydroxyproline and proline, match the characteristic pattern for collagen (Kuhn 1982, White *et al.* 1978, Woodhead-Galloway 1980). On the basis of these analyses we may assume that the product of our extractions is gelatin from collagen and that it contains no other protein products. Reproducibility for Grootes' method is shown by six separate extractions from the same bone which gave an average $\delta^{13}C$ value of $-20.65 \pm 0.09‰$ (Chisholm *et al.* 1983).

Originally the NaOH soak was used in collagen extractions to avoid contamination by humic and fulvic acids (Bumsted 1984, Häkansson 1976). Stevenson (1982) mentions that HCl extractions may remove up to 5% of the organics from soil samples, including some low molecular weight fulvic acids (*ca.* 200 daltons), which indicates that some are acid-soluble. However, with the exception of these potential contaminants, all other humic and fulvic acids are soluble in alkali and not in acid (Stevenson 1982) so that maintenance of an acid environment should

Table 2.4. *Amino acid analysis of a typical sample extracted using Grootes' method*

Amino acid	Expected values[a]	Sample values[a]
Hydroxyproline and proline	21.6	19.6
Aspartic acid	4.6	3.4
Threonine	1.6	2.0
Serine	3.1	3.0
Glutamic acid	7.5	6.7
Glycine	33.0	32.1
Alanine	11.4	11.4
Valine	2.3	0.9
Methionine	0.6	0.4
Isoleucine	1.2	1.1
Leucine	2.5	2.5
Tyrosine	0.4	0.3
Phenyalanine	1.3	1.0
Lysine	3.5	2.7
Histidine	0.5	0.4
Arginine	.5.2	4.8
NH_3	—	7.7

[a] Expected values are derived from Kuhn (1982) and individual residues are expressed as percentages of the total residues.

keep them out of solution throughout the process. Thus, repeated acid treatments should extract all of the soluble fulvic acids leaving behind only those that are insoluble. Since the humic and heavier fulvic acids are acid-insoluble, and since we are looking for intact collagen molecules or the characteristic large peptides (of about 30,000 and 60,000 daltons) that are initial breakdown products of collagen, then a simple molecular sizing process following the hot water treatment should separate the target protein from lighter contaminants.

Further reasons for avoiding an NaOH wash are that it may noticeably decrease the gelatin yield (P. Grootes 1980, personal communication) and that it may affect the isotopic character of the gelatin. Chisholm *et al.* (1983a) found that use of the NaOH wash resulted in $\delta^{13}C$ values that had greater variability than, and differed from, results obtained by Longin's and Grootes' methods (Table 2.5). DeNiro and Epstein (1981) found a shift of about 0.7‰ between NaOH treated and untreated fresh bone samples. While the reasons for this pattern are not clearly understood, there are a few factors that may explain it. Different amino acids have different $\delta^{13}C$ values (Abelson and Hoering 1961, Hare and Estep 1982, Macko *et al.* 1982a,b). If these amino acids are

Table 2.5. *Differences (in ‰) between extraction methods*

Sample	|G−L|	|G−N|	|L−N|
1	0.1	0.2	0.3
2	0.0	0.1	0.1
3	0.1	0.1	0.0
4	0.1	0.1	0.0
5	0.0	0.4	0.4
6	0.1	0.8	0.7
Average	0.07±0.05	0.28±0.28	0.25±0.27

G = Grootes' method
L = Longin's (1971) method without an NaOH wash
N = Longin's method with an NaOH wash
Source: Chisholm *et al.* 1983a.

selectively removed from collagen, the overall collagen $\delta^{13}C$ value could be biased. We also know that NaOH affects some amino acids more strongly than others (Meister 1965, Veis 1964), particularly arginine and tyrosine (Easthoe and Leach 1977), and serine and threonine which have $\delta^{13}C$ values as much as 10 to 12‰ heavier than the other collagen amino acids (Hare and Estep 1982, Macko *et al.* 1982a,b). Easthoe and Leach (1977) indicate that gelatins are slightly poorer in the rarer amino acids and richer in the common ones than the original corresponding collagens. It is likely that alkali treatment selectively removes peptides poorer in hydroxyproline and richer in tyrosine (Easthoe and Leach 1977). Thus the use of an NaOH treatment may selectively bias the collagen $\delta^{13}C$ results, although this needs further investigation. If this is the case, it may explain the postulated diagenetic alteration of the isotopic character of buried collagens noted by Land *et al.* (1980) and DeNiro (1985). In both cases an NaOH wash was included in the extraction process. Of interest is the fact that all the altered $\delta^{13}C$ values reported by DeNiro (1985) appear to be isotopically lighter than those for other individuals of the same species. Also, 23 of the 25 aberrant C/N ratios reported (DeNiro 1985) deviate in such a direction as to indicate either the loss of nitrogen or the addition of contaminant carbon. It is possible that DeNiro was not observing evidence for diagenetic change, but for bias introduced by sample pretreatment. This problem also requires further investigation.

Bumsted (1984) has determined that NaOH washes are detrimental to collagen extraction and has used an Amberlite XAD-2 resin column to remove contaminants from the gelatin. However, the $\delta^{13}C$ values were altered by as much as 1.5‰ with this approach (Bumsted 1984:82–3), possibly due, in part, to contamination from column degradation products. Many resins gradually degenerate and can contribute carbon to samples being analysed (D. Eckert, Beckman Instruments 1982, personal communication). Alterations of this nature are unfortunately not acceptable if we wish to reduce errors to minimal levels.

VARIATION IN DIETARY SPECIES

The first step of any complete paleodiet study must be the determination of the dietary alternatives. Knowledge of the local biota will provide a list of plant and animal species available, which may in some cases be sufficient information for outlining the choices in the diet. However, it is likely that additional data will be required in order to determine what the alternatives are, and whether they are easily distinguishable by $\delta^{13}C$ values. Ethnographic reports often provide information on species consumed, methods of capture and harvest, and so on, but generally do not indicate the relative importance of the various species they discuss. Archaeological faunal and floral analyses may allow some quantification of the recovered materials, thus giving an initial impression of importance. However, the vagaries of preservation, sampling, and recovery may make the archaeological data unreliable for use in quantified diet reconstructions. Such information can, however, delimit the dietary alternatives and thus provide a necessary starting point for isotopic analysis studies of diet.

Although we may be able to control for variation in collagen resulting from diagenesis, and in the analytical techniques, there is still a large (perhaps the largest) component of variation inherent in the dietary alternative species themselves. These variations may arise from a number of natural causes, such as temporal shifts in isotope ratios for the carbon reservoirs (Stuiver *et al.* 1984). Such fluctuations would be reflected in food species and their consumers and could, if large enough, obscure temporal shifts in diet proportions. Data presented by Broecker and Peng (1982: Figs. 10–19), Craig (1954), Jansen (1962), and Leavitt and Long (1986: Fig. 4), suggest that prior to about 1860 the mean curve for tree ring $\delta^{13}C$ values was effectively flat, but that it fluctuated by up to 1‰. The burning of fossil fuels since about 1860 has added carbon to the atmospheric and oceanic reservoirs and resulted in a gradual non-linear shift in $\delta^{13}C$ values (Stuiver 1978: Fig. 3). Since isotopic paleodiet studies are based in part on comparisons of modern diet alternatives with those of prehistoric consumers it is essential that this fossil fuel induced shift in $\delta^{13}C$ must be considered when data is being interpreted. This problem, which was pointed out by Pedersen (1986, personal communication), has not been considered in previous isotopic studies of paleodiet. At the moment the best estimate for the magnitude of that shift is that both atmospheric and near-surface ocean average $\delta^{13}C$ values are about 0.7‰ lighter for modern samples (Broecker and Peng 1982, Stuiver 1978). While there is no stated uncertainty for this shift, visual inspection of Stuiver's (1978) graph suggests that it should be about ± 0.2‰.

In the terrestrial environment, geographic and seasonal variations in the proportions of C_3 and C_4 grass species (Terri and Stowe 1976, Tieszen *et al.* 1979a) will affect grazing herbivores (Chisholm *et al.* n.d.) and may be passed up food chains. Data from Bumsted (1984) and Schwarcz *et al.* (1985) indicate geographic differences in C_4 species, particularly maize. On a local level, Lowden and Dyck (1974) have observed differences in CO_2 values that may be related to the respiration of tree species. Species growing beneath heavy tree canopies often exhibit a difference in the isotopic ratios of the CO_2 that they consume (van der Merwe 1982). This variation may occur on a seasonal basis, depending upon the growth cycle of the trees in the area and on their respiratory rate. It will be reflected in herbivores that eat the local species and will be carried up the food chains. While geographic differences in $\delta^{13}C$ values for diet species are not yet well mapped, it is clear that they do exist and need to be examined further.

Species that migrate over long distances, through potentially varied environmental conditions, will reflect the average values of the reservoirs through which they pass. In the North Pacific, salmon are the most obvious examples of migratory species. Species such as tuna which also migrate widely have their northern limits in the coastal region of British Columbia and as a result should exhibit values reflecting a mixture of the local and a more southerly reservoir which may differ somewhat from the local one in isotope ratios.

Grazing species subsist on those foods that are available to them. Throughout the year there may be shifts in the relative proportions of different food species present in the local ranges (C_3 versus C_4 plants for example), or the grazers may migrate to new ranges, and this will be reflected in their isotopic averages. Differences in foraging behaviors for various herbivores within the same area may give them different average isotopic ratios. These differences in the diet species will contribute to variation in the overall averages for dietary alternative groups and hence to variation in the results for local humans that rely on the grazers.

The major difference between terrestrial and marine food species results from their respective atmospheric and oceanic carbon reservoirs. The oceanic reservoir itself exhibits differences that may show up as geographic variation. The average value for this reservoir as determined by Craig (1953) is $\delta^{13}C = 0‰$, but Stuiver (1983) has found that the average value for the North Pacific is closer to $+1.0‰$. Obviously these variations in reservoir value will be reflected in local or regional food chains that obtain their carbon from the oceanic reservoir.

Fontugne and Duplessy (1981), Degens *et al.* (1968), Eadie and Sackett (1971), Sackett *et al.* (1965), and Wong and Sackett (1978) have observed a relationship between water temperature and $\delta^{13}C$ values for marine plankton, and presumably for food chains that rely on them. This is no doubt one of the mechanisms that generates differences in values between areas since the water temperature does vary, often widely, between different geographic regions. Seasonal upwelling of colder water along coastal zones will affect local temperatures and may also introduce carbon that is isotopically different from that of the local surface waters.

A possible factor in temperature-induced differences in $\delta^{13}C$ values is the lipid content of the specimens examined. Lipids, as we know, are isotopically lighter than protein and carbohydrates. If lipids are present in greater abundance, then that organism will show a lighter isotopic average than one with a lower lipid content. In colder temperatures an organism has higher energy requirements than in warm conditions. Much of the energy for an organism is obtained through dietary and stored lipids. In colder regimes the lipid content of the organism will be higher, resulting in an isotopically lighter average (McConnaughey and McRoy 1979). Fontugne and Duplessy (1981) indicate that samples (from which lipids were *not* removed) from colder surface temperature areas were isotopically lighter, as expected. Unfortunately we have no data on the relative lipid content of the various samples analysed. We do know that the proportions of lipids versus proteins is highly variable in fish species (Geiger and Borgstrom 1962).

Another factor that may influence the isotopic carbon in marine species is the terrestrial run-off of biogenic carbon. This is a problem particularly for inter-tidal and estuarine species (Haines and Montague 1979, Rau *et al.* 1981, and others), but should not noticeably affect pelagic and migratory marine species. If these species are part of the local human diet, as they commonly are, then we can expect greater variation in dietary average values for the coastal areas. Biogenic run-off also influences the $\delta^{13}C$ values of freshwater species, giving them values similar to the terrestrial species in the area (Chisholm *et al.* 1982).

The potential existence of these regional differences in reservoir and food species values means that it is necessary to sample dietary alternative species within the study area. We cannot assume literature values to be correct from one area to another.

The trophic level difference of 1‰ between diet species and consumers reported by DeNiro and Epstein (1978b) has also been observed in field situations by McConnaughey and McRoy (1979), Bender *et al.* (1981), Tieszen *et al.* (1983), and others. Schoeninger (1985) notes this difference in her results from Kenya and in a world-wide sample but argues that the observed difference is not significant. One difficulty with her results lies in the large standard deviations associated with the sample means for the different levels. The fact that the samples are from a number of different areas of the world likely accounts for much of this variation (and illustrates the problem of geographic differences), as does the small number of samples. Studies that document trophic-level differences can only be valid when the diets of the study animals are monotonous or well controlled. Wide geographic or temporal differences will not guarantee this.

Results from the British Columbia coast (Chisholm *et al.* 1983b), where samples were taken from restricted locales, are shown in Table 2.6. Although the sample sizes are small, trophic-level differences are apparent for the terrestrial species and the two levels of marine carnivores. The marine omnivores show varied results which reflect different sampling locations relative to a major source of terrestrial biogenic carbon influx (the Fraser River). Further variation will result for consumers that are eating a mixture of species of the same basic type, but from different trophic levels. Individuals may show slightly different results if they sample the trophic levels to different degrees, or include foods from different ecological situations, i.e. inter-tidal, benthic, and pelagic. This mixing of trophic levels, the small size of the trophic-level

Table 2.6. *British Columbia coast dietary species samples*

	Sample	n	$\delta^{13}C$(‰) ± 1σ
Terrestrial			
	Herbivores	27	−25.5 ± 1.4
	Omnivores	2	−24.3
			1.2
Marine Omnivores[a]			
	Molluscs	4	−18.0 ± 0.5
	Littoral	2	−20.0
			2.0
Marine Carnivores[b]			
	Primary	5	−18.7 ± 1.4
	Secondary	12	−17.4 ± 1.2
			1.3

[a] Molluscs are from open beach areas while littoral species are from near the Fraser River mouth.
[b] Primary carnivores are smaller fish that eat zooplankton and other small herbivore species. Secondary carnivores include larger fish, such as salmon, that eat small fish.
Source: Chisholm *et al.* 1983b.

increment, and the relatively large variability in dietary alternative averages indicate that Schoeninger (1985) is correct in suggesting that we will have great difficulty in using $\delta^{13}C$ results to distinguish between meat or vegetarian diets in early humans.

PREPARATION OF DIETARY SAMPLES

Since foods are generally either plant, animal muscle, or animal organ tissues, and not bone, we should use those materials to determine average values for dietary alternatives. As animal soft tissues and vegetal materials do not usually preserve well, we are unfortunately limited to the use of modern analogs of identified prehistoric food species. Bone samples from modern individuals may be compared to preserved bone from the same species to establish temporal control over the diet species $\delta^{13}C$ values. Use of previously published data, particularly on plant species, may introduce error into the analyses. Such data are often taken from tissues that may not have been eaten by either humans or animals, or if eaten, did not contribute to the protein metabolism of the consumer.

Because lipids do not contribute significantly to protein formation, other than as an energy source, we are concerned with only the protein and carbohydrate components of food species. Therefore, the lipid component should be extracted and discarded before analysis. This step is also important because of the differences in isotope ratios observed between lipids and other components.

At Simon Fraser University, the dietary sample preparation procedure includes a chloroform extraction (Bligh and Dyer 1959). A mix of chloroform, methanol, and water is used to extract lipids from homogenized samples. The process, carried out in a separatory funnel, is repeated twice to ensure completeness. Since use of a third extraction step has not yielded any further lipids the two-step process is assumed to be sufficient. Lipid-free samples are dried and about 5 mg are loaded into combustion tubes for analysis.

VARIATION IN INTERPRETATION OF RESULTS

As discussed earlier, if a consumer samples both C_3 and C_4 species in its diet, the $\delta^{13}C$ value for its bone collagen will lie between the extremes of about −21.5‰ and −7.5‰. A simple linear interpolation, locating the sample value between the two extremes, will result in an estimate for the relative amounts of C_3 and C_4 species in that particular consumer's diet (Fig. 2.2).

Papers by van der Merwe and Vogel (1978) and by Chisholm *et al.* (1982, 1983) used end-point values of $\delta^{13}C = -20‰$, −7‰, and −13‰ for the C_3, C_4, and marine diet consumer collagens, respectively. Differences from the values listed previously (Table 2.1) are partly due to the use of inappropriate data from the literature. In particular, the choice of −20‰ for the C_3 consumers' collagen end-point was based on a summation of results taken from various issues of *Radiocarbon* (van der Merwe and Vogel 1978). This value was adopted by Chisholm *et al.* (1982, 1983) as the best available and was supported by results for a number of Archaic Period (pre-maize) individuals from two sites on the Ottawa River in Canada, that gave an average $\delta^{13}C$ value of −19.6‰ (Chisholm *et al.* 1982, 1983). However, these samples, and those used by van der Merwe and Vogel (1978), represent people who likely had some access to marine species, and thus would reflect a mixed and not a pure C_3-based diet. Other samples from

Archaic Period sites in Ontario and the northeastern U.S. provide $\delta^{13}C$ values that cluster around −21.5‰ (Bender *et al.* 1981, Schwarcz *et al.* 1985), in agreement with predicted values (Table 2.1). It is thus evident that earlier usage of −20‰ to represent the consumers of purely C_3-based diets was incorrect and that a $\delta^{13}C$ value of −21.5‰ is more appropriate. Selection of the correct end-points for C_4 and marine consumers is also problematic because it is difficult to find human consumers that have only C_4- or marine-based diets. Further complications arise from apparent geographic differences in C_4 species, particularly maize (Bender 1968, 1971, Bumsted 1984, Schwarcz *et al.* 1985). These variations may result from interlaboratory calibration errors (Chisholm *et al.* 1983, 1983a, Mann 1982), from the presence of lipids, or from real geographic influences.

A rounded value of $\delta^{13}C = -13$‰ was used for consumers of purely marine diets by Chisholm *et al.* (1982, 1983), based on Tauber (1979) and measurements from the British Columbia coast. Since a number of the results from British Columbia fall below this value, it too is probably in error. A value of *ca.* −12‰ or −12.5‰ is likely more appropriate. The geographic problems that apply to C_4 species also apply to marine species.

Fortunately there is an easy route around these difficulties. Instead of locating our unknown sample value between end-point values for the human consumers of purely C_3-, C_4-, or marine-based diets, we could determine the average diet value for our known consumer and then locate that value relative to the dietary alternative average values. To do this, we apply the "ΔDC" value to our unknown sample results in order to determine their dietary average values. These values are then located between the locally determined dietary alternative averages to determine diet proportions (Fig. 2.3). In this way we do not require consumer end-point values, although it would still be useful to have a better idea of the correct end-points for pure diet consumers in order to determine the diet proportions of isolated individuals, without having to do a complete survey of local dietary alternative species.

Based on field data, the increment between the average diet and the bone collagen of the consumers, called "collagen enrichment" or "ΔDC," is about 5‰ (Chisholm *et al.* 1982, van der Merwe and Vogel 1978). DeNiro and Epstein (1978b) found a somewhat different "ΔDC" value of about 3.0‰ based on a study of two groups of three mice each on two different diets. This result was altered to 3.9‰ after further

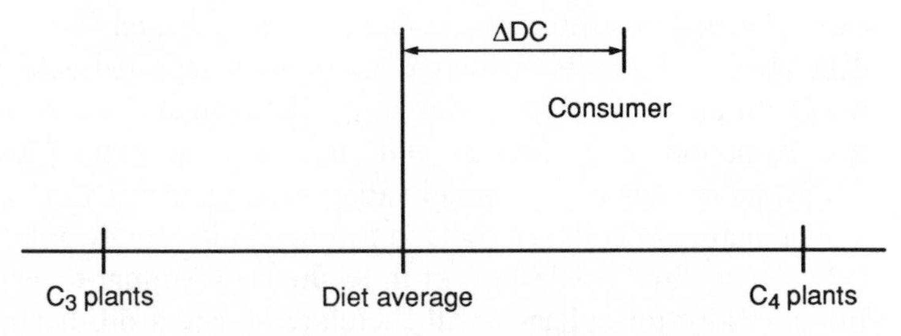

Fig. 2.3 Using "ΔDC" and diet alternatives to estimate proportions

investigation (DeNiro and Epstein 1981). The difference between these values may result from the removal of lipids from dietary samples used in the mice study (DeNiro and Epstein 1978b) while this was not done in the field samples. If lipids were removed from diet species then their average values would be heavier, and thus closer to the consumers' value, resulting in a smaller "ΔDC" value. Further research is necessary to clarify this value.

The overall error on the proportion determinations will be reached by algebraic combination of the errors associated with (1) the sample measurement, (2) ΔDC, and (3) either the consumer end-points or the two dietary alternatives being compared. For marine versus terrestrial comparisons on the British Columbia coast the calculated error on proportion estimates is about ±8% (Chisholm *et al.* 1983). For C_3 versus C_4 comparisons, since the difference between end-points is greater than in marine versus terrestrial comparisons, the overall error should be about ±5% (Chisholm *et al.* 1983). The previously mentioned example result of $\delta^{13}C = -11.0‰$ thus indicates a diet that was 75±5% C_4 in content.

SUMMARY AND CONCLUSIONS

This discussion has considered the various stages at which variation may be introduced into stable carbon isotopic reconstructions of paleodiet. The conclusions reached are summarized below.

Care must be taken to ensure complete combustion of carbon samples for analysis, but large, complicated, and expensive systems should not be necessary. While standards do exist for calibrating instruments, there are as yet none in common use for calibrating the extraction and measurement process for bone collagen. These should be developed and results of their measurement reported with analytical results to allow accurate comparisons between studies. Nevertheless, the extraction, combustion, and measurement process should not contribute greatly to the overall variation in these analyses.

The nature of collagen metabolism precludes significant differences between age and sex groups of individuals on similar diets. Differing isotope ratios for collagen will therefore be based on dietary and not metabolic differences, which may reflect culturally or individually controlled biases, or differing availability of foods.

Except in cases of protein deficiency, the amino acids that form collagen should come from ingested protein and carbohydrates, which have similar $\delta^{13}C$ values. Lipids, which differ significantly from proteins and carbohydrates in $\delta^{13}C$ value, must be removed before analysis, particularly from dietary alternative species. Diagenesis seems to remove the lipids from archaeological bones, but this may vary for different environments and must be confirmed.

Collagen is an extremely stable and insoluble macromolecule and preserves its structure and character well under many depositional conditions. If intact collagen is recovered from a buried bone sample and all contaminants are removed we can be certain that it has retained its isotopic character. To ensure this we must be certain of the sample extraction techniques used. While further confirmation is still necessary, the extraction method suggested by Grootes provides a simple and successful means of extracting collagen from bone samples. The addition of a molecular sizing step may be appropriate for dealing with possible fulvic acid contaminants. Use of NaOH washes and resin column treatments are detrimental to the extraction process, potentially altering $\delta^{13}C$ values and giving results which may be confused with diagenetic effects.

Because of the differences observed for dietary species, geographically, between trophic levels, and so on, we cannot use samples from widely separated areas to construct a general average for diet species. To ensure the correct values, with minimum variations, for dietary averages it will be necessary to sample diet species locally.

It is clear from the above discussion that there are still a number of problems relating to diet reconstructions via isotopic analysis that must be solved before the technique produces optimal results. In particular, the value for "ΔDC" must be accurately determined, an appropriate set of standards must be developed for checking the method, and extraction methods must be confirmed sufficient.

In conclusion, if we intend to apply isotopic analysis meaningfully to archaeological problems, it is essential that we understand and minimize the associated variations and arrive at reasonable error estimates for our results. With appropriate and careful application of methods this is quite possible.

ACKNOWLEDGMENTS

Isotopic studies carried out at Simon Fraser University have involved a number of people, particularly D. Erle Nelson, Keith A. Hobson, and Nancy C. Lovell. Tom Brown, John Southon, and John Vogel have also provided useful advice and assistance. Henry P. Schwarcz provided access to a Micromass 602D mass spectrometer at McMaster University, and Martin Knyf assisted with, and carried out a number of measurements. All of these colleagues provided useful discussion and comments. Financial support has been provided by Natural Science and Engineering Research Council grants to D. Erle Nelson.

ADDENDUM

Since this paper was originally prepared there have been improvements in the methodology. A modified and better extraction method for collagen has been reported by Brown *et al.* (1988) which solves the handling problem caused by the hygroscopic character of the free amino acids and small peptides. Koike and Chisholm (1988) have reported a value for ΔDC of about 4.2‰ using lipid-free samples from Japanese Macaques. This concurs generally with as yet unpublished results discussed by Chisholm (1986). Finally, the method for extracting lipids from diet species samples (Bligh and Dyer 1959) mentioned above has been modified by using just a 2:1 mixture of chloroform and methanol, without water (Koike and Chisholm 1988), as it was found that use of water with an acid pH could lead to inconsistent results. An alternative method is to use acetone for lipid removal which has the added advantage of drying the samples at the same time.

References

Brown, T. A., D. E. Nelson, J. S. Vogel and J. R. Southon. 1988. Improved collagen extraction by modified Longin method. *Radiocarbon* 30(2): 171–177

Chisholm, B. S. 1986. Reconstruction of prehistoric diet in British Columbia using stable-carbon isotopic analysis (Ph.D. dissertation, Department of Archaeology, Simon Fraser University)

Koike, H. and B. Chisholm 1988. An application of stable-carbon ratios for the diet analysis of wild mammals. *Saitama University, College of Liberal Arts Bulletin* 6: 107–115. (In Japanese, with English abstract.)

3
Reconstructing prehistoric human diet

MARGARET J. SCHOENINGER

Department of Anthropology
University of Wisconsin–Madison

We are what we eat. If only we could put realistic figures in both sides of the equation implied by this statement, we could begin to reconstruct prehistoric human diet. With such knowledge, aspects of prehistoric subsistence strategies could be inferred which, in turn, could provide clues about group size, sexual division of labor, and settlement patterns. Identification of specific foods and the proportions in which those foods were consumed would contribute data to test the recent proposition that, prior to agriculture, human diet consisted largely of lean meat and non-starchy vegetables (Eaton and Konner 1985). These authors have suggested that the frequency of diseases such as atherosclerosis and bowel cancer in living populations is due, in part, to our dietary dependence on the products of plant and animal domestication, i.e., starch and fatty meat. They compiled dietary evidence from present-day hunter-gatherers to support their proposal, assuming that hunter-gatherers who lived prior to the Neolithic period would have consumed the same type of diet. Information on the diets actually consumed by prehistoric people would be an invaluable contribution to this issue.

In order to begin addressing such questions, however, the components of prehistoric human diet must be identified and the relative proportions of these components in diet must be ascertained. Analyses of floral and faunal remains recovered from archaeological middens can identify the dietary components available but seldom can such analyses indicate the actual contribution of individual components to diet. Further, diets of individuals cannot be estimated from faunal and floral remains alone. Thus, it is not possible to identify associations between diet and certain attributes of an individual, such as status, age, sex, or pathological state.

Several recently proposed methods based on bone composition have held the promise of providing information about diets of individuals. The basis for these methods of diet reconstruction is the demonstration that certain food categories differ from one another in specific aspects of their composition. For example, C_3 and C_4 plants differ from each other in the stable carbon isotope ratios in their tissues (summarized in van der Merwe 1982). Marine and terrestrial foods also have been shown to differ from each other both in stable carbon and nitrogen isotope ratios (Chisholm *et al.* 1982, Schoeninger and DeNiro 1984, Tauber 1981, Wada *et al.* 1975). Foods derived from animal sources differ from those obtained from plants in both strontium concentration and in stable nitrogen isotope ratios (Schoeninger 1979b, 1985, Schoeninger and DeNiro 1984, Sillen and Kavanagh 1982).

Further, the composition of bone reflects these observed differences in food composition (DeNiro and Epstein 1978b, 1981). For example, bone collagen stable carbon isotope ratios of animals feeding on C_3 plant material (such as most tree leaves) reflect the C_3 signature, whereas the ratios in animals feeding on C_4 plant material (such as many tropical grasses) will reflect the C_4 signature (Vogel 1978). Animals feeding on marine plant or animal material differ in both carbon and nitrogen stable isotope ratios from those feeding on terrestrial foods (Schoeninger and DeNiro, 1984). Bone collagen stable nitrogen isotope ratios and bone strontium concentrations in known herbivores and carnivores reflect the difference in isotopic ratio and trace element concentration in plants versus meat (Schoeninger 1979b, 1985, Sillen and Kavanagh 1982). Bone collagen stable carbon isotope ratios, on the other hand, do not reflect this particular difference in food composition (van der Merwe 1982, citing Vogel, personal communication). There is a rather large fractionation effect on carbon stable isotope ratios during the metabolism of food in collagen formation (3–5‰; DeNiro and Epstein 1978b, Vogel 1978). Between food and muscle of the animal, however, the magnitude of the fractionation is much smaller (DeNiro and Epstein

1978b, Tieszen *et al.* 1983) with the result that muscle in an animal has a $\delta^{13}C$ value which is 3–4‰ less positive than its own bone collagen. A carnivore feeding on flesh will consume a diet that is only 1‰ more positive than the plants which nourished the herbivore. Thus, carnivore bone collagen exhibits a $\delta^{13}C$ value on the order of 1‰ more positive than that of the herbivore upon which it fed (McConnaughey and McRoy 1979, Schoeninger and DeNiro 1984). For example, a herbivore feeding only on corn with a $\delta^{13}C$ value of −12.5‰ will have a bone collagen value of around −7 to −6‰ and flesh of around −11 to −10‰. A carnivore feeding on herbivore flesh of −11‰ will have a bone collagen value of around −6 to −5‰.

Thus far, analyses of bone from contemporary animals with known diets and from recent human populations with written dietary histories have produced results promising for these methods of dietary reconstruction. An excellent example of the application to protohistoric groups is the recent paper by Ambrose and DeNiro (1986a). These authors demonstrate that groups of pastoralists, agriculturalists, and combinations of these two subsistence patterns in East Africa, can be distinguished from each other on the basis of the stable isotope ratios of carbon and nitrogen in their bone collagen. Previous studies have demonstrated that these isotopic ratios also reflect expected dietary dependence on marine fish versus dependence on terrestrial plants and animals (Chisholm *et al.* 1982, Schoeninger *et al.* 1983, Tauber 1981, Walker and DeNiro 1986).

The applications of carbon stable isotope data to the prehistoric record have been intriguing. Tentative solutions have been proposed for the timing of the development of maize agriculture in Meso-America (Farnsworth *et al.* 1985), its use in South America (van der Merwe *et al.* 1981), and its introduction into North America (Bender *et al.* 1981, Lynott *et al.* 1986, van der Merwe and Vogel 1978). In addition, dependence by prehistoric groups on coastal marine resources has been estimated in northern Europe (Tauber 1981), North America (Walker and DeNiro 1986), South Africa (Sealy and van der Merwe 1986), and coastal Australia (Hobson and Collier 1984). The application of nitrogen isotope data to prehistoric samples where alternative sources of dietary information are lacking has not been as successful (Schwarcz *et al.* 1985). This point will be discussed in greater detail below.

The reconstruction of diet using trace elements has also been problematic. Sillen (1981a,b) demonstrated a significant separation, on average, of bone strontium levels in herbivores and carnivores at Hayonim cave in Israel. Human skeletons recovered from the same archaeological level had bone strontium concentrations which fell in the area of overlap between herbivores and carnivores. Other investigators have not been as fortunate. Katzenberg and Schwarcz (1984) could not distinguish between herbivores and omnivores on the basis of bone strontium levels at archaeological sites in Canada. Price *et al.* (1985a) report a huge range of variation in bone strontium levels of a population of wild shot white-tailed deer. When this range is compared with bone strontium levels of prehistoric humans in some studies (including Katzenberg's) the slight shift in means observed between time levels could be explained as sampling error. In some studies, the human bone strontium levels are higher than those for known herbivores (Decker 1986, Schoeninger 1981).

One proposed explanation (Schoeninger 1985) is that we do not yet have enough information on the distribution of strontium through single ecological systems, and for this reason, we do not know in which cases the method is applicable. Elias *et al.* (1982) report bone strontium concentrations in animals from different trophic levels within a single system, but very few individuals were analysed from each species and from each trophic level. Similar criticism can be made of the set of Iranian animals analysed by Schoeninger (1982). In other words, the variation within each dietary category is not well documented. Thus, although the means of two categories may differ significantly, particular diet items within each of two categories might be similar in strontium concentration. It is possible that the large range of variation in the deer mentioned above (Price *et al.* 1985a) is a reflection of high soil and groundwater levels of strontium or of uneven distribution in concentration of soil strontium throughout the home ranges of the deer. It is well known that major differences in background strontium occur between geographic regions (Schoeninger 1979, Sillen and Kavanagh 1982).

Preliminary data (Fig. 3.1 and Table 3.1) from an area called Buluk in northern Kenya, suggest that the situation may be more complex than has been appreciated up to this point. Bone samples from one human and from individuals representing several species of fauna, including both wild and domesticated animals, were collected near a waterhole located in a desert area north and east of Lake Turkana, close to the Ethiopian border. The bone is from animals and humans that live in the

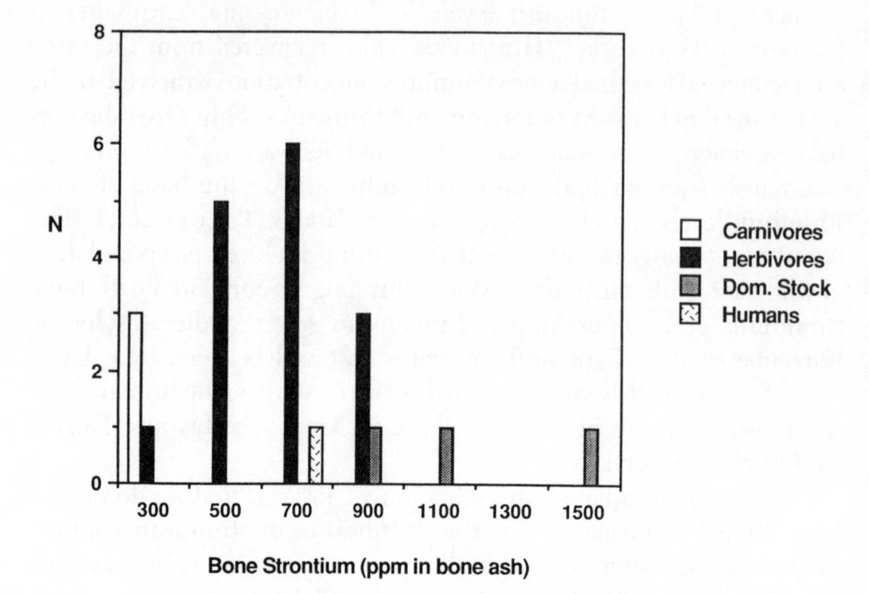

Fig. 3.1 Bone strontium concentrations in samples from Buluk in northern Kenya. Human, wild fauna, and domestic fauna are included. When compared with the wild fauna (Carnivores and Herbivores), the human diet appears to have been herbivorous; when compared with the domestic fauna (Dom. Stock) it appears to have been carnivorous; and when compared with wild carnivores and domestic fauna, it appears to have been omnivorous.
Note The intervals are labeled such that 300 ppm refers to 300 to 499 ppm, etc.; see Table 3.1 for specific values

area today and depend on the waterhole as their source of drinking water.

The sample sizes within each species and representing each dietary category are small, although the total sample size of fauna is larger than that analysed for most archaeological purposes. In any case, a point important to this discussion is obvious. If the single human sample is compared with wild fauna (labeled Carnivores and Herbivores in Fig. 3.1), it appears that the individual should be considered firmly within the herbivore feeding pattern. If, however, the comparison is made with domestic stock (sheep, labeled Dom. Stock in Fig. 3.1), the human

Table 3.1. *Buluk fauna: concentration of strontium in bone ash*

GROUP	Scientific and common names	Sr (ppm) in bone ash
CARNIVORES		
	Crocuta crocuta	389
	Spotted hyaena	
	Lynx caracal	364
	Caracal	361
HERBIVORES		
	Giraffa camelopardalis	450
	Giraffe	
	Tragelaphus strepsiceros	758
	Greater kudu	706
	Oryx beisa	972
	Oryx	
	Madoqua phillipsi	614
	Dik dik	754
		526
		858
		717
		576
		766
		533
		569
	Litocranius walleri	966
	Gerenuk	957
DOMESTIC STOCK		
	Ovis aries	1203
	Sheep	2257
		1591
	Bos	1034
	Cow	
HUMAN		
	Homo sapiens	827
	Human	

appears to have been carnivorous during life. A third possibility arises if the comparison is made between the human, on the one hand, and the carnivores and the domestic stock on the other. In this case, the human appears to have been an omnivore who ate equal amounts of meat and vegetable material. Obviously all of these interpretations cannot be correct. Yet, depending on the faunal samples chosen (or available) for analysis, any one of these would appear reasonable.

Thus far, there have been no published reports of bone collagen stable isotope ratios of carbon and nitrogen in terrestrial fauna from a single ecosystem. The recent paper by Ambrose and DeNiro (1986b) reports on samples from a broad geographic area. Results reported in Heaton *et al.* (1986) indicate that some geographic variation unrelated to diet may occur in the $\delta^{15}N$ values of bone collagen. Thus, such single ecosystem studies are essential. This is true especially in view of the proposal that one possible means of estimating the meat to vegetable proportions in human diet is to compare nitrogen stable isotope ratios in humans with those in known carnivores and herbivores (Schoeninger 1985).

Again, preliminary data suggest that this approach may not be as productive as originally hoped. Results from a larger project are presented in Fig. 3.2A and Table 3.2. The faunal samples were collected along the eastern shore of Lake Turkana in northern Kenya. The human data points are replotted from Ambrose and DeNiro (1986a). Four species of carnivores are represented (Table 3.2). Using the average of individuals within each species as a single value representing each species, the average $\delta^{15}N$ value of the four carnivore species was calculated to be +12.5‰. Three species of herbivores are represented; the average $\delta^{15}N$ value of the three species is +10.4‰. Thus, as in previous reports (Schoeninger 1985, Schoeninger and DeNiro 1984) carnivores are enriched relative to herbivores. The actual enrichment value cannot be determined from these data because the species represented do not reflect feeding relationships. For example, it is unlikely that the caracal (a small felid) would feed upon any of the large-bodied herbivores included in Table 3.2. Even so, a clear separation occurs between herbivores and carnivores in this trophic system.

In terms of carbon, the two species of grazing herbivores (topi and Burchell's zebra) have $\delta^{13}C$ values that are enriched relative to the browsing herbivore (gerenuk) by about 10‰. This reflects the C_4 composition of the grassland and the C_3 composition of the available browse reported by Tieszen *et al.* (1979a). It is interesting to note the intermediate position of the carnivores, indicating a feeding strategy which must include herbivores that feed on C_3 plants and also ones that feed on C_4 plants.

It was expected that humans with omnivorous diets would have nitrogen stable isotope ratios that would fall in between the end-points represented by the carnivores and herbivores. Rather than this occurrence, however, the mean and end-points of the $\delta^{13}C$ and $\delta^{15}N$ values of Turkana pastoralists reported by Ambrose and DeNiro (1986a) are far more enriched in nitrogen than expected. The $\delta^{15}N$ values of the human samples fall above the herbivore distribution and the mean value is equivalent to the most enriched carnivore.

Plotting human and fauna $\delta^{15}N$ values from systems other than the one at East Turkana indicated that the extreme nitrogen isotope ratio enrichment observed in humans from East Turkana is not unique (see Fig. 3.2B and C). Figure 3.2B (labeled *Terrestrial Trophic System*) is a plot of isotope data from recent prehistoric agriculturalists from one of the pueblos in the southwestern U.S. and of herbivorous and carnivorous fauna from the western portion of the U.S. The data are replotted from Schoeninger *et al.* (1983), Schoeninger and DeNiro (1984), and Schoeninger (1985). Figure 3.2C (labeled *Marine Trophic System*) includes data from Eskimo and N.W. Coast salmon fishers plotted with data from the marine fish and mammals collected along the California coast. The data here are replotted from Schoeninger *et al.* (1983) and Schoeninger and DeNiro (1984). In this figure, primary carnivores refer to invertebrate feeders such as walrus; secondary carnivores refer to vertebrate feeders such as seals and toothed whales.

In both cases, humans are more enriched in nitrogen than expected from ethnographic information about their diet. The pueblo agriculturalists, reported to have eaten about 80% corn (Wetterstrom 1986), should have human bone collagen with nitrogen stable isotope ratios close to the herbivore mean. On the contrary, the data indicate that the average value for humans is closer to that of the carnivores. Estimating human diet from these data would lead to the conclusion that humans ate nearly as much meat as did the carnivores. The data plotted in Figure 3.2C suggest that Eskimos and N.W. Coast fishers ate only top carnivores such as toothed whales. Since ethnographic evidence indicates that other animals lower in the trophic pyramid were actually dietary staples, it appears that a simple mixing line model is not sufficient in estimating human diet from nitrogen isotope ratios. A similar conclusion was reached by Bumsted (1983) with respect to carbon isotope ratios as predictors of the percentage of C_3 and C_4 plants in human diet.

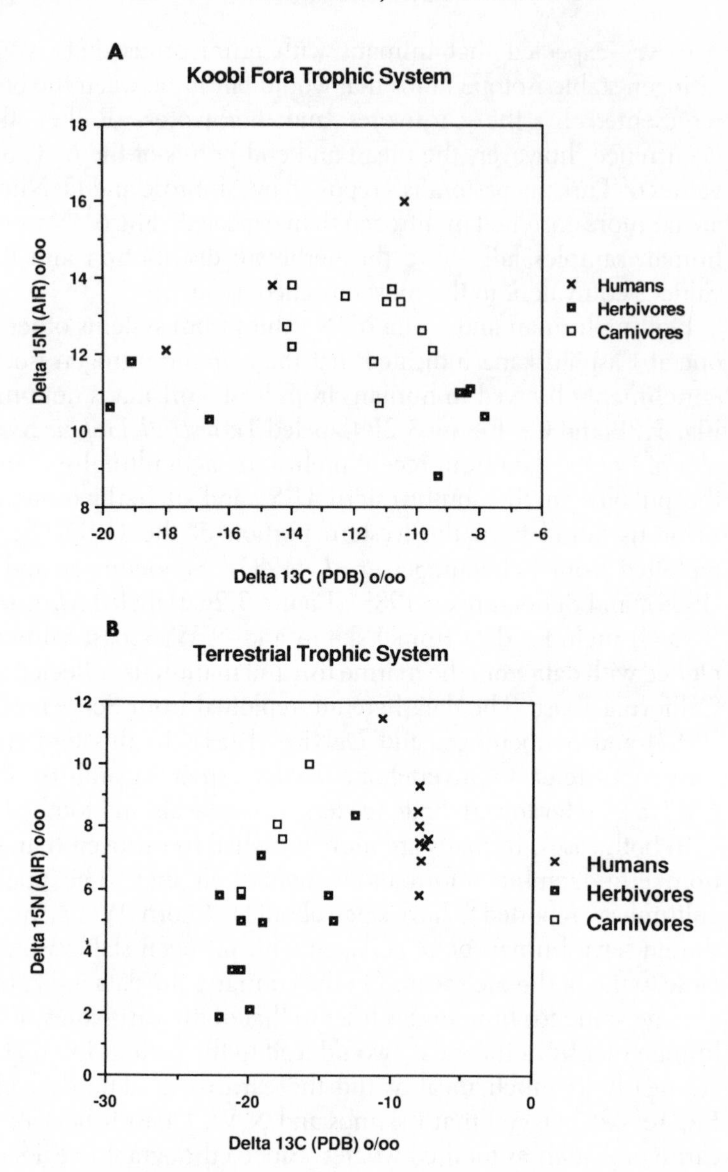

The explanation for these unexpected patterns may lie in recognizing the underlying assumption in this model. It assumes that human bone collagen $\delta^{15}N$ values will fall on a mixing line between 0 and 100% of calories from meat. Because virtually all of the nitrogen in food comes from protein whereas calories can be derived from protein, carbo-

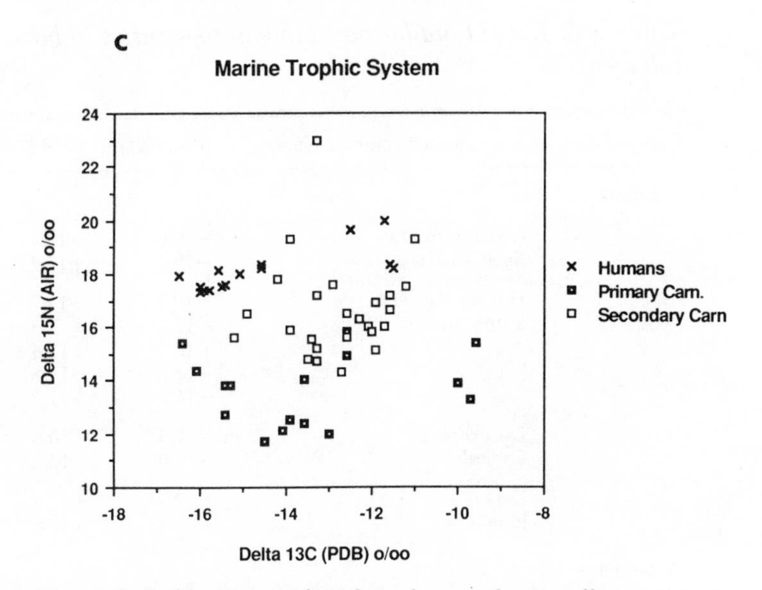

Fig. 3.2 Stable isotope data from human bone collagen samples plotted with those from fauna of known diets.
A. Koobi Fora Trophic System. The humans, taken from Ambrose and DeNiro (1986a), are pastoralists who live near Lake Turkana in northern Kenya. Rather than displaying $\delta^{15}N$ values intermediate between the herbivores and carnivores, the human values lie within the carnivore range.
B. Terrestrial Trophic System. The samples, both human and fauna, are from the southwestern portion of the United States. The humans are pueblo agriculturalists; yet, in nitrogen isotope ratios they appear to be more carnivorous than herbivorous.
C. Marine Trophic System. The samples, both human and fauna, are from the northwest coast of North America. The fauna represent invertebrate feeders such as walrus (primary carnivores) and vertebrate feeders such as seals and toothed whales (secondary carnivores). Although the humans obtained food items from both trophic levels, the nitrogen isotope ratios of human bone collagen suggest that all foods were selected from the top of the trophic system.

hydrates, and lipids, the true mixing line for $\delta^{15}N$ values should be 0 to 100% protein. It is possible that given the relatively protein-rich diet of humans, the great majority of nitrogen incorporated in collagen comes from unaltered amino acids rather than through transamination. Reports in the literature (Gaebler *et al.* 1966, Macko *et al.* 1982a)

Table 3.2. *Koobi Fora fauna: stable isotope ratios in bone collagen*

Group	Scientific and common names	$\delta^{13}C$ (‰)	$\delta^{15}N$ (‰)
Carnivores			
	Crocuta crocuta	−9.6	+12.9
	Spotted hyaena	−10.5	+12.7
	Hyaena hyaena	−10.8	+13.7
	Striped hyaena	−12.3	+13.5
		−10.5	+13.4
		−14.0	+13.8
		−11.0	+12.7
	Lynx caracal	−11.5	+10.6
	Caracal	−14.0	+12.2
	Leo leo	−9.8	+12.6
	Lion	−11.4	+11.8
		−9.5	+12.1
Herbivores			
	Equus burchelli	−9.3	+8.8
	Burchell's zebra		
	Damaliscus korrigum	−8.6	+11.0
	Topi	−8.3	+11.7
		−8.4	+11.0
		−7.8	+10.4
	Litocranius walleri	−16.6	+10.3
	Gerenuk	−19.1	+11.8
		−19.8	+11.8

disagree whether lack of transamination would result in $\delta^{15}N$ depletion or accumulation. For this reason, the mechanism underlying this observed enrichment in humans relative to other animals is not clear.

Given the level of our analyses we can assume that nitrogen from plant protein has a possibility of being incorporated into bone collagen equal to that of nitrogen from animal protein. Although most nutrition texts state that meat protein is more efficiently absorbed than plant protein, the difference is not large enough to affect the estimation, given the overall variation in isotope ratios between individuals (DeNiro and Schoeninger 1985).

DIET RECONSTRUCTION USING FOOD COMPONENT DATA

Pecos Pueblo

The data presented here were obtained from a study undertaken in collaboration with Dr. Katherine Spielmann of the University of Iowa. Preliminary results have been presented previously (Schoeninger and Spielmann 1986). A complete report on diet at the pueblo through the time of occupation will be presented elsewhere (Schoeninger and Spielmann, in preparation).

The ruins of Pecos pueblo are situated near the present city of Santa Fe, New Mexico. It was a prehistoric agricultural village situated on a small mesa with agricultural fields in the surrounding lowlands. Occupied for at least 500 years beginning around A.D. 1300, its inhabitants were agriculturalists who hunted for antelope and deer or obtained bison meat through trade with plains-dwelling hunter-gatherers (Spielmann 1982). In addition, they probably gathered wild plants such as pinyon nuts, chenopodium, amaranth, and Indian rice grass (Wetterstrom 1986).

An outline for diet estimation at Pecos was taken from a recent report of a study of plant and animal material recovered from Arroyo Hondo pueblo (Wetterstrom 1986) located near Pecos. Although situated in a somewhat more marginal local environment than Pecos, Arroyo Hondo presents a picture similar to that at Pecos. Using estimates of amount of available arable land, of the land's productivity, and of population size, Wetterstrom calculated the percent caloric contribution for each cultivar grown in the area. Using similar estimates based on population density of each species of animal living in the area and the density expected for the wild plants, she calculated the calories which could have been contributed by each type of animal and each species of wild plant. The floral and faunal remains recovered from Pecos pueblo included the same items which Wetterstrom (1986) reports from Arroyo Hondo pueblo, with the exception that a large quantity of bison bone was recovered from Pecos (Spielmann 1982). Bison was uncommon at Arroyo Hondo.

Using Wetterstrom's estimates for Arroyo Hondo pueblo, a table was constructed listing food items with estimates of their importance in diet (Table 3.3). At Arroyo Hondo, maize could have been produced in

Table 3.3. *Food items at Pecos pueblo*[a]

	% Calories in diet	Cal/100 g[b]	Prot/100 g[b]	Prot/100 cal
Cultivated Plants				
Maize (*Zea mays*)	up to 100%	348	8.9	2.6
Beans (*Phaseolus vulgaris*)	up to 20%	118	7.8	6.6
Squash (*Cucurbita sp*)	Unimportant	–	–	–
Wild Plants: Weedy Annuals				
Cheno Ams:				
Amaranth seeds (*Amaranthus sp*)		36	3.5	9.7
and	Up to 15%			
Chenopodium seeds (*Chenopodium sp*)		320	13.3	4.2
Sunflower (*Helianthus sp*)	Unimportant	–	–	–
Other Wild Plants				
Fruits:				
Prickly Pear (*Platyopuntia sp*)	Unimportant	–	–	–
Cholla (*Cylindropuntia sp*) etc.	Unimportant	–	–	–
Indian rice grass (*Oryzopsis hymenoides*)	Unimportant	–	–	–
Pinyon (*Pinus edulis*)	Up to 15%	635	13	2.0
Fauna				
Hares (*Lepus californicus*) and Rabbits (*Sylvilagus audubonic*)	Unimportant	–	–	–
Mule deer (*Odocoileus hemionus*)	up to 10%	–	21.0	16.7
Turkey (*Meleagris gallopavo*)	Unimportant	–	–	–
Pronghorn antelope (*Antilocapra americana*)	Up to 5%	126	21.0	16.7
Bison (*Bison bison*)	Up to 10%	138	25.0	18.1

[a] See text for discussion
[b] Values taken from Watt and Merrill (1975), Styles (1986), Sokolov (1986)

sufficient quantities to provide up to 100% of required calories during years with moderate rainfall. Since the area surrounding Pecos is not as dry as that at Arroyo Hondo, it is reasonable to assume that in normal years the inhabitants at Pecos could have produced sufficient maize to meet energy needs. In fact, Spielmann (1982) has argued that beyond meeting their own energy requirements, the people of Pecos produced enough maize to use in trading for bison meat with plains-dwelling hunting-gathering groups. This is not a suggestion that maize actually provided all of the calories in the diet of the inhabitants at Pecos. Given the well-documented nutritional insufficiencies of a total maize diet it is considered unlikely that the inhabitants of Pecos subsisted on a monotonous diet of maize.

The estimates of other food items are used to suggest limits on the amount of maize in the diet. Wetterstrom (1986) reports that enough beans could have been grown to provide up to 20% of total required calories, yet ethnographic evidence argues against the consumption of such a large amount of beans. For this reason, she suggests that only a small fraction of the calories would have come from beans. Wetterstrom considers that squash is "unimportant" (less than 1% of total calories) because it does not grow well in the area surrounding Pecos and Arroyo Hondo. On the other hand, some of the weedy annuals (e.g. chenopodium and amaranth) could have provided up to 15% of total calories because they are ubiquitous in disturbed environments in the area. Sunflower, wild cactus fruits, and Indian rice grass are thought to be unimportant based on ethnographic evidence even though they probably were eaten in certain seasons. Pinyon, on the other hand, could have been a substantial source of calories. Even though good yields could be expected only once in six years, the nuts can be stored and thus used over the whole six-year period. Of the various types of fauna, only mule deer and, to a lesser extent, antelope, were considered to have contributed significantly to the diet at Arroyo Hondo. Wetterstrom argues that in the area surrounding Arroyo Hondo (and similarly for Pecos) turkey, rabbit, and hare probably provided less than 1% of the total calories. Bison has been added to the list of diet items at Pecos because the faunal remains from Pecos indicate that bison was an important meat component in the diet.

Samples of several diet items were obtained from areas near Pecos and Arroyo Hondo pueblos. These samples were analysed for nitrogen stable isotope ratios (Table 3.4). Carbon stable isotope ratios of plants were

Table 3.4. *Stable isotope ratios of C and N in food items from Pecos pueblo*

Food	$\delta^{13}C$(‰)	$\delta^{15}N$(‰)
Maize (*Zea mays*)	−12.5	+ 8.2
Beans (*Phaseolus vulgaris*)	−26	0.0
Amaranth seeds (*Amaranthus sp*)	−12.5	+11.1
Chenopodium seeds (*Chenopodium sp*)	−26	+ 7.4
Mule deer (*Odocoileus hemionus*)	−21.5[a]	+ 5.0
Pronghorn antelope (*Antilocapra americana*)	−22[a]	+ 5.6[b]
Bison (*Bison bison*)	−13.2[a]	+ 5.6

[a] The $\delta^{13}C$ values for meat were estimated by subtracting 4‰ from the $\delta^{13}C$ values measured in bone collagen in each animal. DeNiro and Epstein (1978[b]) report that muscle tissue is about 4‰ less negative than bone collagen. The $\delta^{13}C$ value of antelope bone collagen was provided by N. van der Merwe. Since $\delta^{15}N$ value of bone collagen is extremely close to that of muscle tissue (DeNiro and Epstein 1981), the $\delta^{15}N$ value measured in bone collagen is used as an estimation for the value in meat.
[b] Value based on that of bison.

taken from the literature (van der Merwe 1982) as were the nitrogen stable isotope ratios of pinyon and beans (Virginia and Delwiche 1982). Collagen from bison, antelope, and mule deer bone was extracted and analysed as described below for the human samples. The results of these analyses are shown in Table 3.4.

Using these data it is possible to estimate the stable isotope ratios of nitrogen and carbon that would be produced in the bone collagen of humans eating particular combinations of diet items. For example, using Wetterstrom's (1986) estimates for human diet at Arroyo Hondo pueblo, a diet consisting of 5% beans, 5% amaranth, 5% chenopodium, 15% pinyon nuts, 5% mule deer meat, and 5% antelope or bison meat can be proposed (see Fig. 3.3A and B and Table 3.5). Such a diet would provide 60% of its calories as corn. Table 3.5 lists the weighted $\delta^{13}C$ and weighted $\delta^{15}N$ values for each component of diet. The weighted $\delta^{13}C$ value is calculated as:

Weighted $\delta^{13}C$ = % calories food item × ($\delta^{13}C$ food item + f.f.)
where f.f. = fractionation factor.

In the case of C_4 plants (maize and amaranth), the fractionation factor used is 6‰ (following Bumsted 1983); thus the percentage of calories in the diet is multiplied by −6.5‰ (−12.5 + 6). The fractionation factor between C_3 plants and bone collagen is 5‰ (van der Merwe 1982) and the same fractionation factor is assumed between meat and bone collagen. A fractionation factor of +1‰ is used between the value for collagen reported in the table and the bone collagen value expected to be produced from the meat (flesh) represented by that bone collagen. Bone collagen $\delta^{13}C$ values of animals from adjacent trophic levels differ by approximately 1‰. As discussed earlier, this occurs because flesh is approximately 4‰ more negative than bone collagen (DeNiro and Epstein 1978b) and a 5‰ fractionation occurs between flesh and the bone collagen of the animal that eats the flesh.

In the case of carbon, the delta value of each food item is multiplied by the percent calories in diet in order to estimate the contribution of that food item to the $\delta^{13}C$ value of the total diet. Carbon atoms can be obtained through the metabolism of carbohydrates, lipids, and proteins, since all these molecules contain carbon. For this reason, the weighting used for estimating the $\delta^{13}C$ value of the diet is calculated using total calories.

Nitrogen atoms, on the other hand, are located only in protein. For that reason, the percent protein of each food item was calculated using nutrition tables (Watt and Merrill 1975). In calculating expected $\delta^{15}N$ values, the delta value of each food item was multiplied by the percent protein in diet in order to estimate the contribution of that food item to the diet as a whole. Thus:

Weighted $\delta^{15}N$ = % protein food item × ($\delta^{15}N$ food item + f.f.)
where f.f. = fractionation factor.

The fractionation factor between all foods and bone collagen is 3‰ (DeNiro and Epstein 1981).

From the total skeletal sample at Pecos, over 100 individuals were analysed for bone strontium levels, 15 were analysed for bone collagen $\delta^{13}C$ values, and 31 were analysed for bone collagen $\delta^{15}N$ values.

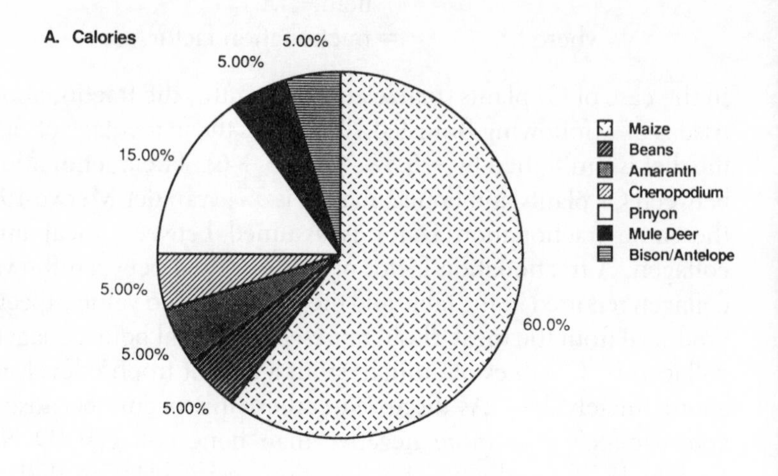

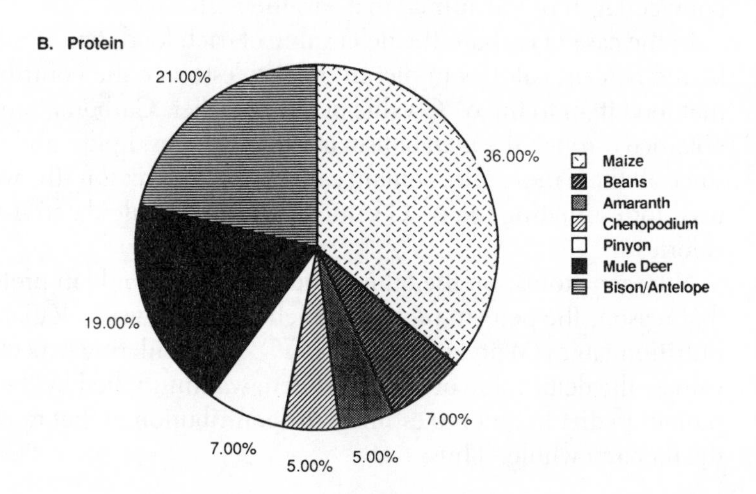

Fig. 3.3 Diets proposed for the inhabitants of Pecos pueblo.
A. The contribution of individual diet items to the total caloric content of a diet containing 60% of its calories as maize.
B. The protein content of the diet in A. Note the change in representation of meat between the two figures. This will affect the final nitrogen isotope ratio of diet as explained in the text.
C. The caloric content of a diet containing 80% of its calories as maize.
D. The protein content of the diet in C.

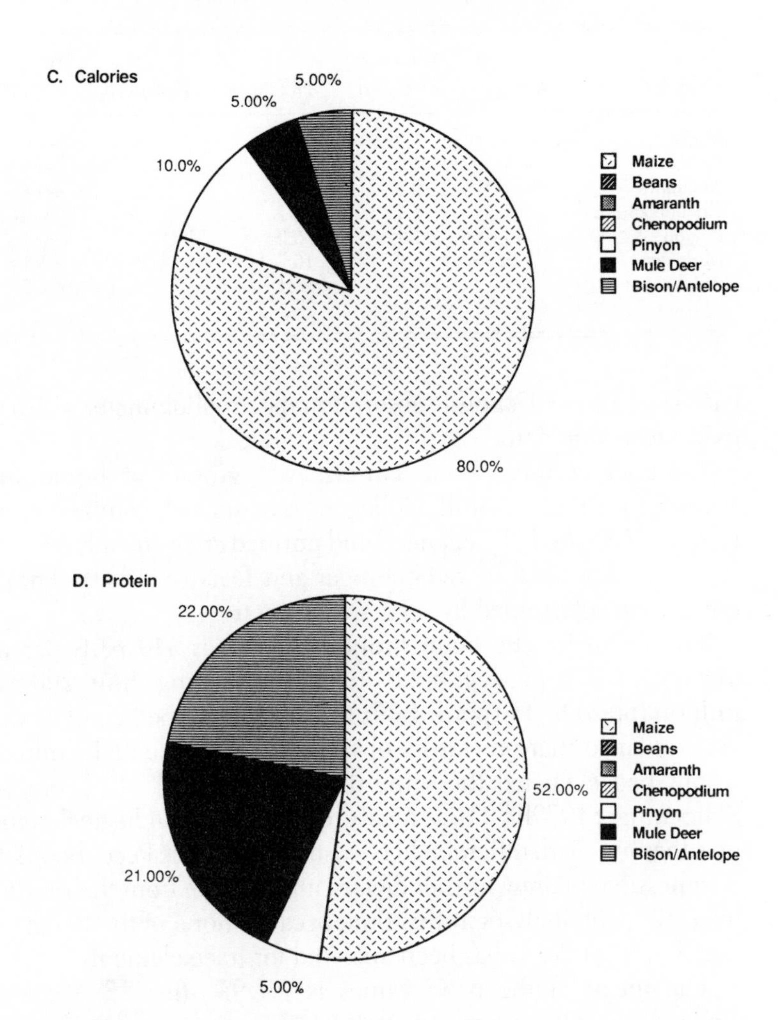

Portions of each sample were cleaned mechanically; cancellous bone was removed because it tends to trap soil. The remaining cortical bone was then cleaned in double-distilled, de-ionized water in an ultrasonic cleaner. After drying to a constant weight in a low temperature oven, the bone was ground either in a ball mill grinder or by hand with a mortar and pestle, taking care to avoid heating the bone. Sample preparation for elemental analyses was the same as that described in an earlier paper by Schoeninger (1981). Bone samples were analysed for strontium using

Table 3.5. *Proposed diet at Pecos: estimate #1*

Food item	Calories (%)	Weighted $\delta^{13}C$ (‰)	Protein (g)	Protein (%)	Weighted $\delta^{15}N$ (‰)
Maize	60	−3.9	31.2	36	+2.9
Beans	5	−1.0	6.6	7	0.0
Amaranth	5	−0.3	4.3	5	+0.6
Chenopodium	5	−1.1	4.2	5	+0.4
Pinyon	15	−3.1	6.0	7	+0.1
Mule deer	5	−0.8	16.7	19	+1.1
Antelope or bison	5	−0.8	18.1	21	+1.2

a Perkin-Elmer 403 atomic absorption spectrophotometer with a nitrous oxide/acetylene flame.

A subset of these bone samples was ground at liquid nitrogen temperature in a Spex mill. Collagen was extracted, combusted, and the resulting CO_2 and N_2 separated and purified cryogenically in a vacuum system as described by Schoeninger and DeNiro (1984). The isotope ratios were determined by mass spectrometry.

The mean for the bone strontium levels is 340 parts per million (n = 103, s.d. = 60, c.v. = 17%). The values range from 200 parts per million (ppm) to 450 ppm. Both the range and coefficient of variation are similar to that previously observed in a sample of 19 mink, all of whom had been fed the same diet ($\bar{x}$ = 336, s.d. = 75, c.v. = 22%; Schoeninger 1979b). These measures of variation indicate that there are no subgroups with different diets existing within the Pecos population. It is impossible to draw further dietary information from the results of the trace element analyses at this time because none of the fauna or plant material from Pecos has been analysed for trace elements.

The mean of the $\delta^{13}C$ values is −7.9‰ (n = 15, s.d. = 0.6‰, c.v. = 8%). The mean of the $\delta^{15}N$ values is +9.1‰ (n = 31, s.d. = 0.7‰, c.v. = 7%). Comparing these data with the estimated value from the diet proposed above (Table 3.5), several things are obvious. First, the combination of meat and plant material in Wetterstrom's proposed diet should produce a bone collagen $\delta^{15}N$ value virtually identical to that actually observed in the analysed Pecos skeletal samples. This suggests that the people at Pecos ate no more than about 10% of their calories as meat. This agrees with previous estimates based on ethnographic reports (Spielmann 1982). Increasing the amount of

Table 3.6. *Proposed diet at Pecos: estimate #2*

Food item	Calories (%)	Weighted $\delta^{13}C$ (‰)	Protein (%)	Weighted $\delta^{15}N$ (‰)
Maize	80	−5.2	52	+5.8
Pinyon	10	−2.1	5	+0.2
Mule deer	5	−0.8	21	+1.9
Bison	5	−0.5	22	+1.7

meat would increase the weighted $\delta^{15}N$ value markedly because the high protein content in meat affects the final value to a great extent. Secondly, given the high protein content and $\delta^{15}N$ value of amaranth seeds (Tables 3.3 and 3.4), it is unlikely that diet could have included much more than the 5% amaranth that is suggested. Thirdly, the $\delta^{13}C$ value obtained from the Pecos skeletal sample suggests that the C_4 component of the proposed diet is grossly under-represented in this proposed diet (diet #1) because such a diet should produce bone collagen with a $\delta^{13}C$ value of −11.0‰ whereas the measured value is actually −7.9‰. The ways of increasing the C_4 component are to increase amaranth, bison, or maize. For the reasons discussed previously, it is unlikely that amaranth was used to an extent greater than that already suggested. In fact, given its high protein content and $\delta^{15}N$ value it is reasonable to drop amaranth altogether. The only way to increase the contribution by bison would be to decrease the contribution by mule deer because the overall percentage of meat cannot be increased without raising the expected $\delta^{15}N$ value to an unacceptable amount. The most reasonable solution appears to be an increase in the amount of corn in the diet (see Table 3.6). Beans were dropped from this second proposed diet in order to simplify the calculations.

Increasing the representation of corn in the diet to 80% of total calories should produce human bone collagen with a $\delta^{13}C$ value of −8.7‰. This is still 1‰ less positive than that actually observed at Pecos, indicating that the C_4 component must be increased even more. Replacing the mule deer with bison meat produces a $\delta^{13}C$ value of −8.2‰ (Table 3.7). This appears to be the most reasonable way of increasing the $\delta^{13}C$ value of the diet. The alternative, i.e. increasing the amount of corn, is less attractive since it contradicts ethnographic evidence of the diets of the pueblo groups.

One slight problem, however, is that the new diet produces a $\delta^{15}N$

Table 3.7. *Proposed diet at Pecos: estimate #3*

Food item	Calories (%)	Weighted $\delta^{13}C$ (‰)	Protein (%)	Weighted $\delta^{15}N$ (‰)
Maize	80	−5.2	48	+5.4
Beans	5	−1.0	8	+0.2
Pinyon	5	−1.1	2	+0.1
Bison	10	−0.8	42	+3.6

value of +9.6‰ which is more positive than the mean $\delta^{15}N$ value actually measured (although it is within the range of values obtained). Replacing a portion of the calories contributed by pinyon with beans would lower the $\delta^{15}N$ value in two ways. First, it would be lowered because the $\delta^{15}N$ value for beans is about 1‰ more negative than that of pinyon, and secondly, the percent protein contribution by beans would be greater, thus giving the more negative nitrogen a greater impact. These proposed changes would result in the diet shown in Table 3.7 and Fig. 3.3C and D.

In this diet, the percent protein contributed by the beans/pinyon portion has doubled, and the overall $\delta^{15}N$ has been decreased by 0.3‰. This is in the right direction even though the magnitude is not large enough to achieve the measured $\delta^{15}N$ value of collagen.

Dutch Whalers

The data discussed below were obtained from a collaborative project with Drs. George Maat and Louise H. van Wijngaarden-Bakker as part of an investigation by the Arctic Centre of Ryksuniversiteit Groningen into the development of Dutch whaling during the seventeenth and eighteenth centuries. From a total of 200 Dutch whalers buried on a small island near Spitsbergen, Dr. George Maat excavated, studied, and took bone samples from 50 skeletons (Maat 1981, 1984). Low temperatures in this area, located within the Arctic Circle, ensured the best possible preservation.

Of these 50 skeletons, 44 were analysed for bone strontium levels in the manner described previously in this paper. The 44 bone samples had an average value of 184 parts per million (ppm) strontium in bone ash. The standard deviation is 46 ppm and the coefficient of variation is 25%. The variation within this set of results is similar to that observed in the analyses of bone from 19 mink raised on a monotonous diet ($\bar{x} = 336$, s.d. = 75, c.v. = 22%). Although the absolute value of the mean in the mink sample is higher than that in the human sample, the range of bone strontium levels in both the whalers and the mink is about 200 ppm. Further, the coefficient of variation is similar in both sets. This similarity in statistics describing variation indicates strongly that only one type of diet was shared by all of the whalers. In other words, each individual ate roughly the same proportion of meat and vegetable products as was eaten by all other whalers. This suggestion is supported by the written accounts describing the living situation of the whalers. Nothing more can be said concerning diet among the Dutch whalers, based on bone strontium levels, because comparative fauna from the area have not been analysed.

A small number of skeletons were also prepared for stable isotope analysis of bone collagen as described previously in this paper. The range, standard deviation and coefficient of variation for both $\delta^{15}N$ and $\delta^{13}C$ values were so low that additional samples were not analysed. The mean $\delta^{15}N$ value for six whalers was +12.2‰ (s.d. = 0.9‰, c.v. = 7%, range = 2.0‰). The mean $\delta^{13}C$ values for six whalers was −19.2‰ (s.d. = 0.5‰, c.v. = 3%, range = 1.5‰). The comparable values describing variation in the sample of mink fed monotonous diets are very similar (DeNiro and Schoeninger 1985). In the previous study, bone samples from 19 mink had a range of 1.5‰, standard deviation of 0.2‰, and a coefficient of variation of 2% for carbon. The equivalent nitrogen values were: range = 2‰, standard deviation = 0.4‰, and coefficient of variation = 4%. Van Wijngaarden-Bakker conducted excavation in the whaling stations near Spitzbergen and also studied the ships' records that described foods carried on board ship. According to the resulting overview by van Wijngaarden-Bakker and Pals (1981), whalers subsisted largely on bread, cheese, salted or smoked meat and fish, groats, peas, and beer. A single whaling journey lasted four to five months. Thus, depending on whether a whaler joined one or two such expeditions each year, he could spend up to two-thirds of the year away from the Netherlands. Given that the origin of most whalers was the poorer regions of the country (Maat 1981), it is expected that the diet of individual whalers during their time at home was similar to that which they had on board ship (van Wijngaarden-Bakker, personal communication). Based on the above, a compilation of food items eaten by the whalers can be produced (see Table 3.8). The high percentage of cow

Table 3.8. *Composition of food items eaten by Dutch whalers*

	Cal/100 g[a]	Prot/100 g[a]	g Prot/100 cal	$\delta^{13}C$	$\delta^{15}N$
Fish					
Cod, salted	130	29.0	22.3	−12.5	+13.8
Pork					
Composite of lean cuts w/bones and skin	1028	62.2	6.0	−21	+ 5.5
Beef					
Carcass, standard grade	225	19.4	8.6	−21	+ 5.5
Rye (flour)	1588	51.7	3.3	−26	+ 5.1
Barley (whole)	348	9.6	2.8	−26	+ 5.1
Beans	348	20.4	5.9	−26	0.0
Peas	340	24.1	7.1	−26	0.0

[a] Values taken from Watt and Merrill (1975).

ribs and vertebrae recovered in the archaeo-zoological remains led van Wijngaarden-Bakker to conclude that the salted meat stored on the ship was produced from the cheapest cuts of beef. Almost all bones of pig are represented which suggests that whole carcasses were included rather than selected portions. Recovered plant remains and recorded lists of foodstuffs indicate at least two cereal species were taken as provisions. Rye was used as flour in baking bread. Barley (possibly mixed with wheat) was eaten as groats for porridge. Remains of two types of pulses were also recovered, horsebeans (*Vicia faba*) and peas (*Pisum sativum*). Some fruits were also included but probably constituted only a trivial portion of the diet. Fresh meat from reindeer may have been eaten, but the amount included in diet is unknown. In all likelihood such additions were few and far between since the whalers would not have been given free time for hunting. Table 3.8 includes the composition of food items considered to be most similar to that eaten by the whalers.

The $\delta^{13}C$ and $\delta^{15}N$ values obtained from human bone collagen can be used to produce estimates of diet including the identified floral and faunal remains. It is obvious that no single diet can be proposed which uniquely produces the measured bone collagen isotope ratios. Even so, limits on the percent caloric representation of particular diet items can be identified when violation of those limits would result in bone collagen isotope values that are different from those actually measured in bone. Table 3.8 includes $\delta^{13}C$ and $\delta^{15}N$ values for each food item. The $\delta^{15}N$ and $\delta^{13}C$ values for the animal foods are taken from

Schoeninger and DeNiro (1984). The value for fish is the average value observed in collagen of ten marine fish, and the value for pork and beef collagen is the average for six large-bodied herbivorous mammals from C_3 environments. The $\delta^{15}N$ value for rye and barley is the average of non-leguminous domesticated food plants reported by DeNiro and Hastorf (1986). The $\delta^{15}N$ value for beans and peas is the average for nitrogen-fixing plants reported by Virginia and Delwiche (1982). The $\delta^{13}C$ value for all plants is the average value for C_3 plants as reported by van der Merwe (1982).

As discussed above for the Pecos sample, diets can be calculated and the $\delta^{13}C$ and $\delta^{15}N$ values expected in resultant bone collagen can be proposed. In calculating the $\delta^{13}C$ of bone collagen, the percent calories for each food item is used for weighting because all components of diet contain carbon. Between plant $\delta^{13}C$ and bone collagen $\delta^{13}C$, a fractionation factor of +5‰ is used based on Vogel's field studies of large-bodied animals (cited by van der Merwe 1982). A fractionation factor of +1‰ is used between the value for collagen and diet for reasons discussed previously. In each case the following equation was used:

$$\text{Weighted } \delta^{13}C = \%\ \text{calories food item} \times (\delta^{13}C\ \text{food item} + \text{f.f.})$$

where f.f. = fractionation factor.

The equivalent equation for calculating weighted $\delta^{15}N$ values uses percent protein as shown for the Pecos sample. For all food categories, the fractionation factor between diet $\delta^{15}N$ and bone collagen $\delta^{15}N$ is +3‰ as discussed above. Thus:

$$\text{Weighted } \delta^{15}N = \%\ \text{protein food item} \times (\delta^{15}N\ \text{food item} + \text{f.f.})$$

where f.f. = fractionation factor.

For the purposes of proposing diets, some food items in Table 3.8 were combined. Pork and beef were combined into a "meat" category for two reasons. First, during the seventeenth century pigs would not have been fattened to the extent that they are today. Thus it was assumed that the protein per 100 calories of pork and beef would be more similar to each other than shown in Table 3.8, which is taken from analyses of contemporary samples (Watt and Merrill 1975). A value of 8 grams of protein per 100 calories was used in the calculations presented below. Secondly, the $\delta^{13}C$ and $\delta^{15}N$ in both pork and beef were estimated as

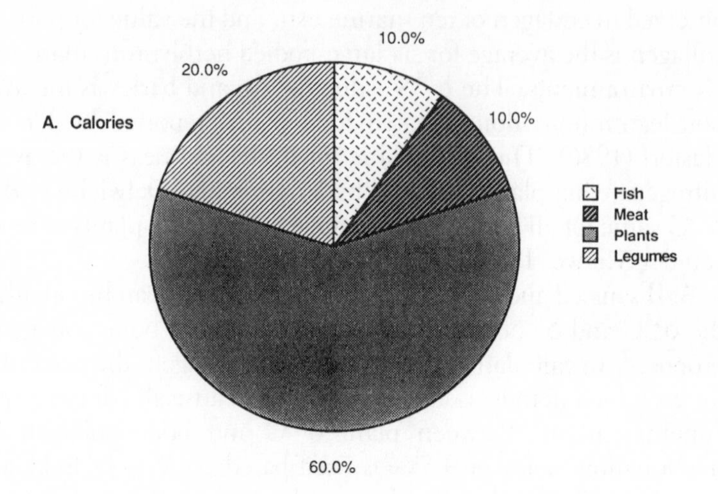

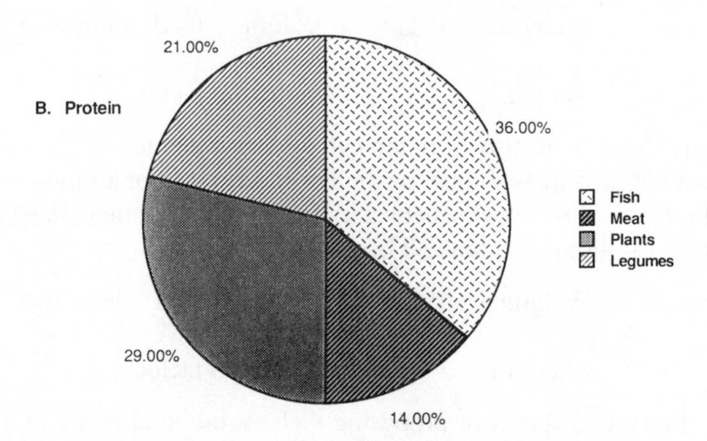

Fig. 3.4 Diets proposed for Dutch whalers.
A. The contribution of individual diet items to the total caloric content of the diet.
B. The protein content of the diet in A. Note the marked change in representation of fish between the caloric and the protein proportion of diet.
C. The caloric breakdown of a diet with a greater portion of the calories provided from fish.
D. The protein content of the diet in C.

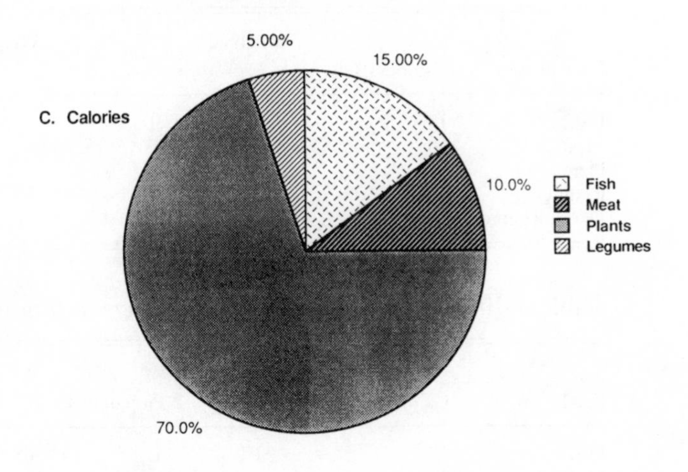

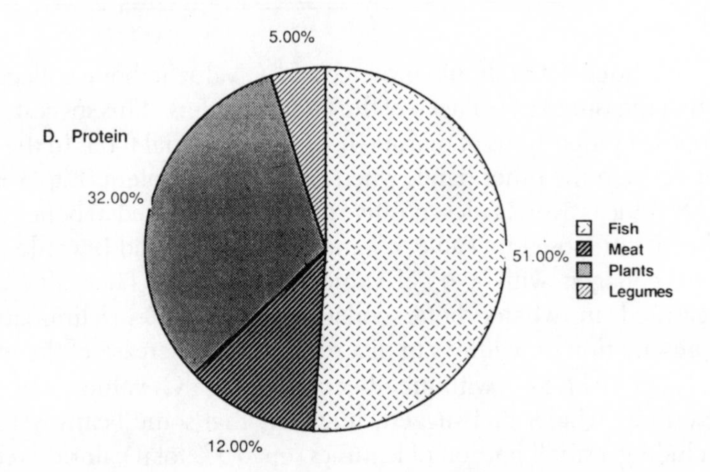

identical because both pigs and cows are herbivores; thus the average value from a previous study was used for both. For the same reasons, rye and barley were grouped as "plants: non-legumes" (3 grams of protein per 100 calories) and beans and peas were grouped as "plants: legumes" (6.5 grams of protein per 100 calories).

Using these values, a diet in which about 20% of total calories are derived from meat and fish can be proposed (see Table 3.9 and Fig. 3.4A

Table 3.9. *Proposed diet of Dutch whalers: estimate #1*

Food item	Calories (%)	Weighted $\delta^{13}C$ (‰)	Protein (%)	Weighted $\delta^{15}N$ (‰)
Fish	10	− 0.8	36	+6.0
Meat	10	− 2.0	13	+1.1
Plants: non-legumes	60	−12.6	29	+2.3
Plants: legumes	20	− 4.2	21	+0.6

Table 3.10. *Proposed diet of Dutch whalers: estimate #2*

Food item	Calories (%)	Weighted $\delta^{13}C$ (‰)	Protein (%)	Weighted $\delta^{15}N$ (‰)
Fish	15	− 1.2	51	+8.6
Meat	10	− 2.0	12	+1.0
Plants: non-legumes	70	−14.7	32	+0.2
Plants: legumes	5	− 1.1	5	+0.2

and B). Such a diet should produce a $\delta^{13}C$ value in bone collagen close to that measured in collagen of the Dutch whalers. This suggests that the proposed proportions of marine (fish) and terrestrial foods in the diet are correct. On the other hand, when considering protein (Fig. 3.4B), the $\delta^{15}N$ value is over 2‰ less positive than that measured in bone collagen. The diet proposed in Table 3.9 and in Fig. 3.4A and B would produce bone collagen with a $\delta^{15}N$ value of +10.0‰. The value actually measured in whaler bone collagen is +12.2‰. Eliminating the representation of legumes in diet results in an increase of the weighted $\delta^{15}N$ to +11.8‰ without affecting the $\delta^{13}C$ value. The reports describing whaler diet suggest, however, that some beans were eaten. Including a small portion of legumes (up to 5% total calories) requires a slight increase in the amount of fish (see Table 3.10 and Fig. 3.4C and D) in order to produce an expected bone collagen $\delta^{15}N$ value of +12.4‰ and a $\delta^{13}C$ value of −19‰.

CONCLUSIONS

In the preceding pages two approaches to the reconstruction of prehistoric human diet were presented and discussed. In the first, bone strontium concentrations and stable isotope ratios of carbon and nitrogen in bone collagen from fauna of known diet and from humans were compared. It was assumed that human bone strontium and nitrogen stable isotope ratios would have values intermediate between herbivores and carnivores. The specific position was anticipated to depend on the amount of carnivory and herbivory practiced by particular humans or groups of humans. A comparison of preliminary data on fauna from the two separate regions east of Lake Turkana in Kenya with data on humans from the same regions do not support this assumption. Bone strontium levels in wild fauna bracket the human data, suggesting that the humans were omnivorous. The domesticated fauna, on the other hand, have bone strontium levels that are much higher than humans which makes it appear that the humans were carnivorous. Choosing the proper faunal sample for comparison with humans appears to be critical in attempts to use bone strontium levels in assessing dependence on meat by prehistoric people.

The nitrogen isotope data are also less than clear cut. When $\delta^{15}N$ values of bone collagen from humans are plotted with those from fauna, humans have values near the extreme of the positive end of the range of faunal nitrogen isotope data. Examples were presented from three different regions of the world including northern Kenya, the southwestern United States, and the northwest coast of North America. These examples reflect three different subsistence strategies: pastoralist, agriculturalist, and hunter-gatherers. It is suggested that the explanation may lie in the fact that humans subsist on diets that are relatively high in protein and that the extractable protein can be obtained from plants as well as from meat. Thus, the proper comparison should be with the amount of protein rather than calories. The original expectation that human data would be intermediate between herbivores and carnivores includes the implicit assumption that nitrogen can be obtained from all food components. The only way that an atom of nitrogen analysed in collagen could have originated in the carbohydrate or lipid portion of diet is through transamination of that atom from a protein amino acid to a molecule from one of the other two components. It may be that with excess protein in diet, as is true for most humans and for carnivores, this transamination does not occur. There are conflicting reports in the literature concerning the expected effect of transamination on $\delta^{15}N$ enrichment. In any case, the major source of nitrogen is protein and the proper comparison is with 0 to 100% of total protein whether that protein comes from plants or animals. This assessment of the source of nitrogen is used in the second (more successful) approach to reconstructing human diet.

Several diets were proposed for the prehistoric population at Pecos pueblo in New Mexico and for recent whalers from the Netherlands. The method for proposing each diet consists of combining information gained from identification of excavated food items with the results from stable isotope analysis of those food items. The results of trace element analyses for bone strontium were used as an indication that no major differences in diet existed within subsets of either population. Following this, diets were proposed that would produce $\delta^{15}N$ and $\delta^{15}C$ values in bone collagen similar to those actually measured in human bone from these two populations. Although it is recognized that no single diet will fulfill the requirements for producing measured isotope values, limits on certain food items can be assessed.

The results presented above suggest that within limits we may be able to propose reasonable diets for prehistoric human populations. It is obvious that there are still several areas requiring further investigation before we can pursue this activity with confidence. First, we must increase the number of analyses of food items which would have been available to the human populations. Secondly, we must know more about the metabolism of specific food items. It seems likely that all sources of protein could provide amino acids which are incorporated into bone collagen. On the other hand, it is unclear whether the carbon can come from all major components of diet or only protein. Could it be that there are differences in the carbon source depending on total calories in diet or on diet composition? We do not know at this point.

Even so, it appears that we will be able to propose diets, and once that happens we can begin to address the more interesting questions. We can investigate whether or not dietary changes precede, follow, or are unpatterned in relation to economic and organizational changes that have been observed in prehistoric communities. Further, we can assess more rigorously the role of specific diets in relation to particular health states observed in the prehistoric record.

ACKNOWLEDGMENTS

I wish to thank Kate Spielmann, George Maat, Loes van Wijngaarden-Bakker, Kay Behrensmeyer, Alan Walker, the staff at the Pecos National Monument, and Wilma Wetterstrom for providing samples analysed in this project. Richard Leakey and Aila (my Kenyan field associate) made possible the collection of the samples from Koobi Fora and their support is greatly appreciated. Further thanks are due to Kate Moore Hiebert, Kate Spielmann, Bruno Marino, and Mark Schurr for sample analysis. Kate Moore Hiebert, Lane Beck, Christopher Peebles, and an anonymous reviewer read previous drafts of the manuscript and made substantive comments. Finally, my thanks to Douglas Price and Marion Wingfield for their patience and to William H. Saunders for his question to me at a Gordon Conference which led to the approach presented in this paper. This research was funded by NSF grant BNS-85-09753 and NIH Biomedical Research Support Grant #RR 5378.

4
The development of maize agriculture in the Viru valley, Peru

JONATHON E. ERICSON

Program in Social Ecology and Department of Anthropology
University of California at Irvine

MICHAEL WEST

Los Angeles County Museum of Natural History

CHARLES H. SULLIVAN
HAROLD W. KRUEGER

Geochron Laboratories

Are there similarities in the rates of development of agriculture among widely divergent prehistoric cultures? Are there similar levels of dependence on a restricted number of domesticated species among prehistoric societies? What are some of the pooling or food-sharing principles involved in early agricultural societies? These are basic questions of human ecology with respect to understanding past human–plant relationships as well as the dynamics of development of complex societies.

Beginning in 1975 using the Viru valley as a test case, these basic questions were put to study (Ericson *et al.* 1980, 1983). The completion of this paper was delayed, in part, to await comparative cross-cultural data published by independent researchers. There is now sufficient data to obtain a preliminary resolution of the above questions involving the development of prehistoric maize agriculture in a north Peruvian coastal valley.

THE VIRU VALLEY

Viru is a small river drainage crossing the north-central part of the Peruvian coastal plain, approximately 40 kilometers south of the modern city of Trujillo. Its two combined basins, Viru and Huacapongo, enclose an area of approximately 150 square kilometers. Willey (1953) estimated that at its peak the population of the Viru could have been 25,000.

Tosi (1960) classifies the Viru environment as a Sub-Tropical Desert Formation, created by the inhibition of rainfall that results from a temperature inversion when cool, moisture-laden clouds move off the ocean over a warm land mass. Since there is no precipitation, except under extraordinary circumstances, the principal source of water is the Viru River. The hydrographic regime is dependent on seasonal rainfall above 2500 meters in the mountains. More than 80% of the annual flow occurs between January and May. The run-off is unpredictable, with significant fluctuations. Long-term cycles are connected to variations in the ocean currents. A dramatic decline in run-off occurs from June to December, which corresponds to cessation of rainfall in the mountains.

Summer (January–April) is the most favorable season for cultivation since temperatures are higher with long periods of sunlight. During the winter (June–August) temperatures decline, mainly in the lower valley where humidity reaches its maximum, fostering growth of pathogens and insects. The upper Viru and Huacapongo basins are protected from cool sea winds by the foothills. As a consequence the upper valleys enjoy a consistently more favorable climate. In addition, the rising hot air breaks up the cloud cover. The lower Viru basin bears the brunt of cool, salt-bearing winds, and is more humid and receives far less sunlight during the winter. In short, the upper valley is particularly conducive to maize agriculture as it has a long continuous growing season, deep, well-drained soils, abundant water, and warmth. The lower valley has a variable growing season.

Archaeological investigations began with the surveys of Kroeber (1930) and the excavations of Bennett (1939) and Larco Hoyle (1945). The archaeological record has been established as a result of two major studies, the Viru Valley Project (Bennett 1950, Bird 1948, Collier 1955, Ford 1949, Strong and Evans 1952, Willey 1946, 1953) and the Puerto Moorin Cultural Ecology Project (Ericson *et al.* 1978, 1979, 1980, 1983, Mangrum 1974, Reitz 1979, Singer 1976, 1977, 1978, West 1970, 1971a,b, 1974, 1976, 1977, 1979, 1980a,b, West and Whittaker 1979).

A map of the Viru valley and the archaeological sites mentioned herein is presented in Fig. 4.1. The site types and subsistence orien-

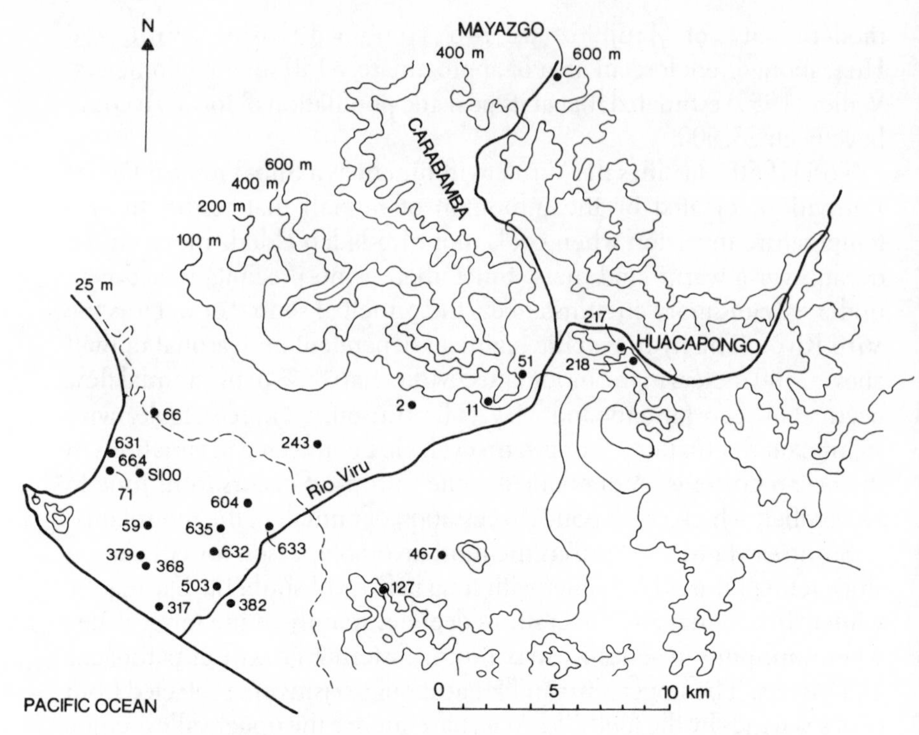

Fig. 4.1 The Viru valley, Peru

tation for these sites are summarized in Table 4.1. Site descriptions and other information may be found in the appendix to this chapter.

DIETARY RECONSTRUCTION OF PREHISTORIC PEOPLE OF THE VIRU

The study of prehistoric human diets depends on many related factors. Moreover, with few exceptions, it is likely that reconstructions of ancient dietary patterns using only floral and faunal remains will result in impressionistic models rather than solid, reliable ones. Of course, much of the problem is due to the varying degrees of preservation that characterize the different types of foods that may have comprised any particular prehistoric diet. Bone and shell are obvious candidates for preservation under a wide variety of conditions; however, softer organic remains such as vegetable foods normally do not fare so well. In recent times, investigators have turned to alternate sources for additional

Table 4.1. *Site type and orientation of prehistoric sites*

	Cemetery	Domestic	Orientation	
			Coast	Inland
2	*		*	*
11	*		*	*
51	*	*	*	*
59	*	*		*
66	*	*	*	
71	*	*	*	
127	*	*	*	
217	*			*
218	*			*
243	*	*	*	
317	*	*	*	
368	*	*	*	
379	*	*	*	
382	*	*	*	
604	*	*	*	
631	*	*	*	
632	*	*	*	
633	*	*	*	
635	*	*	*	
664	*		*	
700	*			*
SI100	*		*	

information that can provide valuable clues as to the composition of a group's diet. Flotation techniques, coprolite and pollen analysis, and the assessment of carbon and nitrogen isotopes have been employed. Also, the frequency of occurrence of particular classes or assemblages of implements and facilities are indicative of the relative importance given to particular foods.

The north coast of Peru provides an environment that is very conducive to preservation of literally all classes of organic remains. Nevertheless, there is still quite a disparity in the rates of preservation within any class of food and between classes as well. Any reconstruction is also plagued with variations created by seasonality (see Farnsworth *et al.* 1985). Therefore, it would appear that in most cases the best one can do is note the presence or absence of certain foods without gaining a truly accurate picture of their relative importance in the diet. However, the Viru data do provide indicators of dietary trends. The following tables (Tables 4.2–4.7) describe the results of an attempt to assess the nature of prehistoric diets in the Viru valley over a span of nearly 1500 years (400 B.C.–A.D. 1000).

In most of the cases of randomly selected lower valley sites (V-105, V-243, V-317, V-368, V-379, V-467, V-503, V-519, V-598, V-604, V-631, V-632, V-633, V-635) the samples were drawn from single stratigraphic excavations that are best described as "cores" through deep occupation, often over 5 m in depth. On the other hand, several others (V-66, V-127, V-432, V-434) represent the results of more extensive recoveries. For example, in the case of V-66, it is estimated that over 85% of this shallow site was sampled with complete recovery. Fortunately, excellent preservation was encountered and V-66 offers our best opportunity to observe the problems associated with diet reconstruction using organic remains.

Twenty-five coprolites were analysed from the Puerto Moorin coastal site, V-66. The results of the analysis are presented in Table 4.2. Plant fibers and charcoal were present in most of the coprolites. Bone fragments, shell, seeds, hair, and fish vertebrae were also observed in descending order of frequency. Sand and silt were also present. These data demonstrate both the degree of preservation of organic remains and the variability of diet for the inhabitants of V-66.

Since the coprolite represents a sample diet of 24 hours or less, the foods eaten during that time can be evaluated. Fire is being used to process some of the foods. Plant foods are generally eaten with meat or fish protein – indicated by bone fragments, fish vertebrae, and shells. Bone fragments representing vertebrate protein consumption are usually not consumed with shellfish, except in Sample 41. Vertebrate protein and shellfish are most likely cooked, as evidenced by charcoal, or eaten with charred vegetables, except in Sample 37. In general the V-66 diet looks like it is varied. It does not appear that a communal or "pepper pot" type of food preparation is represented by these data, since shell, bone fragments, plant fibers, and charcoal would be frequently associated in that case.

The plant food remains in the V-66 coprolites are quite diverse, as shown in Table 4.3. Maize is present along with known complements of domesticated plants such as beans, potatoes, and peanuts. The presence of maize, and potentially other C_4 plants in the Chenopodiaceae and Gramineae families, is noted and has importance in interpreting the results of stable isotope analysis.

The diachronic incidence of domesticated and wild foods that were recovered from excavated sites and coprolite analysis is presented in Table 4.4. The diversity and preservation of food remains at V-66

Table 4.2. *Coprolite contents of samples from V-66 (Puerto Moorin)*

Sample no.	Plant Fibers	Bone Fragments	Charcoal	Seeds	Hair	Fish Vert.	Shell	Sand	Silt
1	*	*						*	
2			*	*	*				
8			*	*					
9		*	*	*		*			
10			*			*	*	*	
12		*	*	*					
19	*		*					*	
21		*		*					
22			*	*	*				
26		*		*					
27		*	*	*					
28		*		*					
29	*							*	
31		*		*					*
32		*	*	*					*
34		*							
35		*							
36		*	*	*					
37		*						*	
38		*	*	*					
39		*		*	*			*	
40		*	*	*					
41		*	*	*				*	
48		*		*				*	
50		*	*	*					

All coproplite samples were recovered from the exterior wall base (L-shaped) and interior garbage pit cut in kitchen area. The coprolites represent terminal occupation of this shallow site.

relative to other sites is noted. This may also be a consequence of the sampling procedures employed at each site. For example, recovery techniques at each site were identical, whereas sampling unit frequency varied greatly from site to site. One-quarter inch mesh screen was used for all excavated materials. Maize is represented at most sites throughout time. The recovered cobs provide an important and continuous record of hybridization and use of maize in the Viru valley (Bird 1978). Amaranthus and quinoa occur infrequently in the coprolites over time. Legumes, particularly beans, occur frequently in the excavated samples. Squash and other fruits are also frequent.

The arid and barren coast of Peru contrasts with the extremely abundant marine fauna. Prior to the domestication of animals and

Table 4.3. *Possible vegetable remains as evidenced by coprolites from V-66 (Puerto Moorin)*

Family	Food	Comments
Solanaceae	aji[a]	
	potato	
	pepino	
Chenopodiaceae	quinoa	
	bledos	
Gramineae	bamboo	
	cana brava	
	reed grass	
	maize	
Leguminosae	peanuts	
	jack bean	
	pacae[a]	
	lima bean[a]	
	frijol[a]	
	algarrob	
Compositeae	flower	*Mutisia hirsuta*
	yacon	
	dye	*Baccharis prostrata*
Convolvulaceae	camote[a]	
Umbelliferae	celery	misidentifiable as yuca
Cyperaceae	*Cyperus*	rhizomes are edible
	Scirpus	
Typhaceae	cattail (*Typha*)	rhizomes are edible
Sapotaceae	lucuma[a]	
Bromeliaceae	*Tillandsia*	used for pillows and mummies
Potamogetonaceae	*Potamogeton*	pond weed (probably due to pollen rain)
Polemoniaceae	*Cantua*	national flower of Peru – mountainous
Polypodiaceae	fern?	
Malvaceae	cotton[a]	
Proteaceae	dye	
Salicaceae	*Salix*	Willow (probably due to pollen rain)

Food remains from V-66 not evidenced in coprolites: guanabana, chirimolla, coca, ciruela, avocado and *campomanesia lineatifolia*.

[a] Remains incomplete to proceed to lower taxonomic identification.

staple food plants such as maize, inhabitants of the Viru valley relied heavily upon marine fauna supplemented with horticulture-gathering (Willey 1953:390). Thereafter, residents shifted subsistence to domesticated terrestrial animals and intensified cultivation. The extent to which marine and terrestrial fauna were consumed at a Puerto Moorin phase agricultural site (V-434) has been described by Reitz (1979). V-434 is located 5 km inland and 5 km northwest of the Viru River. The site lies just within the limits of modern cultivation, yet just on the edge of the cultivated area of the prehistoric valley (Willey 1953).

Faunal analysis of the excavated materials of V-434 revealed that the chief source of animal protein was the domestic llama herd. Deer were also eaten, most likely hunted in the nearby lomas (fog-vegetation). Analysed marine fauna suggest exploitation of rocky outcrops and sandy beaches as well as the Viru River delta or nearby lagoon. Apparently, no highland resources and few desert animals were exploited by the inhabitants at this time.

The diachronic variation of fauna recovered from coastal occupation sites is presented in Table 4.5 and shown in Fig. 4.2, and indicates a trend different from that proposed by Reitz (1979). The diachronic variation and consumption of wild terrestrial animals were low relative to domesticated and marine sources. Lizards and rats were used as a food source particularly in the early periods but do not contribute greatly to biomass (West 1980a).

Marine foods tend to dominate among the three faunal food sources for all five periods except the Puerto Moorin. During that time there was a dependency on domesticated animals, particularly llamas. Beginning in the Puerto Moorin period there is an interesting diachronic trend in that domesticated animals appear to decrease through time in all sites occupied during the Gallinazo–Moche period except at V-243. During the Middle Horizon, along the coast, domesticated animals are quite rare. This diachronic trend is one of the more surprising findings among our data.

Marine fauna are divided into three categories: bird, fish and sea mammals, and molluscs. Marine birds constitute less than 5% by weight of faunal assemblages, yet, they are nearly always present. Molluscs or shellfish are an interesting category. During the Early Horizon (V-127) and Middle Horizon (V-317-01, V-317-02, V-368, V-379, V-631) shellfish constitute 70–99% of the total faunal diet by weight. During the intermediate periods, shellfish is much lower and very variable in contribution to the diet. Changes in type and diversity of shellfish are noted from rock-dwelling molluscs such as *Chorus mytilus* during the Pre-ceramic and Initial periods, to modest size sand-dwelling clams, e.g. *Tivela hians* and *Mesodesma donacium* during the early phase (Puerto Moorin) of the Early Intermediate period, to the domination by the small sand-dwelling *Donax* clam in succeeding periods.

Table 4.4. *Diachronic incidence of domesticated and wild plant foods recovered in excavated sites and from coprolite analysis*

	Early Horizon	Puerto Moorin					Gallinazo						Moche	Middle Horizon					
SITE	127	66	432	434	105	467	519	598	604	532	533	635	243(U)	631	368	379	503(U)	317-01	317-02
GRAINS *Amaranthus sp.* Quinoa		*																	
Chenopodium sp. Maize		*																	
Zea Mays	4 cob	200* cob				×	×	×	×	14 cob	×			89 cob	6 cob		6 cob	52 cob	333 cob
LEGUMES *Arachis hyp.* Peanuts	+	250* cob		+		+													
Phaseolus sp. Beans		35g* pod	1s	3s		2s			1s					1s			1s	4s 2.5g pod	3s
Inga sp. Pacae		11f		2f														13f	4f
FRUITS *Annona Cher.* Chirimolla		+												5s= 1f				201s= 8f	51s= 2f
[illegible]		+												357s					

Campomanesia								
Cucurbita sp. Squash	1s	22s*	4s	12	41s	39s	45s	42s
Lucuma bif. Lucuma		1s= 1f*	1s= 1f		20s= 7f		9s= 3f	1f
Persea amer. Avocado	1s= 1f	17f	1f		1.5f			
ROOTS & TUBERS								
Ipomoea Bat. Sweet Potato		*? 2	1					2
Manihot esc. Manioc		10						
Scirpus sp. a small reed		×*						
CONDIMENTS								
Capsicum sp. Pepper		6*			*			
WILD PLANTS								
Prosopis sp. Algarobo	×	13s	×		238s	4s	5326s	5637s
Seaweed		×						

Key

Vegetable foods: × present
* present in coprolite
s seed
f fruit

Table 4.5. *Fauna recovered from coastal occupation sites: meat weight and percentage edible meat using Prang formula*

	Biomass Meat Wt. (kgs)	% Meat
V-127		
Domestic	0.14	14.67
Wild Terr.	0.004	0.42
Marine:		
Bird		
Fish, S. Mam.	0.06	6.31
Mollusc	0.75	78.20
V-66		
Domestic	7.60	68.65
Wild Terr.	0.21	1.89
Marine:		
Bird	0.06	0.54
Fish, S. Mam.	0.257	2.32
Mollusc	2.95	26.68
V-434		
Domestic	19.39	69.94
Wild Terr.	0.55	1.98
Marine:		
Bird	0.49	1.76
Fish, S. Mam.	5.61	20.23
Mollusc	1.68	6.06
V-382		
Domestic	0.55	6.90
Wild Terr.	0.03	0.40
Marine:		
Bird	0.02	0.20
Fish, S. Mam.	3.65	46.10
Mollusc	3.66	46.20
V-604		
Domestic	5.30	25.20
Wild Terr.	0.97	4.60
Marine:		
Bird	0.30	1.40
Fish, S. Mam.	12.53	59.70
Mollusc	1.97	9.40
V-632		
Domestic	5.98	21.20
Wild Terr.	0.74	2.60
Marine:		
Bird	0.88	3.10
Fish, S. Mam.	6.02	21.30
Mollusc	14.60	51.70
V-633		
Domestic	3.02	23.30
Wild Terr.	0.39	3.00
Marine:		
Bird	0.23	1.80
Fish, S. Mam.	1.60	12.40
Mollusc	7.70	59.50
V-635		
Domestic	0.52	6.70
Wild Terr.	0.53	6.90
Marine:		
Bird	0.02	0.20
Fish, S. Mam.	5.31	69.10
Mollusc	1.30	16.90
V-243 (upper)		
Domestic	2.88	46.20
Wild Terr.	0.34	5.40
Marine:		
Bird	0.03	0.05
Fish, S. Mam.	0.67	10.70
Mollusc	2.31	37.00
V-382 (upper)		
Domestic	3.63	11.80
Wild Terr.	0.27	1.00
Marine:		
Bird	0.09	0.30
Fish, S. Mam.	0.56	1.80
Mollusc	26.26	85.20
V-368		
Domestic	0.37	0.30
Wild Terr.	0.10	0.001
Marine:		
Bird	0.01	0.00001
Fish, S. Mam.	0.78	0.70
Mollusc	111.00	98.80
V-379		
Domestic	0.16	0.70
Wild Terr.	0.02	0.10
Marine:		
Bird	0.30	1.40
Fish, S. Mam.	5.30	24.20
Mollusc	16.10	73.60
V-631		
Domestic	1.98	2.70
Wild Terr.	0.07	0.10
Marine:		
Bird	0.81	1.10
Fish, S. Mam.	4.87	6.70
Mollusc	64.80	89.30
V-317 (01,02)		
Domestic	0.44	2.50
Wild Terr.	0.03	0.20
Marine:		
Bird	0.82	4.70
Fish, S. Mam.	3.94	22.60
Mollusc	12.20	70.00

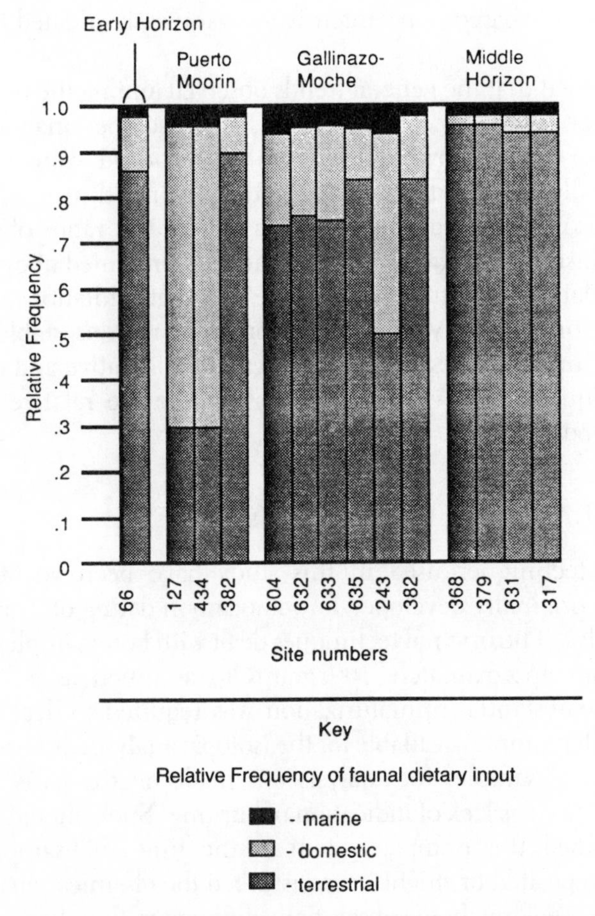

Fig. 4.2 Diachronic variation of marine, domestic, and wild terrestrial fauna for coastal sites

Such changes appear to be related to alterations in the littoral zone at Guañape and increased human exploitation. The reasons for the resurgence of settlement along the coast and use of shellfish during the Middle Horizon in Viru are seen as part of a pattern of readaptation taking place during that time (Julien 1979).

It is important to mention that the coprolite, floral, and faunal analyses presented herein were performed on material recovered from occupation sites. The stable isotopic analyses to be discussed next were performed on human bone recovered from cemetery sites. The dating of these sites is based on intensively radiocarbon-dated ceramic chronology.

It is assumed that the general trends observed among the occupation sites can be used to interpret the stable isotope analyses. It is unfortunate, for our own purposes, that the dead were buried in geographically separated cemeteries rather than within residences or villages. Also, it is impossible to obtain the relative ratios of plants to animals consumed at each site using the data presented above. These biological data demonstrate some of the inherent limitations of dietary reconstruction in the Viru valley. For these reasons stable isotope analysis of human bones is a complementary qualitative and quantitative technique which will allow us to describe the relative ratios of different food groups.

LABORATORY PROCEDURES

Analytical techniques used in this study have been adapted from procedures originally developed for radiocarbon dating of much larger bone samples. The original techniques dealt with bone samples ranging in size from approximately 100 grams to as much as a kilogram. Therefore, substantial miniaturization was required to deal with the much smaller samples available for the isotopic analyses discussed here.

Selection of samples for analysis was made on the basis of visual appearance such as lack of indication of burning. Such alteration might have disturbed the isotopic system at the time the samples were originally deposited or might have disturbed the chemical character of the samples, making them substantially different in their behavior from normal bone. Samples were cleaned rigorously to remove adhering material, rootlets, and other intrusive organic matter. Any secondary inorganic material such as calcite, anhydrite, or gypsum which may have crystallized in the interior cavities of the bone was also removed. After physical cleaning of the bone fragments they were bathed in dilute acetic acid in ultrasound to further free them of loosely adhering material, especially secondary carbonates.

Following gross physical and chemical cleaning, the bone fragments were dried in a vacuum desiccator and ground in a mill to a powder consisting of fragments less than one millimeter in size. An aliquot of this bone powder, usually five grams, was then processed to separate carbon-bearing compounds according to their chemical character. The fractions collected include normal carbonates, carbon dioxide evolved upon the dissolution of bone apatite, and, finally, purified bone gelatin.

The normal carbonates were decomposed by reaction of the powdered bone material with dilute acetic acid (1M) at room temperature in a closed vessel under vacuum. The material was stirred constantly during the 24-hour dissolution procedure and the evolved gases, which are primarily derived from normal carbonates, were collected for subsequent purification and analysis by mass spectrometry.

The solid material remaining after removal of normal carbonates was washed clean of acetic acid and suspended matter by repeated additions of distilled water, agitation, and decantation. The residual solid material was replaced in the closed vessel, the vessel evacuated, and the bone apatite (hydroxyapatite) was reacted with dilute HCl (1M) at room temperature. The carbon dioxide that was evolved from dissolution of hydroxyapatite was collected for analysis by mass spectrometry.

Residual material remaining after bone apatite dissolution was collected on fiberglass filters. This material consisted of raw collagen, any remaining rootlets or cellulose material that had not been originally removed from the sample, any siliceous material that might have remained in the sample after cleaning, and humic acids which may have been present in the sample. The residue on the filter was then boiled in distilled water, made slightly acid with HCl to solubilize the collagen. This hot solution was then filtered and the filtrate containing the soluble collagen, i.e. gelatin, was collected. Humic acids, rootlets or other cellulose material, and any siliceous inorganic material remained on the filter and were discarded. The solution of dissolved gelatin was then evaporated to dryness and the purified bone gelatin which resulted was analysed for its carbon isotopic composition.

The preparation of CO_2 gas for mass spectrometry was carried out as follows. The carbon dioxide obtained from the normal carbonate evolution and from the bone apatite dissolution procedure was purified in a vacuum line to remove water vapor at dry ice temperature and it was then distilled under vacuum to remove any other atmospheric impurities. The purified CO_2 was then analysed to determine its isotopic composition. Bone gelatin samples were burned in a combustion system similar to that of Craig (1953) and CO_2 from the combustion products was purified in a manner similar to that described above.

The analyses were done at Geochron Laboratories using a Micromass 602D mass spectrometer. Results are reported in $\delta^{13}C_{PDB}$ units expressed in parts per mil (‰) compared with the reference standard Pee Dee Belemnite (PDB) and calculated using the following equation:

$$\delta^{13}C(‰) = \left[\frac{(^{13}C/^{12}C)_{sample}}{(^{13}C/^{12}C)_{standard}} - 1\right] \times 1000$$

The overall analytical reproducibility is better than ±0.5‰. Details of this procedure are adequately described elsewhere (DeNiro and Epstein 1978b).

EXPERIMENTAL RESULTS

Human bone samples were collected from the surfaces of looted cemeteries by Ericson in 1977 and by West in 1979, including samples from V-664; by West in 1980, including samples from V-71; and by West in 1983, including samples from V-11, SI00, V-217, and V-218. Looting of the cemeteries had occurred within the last 30–40 years (as reported by Willey 1953) with the exception of V-664 which had been recently looted.

Stable carbon isotope analyses of human bone apatite and gelatin, as well as nitrogen isotope analysis of gelatin, are reported in Table 4.6.

Table 4.6. *Stable isotope analysis of human bone samples from looted cemeteries in the Viru Valley*

Sample No.	Prepared by[a]	Sex	$\delta^{13}C$ Apatite	$\delta^{13}C$ Gelatin	$\delta^{15}N$ Gelatin
Site SI00 (Lower Valley, Middle Horizon)					
1	HWK	F	−5.7	−11.8	+ 9.4
	BO			−11.8; −11.8	
2	HWK	F	−4.8	−10.2	+11.7
	BO			−11.9; −12.0	
3	HWK	F	−5.4	−11.4	+10.3
	BO			−11.0	
4	HWK	M	−6.1	−11.8	+ 8.2
	BO			−10.3	
5	HWK	M	−5.4	−10.6	+11.1
	BO			−10.7	
Site 11 (Upper Valley, Gallinazo-Moche)					
1	HWK	M	−8.2[b]	—	—
	BO			−15.7[c]	
2	HWK	M	−6.4	—	—
	BO			−13.4[c]	

Table 4.6 (cont.)

Sample No.	Prepared by[a]	Sex	$\delta^{13}C$ Apatite	$\delta^{13}C$ Gelatin	$\delta^{15}N$ Gelatin
3	HWK	M	−3.7	− 9.2	+13.2
	BO			−16.8[c];−15.2[c]	
4	HWK		−4.2	−9.3	+13.0
	BO			−9.2	
5	HWK	F	−6.5	—	—
	BO			−12.5[c]	
6	HWK	F	−8.5	—	—
	BO			−16.0[c]	
Site 51 (Upper Valley, Middle Horizon)					
1	HWK	M	−6.7	−11.4	+8.9
	BO			−11.3	
2	HWK	M	−5.4	—	—
	BO			−10.5	
3	HWK	M	−5.8	−10.2	+10.5
Site 59 (Lower Valley, Gallinazo)					
1	HWK	M	−5.7	—	—
	BO			−14.6[c]	
2	HWK	F	−5.6	−10.8	+11.0
	BO			−10.8	
3	HWK	F	−7.3	−11.8	+ 9.8
	BO			−11.9	
4	HWK	M	−6.4	−10.6	+11.5
	BO			−10.7	
Site 71 (Lower Valley, Middle Horizon)					
69	HWK	F	−6.1	− 9.9	+14.2
	BO			−10.0; −10.1	
78	HWK	F	−4.5	− 8.9	+14.8
	BO			− 9.7	
101	HWK	F	−5.4	− 9.9	+13.1
	BO			−10.0	
129	HWK	M	−4.1	− 8.7	+14.8
	BO			− 8.6	
223	HWK	M	−4.9	− 9.1	+13.2
	BO			− 9.4	
304	HWK	F	−5.4	−10.0	+13.0
	BO			−10.0	
396	HWK	M	−7.8	−12.2	+12.5
	BO			−12.8	
410	HWK	M	−4.0	− 8.5	+14.9
	BO			− 8.3	
427	HWK	F	−6.8	−10.9	+14.7
	BO			−10.8	
444	HWK	M	−5.9	−10.6	+14.7
	BO			−10.6	
540	HWK	F	−6.7	− 9.9	+15.0
	BO			−10.0	
624	HWK	M	−4.7	−10.6	+11.9
	BO			−10.6	

Table 4.6 (cont.)

Sample No.	Prepared by[a]	Sex	$\delta^{13}C$ Apatite	$\delta^{13}C$ Gelatin	$\delta^{15}N$ Gelatin
Site 217 (Upper Valley, Middle Horizon)					
1	HWK	F	−5.6	−12.3	+3.2[b]
	BO			−12.4	
2	HWK	F	−6.2	−11.4	+11.1
	BO			−11.9	
3	HWK	F	−6.8	−16.6[c]	—
	BO			−16.7[c]	
4	HWK	F	−7.4	−14.0	+8.0
	BO			−13.5	
5	HWK	F	−7.1	−12.9	+8.3
	BO			−12.8	
6	HWK	M	−5.5	−15.2[c]	—
	BO			−15.9[c]	
7	HWK	M	−5.6	—	—
	BO			−15.6	
8	HWK	M	−5.3	−19.4[c]	—
	BO			−16.7[c]	
9	HWK	M	−8.4	—	—
	BO			−16.5[c]	
10	HWK	M	−4.9	—	—
	BO			−13.4[c]	
Site 218 (Upper Valley, Puerto Moorin)					
1	HWK		—	—	—
	BO			−14.0[c]	
2	HWK		−15.7[c]	—	—
	BO			−18.7[c]	
3	HWK		—	—	—
	BO			−16.2[c]	
4	HWK		—	—	—
	BO			−6.8; −19.9	
5	HWK		−15.2[c]	—	—
	BO			−14.7[c]	
6	HWK		−10.0	−20.6[c]	—
	BO			−17.4[c]	
7	HWK		—	—	—
	BO			−17.5[c]	
8	HWK		—	—	—
	BO			−19.7[c]	
Mayazgo					
1	CHS		−10.30	−16.60	
2	CHS		− 9.79	−15.45	

[a] CHS Sullivan; HWK Krueger; BO O'Brien
[b] Questionable result (analytical reasons)
[c] Poor quality sample
— No data possible; sample inadequate.

Maize agriculture in the Viru valley

Dietary reconstruction by stable isotope analysis is difficult because of the problem of decoupling contributions of the many isotopic reservoirs present in the Viru valley. C_3 plants, maize and other C_4 plants (to a lesser degree), domesticated animals grazing on both C_3 and C_4 plants, and marine animals are four components which contribute carbon to the diet. As already mentioned, estimates of meat and plant ratios are not available for dietary reconstruction. Legumes, marine animals, non-leguminous plants, and animals feeding on non-leguminous plants (see DeNiro and Epstein 1981) are four components which contribute nitrogen to the diet. Interpretation of the stable isotope data for the lower Viru and coastal area is particularly problematic with the large marine inputs observed in the faunal analysis.

Diachronic variations of $\delta^{13}C$ among coastal and inland peoples

The diachronic variations of $\delta^{13}C$ among coastal and inland site populations are shown in Fig. 4.3 and suggest two different patterns. The carbon isotopic ratios of coastal populations do not appear to change much over time. This lack of consistent change is not very

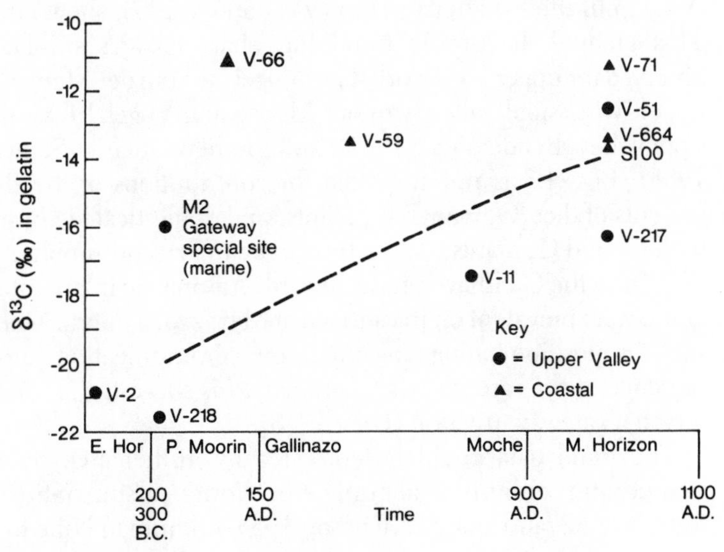

Fig. 4.3 Diachronic variation of $\delta^{13}C$ in the Viru valley (time scale is non-linear)

diagnostic of whether or not maize usage was increasing, because other dietary inputs, particularly marine animal foods or the use of terrestrial animals who themselves ate C_4 plants, could cause the same isotopic effects as increasing maize consumption. Evidence discussed below suggests that at least some of the ^{13}C enrichment in coastal populations is due to seafood consumption. Definitive statements about maize consumption cannot be made using carbon isotopes in bone gelatin.

If we use only the carbon isotope values for apatite to represent the carbohydrate portion of the total diet, as modeled by Krueger and Sullivan (1984), sites V-2 and Mayazgo (V-700) would indicate as little as 10–20% maize in the diet. Most of the other sites would be interpreted as using between 40% and 60% C_4 plants in the total diet. Sites V-71, V-664, and V-11 would indicate C_4 plant intakes of as high as 70%, except that the nitrogen isotopes in bones from these sites indicate that seafood consumption was high, and some carbon from seafoods would be metabolized and simulate C_4 plant consumption. Actual C_4 plant consumption at these sites is likely to have been similar to the other sites which did not indicate high seafood consumption (40–60%).

The diachronic variation of $\delta^{13}C$ among the inland people appears to follow a gradual increase from the incipient phase in the Early Horizon (V-2) until the Middle Horizon (V-51 and V-217), shown in Fig. 4.3. This gradual diachronic trend has characteristics similar to those observed for upper New York state (Vogel and van der Merwe 1977), the upper Mississippi valley (van der Merwe and Vogel 1978), the Mississippi valley (Bender *et al.* 1981), and southen Ontario (Schwarcz *et al.* 1985). Fig. 4.3 is not corrected for contributions of the three components of diet (C_3 plants, C_4 plants, and domesticated animals fed on both C_3 and C_4 plants). We estimate the maize consumption to be 40–50% from the Gallinazo phase onward. Among the inland sites, marine fauna were prevalent on the surface of Mayazgo, a Puerto Moorin phase site. Its position along an important communication corridor and presence of the rare species *Chorus mytilus* suggests the site may have served a gateway function (Hirst 1978).

The trend data could be corrected by further analyses. Nitrogen isotope ratio, strontium/calcium ratio, barium/calcium ratio, and strontium isotope ratio analysis (Ericson 1985) on human bone from inland sites, as well as stable carbon isotope analysis of domesticated fauna, would help separate the contributions of the different components.

Unfortunately, these data are not available for interpretation at this time.

Diachronic trends in carbon and nitrogen analysis

The history of maize in the Viru suggests a gradual increase in yield, particularly after the Gallinazo culture (Bird 1978). Our carbon and nitrogen isotope data (Fig. 4.4) are consistent with a gradual increase in maize consumption, with a marked change observed at the beginning of the Gallinazo phase. This isotopic shift is consistent with floral and faunal data (Reitz 1979), which suggest a shift away from dependence on maritime resources once maize agriculture was well established. Figs. 4.5 through 4.8 are various representations of the carbon and nitrogen isotopic compositions of bone from various prehistoric populations in the Viru area. Fig. 4.5 is a plot of carbon isotopes in apatite and in gelatin, with modeling data from Krueger and Sullivan (1984), and data from several Viru sites plotted.

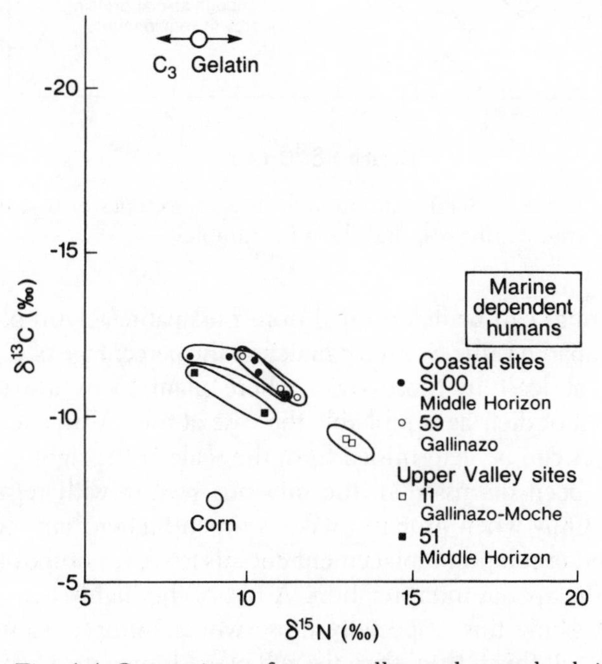

Fig. 4.4 Comparison of upper valley and coastal subsistence over time for four populations using carbon and nitrogen isotopic ratios of human bone, corn, and marine foods

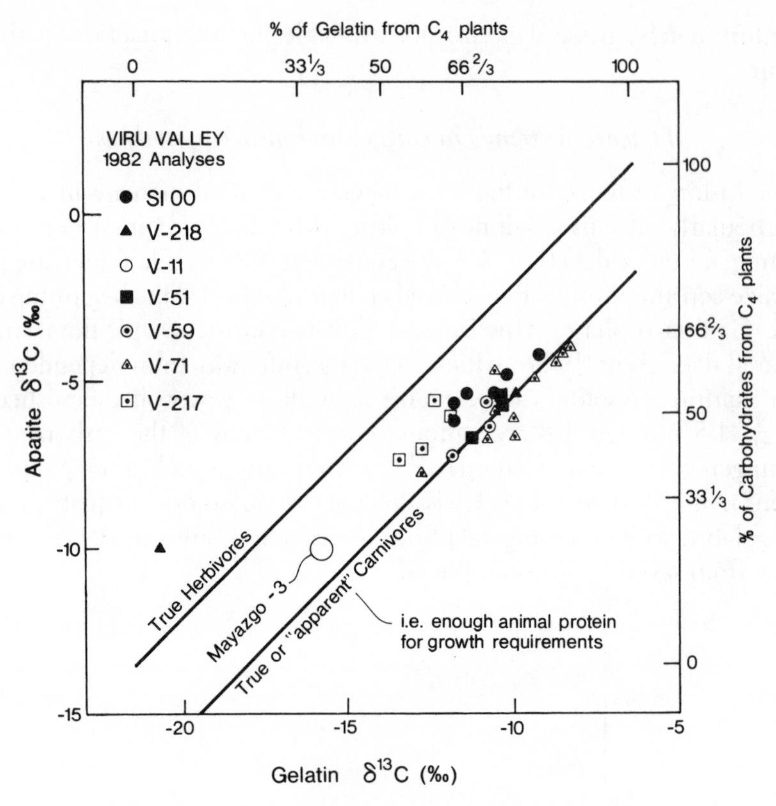

Fig. 4.5 Stable carbon and nitrogen isotopes of true herbivores, true carnivores, and the Viru samples

Two things can be determined from the apatite/gelatin plot in Fig. 4.5. The apatite value by itself can define the percentage of C_4 plants in the diet, at least in those cases where plant foods are the major component of diet, as is probably the case at most Viru sites. Specific percentages can be determined from the scale at the right of Fig. 4.5, and have been discussed in the previous section with regard to site averages. Only when protein intake is much higher than required for growth and execretion replacement does its isotopic composition begin to affect the apatite interpretation. A few of the highly marine sites at Viru may show this, especially those whose nitrogen values exceed about +12. If this is true, then we will overestimate the C_4 plant input because seafood would then become involved in energy metabolism and its carbon would partly end up in apatite, thus simulating a significant portion of the interpreted C_4 input.

The second thing that Fig. 4.5 shows us is how much like a carnivore the individuals were. Herbivores, synthesizing essentially all of their proteins, have a particular isotopic relationship, plotted as the "True Herbivore" line. As an omnivore diet contains more and more high quality animal protein, alleviating the need for synthesis, the apatite/gelatin difference decreases. By the time the diet has perhaps 10% of meat or seafood, all growth and excretion requirements are met and the omnivore appears to be a normal carnivore. If human points fall near the carnivore locus, then we know that dietary protein requirements are being met or exceeded by high quality animal protein even though the vast majority of the diet is still plant foods, involved only in energy production and general metabolism. This latter situation appears to be true of most Viru sites; hardly any individuals appear to be essential herbivores, and most approach being apparent carnivores.

Comparison of upper and lower valleys during the Middle Horizon

A comparison of upper valley and coastal subsistence patterns was made for four Middle Horizon groups. The lenticular shape of each cluster is an interesting pattern which emerges from examination of the comparative data in Fig. 4.6. Although these are small sample sizes there is no *a priori* reason why this pattern should emerge. A lenticular cluster would occur if the C_3/C_4 ratio remained constant and the marine component changed relative to the consumption of plant foods. The lenticular patterns are most likely due to selective choice of protein source, i.e. more or less seafood relative to terrestrial meat, etc. This is further borne out by the distributions of isotopic data from several other sites shown in Fig. 4.7 and discussed below.

Figure 4.7 is adapted from Krueger (1985) and represents the isotopic composition of bone gelatin, with respect to both carbon and nitrogen isotopes, that might be expected from almost any combination of dietary inputs. Fig. 4.7 (a "protein source diagram") uses only analyses of gelatin for both carbon and nitrogen isotopes. The carbon differentiates C_3 from C_4 plant protein sources, as usual, at the base of the terrestrial trophic system. As trophic levels increase to carnivory, $\delta^{15}N$ values

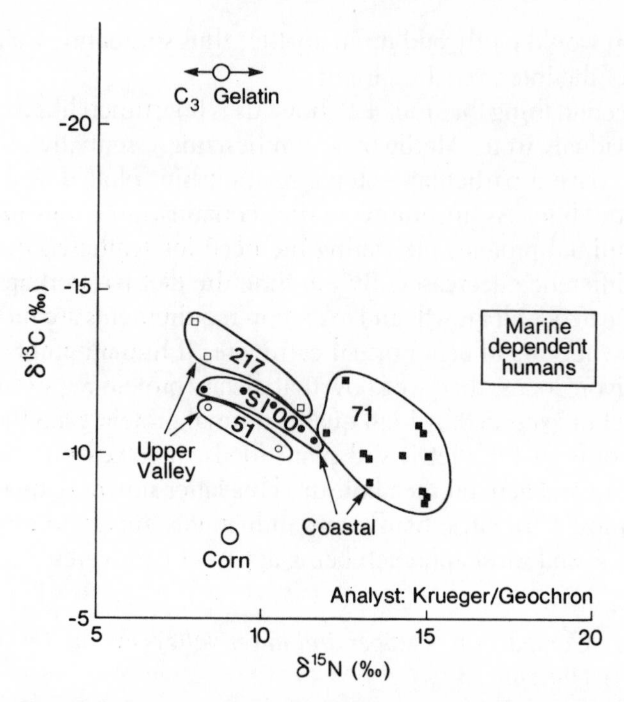

Fig. 4.6 Comparison of upper valley and coastal subsistence patterns of Middle Horizon using carbon and nitrogen isotopic ratios of human bone, corn, and marine foods

increase as shown in the model (although carbon does not change further from the protein of the prey species). When seafoods are added, $\delta^{15}N$ values increase even further, depending upon the trophic level of the seafood in the marine system. With the finite number of end-points now defined, mixing models can be made to represent appropriate dietary protein mixtures. A manuscript describing the full derivation of this model is in preparation by Krueger.

Almost all the Viru sites suggest a healthy input of animal protein, thus the individuals plot mostly in or above the "carnivore" field. All this means is that they had enough to cover growth and excretion needs, and maybe some left over. The sites that plot mostly above the carnivore field clearly had major seafood inputs. Possible mixing line interpretations for site V-71 allow almost any type of seafood input, but the data from sites V-664 and V-11 suggest marine fish rather than shellfish as the marine food end-point.

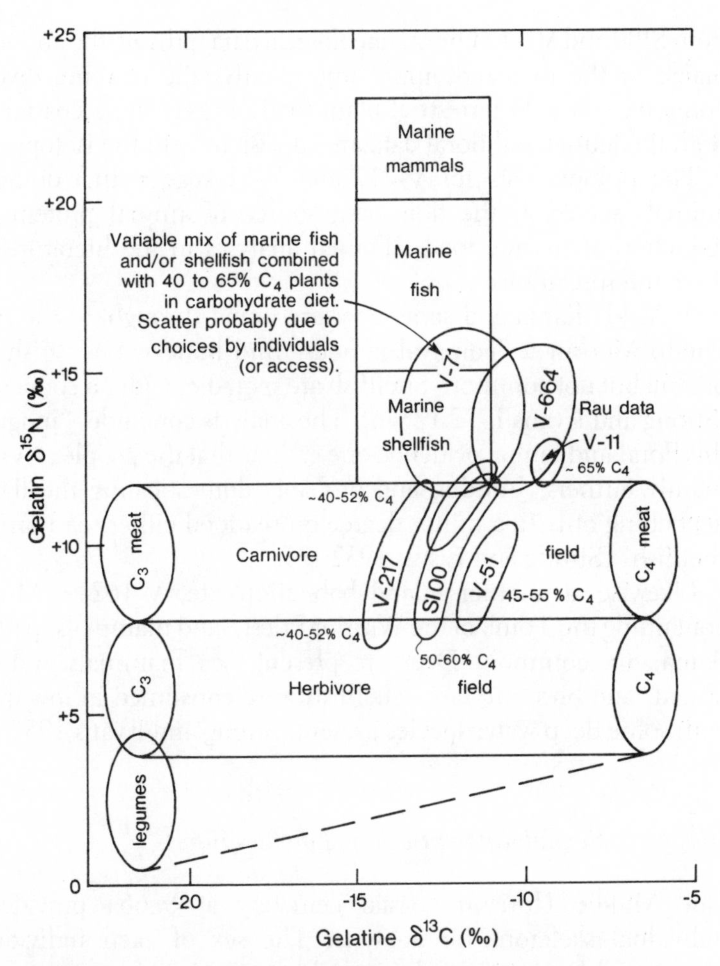

Fig. 4.7 Composite geochemical model of diet based on gelatin $\delta^{15}N$ and $\delta^{13}C$ analysis

The faunal data are qualitatively consistent with the isotopic data. The faunal analysis of four Middle Horizon coastal occupation sites, presented in Table 4.5, indicates that marine fauna constituted a majority of the animal protein with minor amounts of wild terrestrial and domesticated animals represented in the diet. The fauna and isotopic data suggest a marine input for both V-71 and SI00.

The available coprolite and floral data described in Table 4.4 for coastal Middle Horizon habitation sites V-317-01 and V-317-02 are qualitatively consistent with the isotopic data of cemetery population from SI00 and V-71. The archaeological data indicate the abundance of maize in the diet and, more importantly, the extreme diversity of domestic and wild terrestrial plant foods among these coastal people. Both the faunal and floral data are consistent with the isotopic data.

The isotopic data for V-217 and V-51 suggest that domesticated animals served as the dominant source of animal protein, with a reduction of marine foods. Faunal analyses in the literature support these interpretations.

At V-51, llama and some deer are found throughout the site from Puerto Moorin to Tomaval periods. Bird bone is rare. Fish bone is present but not common. Shellfish are sporadic, with no concentrations (Strong and Evans 1952:125–6). The analysts conclude, "judging from this floral and faunal evidence one gathers that the people at V-51 were mainly farmers, hunting and probably domesticating the llama and depending only to a minor degree on sea food either sea lions, fish or shellfish" (Strong and Evans 1952:125).

Likewise at another inland habitation site, V-162, a Moche site containing the Tomb of the Warrior Priest, land mammals, particularly llama, are common. Deer are present, sea mammals and fish are absent, and birds are rare. Shellfish were consumed in low quantities with some deep water species present (Strong and Evans 1952:190).

Sexual differentiation of dietary inputs

One Middle Horizon coastal cemetery at V-664 provided eight individual skeletons for analysis. The sex of each individual was determined by multiple physical characteristics of pelves and crania. Carbon and nitrogen isotope analyses of bone collagen were made. The carbon isotope analysis of bone collagen for the group of three females is $\delta^{13}C = -10.22 \pm 0.43$ and nitrogen isotope analysis is $\delta^{15}N = 14.01 \pm 1.11$. On the other hand, carbon isotope analysis of bone collagen derived from a group of five males is $\delta^{13}C = -10.01 \pm 1.03$ and nitrogen isotope analysis is $\delta^{15}N = 14.52 \pm 1.58$. These data suggest a mixed diet of maize/maize-fed domestic animals and marine food, with a small C_3 component.

Upon plotting the above data (in Fig. 4.8), the female data points were fully circumscribed by the male data. The data suggest several possibilities. One is that males, as a group, had a more varied diet,

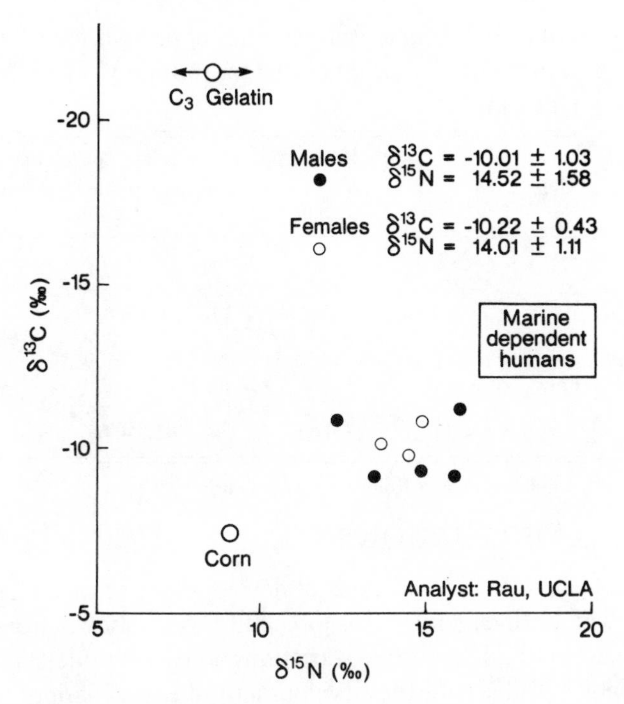

Fig. 4.8 Sexual differentiation of dietary inputs, V-664 (Middle Horizon period)

typified by the analogy that men ate lunch out, perhaps while fishing, foraging, or farming or that they drank more chicha, corn beer (Ericson *et al.* 1983). The female data suggest that food was more generally pooled, perhaps from a communal pot. An alternative view stresses the variability as a function of social hierarchy wherein the consumption of particular foods or classes of foods was gender-prescribed in an institutionalized fashion. We believe that a substantial amount of the scatter of isotopic results at any given site is most likely due to food selectivity by individuals. Not everyone prefers each food equally, or even has equal access to each food choice.

Finally, the dispersion of the V-664 (Middle Horizon) data shown in Fig. 4.8 is quite similar to the dispersion of data observed (Fig. 4.6) for V-71 (Middle Horizon) and the high variances of both isotopes for the male sample relative to the female at this latter site (Table 4.7).

Table 4.7. *Stable isotope ratios of human bone suggesting sexual differentiation of dietary inputs: V-71 (Middle Horizon)*

MALE			FEMALE		
Sample No.	$\delta^{13}C$ Gelatin	$\delta^{15}N$ Gelatin	Sample No.	$\delta^{13}C$ Gelatin	$\delta^{15}N$ Gelatin
129	− 8.7	+14.8	69	− 9.9	+14.2
223	− 9.1	+13.2	78	− 8.9	+14.8
396	−12.2	+12.5	101	− 9.9	+13.1
410	− 8.5	+14.9	304	−10.0	+13.0
444	−10.6	+14.7	427	−10.9	+14.7
624	−10.6	+11.9	540	− 9.9	+15.0
	x=9.95 ± 1.43	x=13.67 ± 1.37		x=9.92 ± 0.63	x=14.13 ± 0.88

Samples were prepared by Krueger or O'Brien

CONCLUSIONS

There appear to be similar rates of development of maize agriculture among widely divergent prehistoric cultures as shown from isotopic data. These gradual diachronic variations help us to understand some of the variables underlying the development of maize agriculture, if not grain-based agriculture in general. There appear to be similar levels of dependence on maize among the sites of the same chronological period. We estimate 40–60% dependence on maize on the basis of stable carbon isotope data, similar to values already reported in the literature. This range appears to be the average upper threshold level of maize consumption for prehistoric populations (Ericson *et al.* 1980, 1983).

There appears to be evidence of dietary variability among males and females for Middle Horizon coastal people. The males have a more varied diet. The females appear to be pooling their food.

The coprolite, faunal, floral, and stable carbon and nitrogen isotope data appear to relate well as independent measures of the following specific trends: (1) maize is used prior to the Gallinazo phase during the Puerto Moorin phase. Apparently, hybridization of corn may have played an important role in increasing the yield in the Gallinazo phase and thereafter. (2) It appears, as already mentioned, that there is a continuous and gradual increase in the use of maize through time. (3) It appears that domesticated animals are quite plentiful during the Puerto Moorin phase, yet decrease through time on the coast. (4) It appears that domesticated animals are quite plentiful throughout time at inland sites. (5) Marine foods are consumed mainly within the littoral zone although some are traded inland. (6) It appears that there are two different subsistence patterns with different foci within the littoral zone and the interior which is consistent with the subsistence economic model presented by West (1971a).

Finally, given the diversity of diet and multiple isotopic reservoirs, the above trends are considered to be hypotheses worth testing with additional samples and analyses including strontium/calcium ratios, barium/calcium ratios, strontium isotope analysis, and pollen transects dated by accelerator mass spectrometry. We consider that only the first page of the first chapter of the book has been written on the subsistence of the Viru valley in all its complexity.

FURTHER CONSIDERATIONS

We see a pattern of gradual development in maize agriculture in the Viru valley and among several other cultures in upper New York state (Vogel and van der Merwe 1977), the upper Mississippi valley (van der Merwe and Vogel 1978), the Mississippi valley (Bender *et al.* 1981), and southern Ontario (Schwarcz *et al.* 1985). This general diachronic trend is an interesting phenomenon, not intuitively obvious. Its existence may stimulate research into the processes underlying the adoption of maize agriculture from incipient agricultural systems.

The Viru valley provides an excellent workshop to examine the development of maize agriculture (because of) tremendous preservation and a long history of archaeological research. In Viru there are a number of factors which may have acted to promote, if they existed, or limit, if they did not, the development of maize agriculture:

(1) The existence of an incipient agricultural technology prior to the introduction of maize acted to promote development.
(2) Advances in storage technology in the form of (solid) ceramics, for storage of seeds for planting and consumption over long periods would have acted to promote adoption.
(3) A basic limiting factor is the nutritional value of maize. As discussed in the next subsection, a case is made for the operation of bilateral hybridization.
(4) Hybridization of maize to increase its yield is another limiting factor. The history of maize hybridization has been reconstructed and will be discussed.

(5) The point at which the natural carrying-capacity of the area (or cross-point) is exceeded is a promoting factor in the development.
(6) There is still the issue of why maize is preferentially selected out of a large array of other plant foods. The micro-climate variation of the Viru may have acted as a selective mechanism for maize development. This variable would have been operational in the other coastal valleys in Peru as well.

It is critical to note that the above factors are not considered an exclusive list of variables. Their presence will promote, not determine, the gradual development of specifically maize agriculture.

Incipient agriculture

The existence of an incipient agriculture technology based on the planting and tending of squash, beans, and a wide array of other plants is well known from the original Viru Valley Project (Bennett 1950, Bird 1948, Collier, 1955, Ford 1949, Strong and Evans 1952, Willey 1946) and more recent research (West and Whittaker 1979). This technology has been used to grow maize since its introduction in the Viru at approximately 1050 B.C. (Bird 1978).

Storage technology

There is some question whether maize was present during the Preceramic period (Bird 1978). On technical grounds, ceramics provided a number of advantages for maize. Ceramics can be used for cooking as well as for dry storage of seeds for planting and/or consumption over long periods of time. Mice, rats, and other rodents are deterred by solid containers.

Archaeologically, we observe an interesting trend in storage technology, as analysed by Ford (1949). Coincident with the rise of maize agriculture in Puerto Moorin, ceramic vessels approximately 30 cm in diameter were a significant type. In the Late Puerto Moorin to succeeding Gallinazo period, the significant ceramic size changed to over 100 cm. At V-503 one of these large vessels was buried intentionally below ground by excavating and then backfilling the space between the vessel and the excavation with sand. A second example of a large subterranean vessel (110 cm wide by 164 cm high) buried in sand was excavated from a Late Puerto Moorin level at V-51 (Strong and Evans 1952:94, 98). At this time we can only infer that these were dry storage vessels and, in fact, were used to store maize or other dry crops. Advances in storage technology such as these would enhance the development of maize agriculture.

Bilateral hybridization

The development of maize agriculture is particularly fascinating in light of the fact that increased dependence on maize can cause a number of different biochemical and physiological perturbations among humans and laboratory animals. These perturbations can be expressed as pathologies in human bone.

Although maize provides a relatively dependable food source, it is a nutritionally deficient staple. Maize is deficient in two of the ten essential amino acids (lysine and tryptophan) and in niacin (Katz *et al.* 1974). Tryptophan is also the precursor to the monoamine neurotransmitter serotonin (5-OH-tryptamine). Rats fed exclusively on a restrictive corn diet develop pain, hypersensitivity, hyperaggressivity, disruption of sleep–wake cycling, and have some appetite disturbance.

Maize can perturb iron metabolism which can result in a number of sequelae including iron-deficiency anemia, porotic hyperostosis, etc. (El-Najjar 1976). Maize lacks phytase, an enzyme that counteracts the effect of phytic acid (Møllgaard *et al.* 1946). Phytic acid affects iron absorption in humans at it acts as a chelating agent to reduce iron bioavailability (Moore 1968). Maize is a source of starch. A dried maize kernel contains by weight 74.5% starch, 6.8–12% protein, 12.0% water, 3.4% fat, and 1% fiber (Heinz 1963). Starch diets are known to inhibit iron absorption (Amin and Hegsted 1971). Given the number of deficiencies of a maize diet, it is not surprising to observe that porotic hyperostosis is found to be significantly higher among children (75.7%) and adults (9.2%) in maize-dependent groups than non-maize-dependent children (23.3%) and adults (3.4%) (El-Najjar 1976).

Apparently the greatest impact of maize-dependence is registered among children. If children were fed a high maize diet such as corn milk or semi-soft mash the effect of the diet would be amplified. Maize-fed children would be particularly vulnerable to iron-deficiency anemia which would retard their growth. Chronic cases of iron deficiency would have resulted in porotic hyperostosis (El-Najjar 1976), described as abnormal bony changes in the skull appearing as spongy or sieve-like porosity in the cranial bones and/or orbits (Angel 1966).

Among prehistoric North American Caddoan cultures along the Red River the health consequences of maize agriculture are quite interesting. Among the pre-agriculturalist, hunter-gatherers, the Fourche Maline, the infection rates of subadults (12.0%) and adults (11.1%) are relatively low with respect to those observed with the introduction of agriculture. Among the Caddo I infection rates were subadult (28.6%) and adult (30.0%) (Rose *et al.* 1984). Likewise, the increase in porotic hyperostosis increases from 1.9% to 15% among these same groups. In time the infection rates begin to drop among the mature agriculturalists during Caddo IV where 15.1% of subadults and 11.9% of adults showed infections. There is also a decline in porotic hyperostosis in conjunction with higher caries rates, suggesting increased iron consumption, e.g. meat. The infant and subadult mortality rates among the prehistoric Caddo follow these trends (J. C. Rose, personal communication).

The increase in the rate of infant/subadult mortality at the initial stage of maize agriculture should have acted to select out members vulnerable to nutritional and health problems encountered by the shift in maize dependence. In time the new population would have characteristics capable of subsisting on a maize diet. In this sense, hybridization here is a bilateral process of human–plant mutualism. These observations are consistent with the hypothesis set forth by Cook (1975) and Cassidy (1972) who suggest that nutrition and health deteriorate with the advent of agriculture. In addition, Cook and Buikstra (1979) suggest that stress will be greatest during the initial introduction of a new subsistence pattern and that it will decrease as the culture adapts to the new ecological conditions.

In the Viru, we have limited information on infant mortality at the transition between incipient and maize agriculture. Bird (1948) reports encountering numerous instances of infants apparently abandoned in refuse built up at V-71. Porotic hyperostosis is observed among many infants in the Middle Horizon (M. West, personal communication).

Hybridization and yield

The yield of a given domesticate can act as a limiting factor. Hybridization of a species plays an important role in altering the yield potential of a given species in a given environment. A history of archaeological maize from the north coast of Peru has been examined (Bird 1978, 1979) and is important to understanding the development of maize agriculture in the Viru valley.

The earliest known maize at coastal sites in Peru is from an area less than 70 km in length which includes Las Haldas, Culebras I, and Huarmey North I (Engel 1970, Kelley and Bonavia 1963, Lanning 1967, Moseley 1975, Wilson 1981). Maize occurs there during the Cotton Pre-ceramic part of the Late Archaic sometime prior to 2000 B.C. Maize next appears in the Early Formative site of Pampa Gramalote in the Moche valley (Wilson 1981). At about 1050 B.C. in this area, the Chavin-like Cupisnique culture, typified by its ceramics, textiles, metallurgy, etc., left four Cupisnique maize types at Huaca Prieta (CU-1, CU-2, CU-3, CU-4) (Bird 1978). South in the Viru valley, the Salinar culture brought higher row-number types (SA-2 and SA-3) at about 200 B.C., which were excavated at Puerto Moorin by M. West.

Suddenly, with the succeeding Gallinazo culture (about A.D. 20, Bird 1979) the high row-number types disappear. With the rise of the Moche in the Viru valley *ca.* A.D. 150 row-numbers fell even more and cobs lengthened. Although no maize from the Middle Horizon (A.D. 550–900) of the Trujillo area (Moche valley) has been studied by Bird (1978), evidence elsewhere points to high yielding, high row-number types like the Salinar hybrid. The interaction of the high and low row-number types may have led to the rapid evolution of Peruvian maize as suggested by Mangelsdorf *et al.* (1967). Further discussion on the evolution of maize is found elsewhere (Bird 1979, Bird and Bird 1980).

The cross-point

The cross-point, or point at which the natural carrying capacity of wild foods is exceeded, is a promoting factor in the continuation and, perhaps, further development of agricultural production. The cross-point is also the point of irreversible change in a system, when humans are truly dependent on food production:

> While people were experiencing increases in fitness by means of coevolved relationships with plants, they were also initiating irreversible changes in their own subsistence systems and in the world in which they lived. They were changing from generalized predators into obligate ones, and because of the

interaction of their changing subsistence patterns with changes in the stability of the ecology from which subsistence was extracted, humans found themselves, perhaps for the first time in their evolutionary career, confronted by a relatively "difficult," "stressful," and unpredictable ecology. (Rindos 1984:143)

Once the cross-point is exceeded, increased agricultural production acts as an extension of carrying capacity. It is an analog of the difference between the highest upper limit of carrying capacity and the normal threshold level achieved by a population. The intensive use of canal irrigation, for example, may be considered as an indicator of reaching or exceeding the cross-point in a given area.

Archaeological evidence from the later Puerto Moorin period indicates a rapidly burgeoning and entrenching population in a relatively short period of time. As an example of punctuated equilibrium, it literally explodes resulting in the Gallinazo culture. This is different from Bennett's (1950) interpretation that the population resulted from an invasion or large immigration at the beginning of the Gallinazo period. The Gallinazo is typified by large populations characterized by marked social stratification, large-scale architecture, large extensive canal systems, high-output craft production, and increased conflict with the neighboring Moche valley. These observed features are coincident with the hybridization of maize observed by Bird (1978).

Micro-environments

As mentioned before, there are differences in climate between the lower Viru valley/coast and upper Viru/Huacapongo as well as a lower valley zone on the lee side of Cerro Compositan south of the river. The upper valley has more sunlight per year, lower humidity, less salt-spray, and fewer high and continuous winds. The soil is deep and well drained. These environmental conditions are more favorable for maize production than the conditions along the coast and lower Viru. The high, intermittent winds, poorly drained soil, high salt-spray, and high humidity (with regard to pathogen growth) would be less favorable for maize production. It is hypothesized that the preferred micro-environment of the upper valley would act to increase the yield of maize relative to other vegetables and plant foods, compared to the lower valley. This increase in yield, particularly if two crops could be planted, would act to differentiate the maize from its competitors. One could envision fresh maize as a gift or item of exchange during the cloudy winter months along the coast.

Some supportive evidence for this hypothesis is the shift in population and its location. The Puerto Moorin settlement pattern is densest in the favorable micro-environments, particularly the upper and middle Viru valley and Huacapongo basin (West 1980a: Fig. 1). In the less favorable environment of the lower valley, Puerto Moorin habitation sites tend to occupy tree-sheltered areas adjacent to riparian zones and transition to the desert edge.

Endnote

The development of agriculture was a very critical threshold in the evolution of modern *Homo sapiens*. Prehistoric dietary reconstruction for its own sake is somewhat limited in application. We would like to continue to focus on and apply our findings to understand the development of agricultural systems and the complex roles of numbers of variables contained within a great variety of hitherto untested cultural models.

ACKNOWLEDGMENTS

We are indebted to the Instituto Nacional de Cultura in Lima and Trujillo, particularly Dr. Hugo Ludena. Human bones and artifacts were removed from Peru under the auspices of the Instituto Nacional de Cultura (Credential no. 003-77-SUB-DCIRBM 9/9/77).

The Milton Fund of Harvard University provided partial support for one of us (JEE) for this research.

We would like to thank the following individuals for sharing their notes and analytical data: Dr. Glendon Weir (Texas A. & M.) for coprolite analysis; Dr. Lawrence Kaplan (Boston University) for legume identification; Dr. Thomas Whitaker (Dept. of Agriculture) for pollen analysis; Dr. S. G. Stephens (retired) for floral analysis; Dr. Robert McK. Bird (Botanical Gardens, Mo.) for maize analysis: Dr. E. Reitz (Florida State Museum) for faunal analysis; and Dr. Greg Rau (Institute of Marine Science, University of California, Santa Cruz) for carbon isotope analysis.

APPENDIX. DESCRIPTION OF THE VIRU VALLEY SITES

Mayazgo V-700 — The Mayazgo complex is situated approximately 8 km up the Carabamba drainage on its east wall. Occupational and burial components appear to date to the latter part of the Early Horizon or beginning of the Early Intermediate period. The presence of diverse littoral zone products in the site and its strategic position within this important connective corridor suggest a gateway function.

SI00 — One of a number of small scattered Middle Horizon burial areas relatively close to the beach zone at Guañape. As in the case of V-71 and V-664, there are many habitation sites dispersed about the surrounding area.

V-2 — Situated on a high sandy stretch above the north edge of the middle valley, this site yielded Early Horizon graves (Larco Hoyle 1945, Willey 1953:60). There are no known contemporaneous settlements in the general region.

V-11 — This Early Intermediate period (Moche) cemetery component (Willey 1953:230) is situated on the sandy northern edge of the valley below an outcrop of Cerro de Las Lanas. It is adjacent to choice irrigation resources and 10 km inland from prime marine zones at Guañape. The presently known pattern of Moche period habitation site distribution suggests that V-11 could have been utilized by a population(s) physically closer to the littoral.

V-51 — The Tomaval fortification is strategically located just below the bottleneck entrance to the upper valley. In addition to the fortification complex, there are village and cemetery components. The latter dates to the Early Intermediate (Moche) and Middle Horizon (Willey 1953:294). Numerous up-valley settlements in the near vicinity may have buried their dead here.

V-59 — This site appears to have been a substantial town or small city during the Early Intermediate period (Gallinazo) (cf. Bennett 1950). Its position in the lower valley would have afforded its inhabitants access to a wide variety of littoral and terrestrial resource zones. At its peak V-59 housed the largest population in the prehistoric period.

V-66
V-105 — Overlooking the lower valley and beach at Puerto Moorin, this extensive site has both village settlement and burial components (Strong and Evans 1952). Inhabitants of the community had access to various littoral zones and high water-table resources (West 1979).

V-71
V-664 — These contiguous cemeteries are 1 km from the present beach near Guañape. They appear to be two of an undetermined series of Middle Horizon burial grounds that intrude in a large Pre-ceramic midden (V-71) locally known as Huaca Negra. There are abundant contemporaneous occupation sites within a radius of several kilometers.

V-127 — This Early Horizon (410 B.C., U.C.L.A. – #1976A) structure is on a well-protected slope on the lee side of Cerro Composítan, south of the river. Originally described and excavated by Willey (1953:58–60), excavation sampling was again conducted in 1975. Floral and faunal materials were recovered from among carbonized middens along several walls. Although its function remains unclear, Willey suggested the rectangular building served as a community center.

V-217 This Middle Horizon cemetery is found at the foot of Cerro Serraque which forms the south side of the upper valley Huacapongo drainage (Willey 1953:294). Settlements of the same period are nearby.

V-218 This Early Intermediate period (Puerto Moorin) burial ground is located in a small outwash emptying into the Huacapongo drainage (Willey 1953:100). The site has been severely modified by erosional forces.

V-243 This site is part of a cluster of late phase (Moche) Early Intermediate period, large family habitations in the lower valley. Its position afforded it easy access to a wide variety of resource zones, especially the littoral.

V-317 Several test pits were placed in habitation areas directly associated with an extensive Middle Horizon water-table farming complex in the lowermost valley near the present delta. Family dwelling units were placed at the edges of each individual cultivation plot.

V-368
V-379 Both are shallow but dense Middle Horizon shell middens situated among old stabilized dunes approximately 2 km inland from the present beach. Their surface extension indicates populations consisting of several family units.

V-382 A test of this site revealed a long history of use as a habitation. Early occupation dates to the beginning of the Early Intermediate period (Puerto Moorin), and terminates in the late phase (Moche) of this period. V-382 appears to be part of a village cluster immediately adjacent to the lowermost course of the river.

V-434 Extensive excavations were conducted in this early phase (Puerto Moorin) Early Intermediate period mound. The site appears to have been the hub of a cluster of contemporaneous family size habitations situated at the north edge of the lower valley. V-434 is characterized by high frequency of llama remains. In addition to widespread domestic activity, there is abundant evidence of specialized craft and industrial operations as well.

V-467 This is a Gallinazo phase Early Intermediate period domestic site located in the favorable micro-climate zone south of the river on the lee side of Cerro Compositan.

V-503 This site is one component in an apparent Puerto Moorin phase, Early Intermediate period village cluster in the lower valley (north) adjacent to the sheltered riparian zone. Its function was clearly domestic.

V-519
V-598
V-604
V-632
V-633
V-635 Probes of these sites revealed middle phase (Gallinazo) occupations of the Early Intermediate period. All are large family habitation components of the dense Gallinazo phase settlement in the lower portion of the valley. The locations of these sites indicate easy access to water as well as diverse littoral resources.

V-631 Excavations were conducted in one part of a compact Middle Horizon village situated less than 1 km from the present beach. This position strongly suggests it was a fishing village, as the area has been a prime fishing ground for the past 4000 years.

5

Natural variation in ^{13}C concentration and its effect on environmental reconstruction using $^{13}C/^{12}C$ ratios in animal bones

NIKOLAAS J. VAN DER MERWE

Department of Archaeology
*University of Cape Town**

Carbon isotope analysis of bone has met with considerable success in reconstructing prehistoric human diets. Another obvious application of bone isotope ratio measurements is environmental reconstruction, based on the analysis of animal bones. To date very little has been done in this direction as environmental problems usually involve many more variables and longer time scales than those encountered in the study of human dietary changes. Case studies of the latter have been carefully selected to measure variations in one dimension – the consumption, say, of maize or salmon – while the rest of the system remains steady, consisting as it usually does of a single biome. In addition, only one animal species (humans) is involved, about which we know a fair amount. Even so, when this species is studied in three ecozones (Sealy and van der Merwe 1985, 1986), the degree of difficulty increases accordingly: a great deal of empirical data is required to replace arguments usually produced from first principles. Studying a suite of animal species across time and space to reconstruct changing patterns in the environment is then that much more difficult.

To achieve successful reconstruction of past environments on the basis of carbon isotope ratios in animal bones requires detailed knowledge in several areas.

* Now at Departments of Anthropology and Earth and Planetary Science, Harvard University.

(1) Natural variations of the $^{13}C/^{12}C$ ratios in the plant food base available to herbivores must be understood or at least empirically known. Such variations are based, in turn, on variations in the ^{13}C content of the atmosphere and in fractionations produced during photosynthesis.
(2) Isotopic fractionation associated with the formation of different animal tissues, whether from plant or animal foods, must be known.
(3) The isotopic character of different biotic communities must be known, as well as the dietary behavior of given animals in such communities.
(4) Operational considerations require the isolation of marker animal species which provide consistent environmental information, and the development of laboratory procedures for measuring carbon isotope ratios in their bones over a long time scale.

These requirements are nothing short of formidable, but at least they do not need to be solved in sequence or simultaneously. If we restrict the time scale to the Holocene, for example, collagen can be expected to be available as sample material in archaeological bone and empirical information about modern biotic communities can be projected into the past with confidence. If the time period under consideration is the Early Pleistocene, however, we are obliged (1) to know a great deal more than we do now about natural variations in carbon isotope ratios, (2) to analyse minuscule quantities of collagen or another sample material, such as apatite carbonate, and (3) possibly to project the dietary behavior of modern animals onto extinct ancestral species.

For all that these problems seem difficult to master now, they are not insoluble. Natural variations in ^{13}C concentration in the atmosphere and in plants can be studied in a variety of situations worldwide. As far as animals are concerned, Africa is a natural area of interest for archaeologists over a longer time scale and is also an excellent laboratory for studying them. The distribution of plant communities on the continent has obviously changed in the course of the Quaternary, but the communities themselves have not changed significantly: they remain the familiar mosaic of forests, savannahs, and arid regions, interspersed with other more minor zones. The modern fauna is rich and diverse, the mammals alone being represented by 740 species and 256 genera

(Bigalke 1978). While this fauna had a high turnover rate during the Pleistocene – 56 genera disappeared and 77 genera appeared for the first time – the majority of the replacements occurred in the Early Pleistocene (Maglio 1978). The presence of nearly a hundred large ungulates gives the African fauna a unique pre-Pleistocene character. Thus, we can approach with some confidence the isotopic study of African fauna as a guide to Quaternary environments.

It is the intention here to scrutinize the requirements listed above and to evaluate the state of our knowledge about them. Such scrutiny demands nothing less than a re-examination of the first principles involved in isotopic studies of bone. Before doing so, it is useful to look at two examples of environmental reconstruction which have already been carried out, in order to form a subjective impression of the difficulties involved in this approach.

ENVIRONMENTAL RECONSTRUCTION: TWO CASE STUDIES

South Africa

The archaeological sequence of Melikane Cave, excavated by Pat Carter in the mountains of Lesotho, spans the last 42,000 years. Vogel (1983) has analysed collagen from six zebra teeth in the sequence, dating between 42,000 and 20,000 years, and compared them with two samples from the last 1500 years. Their $\delta^{13}C$ values average about $-18.5‰$ and $-12.5‰$, respectively. All available evidence shows that zebra are pure grazers, hence these values can be taken to represent two different mixtures of C_3 and C_4 grasses which made up their diets in glacial and recent times, respectively. Using a fractionation value of about $+5‰$ between grass and collagen yields C_3 grass contents for the diet of about 78 and 36 percent, respectively. Two other bodies of data are relevant to these results. Tieszen and his co-workers have demonstrated a clear relationship between altitude (and hence temperature) and C_3/C_4 biomass mixtures on the slopes of Mt. Kenya (Tieszen *et al.* 1979a). Vogel (1983) has calculated the temperature change since the last glaciation at two places in Cape Province by using ^{18}O values in dated underground water (result: $+5.5$ °C) and cave limestone ($+5$ °C). Although the absolute values for temperature and C_3/C_4 mixtures on Mt. Kenya are not available, it should be possible to integrate these bodies of data to provide a detailed description of the upslope migration of C_4 grasses in Lesotho during the Holocene. To do so, however, would require a repetition of the Kenya study in Lesotho, which lies about 30° south of the equatorial Mt. Kenya and consequently has significant seasonal fluctuations in temperature. Other variables in this system which cannot be assessed are the hunting range of the inhabitants of Melikane Cave and the feeding range of the zebra. The two obviously overlapped, but their combined size could have been large enough to include more than one temperature-sensitive vegetational belt on the altitudinal cline.

A much smaller change in the C_3/C_4 grass mixture over the same period is observed at Apollo 11 Cave, a site in southern Namibia excavated by Eric Wendt. This area is desert and lies along the northern periphery of the winter rainfall belt of the western Cape coast. The $\delta^{13}C$ values of zebra tooth collagen from Apollo 11 changed from −14.9‰ during the last glaciation to −12.6‰ in recent times, showing that "the winter rainfall area along the west coast was not extended appreciably further northwards during the last Ice Age" (Vogel 1983). To draw further conclusions about environmental change at Apollo 11 would require analysis of more animal species and comparisons with other relevant biotic communities.

Beringia

During glacial events, accompanied by lower sea levels, a large land area was exposed in the Bering Straits region, extending from the Mackenzie River in Canada across the Yukon and Alaska, to the Lena River in Siberia (Hopkins *et al.* 1982). This region is known as Beringia. Much of it remained unglaciated, due to aridity, and it supported an impressive variety of large mammals. These included mammoth, bison, equids, moose, elk, woolly rhino, bears, and lions. Based on the presence of these animal species and on pollen remains, several conflicting reconstructions of the Late Pleistocene plant cover of Beringia have been proposed, including various types of tundra and grassland. Guthrie (1982) holds that C_4 buffalo grass, as presently found in the North American short-grass prairie, must also have been present, since this grass and the bison herds evolved together. This controversial interpretation requires that the warm growing season in Beringia had to be longer during glacial times than it is today in Alaska and the Yukon.

Bombin and Muehlenbachs (1985) resolved this controversy by analysing the carbon isotope ratios of mummified animals, preserved in the permafrost since Late Pleistocene times. Forty-eight specimens from seven herbivore species were involved (bison, equids, mammoth, caribou, musk-ox, moose, woolly rhino). The sample materials included dry flesh, tendon, hide, hair, and horn sheets, and the average $\delta^{13}C$ value was −22.6‰ (range −21.2 to −23.9‰). These values are typically those of animals with diets consisting exclusively of C_3 plants. Hide and hair have $\delta^{13}C$ values much like bone collagen, since keratin resembles it biochemically. It should, therefore, be expected to measure around −21.5‰, while flesh, with a fractionation of about +3‰, should measure around −23.5‰. The results obtained by Bombin and Muehlenbachs match these values and show that C_4 grasses were absent from Beringia.

In both the South African and Beringian case studies, a number of $\delta^{13}C$ values are assumed accurate: the averages for C_3 and C_4 grasses, for example, and also those for various fractionation effects. These are based on cumulative assessments by several analysts and will be examined further. Both studies also assume that the $\delta^{13}C$ value of atmospheric CO_2 is constant over time. Everyone does, but it may not be true.

AIR CO_2 AND PHOTOSYNTHESIS

The flow chart in Fig. 5.1 provides a model for purposes of discussion about carbon isotope ratios and fractionations in the air–plant–animal chain. It uses $\delta^{13}C$ values of −7‰ for CO_2 in the free atmosphere, −26.5‰ for average C_3 foliage, and −12.5‰ for average C_4 foliage. Variation in these values requires closer attention.

Air CO_2

A value of −7‰ for atmospheric CO_2 is frequently used, but is at best conventional wisdom. It originated as a tentative estimate by Craig (1953), whose nearest measurement was −7.4‰ for Sunday air in Chicago; weekday values varied between −8.1 and −9.9‰. Measurements of the air over La Jolla, Fanning Island in the mid-Pacific, and the South Pole in 1956, provided a Pacific Ocean average of −6.7‰ (Keeling *et al.* 1978). By 1978, this value had been depleted to −7.2‰,

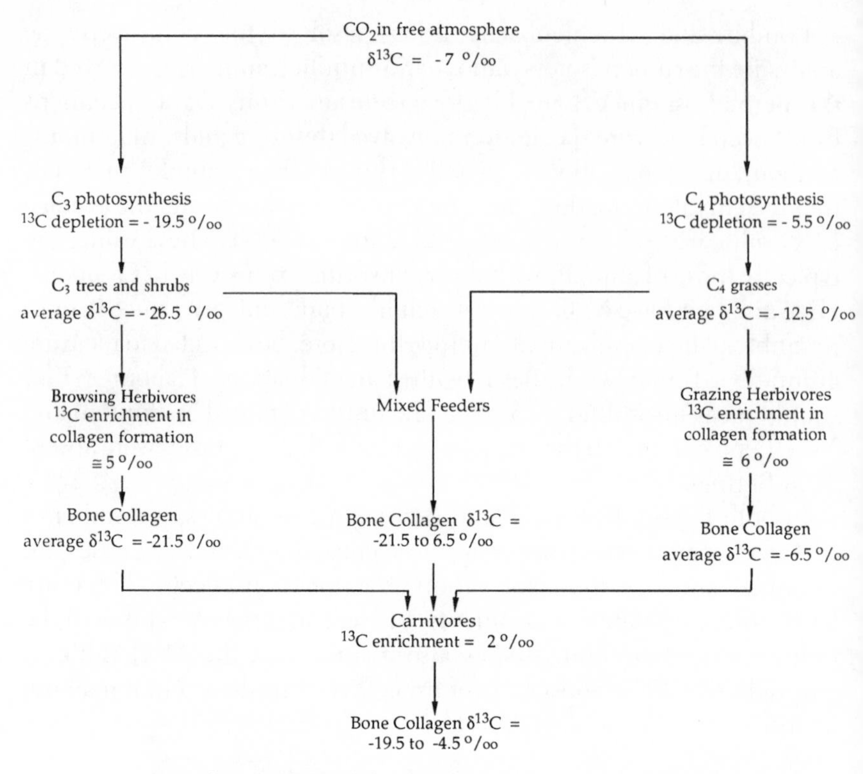

Fig. 5.1 Carbon pathways in a typical African savannah with C_4 grasses and C_3 trees and shrubs, showing fractionation of the $\delta^{13}C$ ratios during different metabolic steps. The basic supply of carbon is atmospheric CO_2; the final product which can be analysed for its $\delta^{13}C$ is the bone collagen of different animals

while the average CO_2 concentration increased from 314 to 334 ppm. These changes can be readily ascribed to fossil fuel combustion, but this is by no means the only source of variation in atmospheric CO_2 and ^{13}C content. Over a longer time scale, equilibrium changes in the ocean–atmosphere–biosphere–cryosphere system probably produced much larger variations in atmospheric ^{13}C content. The CO_2 concentration of air extracted from ice cores taken from the Greenland and Antarctic ice caps is about 300 ppm for the interglacial sections, but only about 200 ppm in the glacial sections (Berner *et al.* 1979). Two opposing models for this variation have been advanced and are discussed in a review article by Broecker *et al.* (1985). Both scenarios predict a change in the $\delta^{13}C$ value of the atmosphere, unfortunately in opposite directions, and both may be wrong. This argument cannot be pursued here, except by way of illustration. In the model favored by Broecker's group, for example, a significant mechanism for reducing atmospheric CO_2 concentration is the "pumping" of carbon from the ocean surface to the depths by marine organisms with $\delta^{13}C$ values more positive than that of air CO_2. Thus the $\delta^{13}C$ values of both the air and marine organisms should decrease with time along with atmospheric CO_2 content. This hypothesis could be tested by measuring the $\delta^{13}C$ values of either ice core CO_2 or of foraminifera of the appropriate age. Since foraminifera do not record the $\delta^{13}C$ value of the atmosphere in a direct way, it would be more appropriate to measure ice core CO_2. While the primary reason for doing so would, no doubt, be the compelling problem of what causes glacial events, the results would have equal importance for the study of carbon isotopes in plants and animals. A variation of more than 1‰ would be significant for environmental reconstructions.

While the long-term global variation in atmospheric ^{13}C content remains to be measured, contemporary terrestrial variations are known and are of considerable importance in local environments. The controlling mechanisms here are the activities of humans and plants. Air CO_2 in our laboratory on campus, which is located on a mountain slope above Cape Town, has a $\delta^{13}C$ value of −11‰. Further upslope, at Rhodes Memorial, the value for the open air is −8.0‰. On top of Table Mountain (altitude 1000 m) it is −7.8‰ which is the value for the local "free atmosphere." The depleted ^{13}C content of our laboratory air is presumably due to the production of isotopically light CO_2 by laboratory workers and acetylene flames. At Rhodes Memorial the depletion is only 0.2‰, which may not be significant, but it could be due to the patrons of the open-air restaurant, the fallow deer (not indigenous), and even the pine trees. Precisely how effective trees can be at diluting the ^{13}C content of air on a local scale is demonstrated in the Amazon forest. A study by van der Merwe and Medina, to be published elsewhere, shows that the $\delta^{13}C$ value for air CO_2 at the top of the forest canopy (height 30 m) is −11‰; in the mat of rootlets and rotting leaf litter on the ground it is −15.5‰. This depleted CO_2 is recycled during photosynthesis in the forest, giving rise to plant foliage with ^{13}C values as negative as −35‰ in the understorey vegetation and −30‰ at the top of the canopy (Medina and Minchin 1980).

Less severe fluctuations of $\delta^{13}C$ values in rural air CO_2 have been measured by Keeling (1961) in both forest and desert in the western United States. At the time of measurement, values varied from about −7.4‰ in the open Arizona desert (Organ Pipe Cactus National Monument) to −10‰ in the redwood forest of Big Sur State Park, California. There was a noticeable diurnal variation in closed forests, with $\delta^{13}C$ values becoming more negative during the night as isotopically light CO_2 respired by the trees raised the total CO_2 content of the air and diluted its ^{13}C content. The average for all Keeling's analyses of rural air is about −7.8‰, the same as that of Table Mountain. The correspondence is entirely coincidental, however; there is clearly no such thing as a consistent $\delta^{13}C$ value for terrestrial air. Each microenvironment has its own average $\delta^{13}C$ value, which is a composite of "free atmosphere" and local CO_2 sources, and which is registered throughout the local biotic community.

Photosynthesis

In the short term, isotopic abundances in air CO_2 are only important if one is interested in photosynthetic fractionation *per se*. The fractionation values for C_3 and C_4 photosynthesis in Fig. 5.1 will obviously vary with the average $\delta^{13}C$ values one accepts for air and foliage. A minor problem here is that mass spectrometric assessments of these values have been carried out over some 30 years. During this time, spectrometer technology and correction calculations have improved, while the $\delta^{13}C$ value for the atmosphere has decreased by 0.5‰ or more. Furthermore, most large-scale studies of plant isotope ratios have been done on herbarium specimens without regard for collection environments. Since the negative end of the spectrum is represented primarily by forest plants, most cumulative averages for C_3 foliage are erroneously skewed in the negative direction by the phenomenon of closed-canopy recycling of CO_2.

An extensive literature is available on $\delta^{13}C$ values in C_3 versus C_4 plants (Bender 1971, Park and Epstein 1960, 1961, Smith and Epstein 1971, Troughton 1971). Particularly useful for this discussion are isotopic studies of grasses, which cover the $\delta^{13}C$ values of C_4 plants fairly extensively and also show that such values are patterned according to environment and the production of malate versus aspartate (Bender 1968, Ellis *et al.* 1980, Hattersley 1982, Smith and Boutton 1981,

Smith and Brown 1973, Terri *et al.* 1980, Vogel *et al.* 1978, Winter *et al.* 1976). Taken as a whole, these studies provide a range of $\delta^{13}C$ values for C_3 plants between −22 and −35‰, with a mean somewhere around −28‰. With some effort, one can eliminate the "forest values," which are usually more negative than −30‰, thereby moving the mean to −26 or −27‰. By restricting consideration to C_3 grasses, which are mostly open-air plants, the mean settles down to −26.5‰. This is not entirely satisfactory, since the procedure excludes trees and shrubs, but is the best we can do for the moment. Now that the mechanisms involved in isotopic fractionation in plants are better understood, new laboratory assessments are clearly necessary.

The $\delta^{13}C$ values of C_4 grasses are quite tightly clustered around a mean of −12.5‰, varying between about −9 and −16‰. This restricted range of values is due to the open-air habitats of these plants, and their lack of discrimination between the isotopes. Fractionation during C_4 photosynthesis is almost entirely due to the diffusional resistance of the leaf surfaces, which accounts for a depletion of about 4.5‰ (Vogel 1980). Fractionation during C_3 photosynthesis is considerably more complex, since the carboxylation reaction contributes a further depletion of about 15‰. Farquhar and a number of co-workers have analysed this phenomenon with considerable success; the most recent theory on the subject (Farquhar *et al.* 1982) suggests that a simple relationship exists between isotopic discrimination and the ratio of intercellular and atmospheric partial pressures of CO_2. The effects of light and dark respiration, in this view, lie entirely in the effects on intercellular CO_2 partial pressure and account for such phenomena as very negative $\delta^{13}C$ values in dense dark forests. In fact, however, such negative values and their altitude gradient, as measured in Amazon forest leaves, is substantially accounted for by the gradient in $\delta^{13}C$ values of the forest CO_2 observed by van der Merwe and Medina. The model for C_3 isotopic fractionation, therefore, still requires some refinement.

The isotopic signatures of CAM plants (i.e. plants with Crassulacean Acid Metabolism, primarily succulents) are not well known at all. These plants are essentially capable of both C_3 and C_4 photosynthesis and consequently exhibit $\delta^{13}C$ values which cover the range of both photosynthetic systems. A single species of CAM plants may vary by more than 10‰ in $\delta^{13}C$ value in different environments, while others are more regular in their photosynthetic behavior. A study of CAM plants on a transect across South Africa (Mooney *et al.* 1977) shows a trimodal distribution of $\delta^{13}C$ values, with peaks at the C_3 and C_4 plant averages and a third in between at about −16.5‰. The implication is that CAM plants can mimic C_3 and C_4 plants, or use both photosynthetic systems to suit environmental conditions. If this is the case, one would expect CAM plants in an otherwise exclusively C_3 biome to have $\delta^{13}C$ values near the C_3 average. In the Amazon rain forest, however, CAM species which normally grow in the savannah have $\delta^{13}C$ values like C_4 plants, once the canopy effect is taken into account. It is clear from these unexpected results that a great deal remains to be discovered about crassulacean acid metabolism. It is tempting to assume that CAM plants are not very important in animal diets and thus to eliminate this uncomfortable group of plants from consideration, were it not for the fact that at least one plant community in South Africa is dominated by them.

ANIMAL TISSUE AND TROPHIC LEVELS

Bone collagen is the standard material for isotopic analysis, since it preserves the original dietary signature essentially as long as the collagen lasts. The only requirement for the analyst is to show that collagen proper is being analysed. This can be done by ensuring that the C/N ratio falls between 2.9 and 3.6, if gelatin extraction is used (DeNiro 1985), or by extracting recognizable collagen through slow decalcification in weak acid. In the latter case, the C/N ratio is invariably correct, but more samples are likely to be rejected as unsuitable.

Two approaches have been used to assess the isotopic shift between food and bone collagen. Feeding experiments with mice (DeNiro and Epstein 1978) and chickens (Bender *et al.* 1981) yielded fractionation effects of only +1 to +2‰. In natural situations, however, the shift between a food-web based on C_3 plants and bone collagen is about +5‰. Values close to this average have been obtained for human hunter-gatherers in the North American Woodlands (van der Merwe and Vogel 1978), for browsing ungulates in South Africa (Vogel 1978), and for a variety of animals with C_3 diets (Sullivan and Krueger 1981). In the case of animals grazing exclusively on C_4 grasses, the shift is about +6‰ (Sullivan and Krueger 1981). Our laboratory has accumulated data on several hundred herbivores from east, central, and southern Africa; the results confirm the reported values of +5‰ for C_3 and 6‰ for C_4 plant diets, provided that animals from forests and CAM-dominated areas are excluded. In all of these cases, of course, the fractionation value is dependent on the average value one accepts for the plant food base.

The differences in isotopic shift between food and bone collagen observed in laboratory animals and in the wild are probably due to the composition of the food. The average $\delta^{13}C$ value between seed protein and foliage of six plant species has been measured at 3.8‰ by Vogel (1982). If the same value holds for leaf protein, it would account for most of the isotopic shift between plant food base and bone collagen, plus about 1‰ enrichment added by the animal's metabolism. The latter resembles the sort of results obtained in feeding experiments, where the food consisted of commercial pellets or maize kernels.

Feeding experiments with large animals and food of known composition and isotopic values could yet prove to be most rewarding. This is evident from the small amount of data available on animal tissues other than collagen – hair, hide, flesh, fat, and bone carbonate – and the isotopic shifts between them in different animals. Of the soft tissues, collagen consistently has the most positive $\delta^{13}C$ value in herbivores; Vogel (1978) found that, in thirteen animals, hair and hide together were isotopically lighter by about 0.6‰, flesh by 2.3‰, and fat by 7.9‰. The variation in this small sample set is fairly large, however, so that the averages are only rough guides. The situation becomes even more complex when carnivores and omnivores are included and when soft tissues are compared with apatite carbonate. Variations in the isotopic shifts between different tissues are introduced by trophic level effects, food composition, and metabolic pathways in animals. Lack of data about these variables has contributed substantially to a debate between Sullivan and Krueger (1981) and Schoeninger and DeNiro (1982), in which variations in the isotopic shift between collagen and apatite carbonate have been ascribed to metabolic effects on the one hand and diagenesis on the other.

The debate in question will have to remain unresolved for the time being, but a substantial amount of new data is available to aid in the solution. Firstly, these data show that the isotopic shift between herbivore and carnivore collagen is about +2‰; between herbivore meat and carnivore collagen it is nearly +5‰. These shifts have been observed in the southwestern Cape Province of South Africa, which is a C_3 biome (Sealy 1984, Sealy and van der Merwe 1986); the results are outlined in Table 5.1. Similar results have been obtained in a study of

Table 5.1. $\delta^{13}C$ *values of bone collagen and meat of animals on different trophic levels: Hopefield, western Cape Province*

		$\delta^{13}C$ (‰)		
		collagen	meat	difference
HERBIVORES:	Hare	−20.0	−22.6	2.6
	Steenbok	−21.2	−23.7	2.6
	Grey duiker	−20.7	−23.5	2.8
	ave.	−20.6	−23.3	2.7
CARNIVORES:	Lynx	−19.2	−21.8	2.6
	Jackal	−17.9	−19.8	1.9
	ave.	−18.6	−20.8	2.3
Tropic level differences:		2.0	2.5	

Difference between herbivore meat and carnivore bone collagen is 4.7‰.
Sources: Sealy 1984, Sealy and Van der Merwe 1986.

gazelles and foxes in Israel. The Israel values follow a predictable gradient from the C_3 plant region in the north to the Negev and Sinai deserts in the south, where C_4 grasses make a significant contribution. The gradient is evident in both herbivores and carnivores, with a constant difference of 2‰ between them. Secondly, the isotopic shifts between collagen, apatite carbonate, and plant food base can now be illuminated. For herbivores, the relationship between collagen and apatite carbonate is linear, the latter being about 7.5‰ more positive in $\delta^{13}C$ value. The isotopic shift between collagen and apatite carbonate in carnivores, however, varies from +3 to +5‰. For omnivores, like baboons, the isotopic shift between collagen and carbonate is about 5‰. These data (Lee Thorp and van der Merwe 1987) tend to support a model for animal metabolism advanced by Krueger and Sullivan (1984). In brief, this model holds that collagen $\delta^{13}C$ values are closely related to food protein, while apatite carbonate values are related to blood CO_2, and thus more closely to carbohydrates.

It hardly needs pointing out that carnivore diets in natural settings can be related to herbivore $\delta^{13}C$ values in only the most general way. Similarly, the model proposed by Krueger and Sullivan will no doubt be substantially changed over time. These remarks underscore our lack of knowledge about animal metabolism and the need for feeding experiments to help improve it.

BIOTIC COMMUNITIES

Successful reconstructions of past environments require detailed information about the natural variations in ^{13}C concentration discussed so far. A short-cut is also possible, however, in that one can study the isotopic character of a modern biotic community and thus be able to recognize it in an archaeological context. This presupposes that former biotic communities are still available for study. In North America this is certainly not the case, due in part to Late Pleistocene extinctions and also to subsequent alterations by humans. In Africa it is still possible and will remain so while national park refuges survive.

Knowledge about the isotopic ecology of African flora is fragmentary. We know more about this subject for South Africa than for any other part of the world, and also a fair amount for Kenya (from Tieszen and his co-workers) and the northern fringes of the Sahara (Winter *et al.* 1976). The rest of the continent is a blank, however, and difficult to fill in from existing plant census data since the literature is indexed by country instead of ecozones (Livingstone and Clayton 1980). A review of the isotopic characters of African plant communities, based on available evidence and interpolations from first principles, has been provided by van der Merwe and Vogel (1983).

A database of $\delta^{13}C$ values for modern and ancient animal bone, mostly from Africa, is being assembled by the Archaeometry Laboratory of the University of Cape Town. These data are obtained from studies conducted for other reasons and consequently have large gaps, but, nevertheless, they provide the beginnings of a system for environmental reconstruction. Other databases exist – J. C. Vogel of the C.S.I.R. Radiocarbon Laboratory in Pretoria has done many $\delta^{13}C$ measurements on animal bone and a few smaller studies have been done in the U.S. Much of this information remains unpublished, because subject journals are not interested in lists of unfocused data. At some time in the near future, this situation will have to be corrected in a manner akin to the publication of radiocarbon dates. Some of the data produced by the Cape Town group have been described elsewhere (van der Merwe 1986). Selected data are discussed here to illustrate $\delta^{13}C$ values for animal collagen in three different plant communities in South Africa.

Table 5.2. $\delta^{13}C$ *values of animal bone collagen from the southwestern Cape coastal belt*[a]

Species	$\delta^{13}C$ (‰)
Tortoise (2 species)	−22.9
Hare (*Lepus capensis*)	−19.0
Steenbok (*Raphicerus campestris*)	−20.7
Springbok (*Antidorcas marsupialis*)	−21.2
Hyrax (*Procavia capensis*)	−20.8
Baboon (*Papio ursinus*)	−20.3
Bat-eared fox (*Otocyon megalotis*)	−19.6
Lynx (*Felis caracal*)	−19.2
Black-backed Jackal (*Camis mesomelas*)	−17.9

[a] This winter rainfall area has over 95% C_3 species.

Sources: Sealy 1984, Sealy and Van der Merwe 1986.

Southwestern Cape Province

The $\delta^{13}C$ values in Table 5.2 are from animals collected on the coastal plain north of Cape Town. This area has a Mediterranean-type climate with winter rainfall and is essentially C_3 in character, with an admixture of CAM succulents and fewer than five percent C_4 species among the grasses. It is not surprising, therefore, that the herbivores have $\delta^{13}C$ values around −21‰. The tortoise (−22.9‰) and hare (−19.0‰) are interesting exceptions. Tortoises invariably have $\delta^{13}C$ values which are substantially more negative than other animals in a C_3 biome; whether this phenomenon has something to do with tortoise metabolism is not known. The hare, primarily a grazer, has a $\delta^{13}C$ value more positive than one would expect for an area with almost no C_4 grasses. This may be the result of CAM plants in its diet. The lack of C_4 grasses is underscored by the bat-eared fox (−19.6), a consumer of termites, which in turn eat grass seeds. Subtracting 2‰ for the trophic level effect yields a $\delta^{13}C$ value comparable to the other herbivores. The same is true for the lynx and jackal. The latter may well include the hare in its diet, thus shifting its $\delta^{13}C$ value toward the positive end of the scale.

Table 5.3. *$\delta^{13}C$ values of bone collagen from animals of the northern and eastern Transvaal*[a]

Species	$\delta^{13}C$ (‰)
Herbivores	
Giraffe (*Giraffa camelopardis*)	−21.6
Grey duiker (*Sylvicapra grimmia*)	−21.5
Elephant (*Loxodonta africana*)	−20.8
Bushbuck (*Tragelaphus scriptus*)	−20.2
Kudu (*Tragelaphus strepsiceros*)	−19.6
Blue wildebeest (*Connochaetes taurinus*)	− 8.5
Tsessebe (*Damaliscus lunatis*)	− 6.8
Carnivores	
Gennet (*Genetta genetta*)	−13.2
Cape hunting dog (*Lycaon pictus*)	−11.8
Leopard (*Panthera pardus*)	−11.0
Spotted hyena (*Crocuta crocuta*)	−10.9
Black-backed jackal (*Canis mesomelas*)	−10.7
Lion (*Panthera leo*)	−10.2
Brown hyena (*Hyena brunnea*)	− 9.5

[a] This area is summer rainfall savannah with essentially no C_3 grasses

Northern and eastern Transvaal

This area includes the Transvaal Bushveld and Lowveld savannah and varies considerably in plant cover, especially as far as shrubs and trees are concerned. The temperatures are uniformly high, however, and the rain falls in summer, thus the grasses are essentially all C_4 species. This sorts the herbivores into browsers, grazers, and mixed feeders, unlike the southwestern Cape example (Table 5.3). The pure browsers (giraffe, duiker, bushbuck) have $\delta^{13}C$ values around −21‰, as on the Cape coast, but a pure grazer like the tsessebe measures −6.8‰. The blue wildebeest (−8.5) is primarily a grazer, but includes some C_3 browse in its diet. The elephant (−20.8) and kudu (−19.6) appear to be nearly pure browsers, but they are actually mixed feeders with a preference for browse when it is available in sufficient quantity.

The carnivores provide an interesting set of results. The gennet (−13.2) is a scavenger and hunter of small animals, while the brown hyena is nearly a pure scavenger. On the basis of its $\delta^{13}C$ value (−9.5), its diet is weighted toward grazing animals. The other carnivores are clustered fairly closely around an average of −11‰. Subtracting 7‰ from this value to correct for two trophic levels leaves −18‰, a plant base to their food-web of about 60 percent C_4 and 40 percent C_3 plants. In this region, the browsers are either very large and difficult to kill (giraffe, elephant) or small and scarce (duiker, bushbuck). This leaves the grazers and mixed feeders as the most likely carnivore prey. When large grazers are killed, the chances for leftovers after one meal are enhanced, thus accounting for the scavenging brown hyena at the positive end of the scale. The most plentiful prey animal in the area is the impala, which has no recognizable dietary preference. Vogel (1978) has shown that impala from a single farm in the Transvaal Lowveld have $\delta^{13}C$ values which vary across the entire spectrum from nearly pure browsers to nearly pure grazers. Impala form harems and bachelor herds for much of the year, which may yet help to account for this peculiar data set. The carnivores presumably do not discriminate according to sex, hence their intermediate $\delta^{13}C$ values.

Impala are the only animals whose $\delta^{13}C$ values indicate such a lack of dietary discrimination. Other species show different values for different biomes, but in a given environment the values for one species are usually clustered. It is precisely this fact which makes environmental reconstruction possible.

Addo National Park, eastern Cape Province

The tight clustering of $\delta^{13}C$ values for a given animal species is illustrated by the data from Addo National Park which appear in Table 5.4. This small refuge lies about 50 miles inland from Port Elizabeth and has a most unusual vegetation cover. The dominant tree species is the spekboom – literally "lard tree" – (*Portulacaria afra*), a CAM succulent with pleasantly sour leaves. It forms about 40 percent of the local plant cover and is a popular browse. Four other CAM species, including an aloe, add another 10 percent to this plant community and are also eaten by browsers. The rest of the plant cover consists of small trees and shrubs, while both C_3 and C_4 grass species are present. This is a peculiar biome by any standard, but particularly so in isotopic terms. The average $\delta^{13}C$ value for spekboom foliage is −17.9‰ and this is evident in the browsers. Assuming that the other CAM plants have similar values, then elephant (−17.2‰) have diets of about 60 percent C_3 and 40 percent CAM plants. Similarly, kudu (−16.6‰) include 55

Table 5.4. $\delta^{13}C$ *values of bone collagen from large mammals in Addo National Park, eastern Cape Province* [a]

		Sample	$\delta^{13}C$ (‰)
Elephant	(*Loxodonta africana*)	# 1	−17.2
		# 2	−17.0
		# 3	−17.4
		# 4	−17.2
		ave.	−17.2
Buffalo	(*Syncerus caffer*)	# 1	−13.5
		# 2	−13.8
		# 3	−13.8
		# 4	−13.1
		# 5	−13.6
		ave.	−13.6
Eland	(*Taurotragus oryx*)	# 1	−19.2
		# 2	−18.4
		# 3	−18.8
		ave.	−18.5
Kudu	(*Tragelaphus strepsiceros*)	# 1	−15.9
		# 2	−15.5
		# 3	−18.3
		ave.	−16.6
Spekboom	(*Portulacaria afra*)	# 1	−18.1
		# 2	−18.2
		# 3	−18.0
		# 4	−16.3
		ave.	−17.9

[a] The dominant tree species in this park is the spekboom (*Portulacaria afra*), a CAM plant, which makes up 40 percent of the plant cover. Four other species add a further 10 percent. Both C_3 and C_4 grass species are present.

percent CAM plants in their diets. Buffalo are pure grazers, hence the local grass cover consists of about 45 percent C_4 and 55 percent C_3 species. Eland are mostly browsers but may also eat grass; their diets cannot be analysed with confidence in this complex biome.

In calculating the CAM components in elephant and kudu diets for Addo National Park, it has been assumed that they do not eat the C_4 grasses. This is a reasonable assumption for an area where trees and shrubs dominate the plant cover. In areas where browse is scarce, elephant and kudu will also eat grass and produce collagen with values similar to those encountered at Addo. Elephant in the Luangwa valley in Zambia, for example, have $\delta^{13}C$ values close to those from Addo. The two biomes are easily distinguished, however, when other species are included, since Luangwa is a mixed woodland savannah.

RECONSTRUCTING ENVIRONMENTS

When confronted with an archaeological faunal assemblage from an unknown African environment, how can the isotopic analyst approach the problem of reconstructing that environment? Firstly, the environment would not be entirely unknown, since the age, site location, and composition of the assemblage would go a long way toward answering the question. Beyond that, a number of general rules can be followed.

(1) The nature of the grass cover can be assessed by looking at the $\delta^{13}C$ values for pure grazers. Zebra, tsessebe, and hartebeest are obvious examples, but there are many more pure or nearly pure grazers.

(2) The nature of the browse can be assessed by analysing pure browsers. Duiker, bushbuck, and giraffe are well-behaved browsers, while elephant and kudu prefer browse if enough is available. An exceptional plant community like Addo Park can immediately be identified when browser collagen values are more positive than about −20‰. Similarly, a forest environment can be identified when the $\delta^{13}C$ values are more negative than about −22‰. Due to recycling of CO_2 under closed canopies, the values for forest elephant, for example, may vary between −22 and −27‰, with animals from the dense tropical rain forests at the negative end of the range.

(3) The density of the tree cover can be assessed by analysing elephant bone. Elephant prefer to browse, but will add grass to their diet to satisfy their prodigious appetites. Their collagen $\delta^{13}C$ values in non-forest environments form a near-linear relationship with tree density, varying between about −22‰ in the northern guinea savannah of Niger and Burkina Faso to −16.4‰ in the grassland of Tsavo Park in Kenya (van der Merwe *et al.* 1986).

(4) The quality of the browse can be determined by looking at the behavior of marker species like springbok and ostrich. Both species prefer browse if it is available and sufficiently succulent. In the Great Karoo, for example, where bushes without thorns dominate, both exhibit $\delta^{13}C$ values similar to pure browsers. In the arid Karoo (northwest Cape Province) and Namibia, where the bushes are prickly and

scarcer, their diets include nearly 50 percent C_4 grass. In open grasslands, springbok have values like grazers; ostrich may as well, but have not been analysed. Kudu show a similar reaction to thorny browse, but they feed higher than about 1 meter above ground, while springbok and ostrich feed below that. In the Kalahari thornveld and central Namibia their diets include more than 50 percent C_4 grass.

(5) While the marker species mentioned here provide significant environmental information, greater precision can be attained by analysing as wide a range of species as possible.

Sample material

Most of the discussion so far has involved bone collagen, although apatite carbonate and mummified soft tissues have also been mentioned. To complete this list one should add ostrich eggshell, which also preserves dietary signatures (von Schirnding *et al.* 1982). The sample material most generally available, however, is bone; thus collagen and apatite carbonate deserve a closer look.

Collagen is certainly the preferred component of bone for isotopic analysis. Handled conservatively, it produces unaltered dietary signatures and can be used with confidence for environmental reconstruction. Its obvious limitation is that it disappears fairly rapidly, especially in hot climates. Systematic information on collagen survival is not available; published results referred to in this paper include analyses on zebra teeth as old as 70,000 years and on bone from extinct North American species. These are the success stories, however; failures are not published. The experience of our research group, particularly when dealing with samples like human ribs (which anthropologists are more likely to part with), has been that collagen is difficult to extract from bones older than 10,000 years. This value is for coastal cave deposits in the temperate southwestern Cape. In open sites along the Ecuadorian coast, collagen unfortunately becomes difficult to isolate before approximately 5000 years b.p., during the critical Valdivia period. These problems can be overcome to some extent by using dense bone for analysis; large mammal teeth are particularly useful. Improvements in mass spectrometer detection limits can also be expected to help. Nevertheless, routine isotopic analyses of very old bones are unlikely with collagen as sample material.

Apatite carbonate survives more or less indefinitely, but is a controversial sample material. It clearly suffers from diagenetic alteration of the original dietary signature. Attempts at removing diagenetic material by chemical means have led to the unresolved debate, mentioned earlier. This problem is not yet solved, but encouraging results have been obtained. Data published elsewhere (Lee Thorp and van der Merwe 1987) show that most of the diagenetic carbonate can be removed; a small amount of diagenetic material remains, which is probably due to isotopic exchange (as opposed to contaminating precipitates). By comparing the $\delta^{13}C$ values for apatite carbonate of animals with known dietary habits over time, this exchange can be shown to take place relatively soon after death – probably as the desiccating collagen opens pores in the bone – and then to slow down or cease. At the site of Klasies River Mouth, the diagenetic alteration of $\delta^{13}C$ ratios in bone apatite 125,000 years old is +2‰. At Makapansgat, three-million-year-old bone has been altered by +4‰. The direction of the alteration is due to the chemistry of the deposits, both of which are cemented by calcium carbonate. The diagenetic alteration can be observed for both grazers and browsers and the isotopic shift between them is as expected for C_4 and C_3 plant consumers. The implication is that the $\delta^{13}C$ values for the rest of the faunal assemblage can be corrected for diagenetic alteration.

CONCLUSION

It follows from the various topics discussed here that a great deal more information is needed about variation of ^{13}C concentrations in the contemporary natural environment. In the course of producing such data, significant contributions to knowledge about the carbon cycle can be expected. Sufficient data are available, however, to undertake reconstructions of past environments, subject to subsequent refinements. This can be done for those parts of the world, like Africa, where former biotic communities are still represented. For Holocene and perhaps Upper Pleistocene events, animal bone collagen can be analysed toward this end. Current work with apatite carbonate holds the possibility that this time scale can be extended to span the entire Pleistocene, and perhaps longer.

ACKNOWLEDGMENTS

I thank my co-workers Richard Bell, Julia Lee Thorp, and Ernesto Medina for the use of data which are as yet unpublished. The research was supported by the Foundation for Research Development of the South African Council for Scientific and Industrial Research.

6
Multi-element studies of diagenesis in prehistoric bone

T. DOUGLAS PRICE

Department of Anthropology
University of Wisconsin–Madison

Analysis of the strontium content of human bone for the reconstruction of past diets is a relatively new technique that relies on the known movement of this element through the food chain. Strontium is an alkaline earth metal that is distributed unequally in trace amounts in the lithosphere (Odum 1951). Naturally occurring strontium enters the food chain through plants. Amounts of strontium are lower in the bones of meat eaters than in those of plant eaters. Thus, the bones of humans (as omnivores) exhibit strontium levels intermediate to those present in herbivores and carnivores, at a level dependent upon the relative contribution of plants and animals to the diet. Several summary reviews of the trace element analysis of bone have appeared (Gilbert 1985, Klepinger 1984, Price *et al.* 1985, Schoeninger 1979a, Sillen and Kavanagh 1982). Bone strontium analysis has been used to examine the relationship between diet and status (Schoeninger 1979b), the relationship between diet and gender (Lambert *et al.* 1979, Price *et al.* 1986), and changes in subsistence (Gilbert 1975, Katzenberg 1984, Price 1985, Price and Kavanagh 1982, Sillen 1981a).

The following pages deal with the question of variability in human bone strontium. An initial section summarizes known variation in bone strontium for modern populations of mammals. Variation in prehistoric burial populations is subsequently discussed. Diet and environment account for some of the differences within these prehistoric populations, but not all. Diagenesis also may have operated to change the pre-depositional composition and condition of the bones. Previous studies of diagenesis are recounted and several new sets of information are brought to bear on the question. Stratified series of bone samples from the Price III site in Wisconsin and Nelson Bay Cave in South Africa are used in a consideration of changes in bone chemistry through time. Adjacent and largely contemporary prehistoric cemeteries near Skateholm in southern Sweden are also compared in terms of bone strontium levels. The levels of bone strontium, calcium, iron, aluminum, and other elements, as well as the ash content of the samples, are considered in these analyses. Each of these studies provides evidence for post-depositional alteration of bone strontium levels. In conclusion, various indices of diagenetic change are considered and evaluated.

VARIABILITY IN BONE STRONTIUM

Although the technique of strontium analysis is relatively straightforward, several questions remain regarding basic principles. Primary sources of strontium in bone appear to be (1) the amounts naturally available in the local environment, and (2) the composition of the diet. There are, however, other factors that contribute to differences in bone strontium, including demographic and physiological conditions and post-depositional chemical change. These additional sources of variability must be understood in order for the results of strontium analysis to be meaningful for the reconstruction of past diet.

Modern variation in humans and other animals

Variation in bone strontium within a population is rather high. Schoeninger (1979b) reports a coefficient of variation (c.v.) of approximately 20% in a modern sample of ranch-bred mink, fed on the same diet. Laboratory rats raised on identical diets exhibit a c.v. of *ca.* 22% (Price *et al.* 1986). These values are *minimal* estimates of variability within a population since (1) there are no differences in diet or environment for these animals, and (2) only minor genetic differences are present within these controlled populations. For an animal population in the wild, Price *et al.* (1985a) report a c.v. of 35% for bone strontium levels in a sample of fifty-three modern white-tailed deer in Wisconsin.

For modern human populations, reported coefficients of variation range from 19.1% among individuals of all ages in Japan (Tanaka *et al.* 1981) to 29.3% or more for individuals from throughout Great Britain (Sillen and Kavanagh 1982). This latter value is likely exaggerated by local strontium differences in the environment among the individuals included in the study. The coefficient of variation within a modern human group within a limited geographic area is likely between 20 and 25%.

This variation is related to age, gender, metabolism, and reproductive status. With regard to age, Lambert *et al.* (1979) found that prehistoric human bone strontium levels decreased through childhood, increased during adolescence, and remained more or less stable between the ages of 20 and 50. Tanaka *et al.* (1981) report a slight, gradual increase in bone strontium with age in a modern sample of Japanese.

Sex-related differences in bone strontium levels are less clear-cut. Lambert *et al.* (1979) found significantly higher strontium values among males in one prehistoric group but not in another. Tanaka *et al.* (1981) report little difference between modern males and females of all ages in Japan. Snyder *et al.* (1964) observed significant differences between the sexes in a study of U.S. individuals between the ages of 20 and 59. Price *et al.* (1986) report females exhibiting higher strontium levels in a majority of prehistoric human populations. These differences are related at least in part to reproductive status, with pregnancy and lactation responsible for increased strontium levels in females.

Prehistoric human variation

Prehistoric human populations exhibit variability in bone strontium that is comparable to modern groups. Burials from archaeological sites throughout the midwestern U.S. exhibit c.v.'s between 10 and 40% (Table 6.1). Differences in bone strontium levels between the sites are likely due to a combination of local environmental strontium levels, regional variation in diets, and diagenesis. These burials date to the Middle and Late Archaic periods, from roughly 8000 to 2700 b.p. Black Earth is a Middle Archaic cemetery and occupation site in southern Illinois. Overall strontium levels are much higher at this site than at others, perhaps as a result of diagenesis. The four Late Archaic period

Table 6.1. *Descriptive statistics for strontium levels in prehistoric human bone from Archaic populations in the midwestern United States (parts per million).*

Site	n	x	s.d.	c.v.(%)
Price III (WI)	53	154.7	33.1	21.4
Reigh (WI)	31	100.2	22.9	22.9
Riverside (W1)	20	86.1	35.1	40.8
Oconto (WI)	32	118.4	26.7	22.6
Chiggerville (KY)	61	541.7	67.3	12.4
Black Earth (IL)	118	1047.0	133.0	12.7
Williams (OH)	10	275.0	101.4	36.9
DuPont (OH)	22	647.2	70.9	11.0
Frontenac Island (NY)	45	541.5	95.8	17.7

sites in Wisconsin exhibit relatively low strontium levels. The Williams site is a Late Archaic Red Ochre ossuary in northeastern Ohio, containing perhaps as many as 1000 individuals. At least 90% of these burials were cremations (Sciulli *et al.* 1982). DuPont and Chiggerville are Late Archaic period sites in Ohio and Kentucky, respectively, and both contain extensive shellfish remains. Consumption of freshwater molluscs at these sites may be in part responsible for the higher levels of strontium that are seen (Schoeninger and Peebles 1981). However, white-tailed deer from both sites also exhibit relatively high levels of bone strontium, suggesting that environmental differences are equally, or more, important than shellfish consumption. Frontenac Island is a Late Archaic site on an island in Lake Cayuga in New York. Many of the artifactual and faunal remains at this site indicated a heavy emphasis on fishing.

STUDIES OF DIAGENESIS

As noted, the majority of pre-mortem variability in bone strontium is the result of either local environmental strontium levels or diet. Some additional minor differences are introduced by individual sex, age, and reproductive status. These minor sources of variability are reasonably well understood.

On the other hand, diagenesis – a potentially significant source of post-mortem variation in prehistoric bone samples – is the subject of considerable debate. A number of studies of fossil and archaeological bone have suggested that strontium is stable in the depositional environment. The 2^+ cation position filled by strontium in bone mineral is very stable (Schoeninger 1979b:304). *In vivo* studies of ^{90}Sr have suggested that it is almost impossible to remove from bone mineral (McLean and Urist 1968). Thus, strontium has *appeared* to be a reliable indicator of pre-mortem conditions as long as the mineral portion of bone tissue was retained.

Toots and Voorhies (1965) observed that the bones of fossil animals had been enriched with iron, manganese, and barium, but comparable changes in strontium levels were not recorded. Parker and Toots (1970) argued that fossil concentrations of strontium were similar to those in the bones of modern animals and, therefore, that diagenetic changes were not affecting strontium levels. In 1980, Parker and Toots reported similar levels of strontium in bone, dentin, and enamel from fossil *Subhyracodon*. Diagenesis, if operating, should have led to observable differences between these materials, since enamel is more resistant to contamination and decomposition.

Lambert *et al.* (1979) reported one of the more detailed studies of diagenesis in human bone. They examined a suite of twelve elements in both bone and adjacent soil at two sites in southern Illinois. Comparison of elemental content revealed that the bone had been enriched with iron, manganese, and potassium from the soil. Magnesium and copper occurred in roughly the same concentrations in both the soil and the bone. Strontium, zinc, calcium, and sodium were found in much higher amounts in the bone than in the soil. The authors concluded that these latter elements are therefore less mobile and more reliable for the study of the pre-depositional condition of the bone.

Several follow-ups to this original study have appeared (Lambert *et al.* 1982, 1983, 1984a, 1985a). In 1982, Lambert *et al.* compared the chemical differences between ribs and femurs from these same archeological sites. They argued that rib and femur tissue should have the same levels of strontium unless diagenesis was operating. The porous, trabecular bone of the rib might be more susceptible to contamination than the denser, cortical bone of the femur.

Analysis of both types of bone demonstrated that the elements generally associated with soil contamination (i.e. iron, potassium, aluminum, and manganese) occurred in slightly higher proportions in the ribs as expected. Levels of calcium and sodium were lower in the ribs than in the femurs. The elements thought to be most closely associated with diet – strontium, zinc, and magnesium – were recorded at comparable levels in both the ribs and the femurs. These results suggested that the "diagenetic loss of material appears not to be as serious a problem as the incorporation of extraneous elements" (Lambert *et al.* 1982:291).

Tanaka *et al.* (1981), however, report significantly lower strontium levels in ribs than in femurs among modern Japanese. On the other hand, Brätter *et al.* (1977) indicate that the strontium content of trabecular bones is higher than cortical material and a function of the mass ratio of *spongiosa/compacta* at the sampling site. It seems clear that there is a difference in the strontium content of rib and femur although the direction is less certain. Thus, the absence of difference originally reported by Lambert *et al.* (1982) may in fact imply that diagenetic changes in Sr are taking place. Strontium levels in the porous rib bone may be enriched by diagenesis. On the other hand, the high coefficient of variation present in the prehistoric samples may mask the rib–femur differences reported by Tanaka *et al.* (1981). Buikstra *et al.* (this volume) note that re-study of matched rib–femur samples shows significant differences in levels of Ca, Na, Sr, Mg, Cu, K, Fe, Mn, and Al. Only Zn and Pb show similar levels in both types of bone. Buikstra *et al.* (this volume) also found that levels of strontium, sodium, and calcium were higher in cortical bone than in the more porous, trabecular samples. The question of rib–femur strontium comparability will certainly require further investigation. It is essential that more reliable baseline information regarding strontium levels in modern ribs and femurs from the same population be assembled as soon as possible.

Electron microprobe analysis of bone cross-sections for evidence of enrichment and/or loss has also been undertaken (Gilbert 1975, Lambert *et al.* 1984a, Parker and Toots 1970). Lambert *et al.* (1984a) observed Fe, Al, K, Mn, and Mg to be concentrated along the margins of the bone section, suggesting that these elements were added as post-depositional contaminants from the soil. Homogeneous distributions of Zn, Sr, Pb, Na, and Ca across bone sections indicated that no post-mortem enrichment had occurred. However, atomic absorption analysis of the soil lying *in situ* directly beneath these bones revealed higher concentrations of Ca and Mg than expected, documenting the depletion of these two elements from bone.

Nelson and Sauer (1984) examined the zinc and manganese content of fifty soil and bone samples from the same burial features at the Black Earth site in southern Illinois. Soil pH at the site was generally alkaline, between 7.0 and 8.5. Very low correlation was observed between manganese and zinc levels in bone and soil and the authors concluded that there was little exchange of these elements between bone and the soil matrix. Data on magnesium, copper, and strontium also showed no association, although sample size prohibited a statement regarding the significance of these relationships.

Contradictory information comes from other investigations. Sillen (1981a) has reported changes in bone strontium and Sr/Ca ratios through time. Sillen examined bone tissue from Natufian (*ca.* 12,000 b.p.) and Aurignacian (*ca.* 20,000 b.p.) layers at Hayonim Cave in Israel. Strontium levels in fox and several species of herbivore bone were distinct in the younger layers at the site but no differences were observed between the older materials. Sillen attributes the equilibration of strontium levels in the older layers to diagenetic changes in bone composition.

Nelson *et al.* (1983a) took a different approach to the question of diagenetic change. Post-mortem chemical alteration was studied through comparison of modern and prehistoric animal bone from the same locality. Differences observed between modern seal and reindeer bone from Greenland disappear in prehistoric samples of the same species. Isotopic analysis of the strontium content led to the conclusion that a large proportion of the stable strontium in the prehistoric material may have been added under post-mortem conditions. Such dramatic evidence for diagenesis has not been reported elsewhere and may reflect specific and unusual depositional contexts in Greenland.

THE COMPOSITION OF MODERN BONE

One way to consider the question of diagenesis is to compare modern bone composition with prehistoric samples. Fresh bone tissue consists of three major components, an inorganic fraction (bone ash), an organic matrix, and water, in the approximate proportion of 17:20:15 (Engström *et al.* 1957). By dry weight, organic materials constitute about 30% and minerals about 70% of bone (Leblond and Weinstock 1976). Collagen, a protein, forms about 85% of the organic portion of dry bone powder (McLean and Urist 1968). Bone ash constitutes $67 \pm 0.9\%$ of whole dry bone (Easthoe 1961:719). Bone ash is largely

Table 6.2 *Ash content of human bone and calcium content of bone ash from prehistoric samples in North America*

Ash Content %	Ca % of Bone Ash	Reference	Site
90.4	37.2 ± 1.9	Price (1985)	Price III (WI)
—	36.9 ± 3.2	Price (n.d.)	Oconto (WI)
—	35.9 ± 3.2	Price (n.d.)	Riverside (WI)
—	35.8 ± 3.0	Price (n.d.)	Reigh (WI)
87.6	38.6 ± 2.2	Price (1985)	Williams (OH)
85.4	38.9 ± 0.9	Price (1985)	DuPont (OH)
86.0	38.4 ± 1.0	Price (n.d.)	Frontenac Island (NY)
89.9	37.8 ± 0.9	Price (n.d.)	Chiggerville (KY)
86.5	41.3 ± 3.6	Price (n.d.)	Black Earth (IL)
82.0	33.8 ± 3.9	Lambert *et al.* (1982)	Gibson (IL)
—	34.9 ± 2.6	Lambert *et al.* (1982)	Ledders (IL)
68.7	38.3 ± 0.6	Katzenberg (1984)	Ossossane (Ont)
70.9	38.8 ± 0.6	Katzenberg (1984)	Kleinburg (Ont)
77.0	38.7 ± 0.4	Katzenberg (1984)	Fairty (Ont)
76.9	38.5 ± 0.3	Katzenberg (1984)	Serpent Pits (Ont)
69.1	38.4 ± 1.3	Katzenberg (1984)	Serpent Mounds (Ont)

— Missing data

mineral in the form of hydroxyapatite, a mixture of calcium and phosphate in a ratio of approximately 2:1 in modern samples. Phosphorus constitutes 15.5–16.4% of bone ash (Easthoe 1961).

The precise amount of calcium in human bone ash is less certain. Several studies of calcium in modern human bone ash indicate an average of approximately 37.3% (38.8%, Baker *et al.* 1946; 37.0 ± 2.0%, Alexander and Nusbaum 1959; 36.0 ± 3.8%, Tipton and Shafer 1964; 37.3 ± 0.7%, Pelligrino and Biltz 1965; 37.5%, Tanaka *et al.* 1981). Thus, the calcium content of modern human bone ash, although apparently somewhat variable, should be approximately 37%. Comparison of calcium levels in modern and prehistoric human bone ash is of interest. Calcium levels in prehistoric human bone samples from eastern North America are presented in Table 6.2. Many of the samples fall close to the modern average. Others, however, show significant deviation. Values from the Gibson and Ledders sites in southern Illinois are very low at 33.8% and 34.9%. The value from the Black Earth site in southern Illinois is very high at 41.3%. Average calcium values for a group of samples thus can provide an important indication of diagenetic enrichment or depletion.

Calcium levels can increase in certain post-mortem situations through the addition of carbonate (Cook and Heizer 1947, Krueger and Sullivan 1984). Such contamination can take at least two forms (Sillen 1981b, this volume). Calcium and carbonate may precipitate as calcite, or the hydroxyapatite crystals in bone may grow through incorporation of carbonate as a substitute for inorganic phosphate (Pelligrino and Biltz 1972). The very high level of calcium in the burials at the Black Earth site, for example, is the result of a high carbonate concentration in the soil which left deposits in and on the skeletal material (Bassett 1982:1029).

The question of differential changes in both strontium and calcium in the post-depositional environment is important. Several authors (e.g. Sillen and Kavanagh 1982) have argued that a ratio between strontium and calcium is the appropriate index for the composition of whole bone in dietary reconstruction. Pate and Brown (1985), however, indicate on theoretical grounds that strontium is generally stable and calcium mobile in post-depositional environments. Their work is based on the examination of the *loci* of strontium and calcium incorporation in the crystalline structure of hydroxyapatite. They suggest a model for the diagenetic replacement of calcium by yttrium in the hydroxyapatite matrix which may account for its mobility relative to strontium. Calcium occurs both in the apatite crystals of interred bone and as a separate mineral phase, filling small voids and fractures. The intercrystalline calcium is mobile in comparison to calcium and strontium found in the crystal structure. Strontium occurs only in the apatite microcrystalline structure and is not found in the intercrystalline spaces (Parker 1965, Parker and Toots 1970, 1974). Strontium/calcium ratios for the assessment of prehistoric materials clearly should not be used if these conditions apply. Certainly the evidence from the case studies presented below documents differential post-mortem behavior for strontium and calcium.

Values for other elements in modern bone ash are presented in Table 6.3. While these values are not exact, they do provide some indication of the concentrations of certain elements. Iron and aluminum are virtually absent in modern bone samples and, thus, in higher concentrations must be present as contaminants (Lambert *et al.* 1979). Zinc values in modern bone are highly variable as they are determined by both local environmental conditions and diet (Beck 1985, Gilbert 1975).

Table 6.3 *Elemental concentrations in modern bone*

Element	Concentration
Na	1.50 ± 0.57%
Sr	120 ± 49 ppm
Zn	210 ± 46 ppm
Mg	4600 ± 1000 ppm
Fe	400 ± 300 ppm
Mn	2–10 ppm
Al	5–110 ppm

Source: Tipton and Shafer 1964, cited in Lambert *et al.* 1985a.

CHANGES IN BONE STRONTIUM

Investigations of strontium diagenesis in bone have often been contradictory. In some studies there appears to be relatively little change in bone strontium levels through time. Toots and Voorhies (1965), for example, reported a difference between grazing and browsing diets in fossil dinosaurs using strontium levels in enamel. In other depositional contexts, however, strontium levels are dramatically altered and variation between trophic levels less pronounced. Such changes may result in increased or depleted levels of bone strontium. Clearly questions regarding diagenesis and bone strontium are far from resolved. In most cases, experimental conditions have not been well designed for the examination of changes in bone chemistry through time. Studies of bone strontium diagenesis have not directly considered alteration under similar conditions of deposition.

Three case studies are presented in the following pages to provide some indication of changes in bone strontium through time and the possible effects of diagenesis. These changes were unexpected, given the similar or identical conditions under which the individuals probably lived. A stratified series of samples of bone from a species of small antelope from a cave in South Africa show interesting changes in strontium through time that may be due to post-depositional effects. Two adjacent, and largely contemporary, cemeteries from southern Sweden exhibit dramatic differences in bone strontium levels that are related to diagenesis. Samples from a prehistoric cemetery in southwestern Wisconsin were analysed as well with regard to this question. Changes in bone strontium levels through several layers of the same burial-feature at this site indicate that diet or diagenesis is responsible.

Analysis

Bone samples were cleaned carefully both with an air abrasive tool and in deionized water in an ultrasonic cleaner, oven-dried to constant weight, and ashed in a muffle furnace at 600 °C for approximately 8 h. Bone ash was ground to powder in an agate mortar and 0.25 g of the ash digested in a mixture of HNO_3 and $HClO_4$ (6:1). Digestion time was *ca.* 3 h at a final temperature of 215 °C. Samples were then diluted to 50 ml with deionized water and analysed by Inductively Coupled Plasma/Atomic Emission Spectrometry (I.C.P./A.E.S.). Nine elements were measured with the I.C.P./A.E.S. including calcium, sodium, strontium, zinc, copper, manganese, magnesium, iron, and aluminum. With typical parameters, I.C.P./A.E.S. provides precision on the order of 1% c.v. (Fischer *et al.* 1981).

Nelson Bay Cave

A series of bone samples from the Nelson Bay Cave in South Africa were analysed. This site contains over 4 m of stratified deposits from the Middle and Late Stone Age (Fig. 6.1). Bone samples were taken from the Younger Stone Age levels, radiocarbon dated from 18,000 b.p. to younger than 5000 b.p. (Klein 1972). The bone samples are from phalanges or astragali of a single species, *Raphicerus melanotis* – the grysbok, a small antelope (Klein 1976). Grysbok bones are found throughout the cave deposits and the species is present in the area today as well. Bone samples from the lower layers of the deposits appeared to be more highly mineralized. All units older than about 10,000 b.p. are below a perched water table in the cave. Pollen and other climatic evidence suggests that vegetation changed from grassier to bushier conditions around 12,000 b.p. in the environment around the cave (R. Klein, personal communication).

Mean values for ash content and elemental concentration by stratigraphic level at Nelson Bay Cave are provided in Table 6.4. Values for calcium are close to the expected average for mammal bone. Ash content of the bone does not vary greatly through the deposits. However,

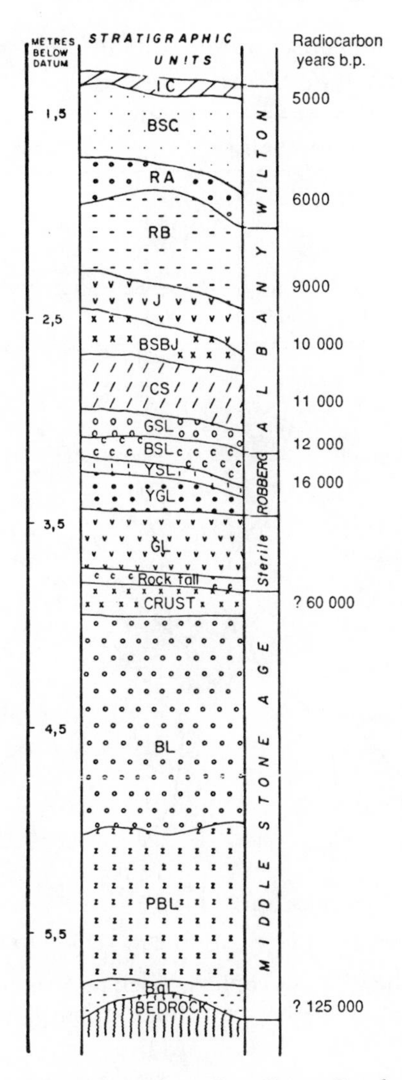

Fig. 6.1 Nelson Bay Cave, South Africa. The stratigraphic sequence and radiocarbon age (from Klein 1972). Used with the permission of *Quaternary Research*

strontium, iron, and aluminum have their lowest levels in the middle layers of the cave. These values are plotted in Fig. 6.2. As can be seen from the plot, the curves for strontium, iron, and aluminum are similar, suggesting that strontium may be a contaminant as well in this particular case. Clearly, Sr levels are varying and show both decrease and increase

Table 6.4 *Mean elemental concentrations and ash content by stratigraphic level at Nelson Bay Cave*

Strat. Level	n	Ca (%)	Sr (ppm)	Fe (ppm)	Al (ppm)	Ash Content (%)
1	5	37.55	1283	244.4	288.3	78.9
2	10	37.93	1052	43.0	138.1	79.3
3	6	37.63	872	60.8	131.5	77.4
4	5	37.09	890	63.8	160.7	82.6
5	4	37.04	961	195.0	255.1	79.8
6	5	37.32	1138	155.0	396.1	82.1

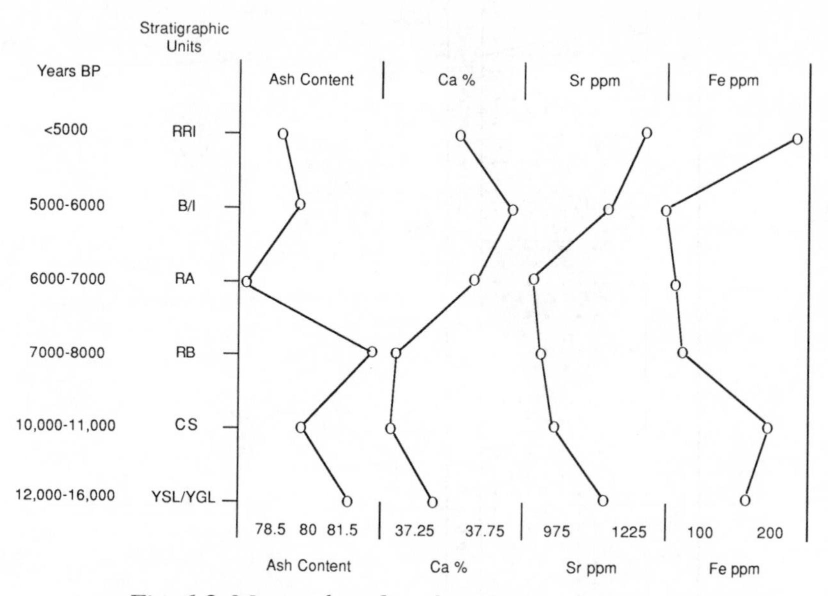

Fig. 6.2 Mean values for ash content, calcium, strontium, iron, and aluminum in grysbok bone from various layers at Nelson Bay Cave

in the deposits. An important question regarding this variation concerns the amount of strontium present relative to other elements.

These data suggest that calcium is fairly stable in the post-depositional environment at Nelson Bay Cave. The average calcium value for all samples is 37.5% with a standard deviation of 1.2%. No pronounced trend can be seen in the plot of calcium values and the correlation between strontium and calcium is very low. Thus it appears that changes in calcium levels are not affecting changes in the relative

Table 6.5 *Correlation*[a] *between elements and ash content in bone samples from Nelson Bay Cave (n=35)*

	Ca	Na	Sr	Zn	Mg	Mn	Cu	Fe	Al
Ca									
Na	0.298								
Sr	0.128	−0.1							
Zn	−0.15	−0.08	−0.05						
Mg	0.223	**0.64**	**0.353**	−0.2					
Mn	−0.11	−0.27	0.067	**0.57**	−0.21				
Cu	−0.21	−0.14	−0.26	**0.329**	−0.09	−0.01			
Fe	−0.08	−0.19	**0.616**	0.253	0.033	0.155	−0.11		
Al	−0.06	**−0.37**	**0.579**	−0.06	0.006	0.202	−0.09	**0.792**	
Ash	−0.2	**−0.34**	0.183	0.079	−0.28	0.114	−0.03	**0.36**	0.281

[a] Values greater than 0.325 are significant at 0.05 and are shown in bold type.

amounts of strontium. The ratio of strontium to calcium in the Nelson Bay Cave deposits shows no patterning. On the other hand, iron, aluminum, and strontium concentrations are enriched. Clearly diagenesis is modifying the amount of pre-mortem bone strontium in the case of grysbok at Nelson Bay Cave. The other elements measured in this analysis (Na, Mn, Mg, Cu, Zn) also show significant variation that is also related to post-depositional chemical change.

A matrix of correlation coefficients among the various elements in all the bone samples from Nelson Bay Cave is presented in Table 6.5. Several interesting patterns emerge from a consideration of these data. The highest correlation seen in this table is between iron and aluminum, indicative of the similar behavior of these two elements which occur largely as contaminants. Strontium values are closely correlated with both iron and aluminum. Other significant positive correlations include strontium and magnesium, and zinc with manganese and copper. Bone ash content is negatively correlated with sodium content and positively correlated with iron. Sodium and magnesium also show a high positive correlation. Parker and Toots (1980) found that sodium was depleted in fossil bone and dentin. However, in the sample from Nelson Bay Cave, sodium values increase through time. Sillen (this volume) suggests that increases in sodium values may reflect the structural incorporation of diagenetic carbonate through recrystallization of the apatite. Correlation coefficients among the elements in samples from the same layer at Nelson Bay Cave do not show similar patterns of significance, suggesting that it is indeed change through time that is responsible for the associations.

Skateholm

Two cemeteries from the Mesolithic period are known from an area near Skateholm in southern Sweden (Larsson 1983, Persson and Persson 1984). These cemeteries are located within 200 m of one another on what were once small islands in the mouth of a bay (Fig. 6.3). Over sixty burials have been excavated at Skateholm I, making it the largest Mesolithic cemetery in Europe. More than twenty-two graves, often heavily stained with red ochre, were recovered from the nearby burial area at Skateholm II. Skateholm I dates from 6250 to 5750 b.p; recent accelerator dates from Skateholm II fall between 6430 and 6090 b.p (L. Larsson, personal communication). Skateholm I is a few meters higher than Skateholm II and likely became the focus of settlement and burial as the lower site was transgressed by the gradually rising level of the Baltic Sea in the early postglacial.

The skeletal materials from these cemeteries have been analysed for both isotopic and elemental content (Price 1986). The $\delta^{13}C$ values from

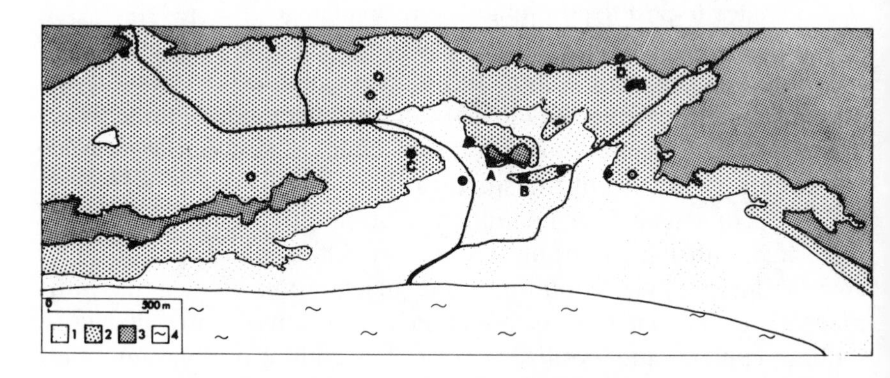

Fig. 6.3 Archaeological sites in the Skateholm area of southern Sweden. Black dots indicate Mesolithic remains; open dots are Neolithic or unknown settlement remains.
Legend A. Skateholm I: B. Skateholm II: C. Skateholm III: D. Ö. Vemmenhög 7: 1. below 3 m a.s.l.: 2. 3–5 m a.s.l.: 3. above 5 m a.s.l.: 4. modern sea level. (From Larsson 1983: 7.) Used with the permission of *Meddelanden från Lunds universitets historiska museum.*

Table 6.6 *Elemental analysis of human bone from Skateholm*

	Age	Sex	Ca (%)	Sr (ppm)	Zn (ppm)
Skateholm I					
	Adult	Female	35.09	749	116
	Adult	Female	36.88	431	195
	Adult	Male	35.48	795	185
	Adult	Female	36.89	506	195
	Adult	Female	37.30	543	175
	Adult	Male	36.85	428	202
	Adult	Female	35.72	603	604
	Adult	Female	31.65	678	277
	Adult	?	31.17	513	447
	Mean	(n=9)	35.23	583	266
	Standard deviation		2.29	133	158
	Coefficient of variation		6.5%	23%	59%
Skateholm II					
	Adult	Male	34.76	805	178
	Adult	Female	28.76	715	113
	Adult	Female (?)	30.14	780	195
	Adult	Male	31.60	832	277
	?	Female	36.53	618	143
	Adult	Female	29.75	723	126
	Adult	Male	32.49	895	225
	Adult	Female	29.35	642	130
	Adult	Female	31.51	910	360
	Mean (n=9)		31.68	769	195
	Standard deviation		2.56	103	81.7
	Coefficient of variation		8.1%	13%	42%

two human bone samples at Skateholm I are −16.8‰ and −20.1‰ (Häkansson 1982, 1984), suggesting a diet based largely on terrestrial foods. Samples from Skateholm II lack sufficient collagen to obtain an isotope ratio. In all likelihood, the lower values for sea foods in the ratios at Skateholm reflect the less saline, relatively fresh waters of the Baltic.

Human bone samples from both sites have been analysed by I.C.P./A.E.S. for nine elements. Descriptive statistics are presented in Tables 6.6 and 6.7. Several elements show pronounced differences in the human bone composition between the two cemeteries. All elements with the exception of Ca and Zn are much more abundant in the remains from the older site of Skateholm II. The higher levels of iron, aluminum, and manganese, for example, suggest that the remains at

Table 6.7 *Elemental analysis of human bone from Skateholm: mean and standard deviation for nine elements at each site*

	Skateholm I (n=9)	Skateholm II (n=9)
Ca %	35.2 ± 2.3	31.7 ± 2.6
Na (%)	0.38 ± 0.04	0.47 ± 0.1
Sr (ppm)	582.9 ± 133	768.8 ± 103
Zn (ppm)	266.4 ± 158	194.0 ± 82
Mg (ppm)	796 ± 144	1060 ± 271
Mn (ppm)	1076 ± 990	1616 ± 885
Cu (ppm)	14.5 ± 4	17.4 ± 6
Fe (ppm)	11257 ± 8042	37973 ± 19872
Al (ppm)	8939 ± 10402	17672 ± 9635

the older site have been subject to more intense contamination. Strontium levels are also higher at Skateholm II.

An initial glance then would suggest that marine foods were more important in the diet at Skateholm II. This is unlikely to be the case, however. The archaeological evidence suggests that marine foods were more common at the younger site of Skateholm I. Over eighty-six different species of animals have been identified from these sites (Jonsson 1987). The percentages of roe deer and freshwater fish are higher at Skateholm II, compared to more abundant saltwater fish, seal, and wild boar at Skateholm I (Larsson 1985).

Bone calcium levels are lower at Skateholm II (31.7%) compared to Skateholm I (35.2%), indicative of greater diagenetic activity at the older site. This reduced calcium content is also reflected in the relative absence of collagen at Skateholm II, noted above. The lower calcium levels at Skateholm II may cause other elements to appear in higher concentrations. Spectrometric measurements are "semi-quantitative," i.e. relative to amounts of other elements in the material under examination. A decrease in the amount of one element means that amounts of other elements may increase in proportion. For example, the levels of iron and aluminum in bone at Skateholm II are exceptionally high. As noted only zinc and calcium occur in lower amounts at Skateholm II; calcium is being depleted; the reasons for the higher levels of zinc are unclear.

Table 6.8 *Correlation[a] between elements in bone samples from Skateholm I and II (n=18)*

	Ca	Na	Sr	Zn	Mg	Mn	Cu	Fe
Ca								
Na	−0.09							
Sr	**−0.49**	**0.66**						
Zn	0.03	−0.02	−0.07					
Mg	0.11	**0.68**	0.42	−0.16				
Mn	**−0.62**	−0.18	0.13	0.22	−0.38			
Cu	−0.17	**0.49**	**0.50**	**0.53**	**−0.50**			
Fe	**−0.76**	0.27	**0.61**	0.07	−0.02	**0.50**	0.25	
Al	**−0.90**	−0.04	0.24	0.07	−0.19	**0.62**	0.12	**0.49**

[a] Values greater than 0.444 are significant at 0.05 and are shown in bold type.

Correlation coefficients (Table 6.8) between these elements for all the bone samples from Skateholm help to document the nature of this relationship. Calcium is negatively correlated with strontium, manganese, iron, and aluminum. As calcium levels decrease in bone, these elements increase. Comparison of the correlation matrices (not shown) for the samples from the individual sites is also informative. At Skateholm I, significant values are found only in a negative relationship between aluminum and calcium and in a positive correlation between magnesium and calcium. At Skateholm II, the negative correlation between aluminum and calcium is repeated and a significant association among strontium, zinc, and copper is apparent.

The behavior of zinc is somewhat puzzling and is not directly correlated with changes in calcium. Zinc concentrations may be higher in carnivores than in herbivores (Rheingold *et al.* 1983, Schoeninger, this volume), as meat is a better source of zinc than plants (Beck, 1985, Gilbert 1975, Klepinger 1984). Zinc values are higher at the younger site of Skateholm I and suggest that meat may have been less important in the diet at Skateholm II.

The Price III site

The Price III site is located on the first terrace of the Wisconsin River in southwestern Wisconsin (Freeman 1966). The cemetery contains some 26 burial features and approximately 130 individuals, including 48 males and 19 females identifiable among the 85 adults. Several of the burial features contain mass interments. Burials occur as cremations, bundles, or primary inhumations. A few graves were sprinkled with red ochre; a number contained rock slabs in the fill. Grave goods were rare; only four projectile points, two antler points, a perforated bear canine,

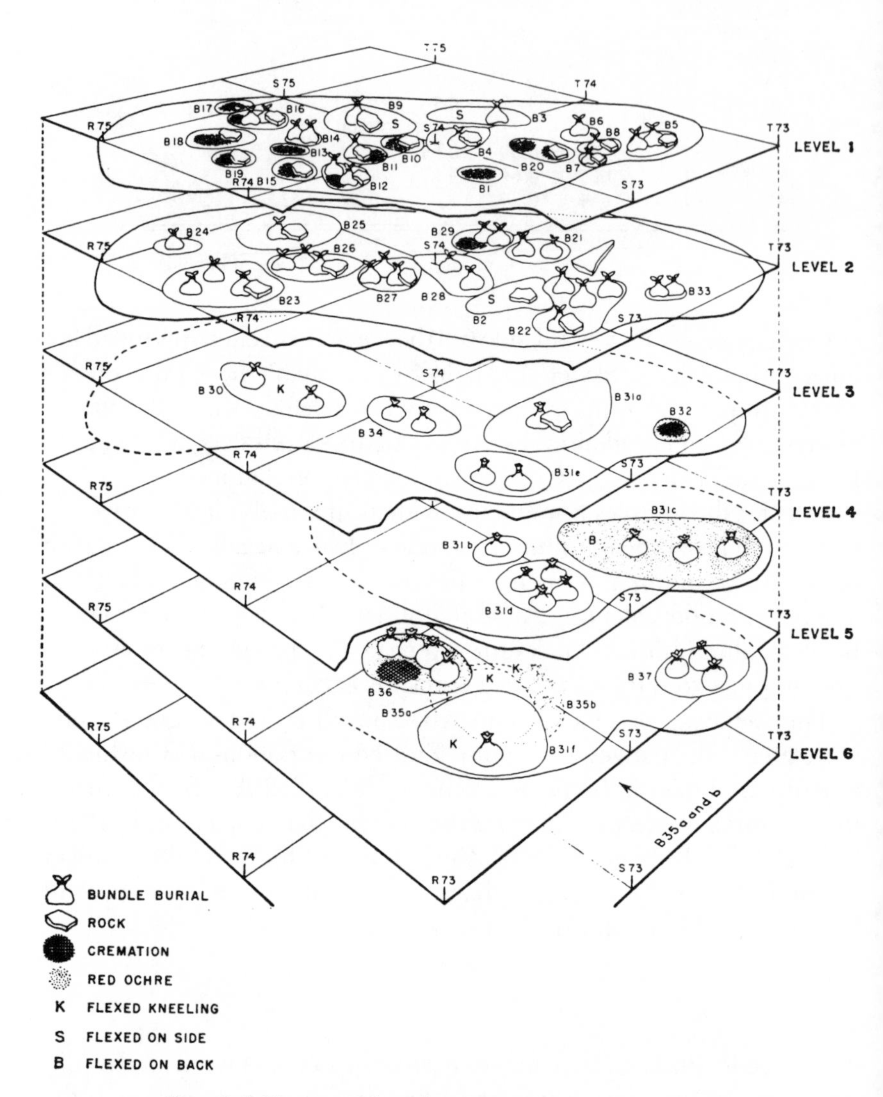

Fig. 6.4 Feature 25 at the Price III site drawn by John Dallman (Freeman 1966). Used with the permission of the Wisconsin Archaeological Society

and a copper fish hook were recovered. Several ^{14}C determinations suggest utilization of the cemetery from approximately 3710 b.p. to 2920 b.p.

The major burial unit at the Price III site was designated as Feature 25. Two-thirds of the individuals (n = 88) from the site came from this single, multi-level burial pit. Six layers were distinguished by the excavators, indicated by depth from surface and the relative vertical position of the burials (Fig. 6.4). Maximum depth of the feature was a little more than 1 m below the ground surface. A series of radiocarbon determinations indicate that the maximum use-life of Feature 25 was likely no more than 500 years (Freeman 1966).

The nature of this burial feature at Price III suggests intermittent use by the same population through time. Depositional conditions in the burial pit are generally constant with little change in soils or moisture. Some changes in the contents of the burials, position of the body, and form of burial can be observed from earlier to later graves. Red ochre is present only in the lower levels; rock mantles occur only on graves in the upper portion; cremations are more common in the upper levels.

Chronological Changes. Average values for a number of elements in bone from the layers of Feature 25 are presented in Table 6.9. Layer 1 is radiocarbon dated to 3280 b.p., layer 2 is dated to 3540 b.p., and layer 3 is 3710 b.p. Fig. 6.5 summarizes both chronology and elemental levels for burials from this feature. The age of the samples decreases from left to right on the graph. Sample sizes are small for several of the levels and the mean strontium ppm for level 6 is not in line. Nevertheless, although the absolute change is minor, the trend of the data shows a clear increase in the average amount of bone strontium per level from

Table 6.9 *Mean elemental concentrations by level in Feature 25 at the Price III site*

	n	Ca (%)	Sr (ppm)	Zn (ppm)	Mg (ppm)	Mn (ppm)	Fe (ppm)	Al (ppm)	Cu (ppm)
Level 1	14	38.06	154	133	2109	386	1236	1715	13.5
Level 2	10	37.76	153	143	2011	584	1103	1466	12.5
Level 3	4	35.90	138	256	2043	650	995	1168	14.9
Level 4	2	35.42	144	450	1832	1011	741	1200	15.1
Level 5	4	35.47	132	173	1888	751	1229	1478	19.6
Level 6	2	36.09	162	365	2077	584	659	917	15.8

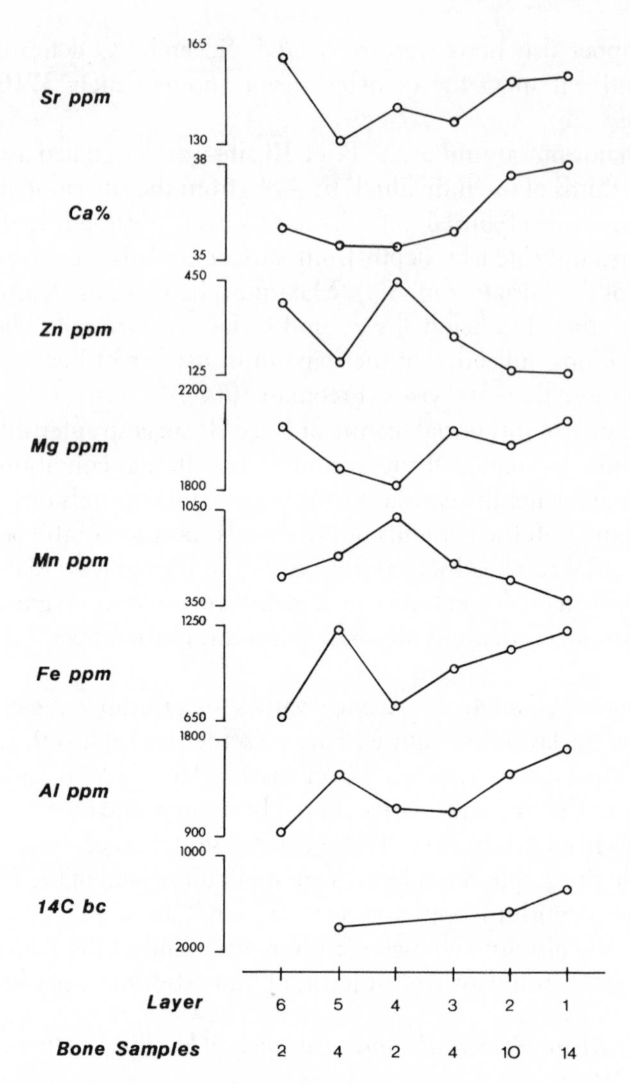

Fig. 6.5 Radiocarbon dates and mean elemental concentrations by layer in Feature 25 (from data in Table 6.9). Radiocarbon dates are indicated in years b.c.

older to younger. Calcium values also show an increase and the curves for magnesium, iron, and aluminum are similar.

Diet and/or diagenesis would appear to be the major factors responsible for the changes observed in bone strontium. This period of prehistory in the midwestern U.S. is characterized as one of transition, with hunter-gatherer societies gradually adopting sedentary village life and beginning to domesticate some plants (Phillips and Brown 1983, Stoltman 1978). Plant foods and/or shellfish may be becoming more important in human subsistence in this period (Price 1985). On the other hand, diagenesis may also be responsible for the gradual increase in bone strontium seen in Feature 25. Older samples may be susceptible to greater depletion via diagenetic activities.

Examination of changes in other elements in the burials from Feature 25 is informative. Calcium values increase almost monotonically from older to younger layers in Feature 25 (Table 6.9). This change is particularly marked between layers 3 and 2 in Feature 25. The average calcium level for all burials from the Price III site is 37.2%, very close to the modern average of 37.3%. Calcium values in the lower levels of Feature 25 fall below this value, suggesting that diagenesis is removing this element from bone. In the upper layers (1 and 2), however, calcium values are greater than this average and some enrichment may have occurred. The loss of calcium, a major constituent of bone mineral, means that other elements will be relatively more abundant while enrichment should reduce the proportion of other elements in the analysis. Thus the results from Feature 25 – where strontium values increase from older to younger, in spite of a concomitant increase in calcium – imply that the actual increase in strontium is even more pronounced than was observed.

Other elements are of interest as well (Table 6.9). Although smooth trends are not present (Figure 6.5), in part because of the small sample sizes, differences between the upper and lower layers of this feature can be seen. Comparison of the average values for layers 1–3 with layers 4–6 indicates that aluminum and iron, elements introduced via contamination from the soil (Lambert *et al.* 1984a), show a distinct increase. Magnesium shows only minor change, while zinc, manganese, and copper show decreases. Zinc concentrations are likely related to meat intake (Beck 1985, Klepinger 1984). This trend is the opposite of the observed changes in strontium. Manganese and copper have been shown to be highly mobile in post-mortem contexts (Lambert *et al.* 1984a). Correlation coefficients between the elemental concentrations in bone samples from the six levels in Feature 25 emphasize these relationships (Table 6.10). Significant negative correlations are observed between calcium and manganese, and between both iron and aluminum and zinc. The only significant positive correlation occurred

Table 6.10 *Correlation[a] between average elemental concentrations by level in bone samples from Price III (n=6)*

	Ca	Sr	Zn	Mg	Mn	Fe	Al
Ca							
Sr	0.56						
Zn	−0.67	0.11					
Mg	0.66	0.62	−0.42				
Mn	**−0.82**	−0.51	0.72	**−0.92**			
Fe	0.48	−0.40	**−0.92**	0.13	−0.46		
Al	0.62	−0.19	**−0.79**	0.06	−0.40	**0.91**	
Cu	−0.74	−0.60	0.12	−0.49	0.42	0.05	−0.16

[a] Values greater than 0.755 are significant at 0.05 and are shown in bold type

between iron and aluminum. Strontium is not significantly correlated with any other element.

Ribs versus Femurs. Some additional information on the effects of diagenesis is available from a consideration of the differences between trabecular and cortical bone at the Price III site. Comparison of the strontium and calcium content of ribs and femurs from all burials is presented in Table 6.11. The mean strontium and calcium concentrations in the two types of bones are very similar. There are, however, differences in the variances of the distributions of these two sets of samples. The standard deviation for Sr levels in the femurs is more than

Table 6.11 *Strontium and calcium levels in ribs and femora at the Price III site*

	Rib	Femur
Strontium (ppm)		
n	14	31
mean	154.9	156.7
s.d.	15.8	39.5
c.v.	10.2%	25.2%
Calcium (%)		
n	14	31
mean	36.98	37.24
s.d.	1.21	2.14
c.v.	3.3%	5.7%

Table 6.12 *Mean bone strontium content in Feature 25 by bone type and feature level*

	Rib	Femur
Upper Level (1–2)	147 ± 11 (n=4)	156 ± 29 (n=14)
Lower Level (3–6)	149 ± 14 (n=16)	136 ± 39 (n=5)

twice that for the ribs. The coefficient of variation is 25.2% for femurs and only 10.2% for ribs. The reason for this difference is unclear. Parker and Toots (1970) suggest that diagenesis may be responsible for higher levels of variability.

Comparison of ribs only from the upper and lower levels of Feature 25 (Table 6.12) indicates no change in strontium level. Although not statistically significant, an increase of strontium is indicated in the femurs from the older to younger layers. The change in femurs is in fact completely responsible for the observed trend in strontium in Feature 25. Such evidence is intriguing and may indicate that diagenetic effects are in fact more pronounced in cortical bone. Future investigation of this question is essential.

Conclusions. Bone strontium levels in Feature 25 at the Price III site change through time. The minor increase in bone strontium contrasts with a general decrease in zinc values, as would be expected if plant and/or shellfish intake were increasing (Beck 1985). Examination of other elements suggests that strontium is fairly stable and reliable in this analysis. The absence of correlation between strontium and elements associated with soil contamination such as iron and aluminum support this interpretation.

MEASURES OF DIAGENESIS

The evidence from Nelson Bay Cave indicates that bone strontium in the grysbok is changing through time in the deposits. This study focuses on the same species in the same geographic area so that changes in bone strontium due to environment or diet are very unlikely. At Skateholm, the differences between the two cemeteries indicate pronounced changes have occurred in bone strontium, likely related to changes in calcium levels. These two cemeteries are almost adjacent and date within a few hundred years of one another. Again, changes in bone strontium due to environment are unlikely. Changes due to diet are possible as seen in the faunal remains from the two sites. However, the expected change should result in increased bone strontium at Skateholm I, not the lower levels that are observed. The Price III cemetery data indicate that bone strontium values increased slightly over a period of no more than 500 years. These samples come from the same burial feature so that environmental differences are very unlikely. Diet or diagenesis must be responsible for the observed changes. Consideration of strontium and other elements through time suggests that strontium values are likely reasonably stable in this case and that the changes, although minor, may indeed be due to diet.

The clear lesson from these studies is that diagenesis must be considered as a potential source of variability in any investigation of bone strontium and paleonutrition. Each burial context must be examined individually to ascertain the extent of diagenetic activity and the degree to which bone has been chemically altered.

The condition of bone in the ground is a consequence of soil acidity, moisture, and temperature (Ortner *et al.* 1972). The decomposition of meat on bone and of the collagen in bone is facilitated by the activity of *Clostridium histolyticum*, governed by conditions of temperature and moisture (Rottländer 1976:86). Protein, which comprises approximately 20% of fresh bone, is hydrolized to peptides which decompose into their constituent amino acids (Ortner *et al.* 1972:514). The rate of removal of these components is in part a function of soil and water activity.

Gordon and Buikstra (1981) document a highly positive correlation between soil pH and bone preservation. White and Hannus (1983) examined the relationship between bone weathering and soil conditions in detail. They concluded that the diagenesis of hydroxyapatite in bone is begun by acids, formed by the microbial decomposition of collagen, as protons replace calcium in the hydroxyapatite. As collagen in the bone is depleted, continued diagenetic change in calcium levels is dependent upon soil conditions. If soils are acidic and protons are available, weathering of the hydroxyapatite may continue. Under burial conditions, hydroxyapatite becomes soluble as pH decreases to 6.5 and is very soluble below a pH of 6.0 (Lindsay 1979). If calcium is present in more basic soils, weathering may cease as calcium levels in the bone are stabilized, again dependent in part on conditions of temperature and moisture (Rottländer 1976). White and Hannus (1983) emphasize the importance of specific depositional contexts in any consideration of diagenesis. Clearly, determination of the soil pH in the depositional environment will provide useful information on the context of diagenesis.

The porous structure of bone tissue is also susceptible to infiltration by foreign materials. Through the use of a microprobe and the analysis of microscopic thin sections, Hassan and Ortner (1977) have demonstrated the presence of a number of physical and chemical contaminants in fossil bone. Contaminants were due either to precipitation from ground water or the physical movement of materials into the bone. Calcium, for example, can be introduced through the precipitation of calcium carbonate in ground water. Inclusions such as quartz were introduced as solid grains. Hyphae (an algal growth), rootlets, and fragments of charcoal were also observed within the bone structure as physical contaminants.

A number of methods can provide some indication of the nature and degree of diagenetic changes in bone composition. As noted in the present study, for example, both the ash content of prehistoric bone and the percentage of calcium in the bone ash provide some measure of diagenetic changes. Specifically, the deviation of calcium values in bone from *ca.* 37% can indicate either enrichment or depletion of that element. Sillen (this volume) discusses the calcium carbonate enrichment of the mineral component of bone.

Lambert *et al.* (1979, 1984a) and others (Gilbert 1975, Katzenberg 1984, Nelson and Sauer 1984), have used the comparison of soil and bone composition in the burial context. The absence of difference in strontium levels between ribs and femurs, and between soil and bone, suggested that strontium was generally stable in the depositional environment. However, their evidence indicated that other elements in bone were significantly enriched or depleted by diagenesis.

Lambert *et al.* (1982, 1985a) have also used the comparison of ribs and femurs from the same site and electron microprobe examination of bone cross-sections in the investigation of diagenesis. Strontium, zinc, lead, and sodium were observed to show homogeneous distributions across the sections, suggesting an absence of diagenesis. Badone and Farquhar (1982) used a microprobe to consider elemental concentrations in bone cross-sections from Old Crow Flats, Yukon, Canada. They suggest that calcium, strontium, and sodium are relatively stable in bone. Henderson *et al.* (1983) used the electron microprobe for bone samples from Olduvai Gorge. Strontium was the least affected by diagenesis in their study. These investigations and others are summarized by Buikstra *et al.* in this volume.

Both Sillen (1981b) and Katzenberg (1984) suggest that the calcium: phosphorus ratio in archaeological bone should be a good index of calcium carbonate contamination. This ratio is approximately 2:1 in modern bone ash. Because phosphorus is a major component of bone ash, it is also important to measure the concentration of this element in samples. Katzenberg (1984:140–5) recorded phosphorus, calcium, and strontium levels (among other elements) in twenty-five human bone samples from five archaeological sites in southern Ontario. One of the samples (SME56) has extreme values for each of these three elements. However, correlation coefficients among Ca, P, and Sr for the remaining samples show a highly significant ($r \geq 0.381$ at $p = 0.05$) positive correlation between calcium and phosphorus ($r = 0.55$), no correlation between strontium and calcium ($r = 0.04$), and a slightly negative, nonsignificant relationship between strontium and phosphorus (−0.23). Such information suggests that phosphorus does indeed play an important role in diagenesis, particularly as a major component of bone ash.

Rottländer (1976:84) has demonstrated that phosphate levels in bone apatite change as a function of temperature. Samples of bone from deeply stratified deposits of almost identical sediments showed changes in the phosphate/calcium ratio that were not correlated with age or the chemical composition of the sediments. Enrichment or depletion of either calcium or phosphorus would result in changes in the concentrations of the other elements present.

Katzenberg (1984) also examined yttrium and zirconium as indicators of contamination. Yttrium is taken up diagenetically as a function of availability in soil and the length of interment (Parker and Toots 1970) and is found in very low concentrations, less than 2 ppm, in fresh human bone. Thus, higher levels of yttrium in bone should be indicative of diagenesis and calcium loss. Zirconium is completely insoluble in water and should not occur in human bone except as a physical contaminant. However, Katzenberg (1984) found zirconium present in prehistoric bone samples from southern Ontario and concluded that some soil particles were present in the bone samples. Strontium was not significantly correlated with zirconium, however, indicating that Sr levels in the bone samples were largely independent of soil contamination. Katzenberg (1984:86–7) suggests a correction factor for bone strontium if physical contamination by soil particles is detected by the presence of zirconium.

Schoeninger (1982) used X-ray diffraction patterns to examine the possibility of diagenesis in samples of human bone from the Upper Pleistocene in the Near East. The technique was used specifically to detect the enrichment of bone mineral through the precipitation of geological apatite or carbonate in ground water. Samples used in this study had been diagenetically altered; both the absolute amount of strontium in bone mineral and the strontium/calcium ratio were changed. Enrichment by geological apatite resulted in an increase in calcium levels and a decrease in the relative amount of strontium in the bone mineral (Schoeninger 1982:46).

It is also possible to consider faunal remains from a site as a baseline of variation for strontium in human bone (Katzenberg 1984, Price *et al.* 1985a). Presumably faunal remains will have undergone diagenetic processes similar to the human bone. Thus, differences between bone strontium levels in a herbivore species, for example, and humans should not be affected by diagenesis or environmental sources of strontium. This index should change only as a result of differences in human diet. In addition, differences between the prehistoric species and the modern animal in the same area may provide some indication of diagenetic changes in bone chemistry.

Sillen (1986, this volume) has recently discussed the possibility of removing certain diagenetic effects through the use of solubility profiles. Initial spectrometric examination of Plio-Pleistocene fauna from the Omo Shugura formation in East Africa indicated no difference between herbivores and carnivores, suggesting that diagenesis had resulted in the equilibration of strontium concentrations in these bones. However, Sillen was able to discover expected differences in strontium levels following a series of washes in acetate buffers. He suggests that diagenetically added minerals exhibit a higher solubility and biogenic elements and thus are removed more readily in acetate washes. Although this technique requires further evaluation, it promises to provide a means for examining earlier hominid materials.

CONCLUSIONS

The possibility of diagenetic change must be addressed in any study of bone chemistry involving the reconstruction of past diet (Nelson and Sauer 1984). There is no longer any question that diagenesis can modify the pre-mortem levels of bone strontium, either through direct changes in strontium levels or through the enrichment or depletion of other elements such as calcium and phosphorus. A variety of measures of the effects of diagenesis are currently available: the comparison of ribs and femurs, of human and animal remains, of elemental concentrations in soil and bone, the use of X-ray diffraction patterns, the analysis of soil pH and moisture, electron microprobe investigations of bone cross-sections, multi-element correlation studies, the determination of index elements such as zirconium and yttrium, the use of the calcium : phosphorus ratio, the measurement of the ash content of whole bone and the calcium content of bone ash, and perhaps the investigation of strontium isotopes. The use of several of these measures and indices should be regarded as mandatory in future studies of bone chemistry and past diet. Certainly, the publication of the concentrations of calcium, phosphorus, iron, aluminum, and ash content is feasible for investigations concerned with strontium and other elements of potential dietary significance. The adoption of such conventions will both improve our understanding of the effects of diagenesis on bone composition and provide more reliable estimates of past diet.

ACKNOWLEDGMENTS

The assistance of Joan Freeman and Melissa Connor in the collection, preparation, and analysis of the samples from Price III is gratefully acknowledged. Richard Klein suggested and collected the samples from Nelson Bay Cave and provided generous assistance in interpreting and understanding their stratigraphic position. Lars Larsson of the University of Lund excavated the Skateholm materials and provided the samples used in this study. Joel Boaz was of major assistance in the preparation of these samples for analysis. John Parsen of the Soil and Plant Laboratory of University of Wisconsin was most helpful as usual. Joe Lambert, Andrew Sillen, and Margaret Schoeninger offered several useful comments and suggestions on an earlier draft of this paper. Funding from the National Science Foundation (BNS-8206415) and the Wenner–Gren Foundation for Anthropological Research made this study possible.

7

Multiple elements: multiple expectations

JANE E. BUIKSTRA

Department of Anthropology
University of Chicago

SUSAN FRANKENBERG

Department of Anthropology
Northwestern University

JOSEPH B. LAMBERT
LIANG XUE

Department of Chemistry
Northwestern University

Since Brown's (1973) pioneering application of trace element analysis to the estimation of dietary patterns for extinct human groups, this technique has excited considerable interest and occasional ire among anthropologists and chemists alike. Brown, influenced by previous paleontological studies such as those of Toots and Voorhies (1965) and Parker and Toots (1970), focused upon the investigation of a single element, strontium, basing her choice on issues of diet and diagenesis. Following her work, a number of scholars have similarly chosen to emphasize stable strontium or strontium/calcium ratios in dietary interpretations, e.g. Katzenberg (1984), Price and Kavanagh (1982), Price *et al.* (1985b), Schoeninger (1979a,b, 1981, 1982), Sillen (1981a), and Sillen and Smith (1984).

Assumptions that must be made in studies of this type include: that the element varies predictably across the ancient diet; that food preparation and storage do not significantly distort the dietary pattern; that the tissues observed reflect dietary levels in life; and that neither post-mortem mortuary practices nor diagenesis have inverted or obscured trace element composition of the tissue at the time of death. Additionally, sampling problems emerge at the population/cemetery level – location of tissue sample, age, and sex, as well as possible status distinctions. Whether or not we can control for variation in geochemical environments and thus meaningfully compare trace element levels across groups also remains a matter of debate (Katzenberg 1984, Lambert *et al.* 1985a, Nelson *et al.* 1983a, Pate and Brown 1985, Price 1985, Price *et al.* 1985a, Schoeninger 1979a,b, 1981, 1982, Sillen and Kavanagh 1982).

While many issues concerning the use of stable strontium to characterize ancient human diets remain unresolved, several workers have looked beyond strontium, attempting to use a broader array of trace (and major) elements to refine estimates of dietary difference, e.g. Bahou (1975), Bisel (1980), Blakely and Beck (1981), Brown and Blakely (1985), Gilbert (1975), and Lambert *et al.* (1979, 1985a). These studies have produced mixed results, primarily due to non-dietary influences upon trace element distributions and imprecise estimations of expected trace element patterns for ancient menus. Measurement and analytical errors are also a matter of concern (Elias *et al.* 1982, Schoeninger 1979a).

Given that only a few trace elements have received as much research attention as strontium – much studied during the 1950s because of concern for atomic fallout – multiple element study is frequently more speculative than research based solely on strontium. The few other relatively well-known metals are those linked to toxicity or deficiency diseases, such as zinc, lead, and iron. Since biomedical research concerning trace elements is currently an active and expanding field, we may anticipate further information concerning trace element distributions among the living as models for the past.

However incomplete our contemporary picture for trace element variation in foods, within and between individuals, and in the environment, we must explicitly seek such information if we are to successfully apply multi-element approaches to the past. The results of exploratory multi-element efforts, technologically relatively simple now with the availability of sophisticated analytical systems, should be constantly tested against expectations based on analyses of foodstuffs, variations in human metabolism (across individuals, age, and sex), and diagenetic changes.

This study is an attempt to interpret the pattern of multiple-element variation in a temporal sequence of paleopopulations from Illinois.

Individuals were chosen based on archaeological context, preservation, and the availability of carbon isotope assays. $\delta^{13}C$ values provide a measure of dietary carbon deriving from C_3 and C_4 plants, maize being the primary C_4 plant in this region (van der Merwe and Vogel 1978). Elements strongly associated with maize in the human diet are expected to co-vary with the ratio. Multivariate statistical techniques are used to examine the observed pattern for variation attributable to diagenesis, environment, diet, or individual life history.

First, we will review studies of paleopopulations that have used multiple elements, focusing upon inferences made about cause in trace element variation. This research is discussed in detail here because it has not been summarized or critically reviewed elsewhere. Secondly, we will develop a set of expectations for fourteen major and trace elements, based on the contemporary biomedical, geochemical, and archaeological literature. In this context, we initially focus upon the impact of diagenesis, as well as illustrate the need for further, in-depth study of non-Western native foods and food-processing techniques. We will then test these expectations against patterns observed in our data set. $\delta^{13}C$ values are included in this phase of analysis as a measure of the maize component of the diet. Given the locale in which our study sample originated, we emphasize the use of terrestrial resources. The potentially confounding effects of marine resources are reviewed by Schoeninger (1979a) for strontium (see also Rosenthal 1963, Schroeder *et al.* 1972).

PREVIOUS MULTI-ELEMENT STUDIES

The following is an overview of previous archaeological studies that investigate more than one trace element. Emphasis will be placed upon the degree to which each investigator attempts to control for diagenesis, the size of the sample, the elements chosen for study, and the research results. In general, all workers assume that variation in elemental levels for human bone reflects dietary intake, although this assumption is rather weak for elements other than zinc and strontium. Estimates of dietary levels are frequently based on assays of Western foods, rather than those likely to have comprised the ancient menu. In other cases, the results are undoubtedly affected by unsuspected diagenetic change or by the small size of the sample. Even so, these pioneering efforts well illustrate the range of important research problems that can be addressed through trace element analysis. Given the limitations inherent in ground-breaking work of this type, interpretations should be accepted only after critical review.

Gilbert (1975, 1977), Bahou (1975)

Gilbert chose to explore the pattern of five trace elements (Zn, Sr, Mn, Mg, and Cu) in the tibiae of three temporally sequential skeletal series from the Dickson Mounds site. These groups were hypothesized to vary in diet, becoming increasingly dependent upon maize agriculture through time: Late Woodland (A.D. 1050; 14 males, 11 females), Transitional (A.D. 1150–1250; 6 males, 9 females), and Middle Mississippian (A.D. 1250–1300; 16 males, 19 females). Associations were sought between trace element frequencies, as determined by atomic absorption spectroscopy, and time, health status, and stature.

Gilbert sought to identify the impact of diagenesis by three methods, First, he examined the trace element frequencies for nine soil samples obtained from within the medullary cavity of certain long bones. This analysis suggested that there were insufficient amounts of Zn, Sr, Cu, or Mg in the soil for enrichment. The highly variable range of Mn led him to conclude that Mn was problematic. Although Gilbert may not have had access to other samples, as we did not in our 1979 study (Lambert *et al.* 1979), it should be noted that soil in direct contact with bone, such as that found within the medullary cavity, would be that most likely to be in equilibrium with adjacent osseous tissue, making it a less than ideal sample for estimating elemental content of the matrix in which the bone was deposited.

His second method for identifying diagenesis was to determine the pH of the soil at the Dickson Mounds site. Gilbert indicates that the soil is slightly acid, with a pH ranging from 4 to 6, usually being slightly above 5. In that the bones appeared to be intact, this estimate of pH (taken by the archaeologist, Alan Harn, at the site) seems rather low. Gordon and Buikstra (1981) observed marked deterioration of adult bones between pH 6 and 7 in a similar context; White and Hannus (1983) cite Lindsay's (1979) observation that hydroxyapatite is relatively insoluble at *ca.* pH 7.5, with solubility increasing rapidly below a pH of 6. Soil acidity can, of course, change through time, thus making contemporary observations imperfect estimates of past conditions. Other factors, such as soil moisture, temperature, and micro-organisms, as well as bone size, are also important in determining bone condition (Hare 1980, Lambert *et al.* 1985b, Parker and Toots 1980, Rottländer 1976, von Endt and Ortner 1984, White and Hannus 1983).

Soil acidity is an important issue, strongly affecting the form that permeation and dissolution may take. *In vitro* studies by Lambert *et al.* (1985b) indicate that in slightly acidic (pH 5–7) contexts, Zn, Pb, and Sr uptake is significant, these elements apparently undergoing marked heteroionic exchange with Ca in the hydroxyapatite matrix. Mg and Mn proportions increase to a lesser extent, with Ca, Na, and K showing little net exchange. At a higher pH in buffered solutions, Zn, Pb, Sr, Mg, Ca, and Na behaved in a manner similar to that at the lower pH. By contrast, K and Mn were taken up more readily. *In vitro* studies by Spadaro (1969) also indicate that, especially at higher pH values, collagen shows more rapid incorporation of ions than apatite.

In his third method for identifying diagenesis, Gilbert used visual examination for hydroxyapatite crystals on six samples and an electron probe on twenty randomly chosen sections. Due to detection limits for the electron microprobe, Gilbert was limited to observations for K, Na, and Mg. All showed a uniform pattern across the section. Gilbert is not precise about the technique used to identify intact hydroxyapatite crystals, though it is certain that one must exercise caution in visual inspection. The presence of intact osteon structure clearly should not be used as an indication that the bone is unaffected by diagenesis. Hassan and Ortner (1977) and Cook *et al.* (1962) report significant replacement of organic matrix by inorganic substances in fossils when optical properties remain relatively unchanged. At a finer level of resolution, Schoeninger (1981, 1982) has provided convincing evidence that X-ray diffraction can be used to distinguish geological from biological apatite.

In general, only the pattern for zinc, expected to decrease through time, conformed to Gilbert's predictions. He concludes that although Cu, Mg, and Sr may be useful in other contexts, where trace element values for prehistoric foodstuffs can be estimated with more confidence and where nuts are not a confounding factor, these elements were not illuminating in this study. He argues that Mn is highly variable due to diagenesis and is therefore not useful. Copper and zinc are shown to be correlated in all except the Transitional sample.

Interestingly, another study using the same Dickson Mounds trace element data produced somewhat more optimistic results (Bahou 1975). In this work Bahou examined change through time, inter-element associations expected due to metabolic antagonisms, and associations with pathology, for the same five elements reported by Gilbert. He reports that Mn, Zn, and Mg all decrease through time, with no observable trends for Sr and Cu. None of the expected correlations between elements is isolated, although Zn is strongly (positively) correlated with Mg and Mn across the pooled sample.

The difference between Bahou's and Gilbert's results apparently derives from the fact that Gilbert chose to use a relatively conservative non-parametric test of significance for F values produced by the ANOVA analysis. Bahou, on the other hand, chose the mean and Student's t. Inspection suggests that the trace element values are not distributed normally and that parametric tests are therefore not appropriate.

Lambert et al. *(1979, 1982, 1983, 1984a,b,c, 1985a,b), Szpunar (1977), Szpunar* et al. *(1978), Vlasak (1983)*

Lambert and co-workers have produced a series of studies concerning trace elements in human remains from west-central Illinois. Initially, this research began with a focus upon dietary, biological, and methodological determinations (Lambert *et al.* 1979, Szpunar 1977, Szpunar *et al.* 1978) with the emphasis shifting to diagenesis (Lambert *et al.* 1982, 1983, 1984a,b,c, 1985a,b, Vlasak 1983) as this emerged as a key issue affecting dietary inferences.

In the first series of studies, a set of twelve elements – Sr, Zn, Mg, Ca, Na, Cu, Fe, Al, Mn, K, Cd, and Pb – was analysed for 136 ribs from the Middle Woodland (150 B.C.–A.D. 400) Gibson and Late Woodland (A.D. 1000–1200) Ledders sites. We also analysed soil samples either recovered from elsewhere in the site (Gibson) or associated with the analysed bones (Ledders). Those elements found in lower amounts in the soil than in the bone were tentatively judged unlikely contaminants: Sr, Zn, Ca, Na, and possibly Mg. The relatively high levels of Fe, Al, and K in the soil and comparable amounts of Cu and Mn make these elements more likely to have infiltrated bone. Manganese is especially problematic due to the large amount found in bone, exceeding expectations based on contemporary samples. Therefore, we concluded that Sr, Zn, Ca, Na, and probably Cu and Mg values were not affected by diagenesis, with Fe, Al, Mn, and K suspect. Soil comparisons between the two sites indicated no significant differences for Sr, Zn, Ca, Fe, Al, and Mn, in contrast to the distinctive results for Na, K, and Cu, with the higher values being from Gibson site. Though this does not control for environmental differences, we concluded that comparisons between sites, even for contaminants, may be valid.

No significant differences by sex were noted for any element at Gibson. As we noted, this may have resulted from equivalent diets or from contamination. Sr, Zn, and Ca differed by sex at Ledders. The higher values for Sr and lower for Zn among the females suggested to us that Late Woodland males may have had disproportionate access to animal protein, or perhaps nuts or legumes.

For Middle Woodland Gibson, differences in elemental frequencies were sought between individuals found in three distinctive types of burial contexts: central log tombs, peripheral graves oriented to the central feature, and other locations. Significant differences emerged only when the pooled tomb and peripheral remains were compared to the category "other." The elements Sr, Zn, Mg, and Na, but not the contaminants, were all lower for those in the "other" category, suggesting that diet differed across these groups. Differential diagenetic effects remain a possibility, given that the "other" category includes bundle reburials. This seems remote, given the similarity in figures for elements most likely to be contaminants. Even so, it should be noted that Blakely and Beck (1982) – see also Beck (1985) – report low concentrations of Zn in remains that had been exposed to the open air prior to interment as bundle burials at Etowah.

With the exception of Al, all elements tend to decrease from infancy through childhood, a trend especially pronounced in Cu. As expected, Ca decreased through adulthood. Elements thought to be contaminants (Fe, Al, Mn, K) increase in frequency through the adult age grades, though this pattern is most obvious in the older site (Gibson). Element values also vary between the mounds at the Gibson site.

Comparisons of Gibson with Ledders indicate significantly higher levels of Sr, Mn, and Mg at the Gibson site. Mn is regarded a contaminant, though the Sr and Mg values may indicate diet-related differences between the two groups.

Extending our concern for diagenetic elements, we compared results for femurs with those of ribs (Lambert *et al.* 1982, 1983). Assuming that no significant differences should occur in element frequencies due to inter-individual variation, we compared averages obtained from forty-seven femurs from Gibson and Ledders sites to those for ribs as reported previously. The fact that Sr, Zn, and Mg show identical values reinforced the notion that these elements were not affected by diagenesis. The values for three elements (Ca, Na, and Pb) were lower in the rib, suggesting the effects of leaching, and four are higher (Fe, Al, Mn, and K), indicating enrichment. Our observations concerning Ca led us to question the use of Sr/Ca ratios in reference to ancient bone. Although the absolute differences, compared by sex, show no intra-site differences, male strontium and female zinc values do decrease significantly through time, from Gibson to Ledders. Magnesium decreases in both sexes.

Microprobe analysis of eight femur sections from Ledders and Gibson detected no significant difference in the distributions of Zn, Sr, and Pb, which contrasts with the build-up of Al, K, and Mn along the outer and, occasionally, the inner surfaces. Manganese penetration of space in the cortex was also detected. Magnesium showed circumferential build-up on the outer portions of certain samples. Calcium and sodium were homogeneous, with minor concentrations of sodium on some surfaces. A significant amount of depletion, however, would have to occur before this process was observable for these major elements.

Controlled study of associated soils (Lambert *et al.* 1984a) served as another test of our models for depletion and enrichment. Samples were taken at 5 cm intervals, over 10 cm measured vertically and horizontally, from the matrix surrounding four burials excavated at the Middle Woodland Elizabeth site. Comparison of soil and bone showed no diagenetic effects for Sr, Zn, Mn, Pb, and Na. Magnesium and Ca apparently are released into the soil from bone, Fe, Al, and K enter the bone from the soil.

We also extended our analysis to include barium and intensified our observation of copper (Lambert *et al.* 1984b). Using the three techniques previously identified, rib–femur comparison, electron microprobe, and sediment analysis, copper was found to be affected by diagenesis. Barium, expected to follow the pattern for strontium, instead appeared to be less sensitive, not discriminating, for instance, between the sexes, at Gibson when contrasted with Ledders site. Barium did concentrate along the surfaces of the femur sections. It was concluded, therefore, that neither copper nor barium would be useful as an indicator of ancient diet as they tended to be subject to leaching.

It was noted, however, that the surface contaminants, manganese excepted, extended no further than 400 μm into the bone, suggesting that it may be rather simple to counter the effect of diagenesis on barium, copper, iron, aluminum, and perhaps potassium, by removing the outer edge of the cortex. Pate and Brown (1985) explain this circumferential enrichment as the result of diagenetic crystallization of amorphous subperiosteal bone.

Bisel (1980)

Bisel's investigation of Ca, P, Zn, Mg, and Sr is embedded in a larger study of health and disease among ancient populations from the eastern Mediterranean region. Sample sizes for most periods are quite small, thus suggesting that sampling bias may severely limit the degree to which Bisel's interpretations may be generalized. Diagenesis is not considered a possible confounding variable, although soil samples are investigated as a means of evaluating the impact of different geochemical environments on consumers at various trophic levels. In general, it appears in her study that there is more difference in trace element levels across geographic zones than through time.

Geidel (1981, 1982), Hatch and Geidel (1983, 1985)

Geidel specifies two arrays of trace elements, four elements in each, which he expects to be associated with plant-dominated (Sr, Mn, V, Ni) and meat-rich (Zn, Cu, Se, Mo) diets. Analysis of 181 femur samples from all ages and both sexes of remains from the Mississippian (A.D. 1300–1550) Dallas and Hixon sites in southeastern North America provided no evidence of Mo, Se, or Ni above the detection level. Although soil samples from the 1930s' excavations were not available, it was argued that the two sites lie in similar environmental contexts and that the sediments are generally neutral to basic. Predictions were that the mound burials would have higher frequencies of the meat-related elements, especially the males with rich grave-good assemblages. Human remains from the village area, as well as the less splendid burials from the mounds should have higher levels of Sr, Mn, and V.

The sub-adults from the village area show higher levels of the plant indicators, though no significant difference was discovered for Zn and Cu. Females show no parallel patterning, although the village males do show higher Zn and V levels than their counterparts from the mound. No differences were observed between the males with impressive grave assemblages, when compared to male mound burials without artifacts or with projectile points only. Village females without artifacts show higher vanadium levels than females with burial goods (pooled village and mound samples). Geidel argues that nut consumption may be confounding the results reported here. In addition, status-related access to food resources for juveniles may be most closely controlled and linked to family affiliation.

The 1981 thesis is summarized by Geidel (1982) and Hatch and Geidel (1983, 1985). In these articles emphasis is placed upon the juvenile differences and the fact that a similar but weaker trend is observable in males. The relatively high zinc value for village males is attributed to nut rather than meat consumption since the vanadium level is also high. Vanadium, as one of the few elements not confounded by consumption of nuts, is used to reliably differentiate between meat and plant (greens, grains, and nut) contributions to the diet. "The best evidence for meat consumption would be very low concentrations of vanadium, which is scarce in meats and somewhat lower in nuts than other plant resources" (Hatch and Geidel 1983:59).

This theme is elaborated in Hatch and Geidel (1985:472) where a series of four expected trace metal patterns associated with specific diets is projected:

(1) Vegetarian without nuts – high levels of manganese, strontium, and vanadium and low levels of copper and zinc.
(2) Vegetarian with nuts – high levels of all five of the elements listed in (1).
(3) Meat-rich without nuts – low levels of manganese, strontium, and vanadium and high levels of copper and zinc.
(4) Meat-rich with nuts – high levels of manganese, strontium, copper, and zinc, but lower levels of vanadium.

The interpretation of results for the Dallas culture from this paper is much the same as cited above for previous studies, except the dominant plant for the village diet is specified to be maize. Also briefly referenced here is work in progress on samples from Copan, Honduras (Hatch and Geidel 1985). The earlier, Pre-classic remains are said to contain significantly more manganese and less strontium than graves from the Classic period. The highest concentrations of Mn, Sr, and V are reported for the most elaborate Classic period grave. Although diagenetic effects for Mn are known, and V is incompletely investigated, this association of Sr with high status may mean that plant resources, such as maize, were considered to be of special worth in this prehistoric Central American culture.

The strongest aspect of these studies is the attempt to develop a formal set of alternative expectations in the use of multiple trace elements. However, this approach is weakened by the facts that the degree to which vanadium in bone reflects dietary levels in humans, and its propensity for diagenesis, are not known. It is argued that vanadium is likely to be high in a plant-dominated diet, although vanadium is apparently relatively abundant in animal fats (Schroeder *et al.* 1963). Manganese, an element that figures heavily in this model, is a likely contaminant, and copper is also problematic without careful control of diagenetic effects. In addition, the possible impact of mollusc consumption is not considered.

Blakely and Beck (1981), Brown and Blakely (1985)

Blakely and Beck (1981) investigated levels of Zn, Cu, Sr, and Mg in a comparison of post-adolescent individuals buried in the village and in Mound C of the Etowah site. The site is located on the floodplain of the Etowah River in the Piedmont region of northwestern Georgia. Mound burials are said to be individuals of higher status, based on the presence of elaborate grave goods characteristic of the Southeastern Ceremonial Complex. Burial goods from village graves are less spectacular. The difference between the two components may either reflect a status difference in contemporary groups or a temporal difference between the two. Variation in the depositional environment may also be a confounding factor. Blakely and Beck choose to accept the questionable assumption that the two components are contemporary, which Beck (1985) does not in more recent work. They test for trace element differences between the village and mound components.

This study is presented as a test of Larson's hypothesis, based on the abundance of exotic materials in Mound C, that status was ascribed at Etowah (Larson 1971). The authors suggest that a difference in diet between the two groups would support this model since, if status was inherited, members of the superordinate class should have enjoyed better nutrition than those of the subordinate category. The authors assume that the effects of diagenesis are minimal, given a pH range of 5.2–6.0. No investigation of soil samples is presented.

Given that adults are used in this study, this is a test for trace element differences that may reflect relatively recent diet – not that during the juvenile period. The assumption that "dietary differences are usually observed between high and low status individuals in both extinct and contemporary ascriptive societies" (Blakely and Beck 1981:428) is crucial to their work and certainly requires further elaboration, distinguishing between rare ceremonial diets, unlikely to be reflected in bone chemistry, and long-term privileged access to foodstuffs (Hatch 1976). The fact that dietary differences exist in some ascriptive contexts does not allow us to assume the opposite in the absence of evidence for dietary differences. Of note is the fact that the most elaborate (male) burial from Mound C showed elevated Zn and Cu levels, with extremely low Mg and Sr, suggesting to the authors that some measure of dietary difference was discernible within the site.

A similar assumption concerning the association of differential dietary practices and social complexity underlies the Brown and Blakely (1985) study of King site, an Early Historic period site (A.D. 1550–1725) located on the Coosa River in northwestern Georgia. Here the two components are clearly contemporary, with grave furniture indicating that high status remains were interred in the public sector – plaza and ceremonial structures – with lower status individuals relegated to the domestic area. Contemporaneity of burial, similarity of soil matrix, and pH above 5.0 suggest to the authors that diagenesis should not have affected their samples.

From a broader array of thirteen elements, results for four – Ca, Mg, Sr, and Zn – are reported here. No significant differences are isolated between the values for the five high status and thirty-eight low status individuals. (Note that the figures reported in Brown and Blakely's Table 1 match the bar graph in their Fig. 2 only for Sr, not for Zn, Ca, or Mg.) These results suggest that the two status groups were enjoying similar diets, rather than a richer and more varied menu for high status folk as expected. A combination of achieved and ascribed status is inferred by the authors.

Beck (1985)

In this study, Beck investigates scatterplots of zinc and strontium values for human remains from three sites archaeologically documented to have had contrasting subsistence regimes: the Middle Woodland Gibson site (hunter-gatherers), the Late Woodland Ledders site (maize horticulturalists), and Etowah (maize agriculturalists). Both Gibson and Ledders sites are in west-central Illinois. Etowah, as noted above, is in northwestern Georgia. In this study, it is assumed that the village burials from Etowah are more recent than those from Mound C.

The scatterplots suggest a highly variable diet for the Gibson sample; variation along the Sr axis is more restricted among the Ledders early horticulturalists. Beck suggests that the consumption of maize affected this result. Males clearly show higher levels of dietary Zn than females, who show elevated values for Sr. This is consistent with earlier analyses by Lambert and co-workers (Lambert *et al.* 1979, 1982) and suggests a predictable gender-based difference in diet. The pattern for Etowah presents much more variation in, and generally higher, Sr values. Some of this can be explained by differences in the geochemical environments for the two sites, although dietary factors, including perhaps the utilization of shellfish (Schoeninger and Peebles 1981) and nuts, should be invoked. Beck discounts increased consumption of animal protein as an explanation for more Zn in the later village sample because the increase is not associated with a decrease in strontium. Beck's use of parametric statistics (*t*-test) as opposed to Blakely and Beck's (1981) non-parametric chi-square likely explains why Beck's analysis shows statistical significance. Given that these data are obviously not distributed normally, a more conservative test for significance would be appropriate.

Katzenberg (1984)

Although Katzenberg's central focus is upon strontium and diet, she also analyses a supplementary array of major and trace elements, primarily as a means of controlling for diagenesis. Ninety-eight ribs from five sites were analysed for Sr and three heavy metals, zirconium, yttrium, and rubidium. Ca, P, Si, Al, Fe, Mn, Ti, Mg, and K determinations are reported for a subsample of twenty-five.

Mean values for calcium and phosphorus were compared to modern observations and an expected Ca:P ratio of 2.16. The prehistoric and modern cases showed close correspondence, reinforcing the argument that little diagenesis had occurred. Analyses of soil samples from the sites showed little variation, suggesting that environmental differences in Sr values did not impact the study. In addition, Sr/Ca ratios for humans depart from those of a sample of deer from the various sites, again arguing that either environmental change or altered conditions of deposition were unlikely to have affected results. Sr does not correlate with the three heavy metals (Zr, Y, and Rb) which are expected contaminants – Y replacing Ca in hydroxyapatite crystal, Zr and Rb being infiltrates of pore spaces. On the assumption that the Sr/Zr contaminants have the same ratio in bone as in the soil, a correction factor is generated and applied to the series. Some samples were affected, but the pattern previously observed was not significantly modified.

Of the other elements, Si, Fe, and Mn appear enriched, when compared to published data and cadaver samples. Potassium seems to have been depleted, though magnesium is within expected values. Silicon and titanium are also assumed not to be of biological significance. A discriminant function analysis using Al, Fe, Mn, and K misclassified only one of the twenty-five samples by site, again suggesting that these are characteristics of the burial environment.

Katzenberg's dietary inferences indicate that the initial maize horticulturalists buried in the pits at Serpent Mounds show elevated Sr levels, beyond those for subsequent or antecedent populations. Assuming that strontium-rich foods include molluscs, nuts, legumes, and leafy vegetables, Katzenberg argues that maize, which is low in Sr, had little impact during the time of its initial appearance, when compared to more recent prehistoric and proto-historic periods. These results are said to conform to Cleland's (1976) focal-diffuse model, with the Middle Woodland adaptation being diffuse, followed by a gradual narrowing of the resource base as maize horticulture develops. Katzenberg states that her results parallel those from Illinois (Szpunar 1977) and Wisconsin (Price and Kavanagh 1982), though they would seem to be just the opposite. In Wisconsin and Illinois, the appearance of maize horticulture is associated with relatively low Sr values.

Benfer (1984)

Benfer reports results of Zn, Ca, and Sr analysis for seventeen femoral samples from the Paloma site, a large Pre-ceramic occupation from the Chilca Valley, Peru. Various components of the site date from 8000 to 4500 B.P. Forty-one soil samples were also analysed, with no correlation found between Sr in bone and soil. A low level correlation does exist for Zn values in these two contexts. No significant relationships were found between bone and adjacent soil samples.

In general, females had less zinc than males, a pattern similar to that reported for the Ledders site (Lambert *et al.* 1979). Utilizing a plot of zinc and strontium residuals, after regression of elemental values against those for calcium, Benfer notes that males, females, and juveniles form distinctive clusters, the last of these showing the highest values for both elements, the females lowest, and the males intermediate. Benfer suggests that strontium will be minimally informative in this context, due to the confounding effects of shellfish consumption. However, it is interesting to note that Sr values do increase with age in this sample, suggesting to Benfer that older adults may consume increasing amounts of fish and molluscs. Trace metals in hair are also analysed in this study to illustrate their potential utility for measuring seasonality and health status.

TISSUE STRUCTURE AND DIAGENESIS

The composition of archaeologically recovered hard tissue is dependent upon conditions at the time of tissue formation, upon exchange during the life of the organism, and finally upon post-mortem changes. The form these alterations take depends upon the structure of the tissue, the environment, diet, physiology, and health status of the living organism, and conditions of the post-mortem depositional environment. In this section we will briefly review pertinent information concerning the structure of bones and teeth, discuss the process of diagenesis, and summarize the results of studies designed to identify and to develop compensating mechanisms for post-mortem enrichment or depletion of elements.

Bone is composed of bone cells, fluids, a mineralized portion, and an organic matrix. (For a more extended discussion of bone structure see Sillen, and Armelagos *et al.*, this volume.) Trace metals are associated with both bone collagen and bone mineral. In general, minerals comprise 70% of bone and organic matter 20–30% (Jowsey 1977, McLean and Urist 1968, Price *et al.* 1985b, Snyder *et al.* 1975). Dental enamel, by contrast, is almost exclusively inorganic. Dentin and cementum more closely resemble bone, in that mineral is embedded in a collagenous matrix with water forming a much more significant component of these tissues. Like bone, dentin and cementum are biologically dynamic throughout life (Snyder *et al.* 1975, Weatherell and Robinson 1973).

The process of accretional incorporation of ions during formation is similar across these tissues and depends upon ion availability, accessibility of the crystallites, and tissue activity (biological). After accretional acquisition has ceased, ionic exchange occurs between the ions of the crystallite surfaces and extra-crystalline water. Three forms of exchange are usually recognized, with decreasing ease of access: the hydration layer, the crystallite surface, and the body of the lattice (Neuman and Neuman 1958, Weatherell and Robinson 1973). Wing and Brown (1979:78) state that "the monovalent ions of potassium, sodium, chlorine, and fluorine diffuse into the hydration shell but do not concentrate there. Multivalent anions and cations of magnesium, strontium, radium, uranium, and carbonate . . . tend to concentrate in the hydration shell . . . Some of these (strontium, radium, and carbonate) enter the crystal surface itself." Within the crystal, divalent ions of Sr, Pb, and Mg can substitute for calcium, fluorine can replace the OH^- ion, and CO_3^{2-} substitutes for PO_4^{3-} (McLean and Urist 1968). During life, as the crystal matures, Sr is increasingly discriminated against in favor of calcium, which may be balanced by preferential release of calcium during *in vivo* resorption (Schoeninger 1979a), though this pattern changes in post-mortem depositional contexts (Pate and Brown 1985). Discrimination against "foreign" ions during crystal maturation means that the older crystals are chemically more pure than those more recently formed.

The relative inaccessibility of the interior mineral structure of dental enamel helps to explain the tendency for concentrations of such environmental contaminants as F, Cl, and Pb to occur on the exterior surface, with the amount of Pb, Fe, and F demonstrated to increase with age in some populations. Although the structure of enamel and dentin are significantly different, there are some patterns of elemental uptake that are similar in both. F, Pb, and Zn, for instance, occur in higher concentrations near the interior (pulpal) surface of the dentin (Weatherell and Robinson 1973).

It should be noted that enamel crystallites are of an order of magnitude smaller than those of dentin, cementum, and bone. For this reason, certain ions such as magnesium would have difficulty entering the enamel matrix. In addition, the larger crystal surface exposure of dentin, cementum, and bone should facilitate elemental exchange compared to enamel (Katzenberg 1984, Parker and Toots 1980, Posner 1969, Sillen and Kavanagh 1982, Weatherell and Robinson 1973). Although Parker and Toots (1980) report that there is little variation between the dentin, enamel, and bone of modern animals for most minerals, they do note that Mg in dentin can be twice that in enamel and bone, and that variation in Sr may be of the order of 10%.

The distinct properties of enamel must be kept in mind when attempting to use teeth as an indicator of diet in the past. Enamel has a distinct chemical history and reflects a different portion of an individual's life than more biologically active tissues, as noted by Sillen and Kavanagh (1982). One should not necessarily expect comparable elemental values across these tissue groups. This point weakens earlier inferences by Toots and Voorhies (1965), Parker (1968) and Parker and Toots (1970, 1974) about strontium's relative stability over time, based on comparable values of this element in teeth, dentin, and bone of Tertiary fossil vertebrates. In fact, Sillen and Kavanagh (1982) argue the opposite: that such comparable values should be taken as an indication of equilibration. The distinctive nature of dental enamel must also be considered when evaluating the work of Elias (1980) and Boaz and Hampel (1978). Questions of context in reference to the Boaz and Hampel study have been discussed by Shipman (1981), Schoeninger *et al.* (1984), and Pate and Brown (1985). Sillen and Kavanagh (1982), Lambert *et al.* (1984b), and Price *et al.* (1985b) address the assumptions made and conclusions reached by Elias (1980).

As bone is created, it progresses through a poorly crystallized, relatively amorphous phase to a crystallized apatite [$Ca_5(PO_4)_3(OH)$] (Katzenberg 1984, McLean and Urist 1968, Posner 1969). These two forms vary in proportion to the age of the individual. Amorphous tissue is more common in juveniles and limited in adults to the endosteal, periosteal, and Haversian canal surfaces. An observed difference in the elemental composition of the non-crystalline and crystalline structures explains age differences in element proportions (Katzenberg 1984, Sillen 1981a, Sillen and Kavanagh 1982). Given that the amorphous phase is more soluble than apatite in adults, it may recrystallize most rapidly after deposition (Pate and Brown 1985). As noted above, this is a possible explanation for the surficial banding noted in microprobe studies of bone, e.g. Lambert *et al.* (1983) and Badone and Farquhar (1982).

Trace elements are differentially distributed through the collagen and apatite portions of bone. Spadaro (1969) and Spadaro *et al.* (1970) identify Al, Pb, Si, V, and possibly Mn and Sr, as being strongly bound to mineral, with copper and most iron associated with the organic matrix. Zinc was present in both, though most closely tied to the mineral phase. While these results are compatible with our knowledge of trace element activity in the human body (Schroeder 1973, Underwood 1977), the implications of these associations are too often ignored in multi-element attempts to assess diets in the past. Clearly, differential diagenesis in the mineral and collagen phases is likely to affect assays of trace element content in bone. As noted by Klepinger (1983), Cu and Fe in collagen may also be lost during ashing procedures.

In archaeological contexts, bone deteriorates from both intrinsic and extrinsic forces. Von Endt and Ortner (1984) argue that intrinsic factors such as recrystallization and hydrolysis of collagen and non-collagenous proteins will proceed in the absence of significant extrinsic factors favoring diagenesis. White and Hannus (1983) emphasize the role of micro-organisms in initiating the chemical weathering of collagen as the initial phase of decomposition, listing water, acid, oxygen, and the calcium content of the soil as key factors influencing bone weathering. The roles of temperature (Hare 1980, Rottländer 1976, Von Endt and Ortner 1984), pH (Garlick 1969, Gordon and Buikstra 1981), and water (Hare 1980) have been considered by various workers. Local environmental factors, such as temperature, moisture, and soil matrix composition, are seen as much more important than time in determining the pattern of bone weathering (Parker 1967, Parker and Toots 1970, 1974, 1980).

It is not known whether or not the minerals released through the deterioration of bone collagen tend to recrystallize within the bone or exit via ground water. Although, as we shall emphasize below, the impact of leaching and enrichment also renders the mineral phase vulnerable to diagenesis, it would appear that the earliest and most extreme impact would be on elements such as copper and iron which are bound to collagen, rendering them less useful in dietary analyses based on elemental content of whole bone ash.

Numerous studies have attempted to identify elements least likely to be subject to diagenetic change, while a lesser number have suggested ways to compensate for such alteration and thus provide a measure of elemental context at the time of death. Techniques commonly used for identifying the effects of diagenesis include comparisons with values obtained from contemporary populations (Gilbert 1975, Lambert *et al.* 1985a, Parker and Toots 1970, 1974, 1980), the comparison of values for bones thought to be relatively permeable with those less subject to diagenesis (Lambert *et al.* 1982, 1984b); analysis of soils surrounding the burial (Becker *et al.* 1968, Benfer 1984, Katzenberg 1984, Keeley *et al.* 1977, Lambert *et al.* 1984a, Nelson and Sauer 1984), comparison of dental and skeletal tissues from the same individual (or species) (Parker and Toots 1970, 1974), and microprobe analysis (Badone and Farquhar 1982, Gilbert 1975, Henderson *et al.* 1983, Lambert *et al.* 1983, 1984a,b,c, Parker and Toots 1970, 1974, 1980, Schoeninger 1979a,b, Waldron 1981).

Of these techniques, comparisons of dental and bony tissues have already been identified as imprecise estimators of diagenesis. Likewise, the comparisons of ribs and bones reported by Lambert and co-workers may have been affected by intra-individual variation in bone remodeling rates and inter-individual variation in elemental content due to either physiology or dietary differences (Katzenberg 1984, Price *et al.* 1985b, Sillen and Kavanagh 1982). In order to clarify this issue, we have reanalysed the data used in our original study (Lambert *et al.* 1979, Szpunar 1977). Previously, we had examined average values across the two bones. We now address matched differences between bones from the same individual.

Szpunar (1977) used samples from twenty-three of the skeletons for which we also have femur data. Levels of Ca, Na, Sr, Mg, Cu, Zn, K, Fe, Mn, Al, and Pb are measured. Given the small sample size, we cannot apply multivariate statistics nor can we assume that our data are normally distributed. Interpretable tests for bone differences are thus restricted to the sign tests. A pair-wise *t*-test for each element is included as an indication of the difference between results for parametric and non-parametric statistics. Descriptive statistics for the raw rib–femur data are presented in Table 7.1; the tests of differences are summarized in Table 7.2.

Pair-wise comparisons using the sign test indicate that rib and femur samples from the same individual differ significantly (at $p < 0.05$) in levels of Ca, Na, Sr, Mg, Cu, K, Fe, Mn, and Al. In other words, similar levels are found across bone type only for Zn and Pb. Levels of Ca, Na, and Sr are higher in the femora than in the ribs, whereas levels of Mg, Cu, K, Fe, Mn, and Al are higher in the ribs. The high levels of the major elements in femora are explainable in terms of the large

Table 7.1 *Descriptive statistics for raw rib–femur data (n=23)*

	mean	s.d.	c.v.	skew	kurtosis	pr(normal)
Rib data						
Ca	317	38.57	12.15	−3.1536	2.6943	0.8894
Na	4356	1072.30	24.62	−0.1369	2.1350	0.7928
Sr	179	77.93	43.45	0.8124	2.3182	0.0001
Mg	5292	3162.45	59.76	1.2920	3.9175	0.0008
Cu	91	24.35	26.82	0.4776	3.8534	0.5811
Zn	311	142.6	45.84	0.3558	2.1578	0.7928
K	560	373.64	66.66	0.6477	2.3428	0.2020
Fe	3349	2186.88	65.29	0.5717	2.2635	0.1586
Mn	341	108.70	31.87	0.5895	2.4078	0.6866
Al	2191	1687.24	77.00	0.7244	2.3619	0.2020
Pb	28	5.73	20.30	−0.8288	3.9259	0.1238
Femur data						
Ca	357	18.20	5.09	1.2144	3.7082	0.2550
Na	5630	1339.92	23.80	−0.2762	2.2980	0.5811
Sr	188	62.59	33.31	1.0168	2.7994	0.0568
Mg	3923	1645.63	41.94	1.1207	3.1702	0.0330
Cu	46	13.01	28.50	0.4831	3.0222	0.8894
Zn	256	158.71	61.92	1.3607	3.7739	0.0251
K	236	358.06	151.92	2.8328	10.2489	0.0000
Fe	196	152.15	77.69	3.0843	13.1691	0.0018
Mn	120	98.03	81.42	1.1212	3.6048	0.0060
Al	152	124.41	81.82	2.9510	11.9432	0.0034
Pb	30	20.33	67.86	0.9574	2.8590	0.0000

amount of dense cortical bone in femora relative to ribs. The high levels of other elements in the ribs may be due to differences in cleaning techniques between samples, and to larger "invasion spaces" or greater permeability for ribs. Given all these differences in element concentration by bone, it is difficult to explain the non-significant differences for Zn and Pb. Similarity in Pb levels may be related to its role as an environmental contaminant and the inability of bone to discriminate against Pb.

Some of these differences may also reflect true distinctions in bone elemental composition at the time of death, as a direct result of differences in remodeling rates and, indirectly, due to diet. As noted by Sillen and Kavanagh (1982), the bones that remodel more slowly, such as the long bones and skull, should give a more accurate representation of long-term dietary habits. In general, adult ribs are thought to remodel more rapidly (2.2–10% per year) than long bones (femur shaft 1.5–2.2% per year; tibia 0.4–2.6% per year) (Snyder *et al.* 1975). Theoretically, we might expect differences to occur due to intra-individual variation,

Table 7.2 *Tests of difference between ribs and femora (pair-wise comparisons)*

	Paired *t*-test				Sign test			
	Mean D	s.d.	*t*	p	*n*/N	Mean *D*	s.d.	p
Ca	−39.78	43.89	−4.3470	.0001	3	.8696	.3444	.0002
Na	−1274.39	1337.21	−4.5705	.0001	4	.8261	.3876	.0013
Sr	−8.52	47.58	−0.8590	.1998	6	.7391	.4490	.0173
Mg	1368.44	3226.13	2.0343	.0271	6	.2609	.4490	.0173
Cu	45.13	23.71	9.1289	.0000	0	.0000	.0000	.0000
Zn	54.91	197.03	1.3366	.0975	9	.3913	.4990	.2024
K	324.78	542.71	2.8700	.0044	3	.1304	.3444	.0002
Fe	3153.44	2160.82	6.9989	.0000	0	.0000	.0000	.0000
Mn	220.65	138.54	7.6382	.0000	1	.0435	.2085	.0000
Al	2039.09	1639.43	5.9650	.0000	0	.0000	.0000	.0000
Pb	−1.74	23.51	−0.3547	.3631	11	.4783	.5108	.5000

even though several studies of modern samples have failed to identify such a pattern (Hodges *et al.* 1950, Yablonskii 1971, 1973, reported in Schoeninger 1979a).

Estimates of expected trace element values in ancient remains, based on determinations from modern samples, should be approached with caution and used only in association with other more reliable techniques such as microprobe analysis. Not the least of the assumptions that must be made in the use of contemporary remains is that there is no instrument error induced through comparisons among several laboratories (Elias *et al.* 1982, Schoeninger 1979a). Katzenberg (1984), basing her argument on modern determinations, advocates the use of an expected Ca:P ratio in hydroxyapatite of 2.16 as one means of identifying diagenesis. While her recent human remains show a closely concordant value of 2.2, Hassan and Ortner (1977) have reported a ratio of 2.5 in the face of obvious diagenesis. The use of Ca:P ratios is explored in more detail by Sillen (this volume).

Complementary investigations of sediment and ground water composition are also important in generating models of diagenesis. Diagenesis has to be recognized as a pervasive and dynamic, though nonlinear process (Parker and Toots 1980, White and Hannus 1983). It is also clear that considerable variation in the degree of elemental exchange occurs between contemporary sites and that models for diagenetic change are not easily transferred between depositional contexts.

Various techniques have been proposed for either eliminating or compensating for the effects of diagenesis. Lambert *et al.* (1983), noting the tendency of affected elements to cluster within the outer 10–400 μm of the femoral cortex, have argued that removal of this layer will eliminate the problem. While this may be a useful strategy for recently buried remains in certain contexts, it is obvious that superficial removal will not compensate in fossil bones such as those reported by Badone and Farquhar (1982) where the penetration of contaminants is characterized by a U-shaped curve. While Lambert and co-workers identified only Mn as a likely penetrant of voids in their millennia-old remains, Parker and Toots (1980) identify Si, Mn, Ba, Pb, and Ca as occupants of voids. Likewise, surficial removal does nothing to compensate for depleted elements, such as Na, Mg, Cl, K (Parker and Toots 1980), or Ca (Lambert *et al.* 1984b).

The use of archaeologically recovered mammals of "known" herbivorous and carnivorous diets has been advocated by various workers as a means of increasing the precision of dietary inference and of identifying values so extreme as to be unlikely results of diet (Brown 1973, Katzenberg 1984, Price 1985, Price *et al.* 1985a, Schoeninger 1979a, b, 1981, 1982, Sillen 1981). As emphasized by Price (1985), Price *et al.* (1985a, b), Schoeninger (1981), and Katzenberg (1984), carnivores are relatively rare recoveries from archaeological sites. Carnivore diets frequently include bone and plant supplementation of meat (Katzenberg 1984, Schoeninger 1981, 1982). These and other workers (Elias *et al.* 1982), advocate the use of herbivore standards for identifying the effects of environmental variation and/or diagenesis. This use of herbivore controls assumes that herbivore diets are relatively homogeneous and have not changed through time and that different human/herbivore land use patterns have not affected results. In addition, it must be assumed that diagenesis has affected herbivore and human bone in an identical fashion (Price *et al.* 1985b, Schoeninger 1981, 1982), which has yet to be demonstrated. As pointed out by Price *et al.* (1985a) and Sillen and Kavanagh (1982), there is an apparent similarity in values for the ratio of Sr in bone to diet in mammals (0.20–0.25). This facilitates the development of herbivore/carnivore baseline values from herbivore bone analysis, and allows evaluation of the relative herbivory of human diets (Price *et al.* 1985a).

Emphasizing that it is important to distinguish between geological and biological hydroxyapatite crystals, Schoeninger (1981) uses X-ray diffraction to differentiate between the effects of diagenesis and diet in samples from the Levant. She thus identifies the effects of carbonate enrichment in samples dating to 30,000–70,000 years and provides a convincing test of the application of this technique to archaeological samples.

Parker and Toots (1980) advocate the use of an "indicator element" as a means of correcting for diagenetic loss. This element must occupy a lattice site within the apatite structure rather than being an inclusion, should not occupy the same site as the element in question, should not be highly sensitive to environmental conditions such as pH, and should be present in small amounts in most ground water. Fluorine is used, for example, to correct for the loss of Na in fossil *Equus* (Parker and Toots 1980:201).

Katzenberg (1984) offers a means of compensating for soil inclusions in her specimens. Assuming that soil particles in the bone have identical proportions of strontium and zirconium, a transition metal and known contaminant, she generates a correction factor based on the ratio of Zr in the soil to that in bone. Strontium values are decreased by this "contamination factor" in sites where Zr is present. This modification did not change the pattern of her earlier inter-site comparisons. Although Katzenberg's technique will work for direct sediment inclusions, neither this strategy nor that offered by Parker and Toots (1980) will compensate alone for the vast majority of changes produced by diagenesis.

Table 7.3 summarizes results from studies of diagenesis, with emphasis upon those reporting more than one element. Although the results of individual reports may be questioned for various methodological reasons, it is obvious that under appropriate conditions the absolute or relative amount of any element – including strontium – can be affected by diagenetic processes. Obviously, each study, whether of one or several elements, must attempt to identify the probable impact of diagenesis on analytical results if the goal is to isolate true dietary differences. As noted by Price *et al.* (1985a:429), "Study of the effects of diagenesis on bone mineral levels is the most critical aspect of bone chemistry analysis at the present time."

OF NUTS AND MAIZE

In order to generate models of expected bone element content due to diet, simplifying assumptions are required. In multi-element contexts

Table 7.3 *Trace elements subject to diagenesis*

Author/ Age of site and Location	Depleted elements	Enriched elements	Stable elements	Method
Badone and Farquhar (1982) *Pleistocene*: Old Crow, Yukon		U,F,Ba,Mn,Fe,V,Sc,Co,Al,Dy,La,Eu,Sm	Ca,Sr,Na	Microprobe
Becker, *et al*. (1968) *>2100* B.P: Peru *Ancient*: N. America *Modern*: Pennsylvannia		Al,B,Fe,Mn,Si,Sr	Cu,Zn	Diachronic comparison
Ericson, *et al*. (1979) *4500–1400* B.P: Peru *Ptolemaic Mummy* *Modern*: U.S. *Modern*: U.K.		Pb,Ba	Bone–tooth comparison	
Hassan and Ortner (1977) *Pleistocene*: N. America *Modern*		Ca		Microprobe
Henderson *et al*. (1983) Olduvai Gorge, Bed III *Modern*		Na,Sc,Cr,Co,Ba,La,Ce,Nd,Sm,Eu,Gd,Tb, Tm,Yb,Lu,Hf,Ta,Th,U	Sr?	Microprobe
Katzenberg (1984) *1900–400 B.P*: S. Ontario	K	Ti,Al,Fe,Mn,Mg?,Zr,Rb,Y	Sr,Mg?	Soil
Klepinger (1983) *2650–2300 B.P*: Morgantina, Sicily	Cd,Mn	Ca,Mg		Diachronic bone com- parison
Keeley *et al*. (1977) *1500 B.P*: *Anglo-Saxon*: England		Mn		Soil

Lambert *et al.* (1979) *2000–900 B.P*: Illinois		Fe, Al, Mn, K	Sr, Zn, Ca, Na, Cu?, Mg?	Soil
Lambert *et al.* (1982) *2000–900 B.P*: Illinois	Ca, Na	Fe, Al, K, Mn	Sr, Zn, Mg	Rib–femur comparison
Lambert *et al.* (1983) *2000–900 B.P*: Illinois		Fe, Al, K, Mn, Mg?	Sr, Zn, Pb	Microprobe
Lambert *et al.* (1984a) *2000–900 B.P*: Illinois	Ca, Mg?, Na	Fe, Al, K, Mn	Sr, Zn, Na, M, Pb, Mg?	Soil, bone comparison, microprobe
Lambert *et al.* (1984b) *2000–900 B.P*: Illinois	Na, Ca,	Fe, Al, Mn, K, Cu?, Ba?	Sr, Zn, Pb?, Mg?	Soil, bone comparison, microprobe
Lambert *et al.* (1984c) *2000–900 B.P*: Illinois		Cu, Ba		Soil, bone comparison, microprobe
Lambert *et al.* (1985a) *2000–900 B.P*: Illinois	Ca, Na, Mg?, K?, Pb?	Fe, Mn, Al, K?, Cu, Ba, Mg?	Sr, Zn, Pb, Mg?	Soil, bone comparison, microprobe and comparison with modern
Nelson and Sauer (1984) *5000 B.P*: S. Illinois			Zn, Mn	Soil
Nelson *et al.* (1983) —: Greenland (seals and reindeer)		Sr		Species comparison
Parker and Toots (1970, 1974) *Tertiary fossils:* Wyoming		F, Y, Si, Mn, Fe	Sr, Na	Bone–tooth, microprobe
Parker and Toots (1980) *Teriary fossils*: Wyoming	Na, Mg, Cl, K	K, Mg, Al, Si, V, S, Mn, F, Fe, Se, Ba, Pb, U, As, La, Y, rare earths, Ca	Sr	Microprobe
Schoeninger (1981) *30,000–70,000 B.P*: Levant		Sr		X-ray diffraction
Waldron (1981) *1700 B.P., 400 B.P*: U.K.		Pb		Microprobe

these typically take a form such as "Three elements in particular – Mg, Sr, and vanadium – are significantly concentrated in plant resources. Two others – copper and zinc – are more commonly available from animal foods" (Hatch and Geidel 1985:472). While the development of a set of generalized expectations will obviously require simplification of dietary complexity, such statements should not be accepted uncritically.

The multi-element studies cited above typically generate sets of expectations for each element or cluster of elements, apply univariate tests across each element, and then explain unexpected results in terms of diagenesis or uncontrolled mineral-rich (or mineral-depleted) dietary items, e.g. nuts or molluscs. It would be preferable, however, to be able to treat multiple expectations simultaneously. This issue is addressed at length in the following section, where our research design is developed. At this point, however, it is important to consider a few key issues concerning specific dietary items.

A further significant problem in elemental studies is the lack of information on expected values for traditional, non-Western dietary items (Beck 1985, Gilbert 1975). For North American workers this problem is acute. Most of the multi-element approaches have been based upon the assays of such workers as Schroeder (1973, and co-workers 1963, 1966a,b, 1972) which show a decided bias toward the Western palate. Examples of information derived from Schroeder's studies for use in evaluating prehistoric trace element values appear in Tables 7.4 and 7.5.

For North American workers, it is especially important to have precise estimates for the elemental content of maize, a dietary item for over two thousand years in the southwestern and, since 1200 B.P., in the eastern U.S. Gilbert, for instance, generated expectations for diet at Dickson Mounds, Illinois, on the basis of a composite "grains and cereals" category which included maize along with wheat, rice, rye, oats, millet, barley, and various breads. Only wild rice and corn are legitimately relevant to prehistoric North American diets, with the hybrid corn values considerably different from those recorded for the composite grain/cereal category shown in Table 7.6.

Other workers, such as Katzenberg (1984) and Price *et al.* (1985a,b), noting this pattern, have characterized maize as a low mineral food. There is, however, reason to question the uncritical application of this generalization to past human groups. First is the question of using

Table 7.4 *Mean concentrations of elements in various food groups*

	Grains and cereals (ppm)	Vegetables[a] (ppm)	Meats[b] (ppm)	Nuts (ppm)
Manganese	7.00	2.50	0.20	17.00
Copper	2.00	1.20	3.90	14.80
Zinc	17.70	6.00	30.60	34.00
Magnesium	805.00	307.00	267.00	1970.00
Strontium	3.00	1.90	2.00	60.00
Vanadium	1.10	1.60	—	0.71
Cobalt	0.43	0.14	0.22	0.47
Molybdenum	1.79	0.51	4.82	—
Selenium	0.15	—	0.92	—

[a] Includes legumes, tubers, and leafy material.
[b] Excludes fish and shellfish
— Insufficient data.
Source: Gilbert 1977.

Table 7.5 *Mean concentrations of nutritionally sensitive trace elements in various food groups*

	Grains (ppm)	Vegetables (ppm)	Meats (ppm)	Nuts (ppm)
Zinc[a]	17.7[d]	3	30–50	30–50
Copper[b]	2	1.2[d]	4	15
Manganese[c]	7	2.5	0.21	17
Selenium[d]	0.15	0.01[g]	0.92	—
Molybdenum[d]	1.79	0.51	4.82	—
Vanadium[e]	1.1	1.47	0.05	0.71
Nickel[f]	0.15–0.35	1.5–3.0	0.13	—

— No data
Source: Geidel 1981, citing
[a] O'Dell and Savage 1960
[b] Schroeder *et al* 1966
[c] Schroeder, Balassa, and Tipton 1966
[d] Gilbert 1977
[e] Schroeder, Balassa, and Tipton 1963
[f] Schroeder, Balassa, and Tipton 1962
[g] Morris and Levander 1970

modern hybrid corn as a standard for ancient maize. Although it would be better for our purposes to have information on the midwestern twelve-row or the eastern eight-row races of corn (Cutler and Blake 1973), the most extensive studies of trace element values for native corn

Table 7.6 *Mean concentrations of trace elements in composite grains*[a] *and hybrid corn*

	Zn (ppm)	Sr (ppm)	Mg (ppm)	Mn (ppm)	Cu (ppm)
Composite Grains	17.70	3.00	805.00	7.00	2.00
Hybrid Corn	3.77	0.52	664.00	1.31	0.46

[a] Maize, wheat, rice, rye, oats, barley, millet, and various breads.
Source: Gilbert 1975, 1977.

Table 7.7 *Approximate percentage of Desired Daily Intake provided by 200 gram portions of U.S.D.A. commodity and Hopi cereals*

	Ca	Mg	Mn	Fe	Zn
Cornmeal (commercial)	1	23	7	36	8
Cornmeal (Hopi)	2	80	18	43	35
Piki bread	40	102	56	121	55
Bivilviki	142	159	57	224	49

Sources: Callaway *et al.* 1974, Kuhnlein 1981

have been conducted among the Hopi of northeastern Arizona (Calloway *et al.* 1974, Kuhnlein 1981, Kuhnlein and Calloway 1979). As Table 7.7 shows, there are distinctive differences between commercially available and Hopi cereals.

Even more striking are the changes which occur during the preparation of traditional Hopi foods such as piki bread (wafer-thin bread prepared with blue cornmeal, ash, and water) and bivilviki (boiled dumpling-bread made with blue cornmeal, ash, and water). In addition to Ca, Mg, Mn, Fe, and Zn, it appears that the culinary ash, commonly made by Hopi from the chamisa (*Atriplex canescens*) or dry bean pods and vines (*Phaseolus* sp.) adds Na, K, Cu, Br, Ru, and Sr (Calloway *et al.* 1974). Although some of this variation may be due to differences in environmental availability of elements between the locations where the commercially available corn and traditional corn were grown, this study points up the need for further investigations of native food resources and food preparation techniques. The use of culinary ash could, for instance, help explain Katzenberg's (1984) results which specify

Table 7.8 *Elemental content of nut resources (ppm)*

	Mn	Cu	Zn	Mg	Sr	V
Composite[a]	17.00	14.80	34.00	1970.00	60.00	—
Composite[b]	17.00	15.00	30.00–50.00	—	—	0.71
Brazil nuts[c]	27.80	23.82	42.30	3175.00	4.04	—
Native N. Am.[c]	14.20	12.71	33.19	1377.00	2.80	—
Brazil nuts[d]	8.00	18.00	41.00	3370.00	77.00	0.01
Native N. Am.[d]	29.98	13.20	38.33	1577.00	2.42	0.02

— no data available
[a] Gilbert 1977
[b] Geidel 1981
[c] Schroeder 1973
[d] Furr 1979

relatively high proportions of Sr among the earliest maize agriculturalists in southern Ontario.

Nuts are also said to confound results, thus providing a convenient caveat for seemingly inexplicable (i.e. high) element levels in bone. One gains the impression from summary Tables 7.4 and 7.5 that nuts should indeed be characterized as concentrating trace elements such as Mn, Cu, Zn, Mg, and Sr, with less extreme effects in V and Co. These data are derived from the work of Schroeder (1973, and co-workers, 1963, 1966a,b, 1967, 1969, 1972). Unfortunately, this composite category includes a number of nut resources not likely to have been utilized by prehistoric North Americans. A more useful comparison is developed in Table 7.8 by focusing on resources found in temperate climate prehistoric North America: walnuts, hazelnuts, and pecans. For comparison, Brazil nuts are also listed, along with the summary figures from Gilbert (1977) and Geidel (1981), who base their values on Schroeder's work. As can be seen, Brazil nuts show a remarkable ability to concentrate trace elements. Data are also included from Furr (1979), who reports on nut resources purchased or grown in a local region: acorn, black walnut, butternut, hazelnut, hickory, and pecan. Particularly significant in this regard is the apparent lack of evidence that Sr is concentrated in nuts documented to have been important in prehistoric diets. V is also in low quantity. As an aside, it should be noted that among the nuts cited here as models for prehistoric North America, acorns appear to be particularly element-poor.

MATERIALS AND METHODS

Sites

The study samples come from west-central Illinois, a region with a long history of archaeological study. Fortunately, geological and geomorphological investigations have also been extensive, thus allowing us to characterize the sediments and soils which form the depositional environment for human skeletal remains (Butzer 1978, Hajic 1981, Rubey 1952, Styles 1985, Willman and Frye 1970). The limestone bedrock (Burlington and Keokuk formations) is covered by a mantle of loess (Peoria loess and Roxana silt) which was deposited during the Wisconsin glaciation (Styles 1985). On the bluff crests, where most of the burial mounds occur, the loessic sediment has weathered to form a variety of soils, some relatively unmodified and having no observable B horizons. Others, more heavily weathered, contain well-developed B horizons with columnar peds. Soil acidity tends to be closely correlated with the degree of soil development, varying between pH 8 and 4.5 on a single bluff crest. Bone preservation, in turn, is closely associated with soil acidity (Gordon and Buikstra 1981).

Fifty mid-shaft femoral samples from three sites have been analysed (Fig. 7.1). The Gibson site (10 males) was chosen to represent a pre-maize baseline case, while the Ledders site (8 males, 11 females) reflects a group in the early stages of maize agriculture, as confirmed by carbon isotope study (van der Merwe and Vogel 1978). A similar pattern exists for the Emergent Mississippian Mound 47 from the Helton site (13 males, 8 females), which shows a finer chronological separation of stratigraphically distinct components than Ledders. Current models for diets among these groups are presented in more detail by Asch and Asch (1985), Buikstra (1984), and Buikstra *et al.* (1986). Radiocarbon dates for the Ledders and Helton sites indicate that they are roughly contemporaneous, dating to between 900 and 1000 years ago (Conner 1984). Although there are no reliable dates for the Gibson site, on the basis of material culture we judge the site to be approximately a millennium earlier than the two maize horticulturalist cemeteries. Individuals were chosen for trace element analysis based on the availability of carbon isotope data from studies conducted by van der Merwe (1978, 1982, personal communication) and van der Merwe and Vogel (1978).

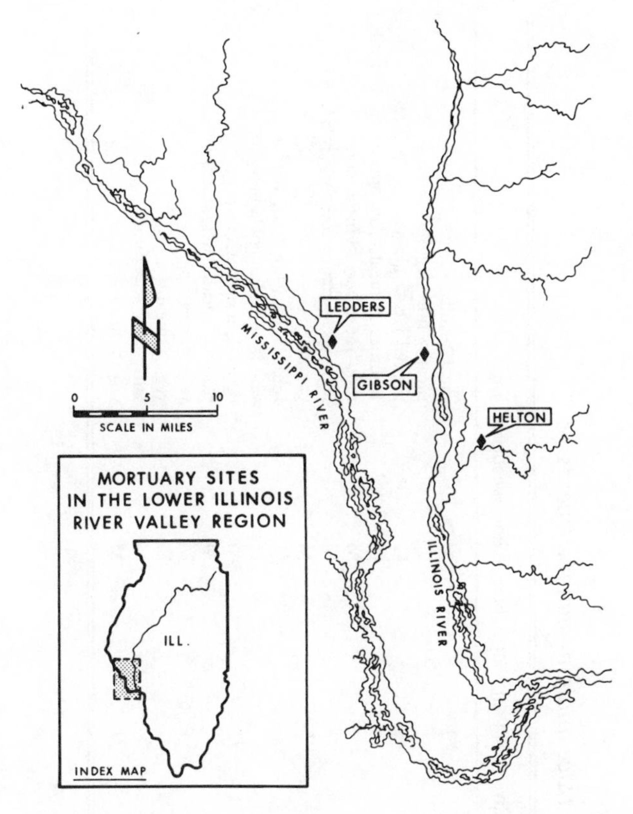

Fig. 7.1 Mortuary sites in the lower Illinois River valley region

Trace elements

The array of fourteen major and minor elements (Zn, Sr, Cd, Pb, Al, Fe, Mn, Ba, Cu, V, Mg, K, Na, Ca) was selected to include those that modern studies had shown to vary by diet, metabolic interactions, and bone component affinities. Elements that had proven to be subject to diagenetic effects in our previous univariate analyses were also chosen. In addition it was anticipated that the age and sex of the remains might influence the levels of certain elements. A summary of anticipated associations based on diet and metabolic antagonisms appears in Table 7.9, along with notes on element affinity for osseous tissue and distribution between the hydroxyapatite and collagen fractions of bone. The following paragraphs further elaborate the basis of our expectations.

Table 7.9 *Expectations for ten trace and four major elements*

	Antagonisms	Age cumulative	% total body in bone	Mineral/collagen	Diet
Zn	Ca,Cu,Fe,Cd,Mn	—	20	M > C	meat > nuts >> veg.
Cu	Zn,Ca,Fe,Cd	—	—	C	meat > nuts, legumes > veg.
V	Fe,Mn,	—	—	C	animal fats > grains, veg. > meat
Fe	Ca,Zn,Cd,Cu,Mn	—	—	C	legumes > meat, nuts, green veg. > fruit
Mn	Fe,Zn,V	—	—	M	nuts, roots, veg. > meat, corn
Sr	Ca,F,Mg	—	99	M	legumes > grains, cereals > meat, nuts
Ba	?Parallels Sr	+	91–93	M	parallels Sr
Cd	Ca,Zn,Cu,Fe	+	—	?	meat > grains > nuts, veg.[a] veg. > meat (except kidney)[b]
Pb	Ca,Fe,Cu,Zn	+	92	M	dependent on environment
Al	F	+	—	M	plants > meat; environment
Mg	Mn,Ca	—	55–58	M	veg. > meat
K	Na	—	—	?	veg. > meat
Na	K	—	38	M	salt >> veg. > meat
Ca	Zn,Sr,Cd,Pb,Mg	neg. assoc.	99	M	veg. > meat

[a] Schroeder (1967) also associates Cd with Zn
[b] Underwood (1977)

Antagonisms. This information is primarily derived from Schroeder (1973, and co-workers 1963, 1966a,b, 1967, 1969, 1972) and Underwood (1977). Antagonisms have been previously sought but not found by Bahou (1975).

Diet. We anticipated that certain elements would be associated with carbon isotope ratios, and that other patterns would emerge that are most readily explained by dietary factors, as suggested in Table 7.9. These expectations are unfortunately weakened by an inadequate knowledge of variation in foodstuffs commonly consumed by prehistoric North Americans.

Diagenesis. These data are based on the information found in Table 7.3. It was anticipated that diagenetic elements would be identified by correlations with other "soil" elements (Lambert *et al.* 1979, 1985a), as well as by consistent associations with specific sites or temporal change.

Percentage of element found in bone. Taken from Underwood (1977), Schroeder (1973), and Snyder *et al.* (1975). Notes are also included concerning affinity for collagen or apatite fractions of bone.

Age/sex specificity. Our study includes only adults, who are anticipated to show minor age-associated patterns. Ca should follow a sex-specific decrease with age. Environmental pollutants such as Pb and perhaps Cd may increase with age though we would not expect this pattern to be so pronounced as in modern samples. Were we including juveniles, especially infants, as we did in an earlier study (Lambert *et al.* 1979) we would anticipate elevated levels of elements such as Cu and Sr in infants. In this preliminary multivariate study, we decided to minimize the variation that might be due to age.

There is currently no consensus concerning expected sex associations for Sr (cf. Price *et al.* 1985a, Sillen and Kavanagh 1982). Although we might expect levels of elements such as Zn, Sr, Fe, and Mn to show sex differences in certain tissues, it is unclear how completely these patterns will be played out in (ancient) human bones.

Chemical analysis

Bone samples were prepared for analysis according to our reported method (Szpunar *et al.* 1978). Samples were cleaned by washing with distilled water, light abrasion with a stainless steel spatula, and repeated washing. The samples were dried, and a portion weighing approximately 4 g was removed from the bone with a saw or percussion hammer and ashed in a Thermolyne Model 20,500 muffle furnace. From the resulting powder, which comprised 70–90% of the gross weight, a 2 g portion was weighed accurately and dissolved in nitric acid. The solution was brought to a volume of 100 ml. The weakest elements were analysed by atomic absorption directly on these solutions (Al, Cd, Cu, Fe, Pb, V). Elements of intermediate sensitivity were analysed after a tenfold dilution of 5 ml of the original solution to 50 ml (K, Na, Sr, Zn). A fivefold dilution was used for Ba and a twofold dilution for Mn. The high sensitivity of Ca and Mg required a 200-fold dilution to bring measurements into a convenient range. K and Na were measured in the emission mode, all other elements in the absorption mode.

The presence of spectral interferences required that different atomic absorption methods be used for the various analyses. Elements without interferences could be measured on a Varian Model 1250 atomic absorption spectrophotometer. Ba, however, has a severe interference from CaOH absorption, so that measurements were carried out on a polarized Zeeman atomic absorption spectrophotometer, Hitachi Model 180-80. The Zeeman method removes most interferences. V has numerous interferences, which were avoided by use of the Zeeman spectrometer. In addition, V had to be measured with a carbon rod atomizer by non-flame methods because of its low sensitivity. Of the remaining elements, Al, Cd, Fe, Mg, Mn, Pb, Sr, and Zn were analysed by the secondary standard addition method to eliminate matrix effects. Analysis of Ca, Cu, K, and Na did not require corrections for matrix effects. Each sample was analysed three times, and the figures in Table 7.10 represent the means of the measurements.

Statistical analysis

The analytical goals of this paper are similar to those of many studies of trace elements in archaeological human bone. We hope to use trace element analyses to make dietary inferences, given an understanding of the metabolic, structural, environmental, and diagenetic processes affecting element concentrations in ancient bone. Like other studies, conclusions regarding diet, physiology, contamination, and diagenesis are ultimately based on the patterning of the trace element results with or against archaeological contextual information and individual skeletal characteristics. Unlike many studies, however, the results of the trace element analyses are treated multivariately. Instead of considering the relationship of each element to dietary and other factors in isolation, relationships among various elements and between trace elements and carbon isotopes are first examined. Composite measures of these inter-element relationships are then used to address the questions of interest. This multivariate approach to trace elements provides new insight into the kinds of information available from archaeological bone samples, but it also renews some of the recent controversies over data structure and statistical techniques found in the literature. Those issues which bear directly on the analytical methods used here include (1) the selection of non-parametric versus parametric tests of difference, and (2) the use of ratios to overcome inter-group variation in diagenesis and contamination.

Selection of non-parametric versus parametric tests of difference is generally based on opinions regarding the form of trace element distributions. Some researchers advocate the use of non-parametric tests on the grounds that trace element frequencies may not be normally distributed (e.g. Klepinger 1984), whereas others adopt parametric tests of difference on the implicit assumption that the elements studied are normally distributed, or that violations of the assumption of normality are inconsequential (e.g. Bahou 1975, Beck 1985). Unfortunately, few non-parametric or parametric studies attempt to discover the actual appearance of trace element distributions, or to assess the effectiveness of transformations to normality. Important exceptions to this situation are Brätter *et al.*'s (1977) study which suggests that trace elements have log-normal or Poisson distributions. Liebscher and Smith (1968, cited by Underwood 1977) argue that essential elements have normal distributions, while the others are skewed. Selecting non-parametric tests on the assumption of non-normality is disadvantageous when the assumption does not hold, because the choice immediately limits the range and strength of statistics available. Selecting parametric tests without consideration of normality, on the other hand, is particularly damaging, since parametric statistics are sensitive to deviations from normality and will produce spurious results when the assumption of normality is violated. Testing whether or not trace element distributions deviate from normality, rather than simply assuming that they do or do not, provides an important and practical criterion for choosing between non-parametric and parametric statistical analyses.

Further considerations for choosing between non-parametric and parametric tests involve the ways in which trace element distributions deviate from normality, and the ways in which such deviations can be corrected. In addition to testing for deviations from normality, the actual form of trace element distributions can be identified by statistically comparing the observed histograms to a series of hypothetical distributions. Once the form of the distribution is discovered, decisions can be made regarding the types of transformation appropriate for normalizing aberrant distributions.

Simple transformations to normal allow us to increase the strength and variety of our statistical analyses without altering the internal structure of the data. Transformations are also advantageous in that they will not alter already normal distributions; they can thus be applied across the entire data set. The present study illustrates a procedure for identifying the form of element distributions, transforming non-normal distributions, and assessing the effectiveness of such transformations. The decision to treat trace elements multivariately (and, therefore, parametrically) follows directly from these preliminary considerations of distribution.

Ratios of various trace elements to Ca are commonly used to standardize observations on whole bone (Sillen, this volume). For studies of bone ash, such standardization is unnecessary and indeed undesirable for both interpretative and general statistical reasons. The use of ratios to overcome inter-group variation in diagenesis and contamination is based on a series of implicit assumptions that Ca frequencies will be affected in similar ways across time and space by various environmental and diagenetic processes, and that despite such processes Ca will bear certain constant relationships to particular trace elements. Unfortunately, as noted above, we have as yet a very incomplete understanding of the effects of diagenesis on individual elements in bone, and an even more incomplete understanding of the effects of diagenesis on inter-element relationships (Lambert *et al.* 1984b, 1985a, Pate and Brown 1985). The number and complexity of assumptions required by an argument in favor of ratios makes it unsound, given our current state of knowledge.

In addition to the problems introduced by diagenetic change, ratios are disadvantageous for several statistical reasons. First, ratios are relatively inaccurate and have larger maximal errors than the direct measurements upon which they are based. Secondly, ratios frequently do not approximate normal distributions. As mentioned above, non-normality can be easily corrected by simple transformations. In the case of ratios, however, the internal structure of the data is altered – ratios obscure the form of the relationship between the variables of which they are composed. Finally, taking ratios of meristic variables or counts can produce discontinuities and peculiarities in their distributions, which are not transformable. The numerical bases for these objections are discussed by Sokal and Rohlf (1969). Similar objections to using ratios as a standardization technique are raised by Atchley *et al.* (1976), Benfer (1984), Gaskings, and Anderson (1976), and Long (1980).

In summary, the choice of statistical techniques should depend on the distributions observed within the data, whereas the use of ratios of various elements to Ca should be avoided, regardless of the observed data structure. With these cautionary rules in mind, we can restate the two goals of the present analysis. First, we want to discover the kinds and directions of relationships among various trace elements and between trace elements and carbon isotopes. Given the multiplicity of, and controversy over dietary, physiological, contaminant, and diagenetic associations between elements, an "open-minded" statistical discovery procedure, requiring no assumptions about the internal structure of the data is appropriate. Principal components analysis meets this criterion, but also requires the assumption of normality. Before applying principal components analysis, then, we will test to see if the data meet this assumption, attempt to normalize the data if they do not, and re-test the data once transformed. Provided that questions regarding normality and inter-element relationships are resolved, the second goal of this analysis, to delineate the relationships between composite measures of elements and various dietary and other factors, can be attempted. The strength of these relationships is tested using one-way analysis of variance, after conducting F-tests for homogeneity of variances. Additional methodological details are discussed below.

Statistical methods and preliminary test results

As discussed above, the analytical framework chosen for the present study is operative only if the data are, or can be made, normally distributed. Normality of the raw trace element frequencies was tested using two different methods. First, partial tests of normality were conducted by calculating Student's *t*-statistics for skew and kurtosis values (from formulae in Sokal and Rohlf 1969) generated by the FREQUENCIES procedure in SPSS, Release 7 (Nie *et al.* 1975) as implemented on a CDC Cyber 760 computer. The null hypotheses for these partial tests of normality were that the calculated values for skew and kurtosis did not depart significantly (at p less than or equal to 0.05) from the hypothetical normal values of zero. The second method for testing normality involved comparison of the observed distributions, rather than their deviations, to a series of model distributions. The models deemed appropriate were the normal and Poisson distributions, and goodness-of-fit was assessed using Kolmogorov-Smirnov (K-S) one-sample tests available in the SPSS NPAR TESTS procedure. In this case, the null hypothesis was one of no significant difference between the observed and model distributions.

It is important to note that, contrary to standard statistical procedure, we wished to accept the null hypothesis of no difference in the K-S tests of distribution. Because statistical tests are constructed with a bias making rejection of the null hypothesis difficult, we had to re-evaluate the significance levels appropriate for assessing goodness-of-fit under the second method. In order to make the tests of distribution more conservative, rejection of the null hypothesis was made easier by relaxing the significance level. A value of p of less than or equal to 0.20 was selected in an attempt to reduce the probability of accepting the null hypothesis when it was false. Of course, this step also increased the probability of type I errors, but in doing so reversed some of the bias in the hypothesis-testing statistic.

The results of both the partial and the distributional tests for normality are presented in Table 7.10. Student's *t*-tests significant at p less than or equal to 0.05 and K-S tests significant at p less than or equal to 0.20 are indicated by asterisks. The results of the *t*- and K-S tests will be compared and used collaboratively, for while the K-S test is a more complete test of distribution, it is a less powerful test of difference than is Student's *t*. From Table 7.10, while Na, Ca, Zn, Sr, K, and Al all appear to be normally distributed under the K-S tests, the partial tests of normality indicate that only Na and Ca possess values of skew and kurtosis which do not depart significantly from zero. In the cases of Pb, Mg, Fe, Mn, Ba, V, and $\delta^{13}C$, on the other hand, both the K-S and *t*-tests indicate deviations from normality. Of these, Pb appears to have a

Table 7.10 *Descriptive statistics for single elements*

	min.	max.	mean	s.d.	skew	kurtosis	normal	Poisson
Na	2525	6310	4798	1021.43	−0.453	−0.762	0.831	3.253*
Ca	337	366	351	7.19	0.146	−0.801	0.866	1.799*
Mg	2222	7698	3402	1053.30	2.356	6.954	1.469	3.742*
Zn	106	419	200	82.36	1.031*	0.234	1.037	3.410*
Sr	104	328	174	50.86	1.408*	1.966*	1.056	2.811*
Cd	24	45	34	4.55	0.765*	0.386	0.950	0.971
Pb	120	188	138	11.57	1.833*	6.281*	1.116*	0.995
K	57	237	101	33.12	1.615*	4.496*	1.037	2.368*
Al	60	342	133	57.91	1.708*	3.791*	0.894	2.929*
Fe	65	417	153	64.44	1.963*	5.245*	1.435*	2.969*
Mn	16	498	138	104.36	1.636*	3.159*	1.133*	3.307*
Ba	72	499	220	99.19	1.205*	1.044	1.118*	3.450*
Cu	38	78	54	9.89	0.769*	0.071	0.867	0.949
V	13	374	110	77.68	1.539*	2.836*	1.092*	3.544*
$\delta^{13}C$	−22	−11	−18	3.04	0.846*	−0.722	1.670*	—

* Values significant at 0.05 (Student's *t*) and at 0.20 (Kolmogorov-Smirnov test).

Poisson distribution. The normality tests also indicate interesting features in the cases of Cd and Cu. These two elements show significant skew under the *t*-test, and fit both the normal and Poisson distributions under the K-S tests.

In summary, the results of the tests for normality suggest that thirteen of the fifteen variables considered are not normally distributed, and thus require transformation before analysis can proceed. To determine what forms the transformations should take, we return to Table 7.10, and consider the directions of skew and kurtosis. Since most of the variables exhibit positive skew, and do not approximate Poisson distributions, log-normal transformations are appropriate. These transformations are applied across the entire data set for reasons discussed previously. Before the log transformations are applied, however, it is wise to eliminate decimal fractions, and it is necessary to eliminate negative values. For these reasons, the Ca, Cd, Pb, and V values are multiplied by a constant of 10, and the $\delta^{13}C$ values (which are reported as a ratio to carbon-12, divided by a standard ratio minus one – see Chapter 2, p. 12) are increased by a constant of 100 and then multiplied by a constant of 10. After this step, transformation of all the variables is accomplished by taking the Naperian logarithm of each value.

After attempting to log-normalize all variables, it is necessary to re-test the element distributions for normality. The same tests of normality

Table 7.11 *Descriptive statistics for transformed elements*

	min.	max.	mean	s.d.	skew	kurtosis	normal
Na	7.83	8.75	8.45	0.233	−0.847*	0.022	0.976
Ca	5.82	5.90	5.86	0.020	0.110	−0.813	0.855
Mg	7.71	8.95	8.10	0.256	1.289*	2.520*	0.990
Zn	4.66	6.04	5.22	0.382	0.451	−0.811	0.640
Sr	4.64	5.79	5.12	0.265	0.780*	0.355	0.764
Cd	3.18	3.81	3.50	0.132	0.404	0.190	0.809
Pb	4.79	5.24	4.92	0.079	1.340*	4.070*	0.975
K	4.04	5.47	4.57	0.297	0.488	0.433	0.696
Al	4.09	5.84	4.81	0.385	0.483	0.224	0.379
Fe	4.17	6.03	4.96	0.365	0.547	0.979	0.864
Mn	2.77	6.21	4.64	0.798	−0.383	−0.284	0.879
Ba	4.28	6.21	5.30	0.422	0.234	−0.133	0.576
Cu	3.64	4.36	3.96	0.178	0.395	−0.402	0.622
V	2.56	5.92	4.46	0.712	−0.239	−0.023	0.555
$\delta^{13}C$	6.66	6.77	6.71	0.037	0.815*	−0.780	1.656

* Values significant at 0.05 (Student's *t*) and at 0.20 (Kolmogorov-Smirnov test)

as used on the original data are applied to the transformed data, except for comparisons to the Poisson model under the K-S tests of distribution. The results of both partial and distributional tests for normality of the transformed data are presented in Table 7.11. As can be seen from this table, all transformed elements approximate normality under the K-S tests, with probabilities for the null hypothesis ranging from about 0.28 to almost 1.00. Under the *t*-tests for skew and kurtosis, on the other hand, a few variables still exhibit significant values at p less than or equal to 0.05. Na exhibits negative skew, Sr is still positively skewed, and Mg and Pb remain both positively skewed and leptokurtotic. The values for skew and kurtosis among these transformed elements are, however, much lower than the original values; in fact, a significant value of negative skew for Na is a new event. Given these trends under the partial tests of normality, and the findings under the distributional tests, we conclude that the transformed variables can be considered approximately normally distributed, and that the parametric form of analysis suggested earlier is, therefore, appropriate.

In order to discover the kinds and directions of inter-element relationships, principal components analysis was conducted on the simple correlation matrix for the transformed data. The analysis was accomplished using the FACTOR procedure in SPSS, in which principal factoring was performed without iteration on the unmodified correlation matrix, and the resulting loadings matrix was rotated using the varimax method. Retention of components was based on the form of scree diagrams of the component eigenvalues, rather than on Kaiser's rule, because of the number of eigenvalues close to, but less than, one. As a result, seven components were retained in the rotated loadings matrices and were used in the calculation of principal component scores for each of the variables. These scores were requested as output, as were the variable communality estimates and both the initial and rotated component loadings matrices. In the end, two principal components analyses were run, one on the entire transformed data set and the other using a reduced set of variables. The reasons for reducing the number of variables and the results of both principal components analyses are presented in the following section.

The second part of the analysis involved using one-way analyses of variance to test for dietary and other differences. The independent variables for these analyses were sex, age, site, and time period. Sex and age were hypothesized as likely dimensions along which metabolic and structural variability in element concentrations might travel. Site provided a dimension for variability in contamination and diagenesis, and time was seen as a likely dimension for dietary differences. The dependent variables in each of the analyses of variance were the principal component scores calculated from the second, reduced-variable, loadings matrix. Principal component scores were used in place of the original variables because they were considered more informative. As composite measures of various variables and their interrelationships, the scores might represent the synergisms and antagonisms which were otherwise not accounted for in the analyses.

The analyses of variance were conducted using the ONE-WAY procedure in SPSS, with a null hypothesis of no difference between subgroups, and a significance level of p less than or equal to 0.10. Applicability of each analysis of variance was assessed using an F-test for homogeneity of variances (from formulae in Sokal and Rohlf 1969) with a significance level of p less than or equal to 0.05. The F-test for homogeneity of variances was selected over Cochran's C and Bartlett–Box F, because the latter statistics are highly sensitive to any deviations from normality and our data may not be completely normalized. The results of the one-way analyses of variance are discussed below.

RESULTS

The results of the principal components analyses are presented in Tables 7.12 to 7.14. Table 7.12, the simple correlation matrix for all transformed variables, depicts the basic relationships upon which components will be defined. It is, therefore, informative to examine the correlation matrix before considering the component matrices. The features of interest in the correlation matrix are (1) the relative independence of Ca, Pb, and $\delta^{13}C$, (2) the intercorrelation of K, Al, Fe, and Mn, and (3) the correlation of one element with a small cluster of others as in the case of Na with Mg and V, of Sr with Mg, Ba, and Ca, and of Zn with Cd and Cu. These and all other asterisked correlation coefficients are significant at p less than or equal to 0.05. The features of interest are discussed in more detail below.

The lack of correlations between Ca and other elements may be due to the fact that Ca, as a major component of bone mineral, is large in amount and varies within narrower physiological limits than do the other elements in the matrix, which are considered trace elements. Additionally, Ca deficiencies and excesses which find their way to bone create recognizable pathologies, and pathologic individuals have been excluded from the present sample. The relative independence of Pb, on the other hand, appears to be due to the way in which Pb is incorporated into bone. Pb is an environmental contaminant which does not "naturally" occur in foods like the other trace elements studied. In the case of $\delta^{13}C$, explanation is not as simple. As a demonstrated dietary indicator (van der Merwe 1978, 1982, van der Merwe and Vogel 1978; see also Klepinger, 1984 for examples), $\delta^{13}C$ should correlate with certain trace elements. There are problems, however, with the way in which $\delta^{13}C$ values are reported which may be obscuring such relationships. $\delta^{13}C$ values are reported as ratios of ratios. Recalling our previous discussion of ratios, it is apparent that treating $\delta^{13}C$ values in this way may re-scale the variable so that its variability in distribution is not comparable to that of trace elements.

The intercorrelation of K, Al, Fe, and Mn is interesting in light of previous findings for these elements. Lambert *et al.* (1979, 1985a) found that these elements were positively associated and suggested that this association was due to their co-occurrence as major soil components. They also found K to be negatively correlated with these elements, a finding not paralleled by the present study. Treating these

Table 7.12 *Simple correlation matrix*

	Na	Ca	Mg	Zn	Sr	Cd	Pb	K	Al	Fe	Mn	Ba	Cu	V
Ca	−.003													
Mg	.481*	.189												
Zn	.189	−.099	.005											
Sr	−.147	−.052	.345*	−.037										
Cd	.043	−.061	−.259	.398*	−.015									
Pb	.202	.194	.162	.004	.134	.017								
K	.110	.155	.147	.466*	−.027	.233	.067							
Al	−.197	−.066	−.455*	.369*	−.168	.561*	−.037	.362*						
Fe	−.121	−.052	−.310*	.585*	−.153	.428*	−.088	.323*	.715*					
Mn	−.066	−.094	−.314*	.625*	−.068	.512*	−.071	.258	.519*	.674*				
Ba	−.490*	.022	−.125	−.072	.436*	.152	−.095	−.007	.042	.053	.041			
Cu	−.156	.140	.180	.324*	.334*	.092	.132	.327*	.114	.034	.111	−.016		
V	−.438*	−.127	−.414*	.105	.178	.188	−.132	−.096	.264	.215	.252	.093	.188	
$\delta^{13}C$	.054	.126	−189	.177	−.107	−.037	.044	−.160	−.152	.011	.173	.041	−.095	.101

elements as a contaminatory unit is further supported by the facts that they do not similarly co-occur in foods, and that they do not play interchangeable roles in bone metabolism or structure. Certain of these intercorrelated elements are, however, also correlated with Zn, Cd, and Cu. The latter three elements form their own correlated unit (which is discussed below), and are rarer and more variable in soils than are K, Al, Fe, or Mn. For these reasons, we believe that either Zn, Cd, or Cu simply shares a similar range of variability with the major soil component elements, and that the other two elements out of that set of three are correlated with the soil elements as a consequence of their correlation with Zn, Cd, or Cu.

The correlations of one element with small clusters of others are more interpretable in terms of presumed dietary, bone-structural, metabolic, and diagenetic relations than were the elements discussed above. Na, Mg, and V are intercorrelated, with V being negatively related to both Na and Mg. The sodium–magnesium relationship makes sense in terms of the similar roles they play in organic salts, but the place of V in this relationship is unclear. Sr is positively correlated with Mg, Ba, and Cu. We expect associations between Sr, Ba, and Mn given the similar reduction of these elements in terrestrial food chains (Elias *et al.* 1982, Ericson *et al.* 1979). The Sr–Cu association is, however, problematic. Zn is positively correlated with Cd and Cu. These associations make sense in terms of the co-occurrence of these elements in various meats and nuts, and the synergism expected between Zn and Cd. We would expect a reversed relationship between Zn and Cu, however, in view of their known antagonism.

Having considered the simple correlation matrix, we can now turn to the principal component analyses and determine which relationships are clarified or reduced to unimportant by this technique. Table 7.13 lists the eigenvalues for and proportion of variance explained by each component in the original and reduced-variable analyses. The cut-off points for components included in the loadings matrices and score calculations are indicated by arrows. The resulting loadings matrices for the original analysis are listed in Table 7.14. Comparison of loadings between the initial and rotated matrices in this table indicates that rotation tends to increase high loadings, whether positive or negative, and to reduce the values of intermediate loadings. Since rotation simply clarifies, rather than changes, the relationships depicted in the initial

Table 7.13 *Summary of component eigenvalues for both analyses*

Analysis of all elements				Analysis excluding K,Al,Fe, and Mn			
Factor	Eigenvalue	% Variance	Cumulative %	Factor	Eigenvalue	% Variance	Cumulative %
1	3.75340	25.0	25.0	1	2.24924	20.4	20.4
2	2.23971	14.9	40.0	2	1.78944	16.3	36.7
3	1.87656	12.5	52.5	3	1.61816	14.7	51.4
4	1.24302	8.3	60.8	4	1.21746	11.1	62.5
5	1.12862	7.5	68.3	5	1.00423	9.1	71.6
6	1.02776	6.9	75.1	6	0.90040	8.2	79.8
7	0.93123	6.2	81.3	7	0.84709	7.7	87.5
►				►			
8	0.63548	4.2	85.6	8	0.58201	5.3	92.8
9	0.57037	3.8	89.4	9	0.38927	3.5	96.3
10	0.46498	3.1	92.5	10	0.21698	2.0	98.3
11	0.37022	2.5	94.9	11	0.18572	1.7	100.0
12	0.29687	2.0	96.9				
13	0.20764	1.4	98.3				
14	0.16790	1.1	99.4				
15	0.08623	0.6	100.0				

Table 7.14 *Component loadings matrices for all elements*

	Initial matrix							Rotated matrix						
	PC1	PC2	PC3	PC4	PC5	PC6	PC7	PC1	PC2	PC3	PC4	PC5	PC6	PC7
Na	−.231	.748	−.346	.006	.295	.135	.120	.040	.781	−.076	−.382	.121	−.162	.218
Ca	−.125	.231	.182	.496	−.670	.022	−.176	−.097	.043	.089	.017	.130	.875	.162
Mg	−.494	.623	.352	−.114	.160	.110	−.146	−.309	.761	.352	.115	−.104	.051	.052
Zn	.675	.467	.062	.106	.321	−.031	−.196	.735	.236	.390	−.019	.228	−.087	−.115
Sr	−.119	−.085	.822	−.017	.342	.172	.126	−.150	.074	.471	.717	−.038	−.239	.193
Cd	.675	.097	.026	−.038	.041	.288	.298	.732	−.053	−.083	.158	−.068	−.115	.231
Pb	−.118	.364	.190	.369	−.160	.026	.735	−.011	.127	.086	−.025	.023	.146	.916
K	.422	.548	.248	−.138	−.279	−.005	−.257	.503	.290	.360	−.039	−.262	.391	−.123
Al	.841	−.006	−.067	−.192	−.280	.004	.179	.798	−.338	−.049	−.080	−.303	.081	.045
Fe	.855	.088	−.112	−.040	−.075	.099	−.047	.852	−.160	−.017	−.047	−.025	.054	−.111
Mn	.809	.093	−.068	.174	.215	.093	−.052	.805	−.103	.093	.005	.272	−.099	−.071
Ba	.121	−.468	.520	.047	−.067	.620	−.131	.083	−.170	−127	.913	.019	.118	−.109
Cu	.211	.259	.660	.082	.009	−.508	−.074	.094	−.087	.876	.031	−.085	.139	.082
V	.413	−.507	.208	.148	.195	−.463	.127	.144	−.727	.347	.026	.151	−.262	.012
$\delta^{13}C$	.039	−.110	.226	.847	.261	.090	−.194	.024	−.069	−.086	−.011	.933	.112	.024

matrix, the rotated matrix values will be used in the remaining discussion.

As can be seen from Table 7.14 (and summarized in Table 7.18), most of the relationships seen in the simple correlation matrix are maintained in the rotated loadings matrix. The fifth to seventh components are single-element factors, reflecting the relative independence of $\delta^{13}C$, Ca, and Pb, respectively. The fourth component represents the association between Sr and Ba as replacers of Ca and dietary co-occurents. The third component is another single-element factor, unexpectedly isolating Cu as varying independently of the other elements. The second component focuses on the "vegetable salts" relationship between Na and Mg and the negative role of V in this relationship. The first component contains the largest grouping of elements and reflects the soil component element associations along with the zinc–cadmium co-occurrence and synergism. These components incorporate all variables except K, and account for approximately 81% of the variance in element frequencies (see Table 7.13).

Given that the first component accounts for 25% of the variance in element frequencies, and that the elements loading high on this component have previously been implicated as contaminants, we decided to eliminate Al, Fe, and Mn and to re-analyse the remaining elements for principal components. K was also eliminated on the grounds that it lacked high loadings on any retained component. The loadings matrices resulting from the revised analysis are listed in Table 7.15. As can be seen in Table 7.13, the revised retained components account for close to 88% of the variance in element frequencies. Elimination of K, Al, Fe, and Mn from the analysis, therefore, appears not to have adversely affected factoring among the non-contaminant elements.

Turning again to Table 7.15 (summarized in Table 7.18) and focusing on the rotated loadings matrix for reasons mentioned above, we see the same relationships as indicated in the original analysis, but with some changes in order of importance. The third and fifth to seventh components are still single-element factors for Cu, $\delta^{13}C$, Ca, and Pb, respectively. The fourth component, however, is now a zinc–cadmium co-occurrence and synergism factor, and the strontium–barium relationship is accounted for by the second, rather than fourth, component. The Na, Mg, and V interrelationships now fall under the first component. The distribution and form of weak, but present, relationships,

Table 7.15 *Component loadings matrices for non-contaminants*

	Initial matrix							Rotated matrix						
	PC1	PC2	PC3	PC4	PC5	PC6	PC7	PC1	PC2	PC3	PC4	PC5	PC6	PC7
Na	−.801	−.077	.355	−.110	.205	.158	.060	.771	−.385	−.082	.172	.138	−.154	.185
Ca	−.220	.228	−.120	.707	−.095	−.378	−.389	.087	.003	.113	−.067	.090	.934	.113
Mg	−.680	.552	−.116	−.168	.042	.169	−.182	.822	.130	.333	−.224	−.112	.056	.057
Zn	.057	.156	.837	−.057	.075	.146	−.226	.130	−.143	.422	.711	.240	−.119	−.130
Sr	.119	.808	−.202	−.145	.177	.273	.153	.123	.745	.455	−.136	−.045	−.223	.192
Cd	.318	.034	.649	−.073	.419	−.399	.011	−.151	.106	−.056	.898	−.111	−.007	.093
Pb	−.327	.339	.121	.414	.078	−.218	.700	.114	−.015	.060	.022	.030	.111	.960
Ba	.562	.344	−.331	.064	.581	−.032	−.157	−.190	.902	−.143	121	.028	.115	−.114
Cu	.129	.678	.341	.060	−.471	−.013	−.141	−.069	.040	.882	.118	−.103	.159	.062
V	.712	.044	.187	.064	−.362	.171	.219	−.737	.041	.363	.050	.138	−.241	.003
$\delta^{13}C$	.080	−.277	.161	.681	.204	.609	−.036	−.080	.001	−.079	.004	.969	.088	.032

as indicated by intermediate loadings, differ markedly from the original analysis. From the rotated matrix in Table 7.15, we see that Na bears a weak and negative relationship to Sr and Ba in the second component, and that Mg, Zn, Sr, and V bear weak positive relationships to Cu in the third component.

The inverse relationship of Na to the Ca replacement ions is perhaps explicable by a diagenetic model for coupled substitution of [Na^+ & CO_3^{2-}] for [Ca^{++} & PO_4^{3-}] (Chickerur *et al.* 1980, Legeros and Tung 1983, Sillen, this volume). The relationships of the various elements to Cu, on the other hand, reflect known antagonisms and dietary co-occurrences. Zn is directly antagonstic with Cu, and is indirectly related, along with V, through antagonisms of Fe or chromium with Cu. The positive signs on the loadings suggest that the indirect relationships are figuring more heavily than the direct antagonism. Sr and Mg tend to occur in relatively high frequencies in vegetable foods, whereas Cu tends to be higher in meats. The observed positive associations between these three elements are expected for non-agricultural, or specifically non-maize, diets when other physiological, contaminatory, and diagenetic factors are held constant.

The principal components analyses thus illustrate patterns of contamination, synergisms/antagonisms, dietary co-occurences, and independence of element variability. They do not, however, provide much information on dietary and diagenetic differences between the subsamples studied. These differences can only be discovered through analyses of variance, which constitute the second part of the present analysis. The analyses of variance are conducted on the principal component scores for reasons discussed previously. The results of the analyses of variance are presented in Table 7.16. Values of the ANOVA F-test significant at p less than or equal to 0.10 and of the homogeneity of variances F-test significant at p less than or equal to 0.05 are indicated by asterisks. The subsample sizes for each analysis are listed beneath each independent variable.

As can be seen from Table 7.16, the scores for component 7 are significantly different (at p less than or equal to 0.10) both between the sexes and between age groups. Together with the mean scores and loadings signs, this suggests that males have greater access to and/or metabolic accumulation of Pb, and that the concentration of Pb in bone is generally age-accumulative. It is important to note, however, that the homogeneity of variances F is significant (at p less than or equal to 0.05)

Table 7.16 ANOVAs *of principal component scores*

	Sex		homog.	diff.	Age			homog.	diff.	Site			homog.	diff.	Time		homog.	diff.
	male	female	F	F	young	middle	old	F	F	Gibson	Helton	Ledders	F	F	M.W.	L.W.	F	F
PC1	.061	−.099	3.529	0.295	−.198	.023	.351	1.606	1.204	.343	.101	−.292	3.940*	1.539	.343	−.086	3.590	1.489
PC2	−.017	.028	1.597	0.023	−.065	.243	−.429	1.554	1.636	.053	.180	−.227	1.673	0.838	.053	−.013	1.612	0.035
PC3	−.103	.169	1.106	0.886	.034	−.006	−.057	1.262	0.031	.304	−.439	.325	2.645	3.902*	.304	−.076	1.442	1.161
PC4	−.201	.327	1.280	3.445*	−.116	.457	−.350	1.886	2.614*	−.247	.064	.059	1.407	0.371	−.247	.062	1.095	0.757
PC5	−.176	.288	1.019	2.624	.032	.259	−.385	2.580	1.429	−.838	.086	.347	13.695*	5.627*	−.838	.210	10.267*	10.486*
PC6	−.039	.062	1.414	0.116	−.118	.029	.189	1.688	0.369	.032	.362	−.417	1.394	3.329*	.032	−.008	1.042	0.012
PC7	.222	−.362	2.929	4.292*	−.144	−.228	.561	5.703*	2.689*	.442	−.166	−.049	2.456	1.308	.442	−.111	1.076	2.522
N=	31	19			23	15	12			10	21	19			10	40		

M.W. Middle Woodland
L.W. Late Woodland

for the Pb component by age ANOVA. This means that the within age-group variances are heterogeneous and that the ANOVA *F*-value is thus questionable. Given the asymmetry of subsamples by age and sex, it is possible that the heterogeneity of variances for Pb by age is due to the interrelationship between Pb concentration and sex. The component 4 scores also differ significantly by both sex and age, though here there is homogeneity of variances. Pulling together the ANOVAs, mean scores, and loadings signs in this case, the zinc–cadmium synergism and co-occurrence is manifested more strongly in females than in males, and more in middle-aged adults than in young or old individuals.

The remaining significant differences in principal component scores between subgroups involve site and temporal unit comparisons. In three of these four cases, however, significant homogeneity of variance *F*-values preclude interpretation of the analyses of variance. The three cases of heterogeneous variances between subgroups are the component 5 by site and by time comparisons, and the component 1 by site comparison. This last comparison shows that Na, Mg, and/or V differ in their range of variability by site, and thus suggests that contaminatory factors have not been completely removed from the analysis. Given the unexplainable relationship of Na to Sr and Ba in the second component, Na may in fact be acting as a contaminant. The component 5 comparisons show that the range of variability in $\delta^{13}C$ values differs by site and by time. The differences in variability for $\delta^{13}C$ may be due to problems in measurement or to narrowing of the resource utilization pattern seen through time, or both. The significant ANOVAs for which heterogeneity of variances is not a problem are the component 3 and 6 by site comparisons. The presence of significant *F*-values for difference in the Cu and the Ca components across sites suggests differences in the diagenesis of these two elements.

In summary, the results of the analyses of variance indicate physiological differences in Pb and Zn–Cd accumulation, and diagenetic differences in Cu and Ca. General dietary differences between temporal groups are not easily discernible, unless heterogeneity of variances and large asymmetries in sample size are disregarded. The presence of heterogeneity of variances in the "vegetable salts," $\delta^{13}C$, and Pb component comparisons does, however, raise two important issues. First, in assigning independent variables on which to conduct analyses of variance, care should be taken so that these variables are also independent of each other. With bone metabolism, age and sex would

Table 7.17 *Principal component scores for Helton individuals by temporal sub-unit*

	burial	sex	age	PC1	PC2	PC3	PC4	PC5	PC6	PC7
Early	HN47–9	f	y	0.533	−0.259	−0.743	−0.367	0.206	−0.366	−0.455
	HN47–16	f	m	1.016	−0.041	−1.302	0.978	1.190	1.647	−0.077
	HN47–20	m	y	0.035	0.057	−0.448	−0.759	1.365	0.134	1.211
	HN47–25	m	m	0.422	1.472	−0.657	0.121	0.814	0.155	−1.503
	HN47–26	m	o	−0.234	−0.205	−1.075	0.374	−0.129	−0.664	−0.090
	HN47–38	f	y	0.590	0.477	−0.114	1.896	−1.106	0.914	0.227
	HN47–44–1	f	m	0.584	−0.148	−0.254	−0.173	−0.974	0.595	−1.052
	HN47–54	f	m	0.403	0.395	0.372	0.393	−0.766	0.171	−1.076
	HN47–60	f	o	−0.183	0.798	1.613	0.835	−0.894	1.597	−0.805
	HN47–61	m	m	−0.783	1.664	−0.140	−0.231	−1.183	−0.265	0.632
	mean			0.240	0.421	−0.275	0.307	0.148	0.392	−0.299
	s.d.			0.526	0.693	0.824	0.775	0.985	0.791	0.884
Middle	HN47–6	m	y	−0.199	−0.034	−0.530	−0.053	−0.271	0.687	−0.582
	HN47–13	f	m	−0.231	0.389	−0.008	1.198	1.981	−1.080	0.271
	HN47–33	m	m	−0.948	0.685	−1.569	1.629	−0.767	−0.270	−0.222
	HN47–37	m	o	−0.169	−1.177	0.125	0.121	−0.601	−1.235	0.054
	HN47–47	m	y	0.980	1.429	−1.590	0.242	−0.701	−0.144	0.451
	HNV2–3–1	m	y	−0.116	1.609	−1.066	−1.075	2.272	0.381	−0.453
	mean			−0.114	0.500	−0.773	0.344	0.319	−0.277	−0.080
	s.d.			0.619	1.022	0.753	0.960	1.414	0.767	0.408
Late	HN47–51–1	m	o	1.767	−2.010	−0.317	−1.347	−0.052	0.948	−0.600
	HNV2–3–2	f	y	−0.507	−0.931	−0.234	−0.957	1.628	2.088	−1.006
	HNS2–6	m	m	1.262	−0.923	−0.430	0.630	1.721	0.147	1.302
	HNV10–1	m	y	−1.238	−0.075	−0.633	−0.877	−1.008	−0.379	0.909
	HNV10–3	m	y	−0.887	0.509	−0.219	−1.228	−0.930	2.562	−0.634
	mean			0.079	−0.686	−0.367	−0.756	0.272	1.071	−0.006
	s.d.			1.347	0.958	0.171	0.798	1.335	1.250	1.036

seem to act simultaneously and collaboratively. Secondly, site and temporal assignments should produce equivalent cell sizes and should be carefully considered relative to one another, so that contaminant and diagenetic differences can be identified and eliminated. In order to detect dietary shifts, then, samples from single multi-component sites appear most useful. Data in this form and in appropriate amounts have generally been difficult to obtain. The present study includes data in this form, but examination of this subset of data for dietary shifts was not fruitful. While the Helton sample could be divided into early, middle, and late clusters on the basis of stratigraphy and ceramic typology, and while mean principal component scores did differ between the temporal subgroups, the ranges of the scores overlapped completely. These data are presented in Table 7.17 for all individuals sampled from Helton. Thus, assessing the utility of single multi-component site comparisons as a control for differences in diagenesis and contamination under a multivariate multi-element approach remains an important but as yet unrealized goal.

SUMMARY AND CONCLUSIONS

In this paper we have presented a multivariate approach to the investigation of multiple trace elements in archaeological contexts. Our review of previous multi-element studies suggested that a multivariate approach would be advantageous, allowing us to consider simultaneously several probable causative factors, such as diet, diagenesis, metabolic antagonisms, age, and sex. Through principal components analysis, following transformation of our data, we confirm the results of several previous studies (Lambert *et al.* 1979, 1980, 1981, 1982, 1983, 1984, 1985a,b) that indicate Al, Fe, and Mn are strongly affected by diagenesis. The positive loadings for all three indicate that they are behaving similarly, defining this cluster as an enrichment factor. A number of other patterns emerge that are likely due to dietary, metabolic, or lifetime exposure factors. These are summarized in terms of the principal components rotated loadings matrices in Table 7.18.

Ca and $\delta^{13}C$ values form independent units of variation, probably due to metabolic buffering in the case of the former, and as yet unresolved computational issues in the latter. Independent variation of Pb, on the other hand, is attributable to its invasive or non-nutritive nature. Sr and Ba co-occur for metabolic and dietary reasons. Na figures

Table 7.18 *Summary of component loadings for both analyses (based on rotated matrices after Kaiser normalization)*

	For all elements	
Component	Elements (highest first)	Interpretation
1	Fe, Mn, Al, Zn, Cd	co-occurrence as soil contaminants, with direct association to Zn–Cd
2	Na, Mg, V(−)	co-occurrence in vegetable foods, possibly as salts; opposite to V, perhaps due to V's association with oils (veg/animal)
3	Cu	variability independent of other elements
4	Ba, Sr	co-occurrence as replacement ions for Ca
5	$\delta^{13}C$	variability independent of other elements
6	Ca	variability independent of other elements
7	Pb	variability independent of other elements

		Excluding soil contaminants (K, Al, Fe, Mn)	
Component	Elements	Internal loadings	Interpretation
1	Mg, Na, V(−)	none	co-occurrence in vegetable foods, possibly as salts; opposite to V, perhaps due to V's association with oils (veg./animal)
2	Ba, Sr	Na(−)	co-occurrence as replacement ions for Ca; negative association with Na problematic
3	Cu	Sr, Zn, V, Mg	large portion of variability independent of other elements; some indication of co-occurrence with Zn and perhaps V in meats/fat; indirect antagonisms with Sr and Mg via Fe
4	Zn, Cd	none	co-occurrence in meats, metabolic-ionic synergism, possible contaminant association
5	$\delta^{13}C$	none	variability independent of other elements
6	Ca	none	variability independent of other elements
7	Pb	none	variability independent of other elements

into the Sr–Ba relationship as a negative factor, perhaps due to diagenetic processes. Metabolic relationships also likely explain the interactions of Cu with Zn and V, though the direct effect of metabolic antagonisms is not evident. The relationship taken into account by the components loadings requires Fe as an intermediary for these antagonisms. Interaction of Cu with Zn and V further appears to involve the parallel dietary levels of these elements, particularly their relative importance in meat. Cd and Zn may also co-vary due to their relative importance in meat, though metabolic or dietary explanations are suggested by the difference between the sexes. Na and Mg present a complementary vegetable component; the negative interaction of V with these elements is perhaps due to dietary factors.

The observed patterning of elements matches our expectations and previous findings. Several expected relationships, however, do not appear through our analyses. First, while the component loadings reflect parallels in relative element concentrations in animal versus vegetable foods, they do not indicate any division between essential versus non-essential elements. For example, associations of Ba with essential alkaline earths and trace metals (found by Schroeder 1973), and co-occurrence of Cd with Pb as non-essential dietary invasions are lacking. Secondly, we isolated no differences in element concentrations attributable to differences in distribution between bone collagen and mineral. This may result from inadequate controls for obtaining collagen versus apatite values, or from a real lack of differences, suggesting that diagenesis has not significantly affected the collagen fraction of these bones. Asymmetric depletion of bone collagen across the sample should appear as a relative reduction in element levels, particularly Cu, V, and Fe, thus forming an indirect measure of diagenesis. Thirdly, although we found age/sex differences in the metabolism of Zn–Cd and Pb, our analyses did not uncover indications of differential buffering, accumulation, or loss in the cases of Ba and Al. Whether these indications are not to be expected, or are hidden by peculiarities of the data set is unclear. The fact that the sample chosen for study represents a period of dietary transition suggests that overall dietary changes may be taking precedence over indications of buffering in the observed element associations. Finally, the initial attempt to integrate carbon isotope values with trace element analysis was unsuccessful, likely due to matters mathematical and perhaps affected also by the small size of the available sample. A larger number of individuals would, no doubt, have provided increased evidence of changing patterns through time, culminating in a richer perspective on diet in ancient human groups, while simultaneously examining related issues of diagenesis and metabolic effects.

Numerous methodological issues have been raised in the course of this study, including the need for large samples, and the testing of distributions of element values for normality. Appropriate transformations are relatively simple to accomplish and allow a much greater range of statistical treatments. In addition, we have emphasized the inevitability of diagenesis, which must be seriously considered in all studies of this type. The multivariate techniques used here provide not only a demonstration of diagenetic effects, but a means for quantifying them given appropriate controls for age, sex, and contamination differences. These methods also hold promise for discovering the relationship of rare earth elements to the more commonly analysed alkaline earths and trace metals. Most importantly, the multivariate approach promoted here can indicate dietary shifts, once the effects of diagenesis and contamination are quantified. A final recommendation for future research is the investigation of trace element values in non-Western resources.

8

Diagenesis of the inorganic phase of cortical bone

ANDREW SILLEN

Department of Archaeology
University of Cape Town
and
Department of Biochemistry
School of Dental Medicine
University of Pennsylvania

"Time the destroyer is time the preserver."

T. S. ELIOT: *The Dry Salvages*

Since calcified tissues are the product of metabolic processes, diet, disease, and other biological phenomena have an effect on their chemistry and structure. Because these effects are becoming increasingly well understood, it is possible to envision substantial gains in our knowledge of the biology and behavior of prehistoric peoples, based on the application of these relationships to prehistoric skeletons. Unfortunately, while calcified tissues may appear to be preserved in the form of fossils, much of the biological information contained in the living organ is at best obscured, at worst destroyed, as a result of diagenesis – the complex chemical changes which usually occur in these tissues after interment.

The potential paleodietary and paleoecological information offered by isotopic and trace-elemental analyses has stimulated research into both the process of diagenesis and the possible means for circumventing the problems caused by the diagenetic contamination of fossil mineral. The purpose of this paper, is, first, to summarize our knowledge of selected aspects of this process, and secondly, to comment on the likelihood of detecting a biological "signal" in certain diagenetically altered fossil mineral. The biological signals which reside in the mineral phase with which this discussion is concerned are (1) Sr/Ca, and (2) $\delta^{13}C$ in apatite. Finally, some implications of the data for future research will be presented.

Given space considerations, and the information which is covered in other papers in this volume, the ensuing discussion will be confined to changes occurring in the *inorganic* phase of bone. Even with this limitation, it is impossible to ignore diagenesis in the organic phase. As the two phases are inextricably linked in life, so the diagenetic modification of one is to some extent affected by that of the other. In this paper I shall discuss diagenesis of the organic phase only to the extent that it directly affects bone mineral.

Moreover, the discussion will concentrate on relatively old fossil mineral in which the vast majority of potential chemical change has already taken place. It is worth drawing attention to this fact at the outset since many researchers who have considered the extent of diagenesis have, in fact, been examining material of widely differing ages. While this observation does not account for *all* of the disparate conclusions (the stated focus of this volume is, after all, variability), it will be shown that the duration of interment is not only a critical variable in diagenesis, but also that diagenetic changes in a given environment may not bear a linear relationship to time. Therefore, conclusions (including those concerning the *process* of change) which might be drawn on the basis of the 20,000 B.P. or 2 my B.P. specimens discussed here will not necessarily be applicable to 500- or even 5000-year-old specimens.

Finally, this discussion will be limited to a particular calcified tissue, mammalian diaphyseal cortical bone. The type of calcified tissue, whether enamel, cortical bone, or cancellous bone, is, of course, another critical variable affecting both diagenesis and the conclusions that have been drawn about it. For example, due to its more open structure, cancellous bone has been shown to be more susceptible to diagenetic alteration than cortical bone (Lambert *et al.* 1982). Conflicting data exists on the suitability of enamel for trace element assays. In the past, it has been suggested that the relatively low porosity of enamel makes it less susceptible than bone to diagenetic change (Parker and Toots 1970, 1980). The high density and low porosity of enamel makes it an attractive candidate for minimal alteration; however, the relationship between trace elements in this tissue and the diet of the living animal is at present poorly understood and likely to be extremely complex (Sillen and Kavanagh 1982). Since early studies on Sr/Ca in fossil food-webs (Boaz and Hampel 1978, Parker and Toots 1980, Toots and Voorhies 1965) did not consider these complications, it is probably inappropriate to draw either positive or negative conclusions regarding the extent of diagenesis from them. While cortical bone is arguably more subject to diagenetic alteration than enamel, it does have the advantage of providing relatively unambiguous dietary information at the starting gate.[1]

While the nature and extent of diagenesis is likely to vary with time, tissue type, and, as we shall see, depositional environment, the possibilities will be limited by the biological template itself. Therefore the process of diagenesis will be discussed in the context of commonly measured properties of bone mineral. Next, known diagenetic changes which obscure biological signals will be presented.

BONE MINERAL AND THE DETECTION OF DIAGENESIS

Living, adult bone consists of about 70% inorganic mineral distributed through an organic matrix. While the exact composition of this mineral is the subject of continuing discussion, most agree that the bulk of it is a non-stoichiometric, carbonate-containing analog of the mineral hydroxyapatite (Posner 1985). (Stoichiometry is the interpretation of mass and energy relationships from chemical equations. Thus, a substance is non-stoichiometric when the determination of its constituent atoms by analytical techniques does not conform to the theoretical values which are to be expected from its chemical formula.)

The unit cell contents of stoichiometric hydroxyapatite are $(Ca)_{10}(PO_4)_6(OH)_2$ as shown in Fig. 8.1. Bone mineral differs from well-formed, stoichiometric apatite in a number of significant ways; much of diagenesis can be seen as a correction of this aberration. For example, bone mineral is generally described as having poor "crystallinity." Crystallinity is a term which connotes both large size and the absence of structural defects, qualities which tend to be found together (Jenkins 1978). Bone mineral crystals are quite small, on the order of 15–79 nm in their largest dimension (*c*-axis) and approximately 5 nm in thickness in their smallest (*a*-axis) (Jackson *et al.* 1978).

The crystallinity of biological and other apatites may be measured by

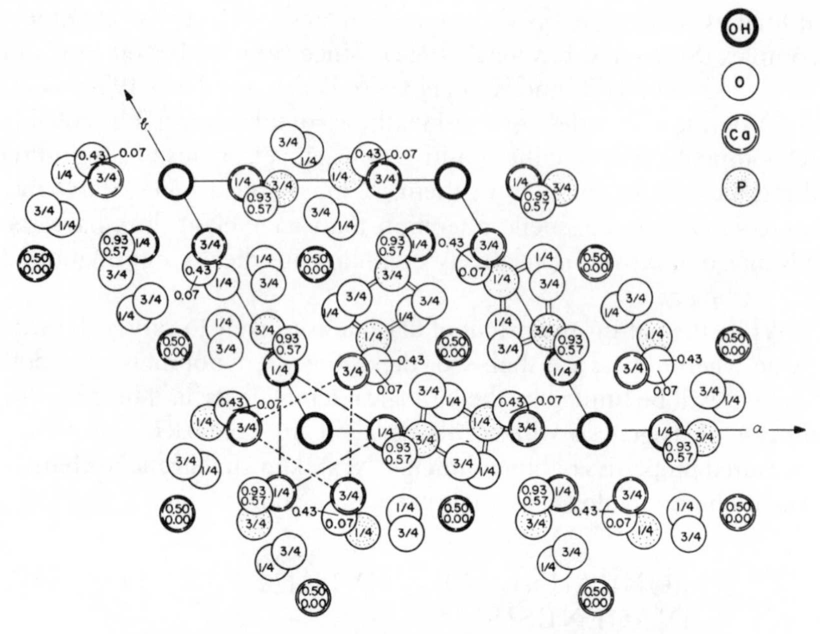

Fig. 8.1 Hydroxyapatite structure projected down the *c* axis on to the basal plane. The *a* and *b* axes, intersecting at 120°, are perpendicular to the *c* axis. These three axes make up the unit cell volume, which contains the formula $Ca_{10}(PO_4)_6(OH)_2$

both X-ray diffraction (XRD) and by infra-red absorption (IR). For the former, the width at half-maximum of the 002 reflection is the most commonly used measurement (Figs. 8.2 and 8.3). In Table 8.1, the crystallinity of some interred bones and fossils is presented.

Two important points emerge from the XRD data in Fig. 8.3 and Table 8.1. First, in many ancient specimens studied to date, only apatite may be identified in the mineral phase. To be sure, other crystal species, e.g. calcite, exist in ancient bones and fossils to varying degrees (Hassan, 1975, Hassan and Ortner 1977, Perinet 1957, 1975, Schoeninger 1982); however, they sometimes exist as minor inclusions which are below the detection limits of XRD (1–5%). For example, no evidence of calcite has been observed in XRD patterns of the Omo Shungura formation fossils examined so far. However, examination of the Ca/P and Ca/CO_3 ratios of highly soluble fractions of this mineral, discussed below, strongly suggests that minor calcite inclusions do exist.

The second observation is that apatite becomes *more* crystalline in the

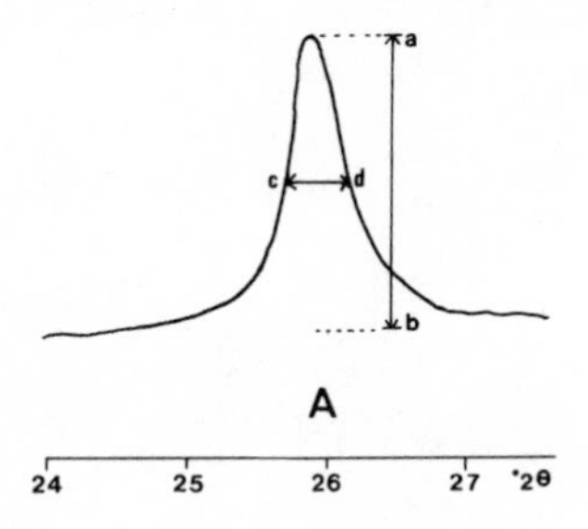

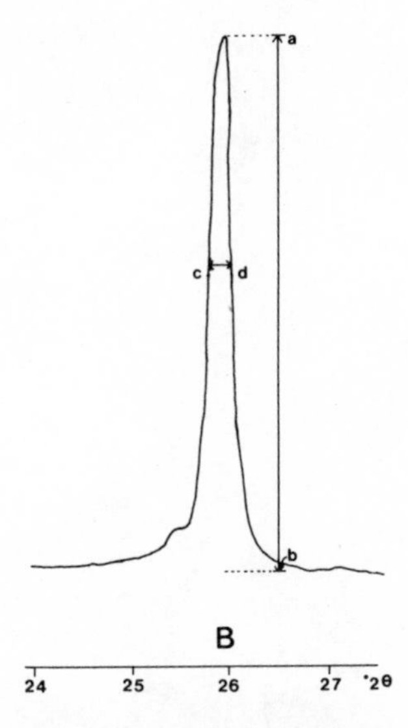

Fig. 8.2 Derivation of crystallinity measurement from 002 reflection with XRD. Crystallinity is measured by calculating the width (c–d) of the 002 reflection at half-maximum (a–b). Two examples are shown (A) poorly crystalline, deproteinized rabbit (modern), and (B) highly crystalline, heavily boiled synthetic hydroxyapatite. The width of the former is much greater.

course of fossilization. While rapid crystallization may certainly occur, this process does not necessarily manifest itself in the first few thousand years of interment. While Fig. 8.3 depicts increasingly sharp XRD patterns, it is clear from Table 8.1 that bones dating from approximately 1000 years ago are not yet affected by this phenomenon. A similar conclusion may be drawn from the X-ray studies reported by

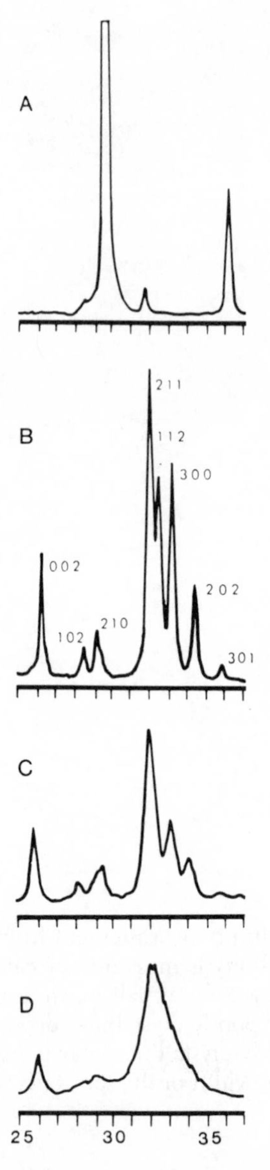

Fig. 8.3 XRD patterns of (A) calcite, (B) well-crystallized boiled hydroxyapatite, (C) Omo Shungura formation fossil cortical bone *Mesochoerus limnetes*, and (D) deproteinized rabbit cortical bone. The fossil mineral is dominantly apatite, with no evidence for calcite

Table 8.1 *Crystallinity of fresh and interred bone powders by XRD*

The values reported represent the width, in °2θ, of the 002 reflection at half-maximum. Sharper peaks are relatively narrow, therefore smaller numbers mean greater crystallinity.

Fresh sheep bone	.448
Deproteinized rabbit bone	.442
Fresh cow bone	.410[a]
Buried elephant bone (*ca.* 10 years old)	.390[a]
Dor human bone (*ca.* 1000 B.P.)	.450
Mammoth, Blackwater Draw (*ca.* 11,1000 B.P.)	.320[a]
Mastadon, Boney Springs (*ca.* 16,500 B.P.)	.350[a]
Homo, Hayonim Cave (*ca.* 20,000 B.P.)	.386
Suid, Omo River basin (*ca.* 1–3 million B.P.) (n=4)	.320 ± .03
Mineralogical fluorapatite	.176
Mineralogical fluorapatite	.190[a]
Boiled synthetic hydroxyapatite	.218

[a] Values from Hassan *et al.* 1977.

Schoeninger (1982). In this case, specimens from the Natufian levels of El Wad (*ca.* 10,000 B.P.) and from the Kebaran levels at Kebara (*ca.* 15,000 B.P.) showed little increase in crystallinity; however, bones from Qafseh (*ca.* 30–35,000 B.P.) were well crystallized.

The infra-red data appear to tell a similar story, although the available data are quite fragmentary. Crystallinity may be measured with IR by examining the splitting of the PO_4 anti-symmetric bending mode peak at wave numbers 550–600 (Blumenthal *et al.* 1975) (Fig. 8.4). Splitting of this peak does not occur in amorphous mineral, since the crystal field is symmetrical in three axes. In crystalline HAP (hydroxyapatite), however, the field (or long-range periodic order) is asymmetric. Because two axes (*a* and *b*) are equivalent and one (the *c*-axis) is different, the peak splits into two modes. The more crystalline the apatite, the greater the splitting of the peak. IR splitting modes also reveal an increase in crystallinity with time (Table 8.2). It is of interest that, as with XRD, crystallinity of apatite appears to increase only *after* some thousands of years of interment. Similar data were collected by Hassan (1975) who found little change in IR splitting modes, even in 10,000-year-old fauna.

In one other way, the difference between bone mineral and apatite diminishes with diagenesis. Bone mineral apatite differs significantly

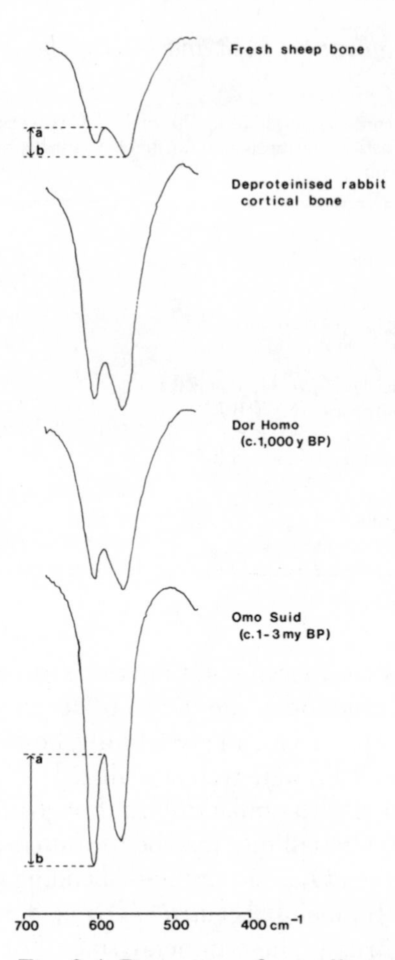

Fig. 8.4 Derivation of crystallinity measurement from IR spectra. Splitting of the PO_4 anti-symmetric bending mode peak at wave-numbers 550–600 cm^{-1} is seen as the distance between "a" and "b." In apatites, the splitting of this peak increases as a function of crystallinity

from stoichiometry; its Ca/P ratio is lower than one would expect from the chemical formula of apatite (2.00 *vs.* 2.15 mass, respectively) (Jenkins 1978, Simpson 1972). The low Ca/P of bone apatite is related to its poor crystallinity; small crystals have relatively high surface-area/mass ratios, and there is generally more latitude for substitution and adsorption at the crystal surface than in the interior. Calcium-deficient apatites have been shown to be relatively highly reactive when exposed

Table 8.2. *Crystallinity of fresh and interred bones based on the IR splitting factor*[a]

Deproteinized fresh bone	1.19
Dor human bone (*ca.* 1000 B.P.)	1.23
Homo, Hayonim B (*ca.* 10,000 B.P.)	1.14
Homo, Hayonim D (*ca.* 20,000 B.P.)	1.28
Omo River basin (*ca.* 1–3 million B.P.) (n=4)	1.42 ± 0.03
Mineralogical fluorapatite	1.52

[a] The splitting of the PO_4 anti-symmetric bending mode at 550–600 cm^{-1}.

to solutions containing calcium. Therefore, with diagenesis, an increase in the Ca/P ratio is to be expected.

An increase in Ca/P in interred bones has indeed been noted in a number of studies and this phenomenon has been put forth as a measure of diagenesis (Sillen 1981b) and even for use as a relative dating technique (Cook and Heizer 1947). Unfortunately, neither study controlled for the presence of calcite which would also markedly raise the Ca/P ratio. Thus, no data currently exist on the Ca/P ratio of interred bone *apatite*. It would be of interest to collect these data and to correlate them with changes in crystallinity and the dietary signals.

Given the limitations of the sample, the invulnerability of apatite during the first few thousand years of interment at some sites is of interest since, in a general way, this coincides with the longevity of collagen. While the rate at which collagen degrades post-depositionally is dependent upon various soil conditions, e.g. pH, temperature, hydrology, etc. (Ortner *et al.* 1972, Salomon and Haas 1967), this process generally takes a few thousand years in the environments in which bones survive at all. For example, when the C/N ratios of interred bones from a variety of archaeological contexts are examined, the ratios reflect those of collagen for some 2–3000 years (Fig. 8.5, after DeNiro 1985). It seems reasonable to hypothesize that crystallographic changes may be accelerated during and after the decomposition of the organic phase, since the apatite crystallites become even more exposed to water and soil ions. In the early post-depositional period, the mineral may be partially shielded from diagenesis by the organic phase.[2]

The manner in which the organic phase decomposes will affect the diagenesis of the inorganic phase. In certain circumstances, notably

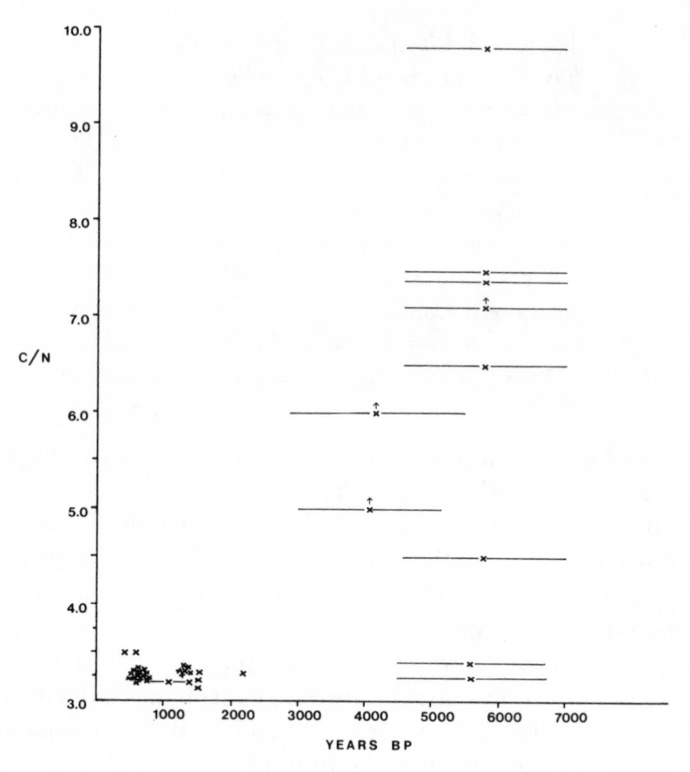

Fig. 8.5 Increase in C/N with duration of interment. Alterations in C/N are generally seen in bones more than 4000 B.P. Data are from DeNiro (1985); burned specimens and specimens originating from peat bogs are omitted from the graph

where soils are moist, fungi and other micro-organisms have been shown to attack collagen (Ascenzi 1963, Morgenthaler and Baud 1957); in turn, these organisms excrete organic acids which cause the dissolution of apatite mineral and the destruction of histological structure (White and Hannus 1983). While new apatite mineral may be deposited in the space vacated by the old mineral, this will not carry a biogenic signal. For example, no histological structure was discerned in Aurignacian bones from Hayonim Cave (*ca.* 17–20,000 B.P.), nor was it possible to identify biogenic Sr/Ca. In dry environments, the action of micro-organisms is less pronounced and the histological structure may survive (Salomon and Haas 1967). However, it remains unclear whether the dietary signals survive as well. In cases where the action of micro-organisms is minimal and microstructure is preserved, diagenesis may involve crystal maturation and new crystal growth, but not necessarily dissolution of the original mineral.

EFFECTS ON THE DIETARY SIGNAL

Given the best-case scenario of minimal dissolution and recrystallization, three properties of apatite will determine both the direction of the diagenetic process and our efforts to deal with it. Firstly, apatite has the capacity to nucleate, or seed, the growth of new crystals (Nancollas and Mohan 1970). Therefore biogenic apatite may seed the growth of diagenetic apatite. Since the pool of ions from which this new mineral grows is not metabolically mediated, it will not reflect any biological signal. As previously stated, other crystal species such as calcite may also exist in ancient bone. However, since both biogenic and diagenetic mineral will be so dominantly apatitic, the practical implication is that the separation of diagenetic from biogenic mineral by physical means, such as density fractionation (Sillen 1981c) or crushing and sieving (Hassan 1975) will fail.

Secondly, apatite, especially the small crystal variety, is prone to substitution by a variety of ionic species; depending upon the conditions of precipitation, the crystal may deviate significantly from the stoichiometric formula described above. (This is to be distinguished from ion exchange, in which one ion may substitute for another after the crystal has precipitated.) The accommodating nature of apatite offers a wide latitude for elemental differences between biogenic and diagenetic mineral. Cation substitutions are relatively straightforward; any alkaline earth with a larger ionic radius than calcium may readily occupy its position (Sr, Ba, Ra), as well as a variety of other metals, notably Pb.

A consideration of the metabolic background for the reduction of Sr/Ca in food chains indicates that, in a natural ecosystem, living bones are deficient in Sr/Ca with respect to groundwater – in other words, groundwater Sr/Ca must be higher than that present in biogenic mineral. We may thus hypothesize that diagenetic apatite that is derived from *groundwater* ions will generally have higher Sr/Ca ratios than biogenic apatite. Where it has been shown that diagenetic apatite has lower Sr/Ca than the biogenic mineral, e.g. the herbivores at Hayonim Cave (Sillen 1981a), it is likely that biogenic material itself is the ionic source. The absence of histological structure in this case indicates that the specimens may have dissolved and recrystallized on a microscopic scale (Sillen 1981c). In these circumstances a simple physiochemical mechanism exists to explain the reduced Sr/Ca; as they grow, crystals tend to exclude strontium in favor of calcium (Likins *et al.* 1960). Alternatively, Lambert *et al.* (1984c) have suggested that the absolute levels of groundwater strontium (which are lower than absolute bone levels) may be a more important determinant than Sr/Ca.

The anion situation is more complex inasmuch as three different positions (the OH^-, the PO_4^{3-}, and the crystal surface) may be occupied. The most important ions to consider in the diagenetic process are F^- and CO_2^{2-}. With regard to F^-, the diffusion of this ion into interred bone from groundwater as a function of time is well established (Hassan 1975, McConnell 1973, Oakley 1964, Parker and Toots 1974b). The F^- ion readily exchanges with OH^- and for various reasons tends to reduce crystal strain and promote crystallinity (Eanes *et al.* 1965, Posner *et al.* 1963). Fluoridated apatites have enhanced crystallinity and reduced surface area (LeGeros 1981, Moreno *et al.* 1977, Nelson *et al.* 1983b).

The incorporation of carbonate deserves special attention since diagenetic CO_3^{2-} will obstruct efforts to recover biogenic $\delta^{13}C$ from apatite. Carbonate may occupy at least two positions in apatite, one structural and one on the surface. The structural inclusion may be coupled with sodium, that is $(Na^+ + CO_2^{2-})$ for $(Ca^{2+} + PO_4^{3-})$ (Chickerur *et al.* 1980, LeGeros and Tung 1983). The effects of this substitution during crystal formation include decreased crystal size, smaller *a*-axes, larger *c*-axes, and a concomitant rise in surface area. In this light it is of interest that an inverse correlation between Na^+ and Ca^{2+} in interred bone has been reported (Buikstra *et al.*, this volume). Increased Na^+ has also been shown in bones from Nelson Bay Cave and this increase was clearly related to other diagenetic phenomena (Price, this volume).

However, the available data do not always indicate a diagenetic increase in Na^+. Reduced Na^+ has also been reported to accompany the process of fossilization (Lambert *et al.* 1984c, Parker *et al.* 1974). Could it be that, in the latter instances, carbonate was not structurally incorporated?

Infra-red studies of synthetic apatites have demonstrated the existence of amorphous or surface carbonate which is not structurally incorporated into the crystal lattice (Termine and Lundy 1973). This carbonate has been shown to be far more exchangeable than structural carbonate (Neuman and Mulryan 1967). For example, Pellegrino and Biltz (1972) studied the release of $^{14}CO_3$ from synthetic labeled apatite into acid buffers. They concluded that "11.2% of the original activity was represented in a freely dissociable form of CO_3^{2-} not intimately associated with the crystal phase." However, 78.5% "was not exchangeable with ions in solution."

Given these considerations, and the observation that total dissolution and recrystallization does not always occur, it would be a mistake to close the book on the likelihood of identifying biogenic carbon in fossil apatite. Research in our laboratory at the University of Cape Town by Julie Lee Thorp indicates that, when appropriate techniques are employed to eliminate exchangeable carbonates, the study of apatite $\delta^{13}C$ may be very promising indeed. A preliminary accounting of the results of this study is discussed in van der Merwe (this volume).

A final property of apatite, relevant to the search for biogenic mineral, is that the anion substitutions discussed above (F^- and CO_3^{2-}) will affect the solubility of the apatite crystallites. Assuming, for the time being, minimal dissolution and recrystallization, a consideration of the differences in solubility behavior of hydroxyapatites, carbonate apatites, and fluorapatites suggests a strategy for the separate elemental analysis of diagenetic and biogenic fossil mineral. These apatites are differentially soluble in acetate buffer in the region of pH 4–5 (Crommelin *et al.* 1983, LeGeros 1981, LeGeros and Tung 1983, Nelson *et al.* 1983b, Okazaki *et al.* 1982a). While apatites generally exhibit aberrant solubility characteristics, it is clear that solubility increases as a function of carbonate content. This is due to the increased crystal distortion resulting from carbonate inclusion in the hydroxyapatite structure (Blumenthal *et al.* 1975). Conversely, the incorporation of F^- into apatite has been shown to result in decreasing solubility as a result of increased crystallinity, reduced strain, and reduced surface area (Eanes *et al.* 1965, LeGeros 1981, Moreno *et al.* 1977, Nelson *et al.* 1983b, Posner *et al.* 1963). When mixtures of apatites of differing solubility are treated with acetate buffer at pH 4.5, the high carbonate apatites dissolve first (Crommelin *et al.* 1983).

Therefore, if diagenetic and biogenic apatites contain differing amounts of CO_3 and F^-, it may be possible to examine these apatites independently on the basis of their solubility differences in acetate buffers. One advantage of this approach is that numerous published studies exist on the behavior of biological and synthetic apatites in similar systems.

SOLUBILITY PROFILES

Since the methods are described in detail elsewhere (Sillen 1986), only a brief description will be given here. Specimens are freezer-milled and 50 mg is placed in an Eppendorf microcentrifuge tube. One milliliter of 100 mM acetic acid/sodium acetate buffer adjusted to pH 4.5 is added to the powder and the preparation is vibrated using ultrasound for exactly one minute, then centrifuged in an Eppendorf microcentrifuge. After centrifugation for 10 seconds, the supernatant is decanted and saved for elemental analysis. New buffer is added to the residue and the procedure is repeated at least 20 times. The series of supernatants thus represent a profile of soluble mineral; the first washes contain the most soluble mineral, washes 5–10 less soluble mineral, washes 10–15 even less soluble mineral, and so on. After 25 washes the least soluble mineral is present as a residue in the centrifuge tube.

To date, two groups of interred bones have been examined using this system: (1) faunal specimens from Hayonim Cave (10–20,000 B.P.), and (2) faunal specimens from the Omo River basin (1–2 million B.P.). For comparison with the fossil material, the behavior of fresh anorganic bone in the solubility profile is presented in Fig. 8.6. It can be seen that the Sr/Ca and Ca/P curves are essentially flat in the critical first five washes; moreover, the Ca/P of the washes hovers around 2.0, the mass Ca/P of fresh bone mineral.

In Fig. 8.7, the Ca/P profile of an Omo suid, *Mesochoerus limnetes* is presented (in duplicate). The specimen has extraordinarily high Ca/P in the first wash, indicating the dissolution of large amounts of calcium carbonate. By wash number four, however, this value approaches 2.0, the Ca/P ratio of bone mineral. The loss of carbonate in the Omo mineral may also be demonstrated with IR spectra (Table 8.3). After 25 washes in pH 4.5 buffer, the CO_2/PO_4 ratio of the insoluble residue, calculated from the respective asymmetric stretching modes, is very similar to that of fresh deproteinized bone.

It would be useful to compare the solubility profiles, Ca/P and Sr/Ca, of Hayonim Cave bones to those of the Omo material; unfortunately these data do not yet exist. Although solubility profiles were recorded for the Hayonim Cave specimens (Sillen 1981c), only 10 washes were

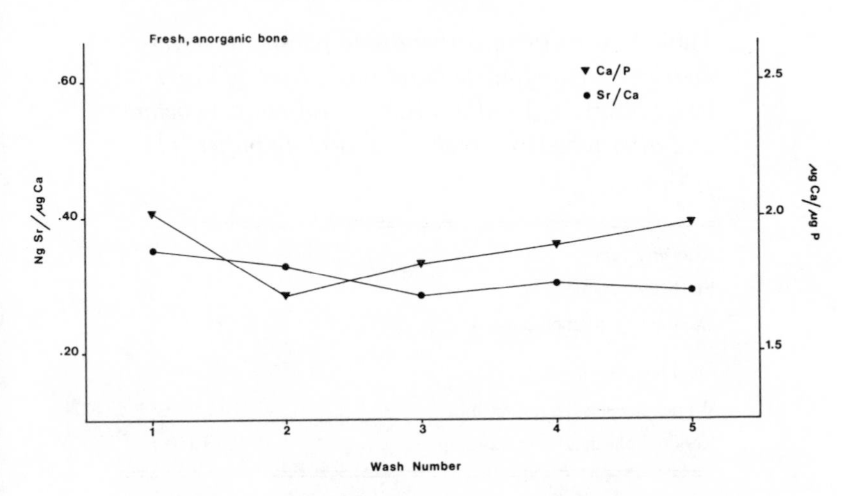

Fig. 8.6 Sr/Ca and Ca/P of fresh, anorganic cow bone in a solubility profile at pH 4.5. Both curves are flat. Moreover, note the Ca/P which hovers at 2.0, the Ca/P of bone mineral

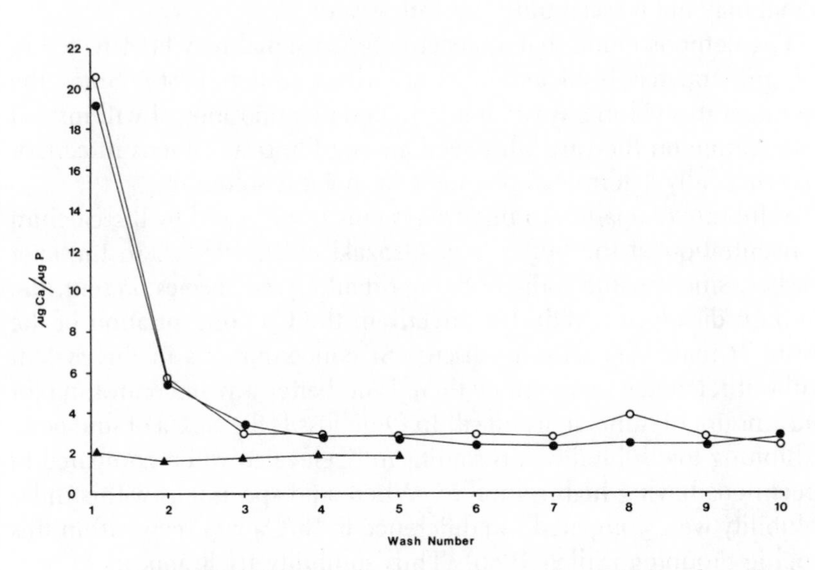

Fig. 8.7 Ca/P of fresh, anorganic cow bone (▲) and an Omo fossil suid (*Mesochoerus limnetes*) (○ and ●) in duplicate. After five washes the Ca/P of the dissolving fossil mineral approaches 2.0, a value consistent with that of bone mineral

Table 8.3. *Ratio of carbonate to phosphate asymmetric stretching mode band intensities*[a] *of Omo River basin (1–3 million B.P.) fossil powders before and after repetitive washing in acetate buffer (pH 4.5)*

Reference values	
Fresh sheep bone	.36
Deproteinized rabbit bone	.43
Omo powders (n=4)	
Whole powders (before washing)	0.80 ± 0.33
Residual powders (after washing)	0.45 ± 0.13

The relative CO_3/PO_4 is decreased in residual powders, indicating the preferencial dissolution of carbonate-containing mineral.
[a] The carbonate and phosphate infra-red band intensities were measured at 1450 and 1000–1200 cm^{-1} respectively.

examined. Subsequent research on the Omo specimens has indicated that the Sr/Ca curves do not stabilize until after 10 washes; a dietary signal may not be seen until the 15th wash.

The demonstration that a biogenic Sr/Ca signal may be detected in this mineral has been presented elsewhere (Sillen 1986). Since the theme of this volume is variability in bone composition, I will instead concentrate on the variability seen among Omo specimens in certain diagenetically determined phenomena, notably solubility.

Solubility of apatites in *in vitro* systems is measured by the calcium concentration of the buffer (e.g. Okazaki *et al.* 1982b). In the later washes, since apatite is the only important crystal species present, the amount dissolved is reflected directly in the Ca concentration of the wash. It makes no sense to discuss Sr concentrations in this system without reference to Ca, since there is no better way of controlling for the amount of mineral dissolved. In Omo fossils the Sr/Ca of suid bone exhibiting low solubility was significantly elevated when compared to specimens having high solubility. When suid specimens with similar solubility were compared, no difference in Sr/Ca was seen within this trophic grouping (Sillen 1986). Thus solubility itself appears to be a determinant of Sr/Ca, and this *varies* within species from the same faunal assemblage. A slightly different phenomenon was seen among the carnivores; in this case, three specimens of *Homotherium* (a large saber-toothed tiger) had reduced solubility when compared to all other carnivore species.

While the explanation for this variability presently eludes us, it is a straightforward matter to investigate since the determinants of solubility, discussed above, are well established. Thus, one research initiative should be the documentation of F^-, CO_3^{2-}, and crystallinity *among* fossil specimens. Indeed, since these differences are sometimes related to species, it may be possible to detect differences in the taphonomic history of these groups of animals. For example, one possible explanation for the differences seen in solubility behavior between Omo *Homotheria* and other Omo carnivores is that these animals lived in different environments and their bones traveled different pathways to the same sedimentary context. Therefore their bones may have undergone different interactions with determinants of solubility, e.g. F^-, in the period between death and discovery.

CONCLUSIONS

The variables that need further consideration in studies of inorganic diagenesis include duration of interment. It is likely that this effect will not be linear, inasmuch as the organic phase of bone may exert some protective effect. If this hypothesis stands, it will also have implications for taphonomic investigations. The period during which bones are most susceptible to destruction has been the subject of much taphonomic concern (Hare 1980, Hill 1980). After an initial five to ten years, the critical period for survival into "fossilhood" may not be the first few thousand years of interment. Instead, the critical period may be afterward, when the organic phase is hydrolyzed but significant mineralization has not yet taken place.

The direction of diagenesis will vary; for reasons related to the action of micro-organisms, some environments will promote recrystallization and others will not. It is tempting to speculate that the apparent stability of the African Rift Valley bone is related to the exceptionally high background levels of F^- in that environment (Cerling 1977). Perhaps in addition to affecting biogenic mineral, the water animals drink affects their diagenesis as well.

In any event, we do not yet have enough information to predict where diagenesis will be completely obliterating, and where it will not. XRD, IR, and CO_2/PO_4 ratios from whole specimens all showed Omo mineral to be highly altered; however, it has been possible to identify a biogenic signal in this material. Indeed crystallinity itself is not an enemy of the biogenic signal; dissolution and recrystallization are. The predictors which may be most useful then are (1) the presence of histological structure, (2) the Ca/PO_4 ratio of washed mineral (i.e. apatite), and (3) the CO_2/PO_4 ratio of washed mineral.

Since recrystallization and the structural incorporation of carbonate may or may not occur, it will be necessary to rethink the research design of studies which seek to determine whether a particular dietary analysis technique, say Sr/Ca or $\delta^{13}C$, may be applied to study the distant past. For one thing, it becomes necessary to define precisely the kind of material on which a study is based, and to limit the conclusions to that material. In the past, disagreements over diagenesis (e.g. Sullivan and Krueger 1981 *vs.* Schoeninger and DeNiro 1982) have, in fact, been based on observations of different specimens, even different species. For another, in order to refine our conclusions, it will be necessary to report descriptive analyses and to address the chemistry of diagenesis itself. As Lambert *et al.* (1984c) have pointed out, a demonstration that a dietary analysis technique does or does not work (cf. Schoeninger and DeNiro 1982, Sillen 1981a, Sullivan and Krueger 1981), no longer seems sufficient; we must also directly address the chemistry of the process.

This chemical information will be useful *whether or not* a dietary signal can be identified, both for its predictive *and* for its taphonomic value. Diagenesis suffers from a bad name; we tend to think of it as the mist on the window rather than part of the view. On the contrary, all of the parameters discussed here (IR, XRD, F^-, solubility, etc.) are determined by the interaction of bone with the post-mortem environment; therefore, they provide quantitative information about that environment and about the survival of bone therein. Although the diagenetic process may destroy the biogenic signals on which we have focused, the taphonomic history of the assemblage may be thereby preserved.

NOTES

1. This discussion is restricted to one paleodietary tracer, Sr/Ca. For studies of fossil apatite $\delta^{13}C$, enamel is in fact the tissue of choice.

2. The relationship of disappearance of the organic phase to mineral uptake would be easily studied using the system described by Lambert *et al.* (1985b). This study measured the ionic exchange with solution of whole fresh bone and archaeological bone specimens. It would be of interest to prepare a series of fresh specimens with a wide range of protein content.

9

Factors affecting elemental and isotopic variation in prehistoric human skeletons

GEORGE J. ARMELAGOS
BARRETT BRENTON

University of Massachusetts, Amherst

MICHAEL ALCORN
DEBRA MARTIN

Hampshire College, Amherst

DENNIS P. VANGERVEN

University of Colorado

The term skeleton is derived from the Greek *skeletos* meaning "dried up" or "withered." While this characterization may describe the attitude of many non-specialists toward bones, the view of bone as a dried-up or withered tissue is far from accurate. In life, bone is a dynamic tissue that has four important functions (Shipman *et al.* 1985). First, it provides support for soft tissues of the body such as internal organs. Secondly, it makes movement possible by providing attachment for the muscular system. Thirdly, it protects organs such as the brain and eyes; and fourthly, the skeleton provides storage for many of the important major, minor, and trace minerals essential for normal bodily function. Calcium, for example, which provides much of the skeleton's strength, is continuously deposited in new bone tissue and then reabsorbed into the circulatory system when needed for critical physiological purposes such as maintaining electrolyte balance and lactation.

Pathological changes in bone, observed in the form of infectious lesions, fractures, and degenerative change, occur when any or all of these four skeletal functions become impaired. The analysis of such changes in the context of bio-social phenomena such as age, sex, and economic stratification can provide the paleopathologist with important insights into the biological and cultural adaptation of ancient human populations.

Traumatic lesions such as depressed fracture of the skull or parry fracture of the forearm (occurring when the arm is raised to ward off or "parry" a blow to the head) are typically the result of interpersonal violence. As a result, such lesions are unlikely to occur with equal frequency among all ages and both sexes within a population. Such lesions typically occur among young adult males, while fractures of the wrist usually result when an individual falls and extends the arm to break their fall. The impact of the fall will frequently fracture the bones at the wrist area. In a sense, the parry fractures are an index of strife while the Colles' or wrist fractures are an index of "klutziness."

Some of the most informative indicators of stress are the result of growth disruptions caused by an interruption of nutrients to the skeleton (Huss-Ashmore *et al.* 1982). Childhood growth retardation, dental hypoplasia (mottling of the dental enamel), and premature bone loss in women and children (osteopenia) have been observed to occur widely among prehistoric human populations.

While it is clear that the range of phenomena of interest to the paleopathologist is wide – extending from depressed fractures of the skull to mottled enamel on the teeth – the avenues of observation were, until recently, quite limited. The paleopathologist, unlike the pathologist, was limited to the physical changes that remained long after the "assault" by club, microbe, or inadequate nourishment had taken place. While the microscope or hand lens was of occasional use, the paleopathologist had little more to go on than what the eye could detect.

Today, modern techniques often borrowed from beyond anthropology are being applied with increasing frequency to the study of paleopathology. Comparative histological and chemical analyses of bone have provided new insights into the dynamics of bone tissue both in health and disease. It is the purpose of this paper (1) to review the normal aspects of bone histomorphology and biochemistry as a baseline for paleopathological inquiry, (2) to consider the methods of analysis by which this new baseline data is obtained, and (3) to evaluate how this new body of data can be integrated into the fundamental questions of human adaptation and evolution. It is our position that the interpretation of changes at the cellular and chemical level, including the analyses of major, minor, and trace minerals and stable isotopes, must be evaluated in terms of taphonomic changes as well as in states of health and disease before their importance to what many view as "archaeological chemistry" can be understood.

HUMAN ADAPTATION PRESERVED IN BONE

The same features of bone that make it resistant to degradation in dry soil are those that also make it an excellent repository of past biological activity. As a highly specialized connective tissue, bone is composed of two separate but completely interactive components, collagen and calcium phosphate salts. This inorganic calcium component and the organic collagen component together form one of the unique biomaterials known to humans. The calcium crystals attach between consecutive collagen building blocks, forming an interlocking molecular structure which has compressional and tensile strength as well as rigidity and hardness. Bioengineers seeking to replicate the structure of bone have likened it to fiberglass, steel-belted radial tires (Halstead 1974), or twisted plywood (Giraud-Guille 1988).

Because of the inorganic and organic properties of bone, biomedical research on its physiological properties has tended to compartmentalize along these two dimensions. This is unfortunate, since the changes of greatest interest to the paleopathologist result from the interaction of bone's organic and inorganic phases. Where principles of bone physiology and morphology have emerged beyond the limits of compartmentalized research, they point clearly to the utility of bone as a remarkably faithful biostructural recorder of metabolic, hormonal, biomechanical, and dietary interactions (Frost 1985).

A review of the diverse physiological activities of bone reveals a system at odds with itself. Bone must be strong, light, mobile, and capable of repair and change (remodeling) in response to stress. It must also serve as the metabolic reservoir for 99% of the calcium and phosphorus in the body, as well as substantial amounts of magnesium, sodium, and carbonate (Raisz 1982).

Further complexity is revealed when growth and development are considered. The initial modeling of the skeleton during fetal life is determined largely by formation of bone on cartilage templates. Incapable of enlargement by internal expansion once mineralization has taken place, bone growth involves a complex process of deposition on outer (periosteal) surfaces and internal (endosteal) resorption, in addition to new bone production at the ends or epiphyses. In order to add tensile and compressive strength but maintain lightness, a network of trabecular (spongy) bone also develops on interior surfaces, particularly near the ends of weight-bearing bones such as the limbs and the interior of vertebrae. However, as with all skeletal structures, the complex network of trabeculae serve a physiological as well as a mechanical function. Embedded with veins and arteries, the extensive surfaces of trabecular bone exposed to the body's circulatory system comprise a major region of mineral ion exchange both to and from the skeleton.

The skeleton, then, cannot be viewed in isolation from the body of which it is a part. We are confronted with a bone–body continuum in life – the paleopathologist is confronted with the skeletal remains of that continuum in the investigation of the dead. Fortunately, the properties of bone that provide its tremendous resilience also preserve its former mechanical and physiological life. In a sense, bone records a physical and chemical "memory" of earlier metabolic and mechanical stimuli in its calcium and collagen configuration.

We are arguing here that the messages locked in the structure can be used as an anthropological library, providing biological data unobtainable from any other source. Because prehistoric bone was part of a living system, it was metabolically tempered, hormonally interactive, nutritionally influenced, and biochemically induced by a living organism that was in turn responding to a broader physical and cultural environment.

While no one would dispute this view, and while histomorphometry of multicellular units of bone has progressed rapidly as a means of reading the structural messages related to the diagnosis of normal and pathological states, skeletal researchers with few exceptions (e.g. Posner 1967) have not linked histomorphometry with molecular or biochemical analyses of collagen proteins in bone. The complex nature of the system remains largely dismembered. To wed the analysis of organic and inorganic phases of bone would indeed provide for a productive and prolific marriage.

ORGANIZATION OF BONE AT THE MULTICELLULAR LEVEL: OSTEONS

Bone dynamics can be considered on several levels: the gross or organ, the tissue, the cellular, and the molecular. On a gross level the skeleton represents a complex organ in constant communication with other bodily systems through its vascular network. Organ level analyses consist largely of measurements of the size and shape of either whole bone or bone sections. Such measurements are assumed to reflect underlying processes of growth and development as well as degenerative changes. Microscopic analyses at the tissue and cellular level reveal processes of modeling and remodeling as these occur throughout the life cycle. The fact that severe disturbance of cell dynamics can exist at the microscopic level without producing measurable changes at the gross level suggests that gross and tissue level changes may be controlled by different mechanisms that can act either harmoniously or independently (Frost 1987).

However, just as the organ and cellular levels may act together or independently, so may the cellular and molecular levels. Depending on the stress or physiological disruption, changes in bone chemistry may or may not produce detectable cell level changes. It seems clear, therefore, that future advances in paleopathological investigation will come with our ability to make definite associations linking these levels of bone response to past patterns of diet and disease.

Bone tissue is built up of a number of lamellae (layers of mineralized bone) in one of three ways. First, lamellae can be stacked flat on one another. This is called circumferential lamellar bone and it is usually found on the outer surfaces of bones. The second type of lamella is that which is found between multicellular units of bone and is called interstitial lamellar bone. Thirdly, lamellae may be arranged concentrically around a central vascular canal (containing a neurovascular bundle). These concentric "packets" of lamellar bone comprise osteons.

Osteons are tissue cylinders which respond to changing physiology and act as homeostatic regulators of calcium metabolism, bone repair, and maintenance. Because osteons are discrete multicellular units of bone, they are generally used in diagnostic procedures. In the femur, osteons measure approximately 0.25 mm in diameter and are easily viewed under low or high magnification (Jowsey 1977). Osteons take a variable amount of time to form. In a ten-year-old child osteons take on average 46 days to attain completeness (Lips *et al.* 1978). The life span of an osteon is also highly variable. Osteons remain viable for many years, since at any given time only 3–5% of the skeleton of a normal adult undergoes active remodeling (Frost 1964).

Osteons have proven to be good foci for histomorphometric studies for the following reasons: (1) they are histologically discrete, (2) they form single dynamic units of bone tissue which are separate yet connected to vascular channels, (3) they are highly vascularized, (4) they are the sites of resorption and formation of bone tissue, (5) they house (in their lacunae) multipotent cells, and (6) they are the major structural units of bone. They, in short, incorporate phenomena relevant to the organ, tissue, cellular, and chemical components of the bone–body continuum.

The human skeleton, containing millions of osteons, is in a state of continuous metabolic reappraisal or bone turnover mediated by two kinds of cells. New bone production is initiated by osteoblasts which are descended from connective tissue stem cells. The resorption of previously formed bone is mediated by osteoclasts which are descended from marrow stem cells (Aitken 1984). Bone remodeling, then, is the result of the collective effects of bone resorption and formation. This process responds equally to the body's need to maintain a physiological concentration of calcium in body fluids, and the need to maintain the structural integrity of bone tissue.

Bone turnover is relatively rapid in trabecular bone and slow in cortical bone. This difference is likely due to the greater surface area of trabecular bone (Darby and Meunier 1981). The activities of osteoblasts and osteoclasts are so closely coupled during the process of bone turnover that new bone formation cannot proceed until there is a certain amount of resorption. The resorptive phase is relatively rapid and is usually completed within a few weeks (Aitken 1984). The formation phase of bone remodeling is relatively slow and can take up to several months to complete an osteon.

Mineralization occurs in relation to resorption and formation. Rates of mineralization vary according to age and health of the individual (Jowsey 1973). Resorption, formation, and mineralization represent a cycle of activity that can take from three months to a year to complete (Frost 1969). Many factors can affect the cycle. One principal factor involves collagen.

Collagen

Collagen makes up 90% of the total organic matrix of bone tissue and it provides an organic framework for the crystal portion of bone (see Eyre 1980 for an excellent review). Crystals attach themselves to collagen, becoming embedded within and along the molecule as mineralization proceeds. The abundance of collagen and its likely importance in connective tissue disease explains the intensity of research focused on this molecule over the last several decades (Gay and Miller 1978).

Beyond its abundance in bone, collagen is the most common protein throughout the human body. It is a major constituent of most connective tissues (Glimcher 1981) – yet characteristic differences exist in the properties of different types of connective tissue. In the past these differences were accounted for by the varying amounts of elastin and mucopolysaccharides or proteoglycans associated with collagen (Lindenbaum and Kuettner 1967). For example, cartilage, about 50% collagen, is more resilient to pressure than other tissues, probably because of its high content of mucopolysaccharides (Bhatenager and Prockop 1966). However, collagen's critical function in tissue remains the same regardless of its structural variety. Collagen maintains the structural integrity of the various tissues and organs of which it is a part. To break a collagen fiber 1 mm in diameter requires a load of 10 to 40 kg (Curry 1962).

In spite of the stability of collagen fiber, its molecular features can be disrupted under relatively mild conditions. For example, when heated in water at pH 7, the fibers undergo an abrupt length decrease at a characteristic temperature (shrinkage temperature, T_s (Gustavson 1956). When a fiber is heated to its T_s at an acid or alkaline pH, it not only shrinks but also goes into solution as a gelatin. Commercial gelatins are often prepared from connective tissues like bone by boiling under either acidic or alkaline conditions. The resulting proteinaceous material constitutes collagen that has been both denatured and partially degraded by hydrolysis of its cross-links and peptide bonds (Gustavson 1956). Polymerization, however, may also occur as the small peptides will recombine easily under appropriate conditions.

Although they maintain similar triple-helical structures and tissue maintenance features, many different types of collagen exist. Researchers classify collagen types on the basis of molecular sequence, size, and tissue (Chung and Miller 1974). The role of collagen types in tissue form and maintenance can vary significantly. Different types of collagen have been attributed to unique tissue features. Bone, primarily composed of Type I collagen, undergoes mineralization (Herring 1972).

CHARACTERIZATION OF THE ORGANIC MATRIX IN EARLY HUMAN SKELETAL MATERIAL

Following the discovery that amino acids are preserved in fossils many millions of years old (Abelson 1954a,b, 1956, Hare and Abelson 1968, Ho 1965, 1967), amino acid geochemistry expanded rapidly (Hare *et al.* 1980, Wyckoff 1972). Originally, researchers had hoped that studying ancient proteinaceous material would further their understanding of biochemical evolution. However, the study of fossil proteins has proven fraught with difficulties, as demonstrated by the conflicting interpretations of results from numerous analyses during the past two decades (Armstrong *et al.* 1983). Amino acid levels in prehistoric bone have varied greatly. In some cases, researchers attributed unusual amino acid profiles to phylogenetic changes (Doberenz and Lund 1966, Dungworth *et al.* 1975, 1976), while others believed that these variations represented diagenesis or post-mortem alterations (Bada *et al.* 1973, Bada and Shou 1980, Hare and Mitterer 1969).

Knowledge concerning post-mortem alterations of bone remains inadequate. The presence of amino acids in fossil bone does not guarantee a well-preserved organic matrix. After death, heat and microbial action initiate protein denaturation. Larger molecules degrade to small peptides of free amino acids, initiating racemization. Environmental conditions further contribute to additional cross-linking or the racemization of small peptides. The analysis of amino acids will not detect these molecular alterations; consequently, such analysis does not offer a flawless indication of protein preservation.

Despite extensive research on fossil amino acid compositions, few studies have utilized polyacrylamide gel electrophoresis or chromatography to evaluate archaeological bone organic matrix preservation. In polyacrylamide gel electrophoresis studies, Tuross *et al.* (1980) found that proteins extracted by a 0.5 M EDTA demineralization and dialysis of bone fragments yielded high molecular weight material that did not migrate. Moreover, general smears were present, indicating extensive organic matrix degradation. Fisher and Termine (1985) have shown that this method of extraction is not ideal. Because the use of bone fragments instead of bone powder requires long-term dialysis which in turn encourages protease activity, less cross-linked proteins undergo degradation to smaller peptides or free amino acids while the more cross-linked proteins remain intact. Consequently, the extraction of collagen from bone fragments as opposed to powder is likely to produce a biased representation of collagen with a higher molecular weight (Tuross *et al.* 1980).

COLLAGEN AND DISEASE

There is another area of research that must be clarified. We need to determine the relationship between diet and the processes of disease and collagen synthesis. The form and structure of collagen is changed significantly by pathologic and physiologic conditions such as scurvy, wound-healing, or post-partum involution of the uterus (Gay and Miller 1978, also see Prockop *et al.* 1979 for an excellent review). These alterations appear on the gross physical, molecular, and chemical levels.

Vitamin D deficiency impairs the mineralization of bone in children (rickets) and adults (osteomalacia) and appears to have multiple effects of collagen synthesis and stability (Barnes and Lawson 1978). For example, decreases in collagen cross-linking can result from either a vitamin D deficiency and/or hypocalcemia (Barnes and Lawson 1978).

Both calcium and phosphate have direct stimulatory effects on collagen and non-collagen protein synthesis in bone (Raisz 1979). Yet, calcium works on both bone and cartilage and has a non-specific cell growth effect (Gay and Miller 1978). Phosphate seems to have a specific stimulatory effect on the osteoblast (Raisz 1979).

Metal ions may affect the structure and function of collagen (Bornstein *et al.* 1966, Schiffman *et al.* 1966, Urist and Abermethy 1967, Wadkins 1968). Researchers have suggested that metallic co-ordination complex formation in cartilage (Dunstone 1959), elastin (Schiffman *et al.* 1966, Veis 1967), and egg-shell matrix (Sinkins and Taylor 1958) is important to the primary calcification process. Similar complexes may be involved in the calcification (or lack thereof) in bone and tendon matrices (Spadaro *et al.* 1970). The specific interactions between collagen and metal ions must be understood before we can assess the role of these ions in connective tissue biology.

Isotopic studies demonstrate that although most adult collagen is metabolically stable, some undergoes rapid synthesis and degradation during life (Kivirikko 1970, Lindstedt and Prockop 1961). Synthesis or degradation of small, metabolically active fractions of body collagen may be critical in several human diseases (Grant and Prockop 1972). Metabolic changes such as an increased rate of synthesis or a decreased rate of collagen degradation may encourage the thickening of basement membranes in diseases such as diabetes (Merimee *et al.* 1970, Siperstein *et al.* 1970) or atherosclerosis.

Further analysis of isolated collagen may entail measuring hydroxyglycine, found elevated in several pathological conditions, including vitamin D deficiency (Barnes and Lawson 1978) and osteogenesis imperfecta (Mechanic 1979). Additionally, hydroxyglycine levels vary with age (Deshmuck *et al.* 1973), perhaps indicating the degree of collagen cross-linking.

Many questions remain. For example, because formation of a collagenous matrix initiates new bone synthesis, and osteoporosis demonstrates no mineralization deficit, collagen synthesis changes may play a role in this condition (Raisz 1979). Continued evaluation of collagen maturation and maintenance may elucidate the processes responsible for this and other bone diseases. Additionally, examining the larger (>200) and less common group of non-collagenous proteins may provide many new perspectives.

During the past two decades, new findings at the molecular, cellular, and tissue level have expanded our knowledge of bone formation and regulation. At the tissue level, the concept of the coupling between osteoclastic resorption and osteoblastic formation in bone remodeling has provided a new way to describe the relationship between bone turnover and skeletal growth (Raisz 1979). In cells, hormonal control of osteoblast responsible for bone matrix synthesis has been examined in detail (Raisz 1983). At the molecular level researchers have studied collagen, the major organic component of bone, determining the sequence of steps responsible for its synthesis. The role of several non-collagenous proteins in bone formation has been studied providing new insights into the mechanisms responsible for mineralization (Termine *et al.* 1981b). Continued examination of the skeletal system will further our understanding of mineralization and related diseases.

TRACE ELEMENTS AND FACTORS AFFECTING THEIR UPTAKE AND BIOLOGICAL ROLE

Biological role of trace elements

Most of the living matter on the earth is composed of a set of the naturally occurring elements called the "bulk" elements. This includes carbon, hydrogen, nitrogen, oxygen, and sulfur, all of which are needed in one's daily diet. Mammalian physiology also required an intake of macrominerals (calcium, magnesium, phosphorus, sodium, potassium, and chlorine) and trace elements (elements occurring at levels less than 0.01% of body mass). It is these latter two categories that have been the focus of skeletal biology and the chemical analysis of bone. Of the many trace elements present in our environment only fifteen are now known to be "essential" for sustaining life processes. These are chromium, cobalt, copper, fluorine, iodine, iron, manganese, molybdenum, selenium, zinc, arsenic, lithium, nickel, silicon, and vanadium (Mertz 1981).

The trace elements serve a number of structural and physiological roles in human biology. Many of their functions relate to the various ionic properties of each trace element with respect to their roles as catalysts in enzymatic systems (Bowen 1966, Underwood 1977). These functions range all the way from maintenance of cell growth and reproduction to brain function and the immunological system. The ionic properties of trace elements that allow them to be taken up in bone can also alter how they are affected upon interment (diagenesis) (Lambert *et al.* 1983, 1985a,b).

Only a few of the trace elements serving as metallo-enzymes have been directly related to the biology of bone. Skeletal defects have been associated with an inadequate cross-linking of collagen, as evidenced by an increase in the solubility of collagen, from dietary deficiencies in copper (Harris 1983). An inhibition of collagen cross-linking has also been associated with low levels of zinc (Fernandez-Madrid *et al.* 1976). In addition, the formation of osteogenic abnormalities has been related to deficiencies in manganese (Underwood 1977). Other trace elements have been connected to the process of bone mineralization and the frequency of caries and dental health (e.g. vanadium and strontium)

(Hadjimarkos 1973, Schneider 1986, Underwood 1977, also see Gilbert 1985).

Trace elements in diet and health

Although essential trace elements do not directly supply energy to the body, they are nevertheless considered a nutrient. Many of the essential trace elements are crucial for the functioning of vitamins, enzymes involved in nutrient uptake and transport, and the biochemical pathways of energy-producing reactions (O'Dell 1985). They can also inhibit dietary intake by affecting taste acuity (hypogeusia) (Bales *et al.* 1986, Henkin 1969).

The dietary source of various trace elements lies in the geochemical environment (soils and ground water) (Bowen 1979), reaching bone via a series of pathways through plant and animal interactions within an environment and related human consumption patterns (Allaway 1977, Hamilton 1979). An understanding of these elemental pathways is critical to interpreting the trace element contents of skeletal remains.

The inhibition of trace element absorption and uptake can be correlated with two major antagonisms, (1) inhibition by other trace elements, and (2) inhibition by other dietary components, e.g. chelating agents and a high fiber intake (Reinhold *et al.* 1976). For example, an excessive intake of zinc can cause a secondary deficiency in copper (Casey and Robinson 1984). The consumption of calcium can aid in the synergistic formation of chelating agents with dietary phytates from grains, forming insoluble complexes that inhibit the uptake of essential trace elements.

A series of pathological conditions can be related to the deficiency of a specific trace element; in addition, a pathological condition can cause a deficiency in a specific trace element. Some research suggests, however, that the bone level of certain trace elements may be unaffected by pathological states. The intake of high levels of a specific trace element can also become toxic to an individual, as was the case for exposure to lead during the time of the Roman Empire (Waldron and Wells 1979). For a discussion of pathological conditions arising from deficiencies in specific trace elements refer to Underwood (1977).

In terms of human health, an interesting component of trace element research is the effect on an individual's immunological system. A deficiency in some trace elements can have an adverse effect on the immunological competence and host defense mechanisms of an organism by inhibiting antibody, lymphocyte, and phagocyte response (Beisel 1982, Treagan 1984). An understanding of these processes has broad implications for the study of etiology of skeletal pathologies.

FUTURE PROSPECTS FOR TRACE ELEMENT RESEARCH

Trace element research should be viewed as an opportunity to gain a chronological perspective on factors affecting human health and nutrition. In this regard Gilbert (1977:96) states:

> Knowledge of the interactions and effects of trace elements upon disease resistance and growth and development may well lead to improved estimates of a population's nutritional and health status. Such information could assist in the mapping of the prehistoric spread of various cultigens and diseases. It might also be possible to plot the adoption/deletion of certain sociocultural traits. For example, status differentiation may be indicated by trace element differences based on disproportionate access to specific food resources. Additional consideration should be given to the antagonisms between and among some of the

Table 9.1 *Ranges of some selected trace element and macromineral concentrations in modern*

	Brown and Blakely (1985:465)	Lambert *et al.* (1985:478) excavated rib	modern rib	Beck (1985:498)	Price (1985:456)	White (1986)	Lambert *et al.* (1985b:88)
Ca	280.000–350,000	330,000 ± 43,000	330,000 ± 38,000		372,000–389,000	192,400–216,150	
P						89,420–118,980	
Mg	775–1450 815–1115	5820 ± 2380	4600 ± 1000			90–540	2560
K		610 ± 364	7000 ± 2900				112
Cl							
*Cr							
*Co							
*Cu							
*I							
*Fe		3460 ± 2320	400 ± 300				
*Mn		338 ± 125	2–10				320
*Mo							
*Se							
*Zn	140–560	320 ± 158	210 ± 46	136.4–284.0		61.0–544.8	293
*As							
*Ni							
*Si							
*V							
*F							
Sr	275–585	192 ± 105	120 ± 49	546.5–638.2	155–647	64.9–154.2	155
Al		2260–1840	5–110				
Ba							
Br							
Cd							
Pb		34 ± 3	47 ± 21				49
Sn							

* Essential trace elements

trace elements, as the presence of antagonisms can aid the researcher in detecting the addition or deletion of certain foodstuffs in the diet.

Trace element analysis should provide an additional database for individuals interested in current issues concerning the epidemiological relationship between humans and the geochemical environment. Table 9.1 presents the ranges of various trace elements as they are found in modern and prehistoric human bone. The results were measured by a number of analytical methods and from materials from throughout the world. The table is not meant to frustrate or discredit the use of trace element analysis within an archaeological context, but rather to make one appreciate the range of factors that could have prompted the variation. This includes the variation in the geochemical environment and in the physiology of individuals, including parameters of age, gender, and factors affecting growth and development. It also serves as a warning for interpreting trace element analysis beyond an intersite comparison of values. To this end it is more important that anthropologists conducting trace element analyses utilize appropriate standards for validating their chemical data and understand the process of chemical measurement (Bumsted 1985).

…rehistoric human bone (all concentrations in ppm)

…mbert *et al.* …979:118)	Ledders	Hamilton (1979)	Price and Kavanagh (1982:75)	Modern (1963)	Becker *et al.* (1969:329) Peruvian (1300 A.D.)	Pennsylvania Indian (1400 A.D.)	Iyengar *et al.* (1978:28–30)
			259,200–480,500				108,000–390,00…
			122,900–243,500				50,000–174,00…
…380	3340 ± 1250		910–8800				700–9370
…84	531 ± 193		74,700–207,400				1470
							632
							0.1–33
							0.029–43.5
7.5	10.5 ± 2.3		12.46–116.50	<5	<3–<5	5	1–25.7
							15
…320	3630 ± 1420		404–4325	4–60	12–100	44	3–2040
…25	410 ± 148			<<5	5–60	<5	0.19–116
							103
							1–8.95
…58	308 ± 129	217.4 ± 35.4–164.6 ± 17.8	85.7–825.6	60–85	25–98	105	50–190
							0.08–4.1
				<5–50	36–155	110	17
				<5–25	<5	<5	0.87–17.6
							2100–28600
…05	158 ± 41	155.9 ± 14.6–138.7 ± 9.0	91.32–362.80	62–130	62–210	375	42.6–237
…840	2360 ± 1020	73.4 ± 16–60 ± 10	543–3301	<5	4–30	74	3–6540
			43.64–521.50				4.12–29
							38
							1.28–4.2
		29.0 ± 3.9–34.5 ± 29		5–110	<5		10–71
				<5–12	9–25		0.8–3.9

CONCLUSION

To understand the complexity of human adaptation in prehistory requires the analysis of skeletal material at a number of levels. Anthropologists have made important strides in incorporating chemical analysis in interpreting diet. The use of major, minor, and trace minerals as well as stable isotopes has provided important tools in reconstructing the adaptation of our ancestors.

The understanding of the dynamics of bone microstructure may help in interpreting the chemical information that is being recovered. The analysis of bone histology is extremely important in establishing the degree of diagenesis that may have occurred. In addition the morphology of bone microstructure can reveal pathological conditions that may affect the metabolism of collagen as well as the bone chemistry. This information may be critical in interpreting the results of chemical analysis.

The advances in the reconstruction of diet will be enhanced by the linking of gross measures of adaptation such as pathology with chemical indicators such as trace minerals and stable isotopes. The co-operation between bone biologists and bone chemists will be mutually beneficial. Together we will better be able to understand how our ancestors lived and died.

10

The chemistry of prehistoric human bone: recommendations and directions for future study

T. DOUGLAS PRICE
GEORGE J. ARMELAGOS
JANE E. BUIKSTRA
M. PAMELA BUMSTED
BRIAN S. CHISHOLM
JONATHON E. ERICSON
JOSEPH B. LAMBERT
NIKOLAAS J. VAN DER MERWE
MARGARET J. SCHOENINGER
and ANDREW SILLEN

The study of prehistoric bone composition lies at an exciting interface between chemistry, physical anthropology, and archaeology. In March 1986, the School of American Research in Santa Fe, New Mexico, sponsored a week-long seminar to discuss this new work. Ten individuals from the above fields convened at the seminar to consider results to date, standards and conventions, problem areas, and future directions. Some of the results of their research have been presented in the preceding pages of this volume. Beyond the more technical papers, however, the seminar felt it would be useful to provide a final chapter in this volume which would summarize some of the debate, consensus, and prognosis that emerged from our meeting. This information appears below in sections entitled *Recommendations* and *Directions for Future Research*. The individual papers in this volume are, in a sense, a summary of things we do know; the directions for future research that appear below involve matters about which we are less certain and need more information.

RECOMMENDATIONS

Our recommendations are organized into three sections: reporting conventions (for isotopes and elements, respectively), reference materials, and needed baseline information about variability in human bone.

Reporting conventions

Isotopes. Carbon isotope ratios should be reported according to the format described in Craig in 1953 (see also Chisholm, this volume) as:

$$\delta^{13}C(‰) = [(^{13}C/^{12}C)_{sample}/(^{13}C/^{12}C)_{standard} - 1] \times 1000$$

Nitrogen isotope ratios should be given analogously (see Chisholm, this volume, Price *et al.* 1985b:429–34). In both cases, the instrumentation should be described. As in any proper scientific report, the methods used in the investigation must be clearly outlined, either in detail or by reference to previous, readily available publications. Any changes or modifications in the current work from the previously published method must be described in the report. Reasonable estimates of error, and their method of derivation, should also be included.

Elements. For elemental analyses, calcium and other major elements should be reported as a percentage (%). Minor, trace, and ultratrace elements should be reported as parts per million (ppm) or μg/g. Composition should be reported as proportions of bone ash or of whole bone. Published reports should make explicit whether the analyses are done on whole bone or bone ash. Bone ash should be characterized as a percentage amount of dried, fat-free bone for each sample. The procedures for drying and ashing should be specified in terms of time and temperature. Error limits (standard deviations or standard errors) should be reported. If available, information on the normality of the data distributions should be reported. In multi-element studies, elemental proportions should be reported as % or ppm, not as ratios with respect to a second element. If ratios are used in element studies, the original values should still be provided for comparison. Instrumentation, reference materials, and standards should be reported (see also Ives 1975).

Because of high coefficients of variability, a number of samples should be used to determine means and variance in analyses for most elements. At least 10–12 specimens per subgroup are preferred. Reports of single analyses or of very small sample numbers are of little value.

Post-mortem changes in the elemental composition of bone are a function of each depositional context and must be considered in each specific case. Measures of potential diagnostic value for diagenesis include differences between ribs and femurs in Sr, comparison with faunal remains, measures of crystallinity, Sr isotopes, C and N for protein in intact bone, Ca/P ratios, and unusual concentrations of Fe, Al, Th, Pb, Zr, V, Y, Rb, and U.

In the report, sites should be carefully described in terms of location, affiliation, and radiocarbon age if available. Bone samples should be reported in terms of the sex and age of the individual, status according to burial characteristics if applicable, quality of preservation, and pathology. Faunal materials and soil samples should be analysed whenever possible. The post-mortem history of the bone samples, if known, should be provided and terms such as "fresh," "buried," "conserved," "preservation treatment," or "prepared" should be defined carefully if used to describe the samples.

Reference materials

The seminar agreed to begin to use a single reference material for both isotope and element analyses. The use of this reference is intended to permit participants to verify preparation and instrument results and to provide values for comparison between laboratories. The only available, and hence the recommended, material is I.A.E.A. Animal Bone (H–5) from the International Atomic Energy Agency, Wagramerstrasse 5, P.O. Box 100, A–1400 Vienna, Austria. Telex: 1–12645. This material is dried, defatted bone powder, produced from selected fresh beef bones. Elemental content has been reported for a number of elements, including As, Ca, Cl, Cd, Co, Cr, Cu, F, Fe, Hg, I, K, Mg, Mn, Mo, Na, Ni, P, Pb, Sb, Se, Si, Sr, V, and Zn.

Baseline information

During the course of the seminar it became evident that our knowledge of the composition of normal human bone is imprecise. While some data on contemporary populations are available, there is a need to update and expand this data base and to develop our knowledge of regional variability in both contemporary and prehistoric populations. For example, reliable information on the amount of calcium and other elements in bone in modern populations is often not adequately reported.

For this reason, one of the recommendations of the seminar was to begin the compilation of baseline data on variation in both prehistoric and contemporary human bone composition, along dimensions such as age, sex, disease, and reproductive status, as well as in terms of variation within a single bone, between the different bones of the skeleton, and between different types of bone tissue – trabecular versus cortical, dentin versus cementum versus enamel, and the protein versus the mineral components, i.e. collagen and apatite. In addition, a number of elements in bone need to be measured from a large sample of individuals to obtain accurate estimates of the mean, standard deviation, and the statistical nature of the distribution. Essential elements such as calcium, zinc, and others are particularly important in this regard. Differences between observed and expected amounts of these elements may provide some indication of the extent of post-depositional changes.

For many, and possibly most, studies, it will be necessary to characterize an individual study region in terms of isotopic ratios in various trophic levels. We should be concerned with geographic differences and environmental factors and how they are reflected in samples. It is important to know if, when, where, and how the methods of extraction and measurement affect normal values for trace elements and isotopes. This requires proper standardization and inter-laboratory calibration and reporting. As a starting point, we need to obtain the baseline data for contemporary samples. If available, information on the normality of the data distributions should be reported. Diagenesis may remove values from these ranges in regular patterns so it will also be useful to examine the ranges of results from archaeological investigations.

DIRECTIONS FOR FUTURE RESEARCH

Isotopes

Multiple isotope studies of bone are recommended. In fact, a combination of multi-isotope characterization in conjunction with multi-element analyses would be the preferred method. The technology for mass spectrometry for analysis will likely produce a revolution in this area within a few years. The following paragraphs are organized by individual isotopes and may indicate some of the remaining questions regarding the relationship between bone chemistry and diet that must be resolved in the coming years.

Carbon isotopes. Studies of the environmental information available from carbon isotope ratios are essential. The possibility of natural variation in the abundance of past carbon dioxide in the atmosphere and in stable carbon isotope ratios must be considered. Studies of fractionation during metabolism must be conducted. Feeding experiments need to be conducted to evaluate the Krueger model which suggests that sources of carbon in collagen and apatite come from proteins and carbohydrates, respectively. Individual amino acids in bone may become important as units of analysis. The carbonate in apatite needs to be further evaluated with regard to its reliability in obtaining a biogenic signal and its relation to diet. Methods for the purification of bone carbonate need to be developed and evaluated.

Nitrogen isotopes. Research on this system is currently in flux. Dichotomies in food systems that were reported initially (i.e. marine versus terrestrial species) are now in question. Much more information is needed on environmental variability in this system. Additional information on the variation within and between populations is essential.

Oxygen isotopes (in PO_4^{2-}). These isotopes in ground water may provide a useful locational signal. Research on the specificity of this system is just beginning.

Sulfur isotopes. This system may offer some possibilities but is one with a low priority. This ratio is difficult to standardize because of air pollution, and the extraction of sulfur from bone requires large samples.

Strontium isotopes. This system is very promising although a great deal of baseline information needs to be developed (see Ericson, this volume). Strontium isotopes are used by geochemists to characterize segments of the landscape on the basis of association with geological substrates of specific age. Strontium isotopes are area specific and may permit a separation of terrestrial and marine species. A different instrumentation than that for light isotopes is involved and decontamination in ultra-clean laboratories is crucial. The process is expensive and slow, permitting only small numbers of samples per study. Much more research is essential in this area.

Lead isotopes. Lead offers a possibility for the examination of past human behavior and is similar to strontium in application. Analyses are difficult to standardize because of pollution. Lead isotopes are the most difficult and expensive of the heavy isotopes to analyse; an ultra-clean laboratory is essential.

Elements

What are the important and reliable indicator elements for diet? A variety of elements have been measured to date in the analysis of the composition of prehistoric bone – Ca, Na, Sr, Cu, Fe, Mn, Mg, Zn, Al, Fe, Ba, and others – but their relationship to diet is often vague. Strontium, zinc, barium, and sodium appear most promising at present as bearers of biogenic signals in bone. Strontium is reasonably well understood but other elements require further documentation of their behavior in the environment, in the food chain, and in depositional contexts. Fundamental studies of trace and ultratrace elements in food and bone are essential to define new, and perhaps more sensitive, indicators of diet and past behavior. Feeding experiments under controled conditions are needed in addition to information on environmental occurrence and availability. Multi-element studies are recommended whenever possible.

CONCLUSIONS

Many of the more important discussions at the seminar concerned the problem areas in this new field: the development of comparable procedures for analysis, the utilization of inter-laboratory reference materials, and the determination of additional sources of variation in human bone, with particular emphasis on diagenesis. Comparability in methods of analysis and in the reporting of results will offer major steps toward more useful and productive investigations. Agreement on the use of common reference materials for all laboratories was reached. A request for a bone tissue standard from the National Bureau of Standards was initiated at the seminar.

There was consensus that too little is known at present regarding the sources of variation in the composition of contemporary human bone. While it is clear that diet is a major contributor, other biological and natural factors are also important. Differences within a population due to metabolism, age, gender, and reproductive status need to be investigated more thoroughly. Variability within a single bone, between types of bone tissue such as dentin, cementum, enamel, cortical bone, and trabecular bone, and within the skeleton of a single individual are also important areas for further investigation.

Diagenetic changes are apparent in most studies of archaeological bone specimens and cannot be overlooked. It is clear that evidence from a variety of archaeological contexts must be considered in order to understand the effects of diagenesis on the reconstruction of past diet. A variety of methods for the determination and measurement of diagenetic changes, with emphasis on multi-element studies, were outlined at the seminar.

We need to develop methods for discovering, and controlling for, the effects of diagenesis which are varied and system-dependent. Post-depositional chemical changes in the mineral component of bone are minor to severe and must always be considered. In the words used at the seminar, "We must look for cures wherever diagenesis rears its ugly head." Diagenetic changes for most isotopes are unknown. For carbon isotopes, diagenesis is possible but likely very minor in bone collagen (see Chisholm, van der Merwe, this volume). Essentially, where collagen is preserved, carbon isotope ratios are reliable. Diagenetic effects may prove to be very interesting in the case of different amino acids in collagen. Diagenetic addition of carbonate to bone may affect isotope ratios in the mineral component (see Sillen, this volume); more study is needed.

New directions for research should also include the consideration of other elements and isotopes, in addition to strontium and zinc, and carbon and nitrogen, as potential indicators of past diet and behavior. One of the recommendations that resulted from the seminar was a request to the National Science Foundation for the establishment of new, well-equipped, dedicated regional laboratories for the study of the chemistry of archaeological bone and related materials. One or more of these facilities should be equipped with an isotope-ratio mass spectrometer for the examination of light isotope variation in bone and other materials.

We now have the ability to consider a variety of subjects concerning the human past. Bone chemistry studies will contribute greatly to a number of important anthropological questions, including the origins and spread of agriculture, the definition of demographic variables and change (e.g. migration, health, status, morbidity, fertility), site catchment analysis, diffusion and migration, climatic and environmental change, geochemistry, paleontology (animal diet, speciation, and extinction), paleoanthropology (e.g. diet, taphonomy, diagenesis, fossilization), and studies of modern health (including the characterization of archaeological populations as a baseline for the effects of modern pollutants, toxic wastes, and natural variability). The education of archaeologists and physical anthropologists regarding the potential for bone chemistry studies, the sample and curation requirements of such methods, and their limitations, is essential.

It is apparent that the study of archaeological bone chemistry is at a turning point, in transition from an experimental procedure to a major research technique. Certainly there is justification for enthusiasm over the potential this methodology will provide for greater resolution in our views of the past. The 1986 seminar in Santa Fe may well have provided the essential groundwork to insure that such investigations continue on firm footing and in exciting new directions.

References

Abelson, P. H. 1954a. Organic constituents of fossils. *Carnegie Institute of Washington Yearbook* **53**:97–101

1954b. Amino acids in fossils. *Science* **119**:576

1956. Paleobiochemistry. *Scientific American* **195**(1):83–92

Abelson, P. H., and T. C. Hoering. 1961. C–isotope fractionation in formation of amino acids by photosynthetic organisms. *Proceedings of the National Academy of Sciences* **47**:623–632

Aitkin, M. 1984. *Osteoporosis in Clinical Practice* (Bristol: Wright)

Allaway, W. H. 1977. Interactions of trace elements. In *Geochemistry and the Environment*, vol. II: *The Relation of Other Selected Trace Elements to Health and Disease* (Washington, D.C.: National Academy of Sciences)

Ambrose, S. H., and M. J. DeNiro. 1986a. Reconstruction of African human diet using bone collagen carbon and nitrogen isotope ratios. *Nature* **319**:321–324

1986b. The isotopic ecology of East African mammals. *Oecologia* **69**:395–406

Amin, E. K., and D. M. Hegsted. 1971. Effect of diet on iron absorption in iron-deficient rats. *Journal of Nutrition* **101**:927–936

Angel, J. L. 1966. Protoic hyperostosis, anemias, malarias, and marshes in the prehistoric Mediterranean. *Science* **153**:750–763

Armstrong, W. G., L. B. Halsted, F. B. Reed, and L. Wood. 1983. Fossil proteins in vertebrate calcified tissues. *Philosophical Transactions of the Royal Society, London* **301**:308–310

Ascenzi, A. 1963. Microscopy and prehistoric bone. In *Science in Archaeology*, ed. D. R. Brothwell and E. Higgs (New York: Praeger)

Asch, D. L., and N. B. Asch. 1985. Prehistoric plant cultivation in west-central Illinois. In *Prehistoric Food Production in North America*. Anthropological Papers no. 75, University of Michigan Museum of Anthropology, Ann Arbor

Atchley, W. R., C. T. Gaskins, and D. Anderson. 1976. Statistical properties of ratios. I. Empirical results. *Systematic Zoology* **25**:137–148

Bada, J. L., and M.-Y. Shou. 1980. Kinetics and the mechanism of amino acid racemization in aqueous solution and in bone. In *Biogeochemistry of Amino Acids*, ed. P. E. Hare, T. C. Hoering, and J. K. King (New York: Wiley)

Bada, J. L., K. A. Kvenvolden, and E. Peterson. 1973. Racemization of amino acids in bone. *Nature* **245**:308–310

Badone, E., and R. M. Farquhar. 1982. Application of neutron activation analysis to the study of element concentration and exchange in fossil bones. *Journal of Radioanalytical Chemistry* **69**:291–311

Bahou, W. F. 1975. The relationships of particular trace elements to various bone pathologies in the Dickson Mounds skeletal population (Senior Honors thesis, University of Massachusetts, Amherst)

Bales, C. W., L. C. Steinman, J. H. Freekand-Graves, J. M. Stone, and R. K. Young. 1986. The effect of age on plasma zinc uptake and taste acuity. *American Journal of Clinical Nutrition* **44**:664–669

Barber, H. 1939. Untersuchungen über die chemische Veränderung von Knochen bei der Fossilization. *Palaeobiologica* 7:217–235

Barnes, M. J., and D. E. M. Lawson. 1978. Biochemistry of bone in relation to the function of vitamin D. In *Vitamin D*, ed. D. E. M. Lawson (New York: Academic Press)

Bassett, E. J. 1982. Osteological analysis of Carrier Mills burials. In *The Carrier Mills Archaeological Project*, ed. R. W. Jeffries and B. M. Butler (Carbondale, Ill.: Southern Illinois University, Center for Archaeological Investigations)

Beck, L. A. 1985. Bivariate analysis of trace elements in bone. *Journal of Human Evolution* **14**:493–502

Becker, R. O., J. A. Spadaro, and E. W. Berg. 1968. The trace elements of human bone. *Journal of Bone and Joint Surgery* **50**–A(2): 326–334

Beisel, W. R. 1982. Single nutrients and immunity. *American Journal of Clinical Nutrition* **35**:417–468

Bender, M. M. 1968. Mass spectrometric studies of carbon-13 variations in corn and other grasses. *Radiocarbon* **10**:468–472

1971. Variations in the $^{12}C/^{13}C$ ratios of plants in relation to the pathway of photosynthetic carbon dioxide fixation. *Phytochemistry* **10**:1239–1244

Bender, M. M., D. A. Baerreis, and R. A. Steventon. 1981. Further light on carbon isotopes and Hopewell agriculture. *American Antiquity* **46**:346–353

Benfer, R. A. 1984. The challenges and rewards of sedentism: the preceramic village of Paloma, Peru. In *Paleopathology at the Origins of Agriculture,* ed. M. N. Cohen and G. J. Armelagos (New York: Academic Press)

Bennett, W. C. 1939. Archaeology of the north coast of Peru. An account of exploration and excavation in Viru and Lambayeque valleys. *Anthropological Papers of the American Museum of Natural History* **37**: part 1. New York

1950. The Gallinazo group, Viru valley, Peru. *Yale University Publications in Anthropology* **43**. New Haven

Berner, W., B. Stauffer, and H. Oeschger. 1979. Past atmospheric composition and climate: gas parameters measured on ice cores. *Nature* **276**:53–55

Bhatenager, R. S., and D. S. Prockop. 1966. Disassociation of the synthesis of sulfated mucopolysaccharides and the synthesis of collagen in embryonic cartilage. *Biophysica Acta* **130**:383–393

Bigalke, R. C. 1978. Present-day mammals of Africa. In *Evolution of African Mammals,* ed. V. J. Maglio and H. B. S. Cooke (Cambridge, Mass.: Harvard University Press)

Biltz, R. M., and D. Pellegrino. 1977. The nature of bone carbonate. *Clinical Orthopaedics and Related Research* **18**:81–90

Bird, J. 1948. Preceramic cultures in Chicama and Viru. *American Antiquity* **13**:21–28

Bird, R. McK. 1978. Archaeological maize from Peru. *Maize Genetics Cooperative Newsletter* **52**:90–92

1979. The evolution of maize: a new model for the early stages. *Maize Genetics Cooperative Newsletter* **53**:53–54

Bird, R. McK., and J. Bird. 1980. Gallinazo maize in the Chicania valley. *American Antiquity* **45**:325–332

Bisel, S. L. C. 1980. A pilot study in aspects of human nutrition in the ancient eastern Mediterranean, with particular attention to trace minerals in several populations from different time periods (Ph.D. dissertation, University of Minnesota, Minneapolis)

Blakely, R. L., and L. A. Beck. 1981. Trace elements, nutritional status, and social stratification at Etowah, Georgia. *Annals of the New York Academy of Science* **376**:417–431

Bligh, E. G., and W. J. Dyer. 1959. A rapid method of total lipid extraction and purification. *Canadian Journal of Biochemistry and Physiology* **37**(3):911–917

Blumenthal, N. C., F. Betts, and A. S. Posner. 1975. Effect of carbonate and biological macromolecules on formation and properties of hydroxyapatite. *Calcified Tissue Research* **81**:81–90

Boaz, N., and J. Hampel. 1978. Strontium content of fossil tooth enamel and diet of early hominids. *Journal of Paleontology* **52**:928–933

Bombin, M., and K. Muehlenbachs. 1985. $^{12}C/^{13}C$ ratios of Pleistocene mummified remains from Beringia. *Quaternary Research* **23**:123–129

Bornstein, P., A. H. Kang, and K. A. Piez. 1966. The nature and location of intramolecular cross-links in collagen. *Proceedings of the National Academy of Sciences* **55**:475–479

Bowen, H. J. M. 1966. *Trace Elements in Biochemistry* (New York: Academic Press)

1979. *Environmental Chemistry of the Elements* (New York: Academic Press)

Brätter, P., D. Gawlik, J. Lausch, and U. Rösick. 1977. On the distribution of trace elements in human skeletons. *Journal of Radioanalytical Chemistry* **37**:393–403

Broecker, W. S., and T.-H. Peng. 1982. *Tracers in the Sea* (Palisades, New York: Columbia University Press)

Broecker, W. S., D. M. Peteet, and D. Rind. 1985. Does the ocean–atmosphere system have more than one stable mode of operation? *Nature* **315**:21–26

Broida, M. O. 1983. Maize in Kentucky fort ancient diets: an analysis of carbon isotope ratios in human bone (M.A. thesis, Department of Anthropology, University of Kentucky, Lexington)

Brown, A. B. 1973. Bone strontium content as a dietary indicator in human skeletal populations (Ph.D. thesis, Department of Anthropology, University of Michigan, Ann Arbor)

Brown, A. B., and R. L. Blakely. 1985. Biocultural adaptation as reflected in trace element distribution. *Journal of Human Evolution* **14**:461–468

Brown, F. S., M. J. Baedaker, A. Nissenbaum, and I. R. Kaplan. 1972. Early diagenesis of a reducing fjord, Saanich Inlet, British Columbia, III: changes in organic constituents of sediments. *Geochimica et Cosmochimica Acta* **36**:1185–1203

Buikstra, J. E. 1984. The lower Illinois River region: a prehistoric context for the study of ancient diet and health. In *Paleopathology at the Origins of Agriculture*, ed. M. N. Cohen and G. J. Armelagos (New York: Academic Press)

Buikstra, J. E., L. Konigsberg, and J. Bullington. 1986. Fertility and the development of agriculture in the prehistoric Midwest. *American Antiquity* **51**:528–546

Bumsted, M. P. 1983. Adult variation in ^{13}C: pre-Columbian North America. *American Journal of Physical Anthropology* **60**:178–179

1984. Human variation: $\delta^{13}C$ in adult bone collagen and the relation to diet in an isochronous C_4 (maize) archaeological population. Publication LA 10259T, Los Alamos National Laboratory, Los Alamos

1985. Past human behaviour from bone chemical analysis – respects and prospects. *Journal of Human Evolution* **14**:539–551

Burleigh, R., and D. Brothwell. 1978. Studies on Amerindian dogs. I:

carbon isotopes in relation to maize in the diet of domestic dogs from early Peru and Ecuador. *Journal of Archaeological Science* 5:355–362
Butzer, K. 1978. Changing Holocene environments at the Koster site: a geo-archaeological perspective. *American Antiquity* **43**:408–413
Calloway, D. H., R. D. Giauque, and F. P. Costa. 1974. The superior mineral content of some American Indian foods in comparison to federally donated counterpart commodities. *Ecology of Food and Nutrition* **3**:203–211
Carbone, V. A., and B. C. Keel. 1985. Preservation of plant and animal remains. In *The Analysis of Prehistoric Diets*, ed. R. I. Gilbert, Jr., and J. H. Mielke (Orlando, Florida: Academic Press)
Casey, C. E., and M. F. Robinson. 1984. Some aspects of nutritional trace element research. In *Metal Ions in Biological Systems*, vol. 16, ed. H. Sigel (New York: Marcel Dekker)
Cerling, T. E. 1977. Paleochemistry of Plio-Pleistocene Lake Turkana and diagenesis of its sediments (Ph.D. dissertation, University of California, Berkeley)
Chickerur, N. S., M. S. Tung, and W. E. Brown. 1980. A mechanism for incorporation of carbonate into apatite. *Calcified Tissue International* **32**:55–62
Chisholm, B. S., D. E. Nelson, and H. P. Schwarcz. 1982. Stable isotope ratios as a measure of marine versus terrestrial protein in ancient diets. *Science* **216**:1131–1132
Chisholm, B. S., D. E. Nelson, K. A. Hobson, H. P. Schwarcz, and M. Knyf. 1983a. Carbon isotope measurement techniques for bone collagen: notes for the archaeologist. *Journal of Archaeological Science* **10**:355–360
Chisholm, B. S., H. P. Schwarcz, and D. E. Nelson. 1983b. Application of stable isotope measurements to paleodiet reconstruction on the northwest coast of North America. Paper presented at the I.C.A.E.S., Vancouver, Canada, August 1983
Chisholm, B. S., D. E. Nelson, and H. P. Schwarcz. 1983c. Marine and terrestrial protein in prehistoric diets on the British Columbia coast. *Current Anthropology* **24**(3):396–398
Chisholm, B., J. Driver, S. Dube, and H. P. Schwarcz. 1986. Assessment of prehistoric bison foraging and movement patterns via stable carbon isotopic analysis. *Plains Anthropologist* **31**:193–205
Christopherson, K. M., and P. O. Pedersen. 1939. Investigations into dental conditions in the Neolithic period and in the Bronze Age in Denmark. *Dental Record* **59**:575–585
Chung, E., and E. J. Miller. 1974. Collagen polymorphism: characterization of molecules with the chain composition {Alpha1(III)}3 in human tissues. *Science* **183**:1200
Cleland, C. E. 1976. The focal–diffuse model: an evolutionary perspective on the prehistoric cultural adaptations of the eastern United States. *Mid-Continental Journal of Archaeology* **1**:59–76

Cohen, M. N. 1975. Some problems in the quantificative analysis of vegetable refuse illustrated by a Late Horizon site the Peruvian coast. *Nawpa Pacha* **10–12**:49–60
Collier, D. 1955. Cultural chronology and change as reflected in the ceramics of the Viru valley, Peru. *Fieldiana Anthropology* **43**. Chicago Natural History Museum, Chicago
Conner, M. D. 1984. Population structure and biological variation in the Late Woodland of west-central Illinois (Ph.D. dissertation, University of Chicago)
Connor, M., and D. Slaughter. 1984. Diachronic investigation of Eskimo diet utilizing trace element analysis. *Arctic Anthropology* **21**:123–134
Cook, D. C., and J. E. Buikstra. 1979. Health and differential survival in prehistoric populations: prenatal defects. *American Journal of Physical Anthropology* **51**:649–664
Cook, S. F. 1951. The fossilization of human bone: calcium, phosphate, and carbonate. *University of California Publications in American Archaeology and Ethnology* **40**(6):263–280
Cook, S. F., and R. F. Heizer. 1947. The quantitative investigation of aboriginal sites: analysis of human bone. *American Journal of Physical Anthropology* **5**:201–219
1953. Archaeological dating by chemical analysis of bone. *Southwestern Journal of Anthropology* **9**:201–220
Cook, S. F., S. T. Brooks, and H. E. Ezra-Cohn. 1962. Histological studies on fossil bone. *Journal of Paleontology* **36**:483–494
Craig, H. 1953. The geochemistry of the stable carbon isotopes. *Geochimica et Cosmochimica Acta* **3**:53–92
1954. Carbon-13 variations in sequoia rings and the atmosphere. *Science* **119**:141–143
Crommelin, D. J., W. I. Higuchi, J. L. Fox, P. J. Spooner, and A. V. Katdare. 1983. Dissolution rate behavior of hydroxyapatite–fluorapatite mixtures. *Caries Research* **17**:289–296
Curry, J. D. 1962. The strength of bone. *Nature* **195**:513–514
Cutler, H. C., and L. C. Blake. 1973. Plants from archaeological sites east of the Rockies. Report no. 1, American Archaeology Division, University of Missouri, Columbia
Darby, A. J., and P. J. Meunier. 1981. Mean wall thickness in formation periods of trabecular bone packets in idiopathic osteoporosis. *Calcified Tissue International* **33**:199–204
Decker, K. W. 1986. Isotopic and chemical reconstruction of diet and its biological and social dimensions at Grasshopper Pueblo, Arizona. Paper presented at the 51st Annual Meeting of the Society for American Archaeology, New Orleans, La., April 1986
Degens, E. T., M. Behrendt, B. Gotthardt, and E. Reppman. 1968. Metabolic fractionation of carbon isotopes in marine plankton, part II:

data on samples collected off the coast of Peru and Ecuador. *Deep Sea Research* **15**:11–20

Delmas, R. J., J.-M. Ascencio, and M. Legrand. 1980. Polar ice evidence that atmospheric CO_2, 10,000 yr BP, was 50% of present. *Nature* **284**:155–157

DeNiro, M. J. 1977. I. Carbon isotope distribution in food chains, and II. Mechanism of carbon isotope fractionation associated with lipid synthesis (Ph.D. dissertation, California Institute of Technology, Pasadena)

1985. Postmortem preservation and alteration of *in vivo* bone collagen isotope ratios in relation to paleodietary reconstruction. *Nature* **317**:806–809

DeNiro, M. J., and S. Epstein. 1978a. Carbon isotopic evidence for different feeding patterns in two *Hyrax* species occupying the same habitat. *Science* **201**:906–907

1978b. Influence of diet on the distribution of carbon isotopes in animals. *Geochimica et Cosmochimica Acta* **42**:495–506

1978c. Fourth International Conference on Geochronology, Cosmochronology, and Isotope Geology. U.S. Geological Survey Open File Report 78–701

1981. Influence of diet on the distribution of nitrogen isotopes in animals. *Geochimica et Cosmochimica Acta* **45**:341–351

DeNiro, M. J., and C. A. Hastorf. 1985. Alteration of $^{15}N/^{14}N$ and $^{13}C/^{12}C$ ratios of plant matter during the initial stages of diagenesis: studies utilizing archaeological specimens from Peru. *Geochimica et Cosmochimica Acta* **49**:97–115

DeNiro, M. J., and M. J. Schoeninger. 1985. Stable carbon and nitrogen isotope ratios of bone collagen: variation within individuals, between sexes, and within populations raised on monotonous diets. *Journal of Archaeological Science* **10**:199–203

Dennison, K. J. 1986. Amino acids in archaeological bone (2). *Journal of Archaeological Science* **13**:393–401

Deshmuck, K., M. Just, and M. E. Nimni. 1973. Comparative study of cross-linking precursors present in rat skin and tail tendons collagen. *Clinical Orthopaedics and Related Research* **91**:186–196

Deuser, W. G., E. T. Degens, and R. R. Guillard. 1968. Carbon isotope relationships between plankton and sea water. *Geochimica et Cosmochimica Acta* **32**:657–660

Doberenz, A. R., and R. Lund. 1966. Evidence for collagen in a fossil bone of the Lower Jurassic. *Nature* **212**:1502–1503

Drucker, P. 1955. *Indians of the Northwest Coast* (New York: Natural History Press)

Dungworth, G., N. J. Vrencker, and A. W. Schwartz. 1975. Amino acid composition of Pleistocene collagen. *Comparative Biochemistry and Physiology B* **51**:331–335

Dungworth, G., A. W. Schwartz, and L. van De Leemput. 1976. Comparison and racemization of amino acids in mammoth collagen determined by gas and liquid chromatography. *Comparative Biochemistry and Physiology B* **53**:473–480

Dunstone, J. R. 1959. Some cation-binding properties of cartilage. *Biochemical Journal* **72**:165–172

Eadie, B. J., and W. M. Sackett. 1971. Stable carbon isotope variations in the Antarctic marine ecosystem. *Antarctic Journal* (United States) **6**:154

Eanes, E. D., I. Zipkin, R. A. Harper, and A. S. Posner. 1965. Small-angle X-ray diffraction analysis of the effect of fluoride on human bone apatite. *Archives of Oral Biology* **10**:161–173

Easthoe, J. E. 1961. The chemical composition of bone. In *Biochemist's Handbook*, ed. C. Long (London: Spon)

Easthoe, J. E., and A. A. Leach. 1977. Chemical constituents of gelatin. In *The Science and Technology of Gelatin*, ed. A. G. Ward and A. Courts (New York: Academic Press)

Eaton, S. B., and M. Konner. 1985. Paleolithic nutrition. *New England Journal of Medicine* **312**:283–289

Eickmeyer, W. G., and M. M. Bender. 1976. Carbon isotope ratios of crassulacean acid metabolism species in relation to climate and phytosociology. *Oecologia* **25**:341–347

Elias, M. 1980. The feasibility of dental strontium for diet assessment of human populations. *American Journal of Physical Anthropology* **53**:1–4

Elias, R. W., Y. Hirao, and C. C. Patterson. 1982. The circumvention of the natural biopurification of calcium nutrient pathways by atmospheric inputs of industrial lead. *Geochimica et Cosmochimica Acta* **46**:2561–2580

Eliot, T. S. 1944. *Four Quartets* (London: Faber and Faber)

Ellis, R. P., J. C. Vogel, and A. Fuls. 1980. Photosynthetic pathways and the geographical distribution of grasses in South West Africa/Namibia. *South African Journal of Science* **76**:307–314

El-Najjar, M. Y. 1976. Maize, malaria and the anemias in the pre-Columbian New World. *Yearbook of Physical Anthropology* **20**:329–337

Engel, F. 1970. *Las Lomas de Iguanily et Complejo de Haldas* (Lima: Universidad Nacional Agraria)

Engström, A., R. Björnerstedt, and C.-J. Clemedson. 1957. *Bone and Radiostrontium* (Stockholm: Almqvist and Wiksell)

Ericson, J. E. 1981. Residence patterns by isotopic characterization. Paper presented at Annual Meeting of the Society for Archaeological Sciences, San Diego, Calif.

1985. Strontium isotope characterization in the study of prehistoric human ecology. *Journal of Human Evolution* **14**:503–514

Ericson, J. E., S. Shirahata, and C. C. Patterson. 1978. Background skeletal lead content in proto-smelting humans: lead analysis of a tooth and femur from a Guanape burial, Viru valley, Peru. Paper presented to the 18th Annual Meeting of the Institute of Andean Studies, Berkeley

1979. Skeletal concentration of lead in ancient Peruvians. *New England Journal of Medicine* **300**:946–951

Ericson, J. E., C. Sullivan, and H. Krueger. 1980. Geographical and temporal gradients of dietary C13/12 in human bone tissue. Paper presented to the 20th Annual Meeting of the Institute of Andean Studies, Berkeley

Ericson, J. E., C. H. Sullivan, and N. T. Boaz. 1981. Diets of Pliocene mammals from Omo, Ethiopia, deduced from carbon isotopic ratios in tooth apatite. *Palaeogeography, Palaeoclimatology, Palaeoecology* **36**:69–73

Ericson, J. E., M. West, C. H. Sullivan, and H. Krueger. 1983. Stable carbon isotopes in prehistoric human bone apatite and collagen from the Viru valley. Paper presented at the XIth International Congress of Anthropological and Ethnological Sciences, Vancouver, B.C., Canada

Eyre, D. R. 1980. Collagen, molecular diversity in the body's protein scaffold. *Science* **207**:1315–1322

Falconer, I. R. 1969. *Mammalian Biochemistry* (London: J. A. Churchill)

Farnsworth, P., J. E. Brady, M. J. DeNiro, and R. S. MacNeish. 1985. A re-evaluation of the isotopic and archaeological reconstruction of diet in the Tehuacan valley. *American Antiquity* **50**:102–116

Farquhar, G. D., M. H. O'Leary, and J. A. Berry. 1982. On the relationship between carbon isotope discrimination and the intercellular carbon dioxide concentration in leaves. *Australian Journal of Plant Physiology* **9**:121–137

Fernandez-Madrid, F., A. S. Prasad, and D. Oberlas. 1976. Zinc in collagen metabolism. In *Trace Elements in Human Health and Disease*, vol. I: *Zinc and Copper*, ed. A. S. Prasad and D. Oberlas (New York: Academic Press)

Fischer, C. G., R. D. Ediger, and J. R. Delany. 1981. An automatic, sequential multielement ICP emission spectrometer. *American Laboratory* **13**(2):346–354

Fisher, L. W., and J. D. Termine. 1985. Purification of the noncollagenous proteins from bone: technical pitfalls and how to avoid them. In *Current Advances in Skeletogenesis*, ed. A. Orney, A. Harele, and J. Sela (Amsterdam: Elsevier)

Fontugne, M. R., and J.-C. Duplessy. 1981. Organic carbon isotopic fractionation by marine plankton in the temperature range −1 to 31°C. *Oceanologica Acta* **4**(1):85–90

Ford, J. A. 1949. Cultural dating of prehistoric sites in Viru valley, Peru. In *Surface Survey of the Viru Valley, Peru. Anthropological Papers of the American Museum of Natural History* **43**. New York

Frayer, D. W. 1980. Sexual dimorphism in the Late Pleistocene and Holocene of Europe. *Journal of Human Evolution* 9:399–415

Freeman, J. E. 1966. Price Site III, Ri 4, a burial ground in Richland County, Wisconsin. *The Wisconsin Archaeologist* 47:33–87

Frost, H. M. 1964. *Mathematical Elements of Lamellar Bone Remodelling* (Springfield, Ill.: C. C. Thomas)

1969. Tetracycline-based histological analysis of bone remodelling. *Calcified Tissue Research* 3:211–237

1985. The "new bone": some anthropological potentials. *Yearbook of Physical Anthropology* 28:211–226

1987. Secondary osteon populations. *Yearbook of Physical Anthropology* 30:221–238

Fry, B., A. Joern, and P. L. Parker. 1978a. Delta C-13 food web analysis of a Texas sand dune community. *Geochimica et Cosmochimica Acta* 42:1299–1302

1978b. Grasshopper food web analysis: use of carbon isotope ratios to examine feeding relationships among terrestrial herbivores. *Ecology* 59:498–506

Furr, A. K., L. H. MacDaniels, L. E. St. John, Jr., W. H. Gutenmann, I. S. Pakkala, and D. J. Lisk. 1979. Elemental composition of tree nuts. *Bulletin of Environmental Contamination and Toxicology* 21:392–396

Gaebler, O. H., T. G. Vitti, and R. Vukmirovich. 1966. Isotope effects in metabolism of ^{14}N and ^{15}N from unlabeled dietary proteins. *Canadian Journal of Biochemistry* 44:1249–1257

Garlick, J. D. 1969. Buried bone. In *Science in Archaeology*, ed. D. Brothwell and E. Higgs (New York: Praeger Press)

Gay, S., and E. J. Miller. 1978. *Collagen in the Physiology and Pathology of Connective Tissue* (New York: Fisher)

Geidel, A. A. 1981. Paleonutrition and social stratification: a study of trace elements in human skeletons from the Dallas archaeological culture of eastern Tennessee (M.A. thesis, Pennsylvania State University)

1982. Trace element studies for Mississippian skeletal remains: findings from neutron activation analysis. *Masca Journal* 2:13–16

Geiger, E., and G. Borgstrom. 1962. Fish protein, nutritive aspects. In *Fish as Food*, vol. II, ed. G. Borgstrom (New York: Wiley)

Gilbert, R. I. 1975. Trace element analyses of three skeletal Amerindian populations at Dickson Mounds (Ph.D. dissertation, University of Massachusetts, Amherst)

1977. Applications of trace element research to problems in archaeology. In *Biocultural Adaptation in Prehistoric America*, ed. R. L. Blakely (Athens: University of Georgia Press)

1985. Stress, paleonutrition, and trace elements. In *The Analysis of Prehistoric Diets*, ed. R. I. Gilbert and J. H. Mielke (Orlando, Florida: Academic Press)

Giraud-Guille, M. M. 1988. Twisted plywood architecture of collagen fibrils in human compact bone osteons. *Calcified Tissue International* **42**:167–180

Glimcher, M. 1981. On form and function of bone: from molecules to organs. Wolff's Law revisited. In *The Chemistry and Biology of Mineralized Connective Tissue*, ed. A. Veis (New York: Elsevier)

Gordon, C. J., and J. E. Buikstra. 1981. Soil pH, bone preservation, and sampling bias at mortuary sites. *American Antiquity* **46**:566–571

Grant, M. E., and D. J. Prockop. 1972. The biosynthesis of collagen. *New England Journal of Medicine* **286**:194–199

Gustavson, K. H. 1956. *The Chemistry and Reactivity of Collagen* (New York: Academic Press)

Guthrie, R. D. 1982. Mammals of the mammoth steppe as paleoenvironmental indicators. In *Paleoecology of Beringia*, ed. D. M. Hopkins, J. V. Matthews, Jr., C. E. Schweger, and S. B. Young (New York: Academic Press)

Hadjimarkos, D. M. 1973. Trace elements and dental health. In *Trace Substances in Environmental Health*, vol. VIII, ed. D. D. Hemphill (Columbia: University of Missouri Press)

Haines, E. L., and C. L. Montague. 1979. Food sources of estuarine invertebrates analyzed using $^{13}C/^{12}C$ ratios. *Ecology* **60**(1):48–56

Hajic, E. R. 1981. Geology and paleopedology of the Koster archaeological site, Greene County, Illinois (M.A. thesis, Department of Geology, University of Iowa, Iowa City)

Håkansson, S. 1976. University of Lund radiocarbon dates IX. *Radiocarbon* **18**:290–320

1982. University of Lund radiocarbon dates XV. *Radiocarbon* **24**:194–213

1984. University of Lund radiocarbon dates XVII. *Radiocarbon* **26**:392–411

Halstead, L. B. 1974. *Vertebrate Hard Tissue* (London: Wykeham Publications)

Hamilton, E. I. 1979. Relations between metal elements in man's diet and environmental factors. In *Trace Substances in Environmental Health*, vol. XIII, ed. D. D. Hemphill (Columbia: University of Missouri Press)

Hare, P. E. 1980. Organic geochemistry of bone and its relation to the survival of bone in the natural environment. In *Fossils in the Making*, ed. A. K. Behrensmeyer and A. P. Hill (Chicago: University of Chicago Press)

Hare, P. E., and P. H. Ableson. 1968. Racemization of amino acids in fossil shells. *Carnegie Institute of Washington Yearbook* **66**: 526–528

Hare, P. E. and M. L. F. Estep. 1982. Carbon and nitrogen isotopic composition of amino acids in modern and fossil collagens. *Carnegie Institute of Washington Yearbook* 82:410–414

Hare, P. E., and R. M. Mitterer. 1969. Laboratory simulation of diagenesis in fossils. *Carnegie Institute of Washington Yearbook* **67**:205–208

Hare, P. E., T. C. Hoering, and J. K. King (Eds.). 1980. *Biogeochemistry of Amino Acids* (New York: Wiley)

Harris, E. D. 1973. Copper in human and animal health. In *Trace Elements in Health: A Review of Current Issues*, ed. J. Rose (London: Butterworths)

Hassan, A. A. 1975. Geochemical and mineralogical studies on bone material and their implications for radiocarbon dating (Ph.D. dissertation, Southern Methodist University, Dallas, Texas)

Hassan, A. A., and D. J. Ortner. 1977. Inclusions in bone material as a source of error in radiocarbon dating. *Archaeometry* **19**:131–135

Hassan, A. A., J. D. Termine, and C. V. Haynes, Jr. 1977. Mineralogical studies on bone apatite and their implications for radiocarbon dating. *Radiocarbon* **19**:364–374

Hatch, J. W. 1976. Status in death: principles of ranking in Dallas culture mortuary remains (Ph.D. dissertation, Pennsylvania State University)

Hatch, J. W., and A. A. Geidel. 1983. Tracing status and diet in prehistoric Tennessee. *Archaeology* January–February: 56–59

1985. Status-specific dietary variation in two world cultures. *Journal of Human Evolution* **14**:469–476

Hatch, M. D., and C. R. Slack. 1966. Photosynthesis by sugar-cane leaves: a new carboxylation reaction and the pathway of sugar formation. *Biochemistry Journal* **101**:103–111

1970. Photosynthetic CO_2-fixation pathways. *Annual Review of Plant Physiology* **21**:141–162

Hatch, M. D., C. R. Slack, and H. S. Johnson. 1967. Further studies on a new pathway of photosynthetic carbon dioxide fixation in sugar-cane, and its occurrence in other species. *Biochemistry Journal* **102**:417–422

Hattersley, P. W. 1982. $\delta^{13}C$ values of C_4 types in grasses. *Australian Journal of Plant Physiology* **9**:139–154

Hayden, B., B. S. Chisholm, and H. P. Schwarcz. 1987. Fishing and foraging: marine resources in the Upper Paleolithic of France. In *Regional Perspectives on the Pleistocene Prehistory of the Old World*, ed. O. Soffer (New York: Plenum)

Heaton, T. H. E., J. C. Vogel, G. Chevallarie, and G. Collett. 1986. Climatic influence on the isotopic composition of bone nitrogen. *Nature* **322**:822–823

Hedges, R. E. M., and C. J. A. Wallace. 1978. The survival of biochemical information in archaeological bone. *Journal of Archaeological Science* **5**:377–386

Heinz, H. J., Company. 1963. *Nutritional Data* (Pittsburgh, Pa: H. J. Heinz Co.)

Henderson, P., C. A. Marlow, T. I. Molleson and C. T. Williams. 1983. Patterns of chemical change during bone fossilization. *Nature* **306**:358–360

Henkin, R. I. 1969. Trace metals and taste. In *Trace Substances in Environmental Health*, vol. III, ed. D. D. Hemphill (Columbia: University of Missouri Press)

Herring, G. M. 1972. The organic matrix of bone. In *The Biochemistry and Physiology of Bone*, vol. 1, ed. G. H. Bourne (New York: Academic Press)

Hill, A. P. 1980. Early post-mortem damage to the remains of some contemporary East African mammals. In *Fossils in the Making*, ed. A. K. Behrensmeyer and A. P. Hill (Chicago: University of Chicago Press)

Hirst, G. 1978. Interregional trade and the formation of prehistoric gateway communities. *American Antiquity* **43**:35–45

Ho, Tong-Yun. 1965. The amino acid composition of bone and teeth proteins in Late Pleistocene mammals. *Proceedings of the National Academy of Science* **54**:26–31

1967. The amino acids of bone and dentine collagen. *Biochimica et Biophysica Acta* **133**:568–573

Hobson, K. A., and S. Collier. 1984. Marine and terrestrial protein in Australian aboriginal diets. *Current Anthropology* **25**(2):238–240

Hodges, R. M., N. S. MacDonald, R. Husbaum, R. Stearns, F. Ezmirlian, P. Spain, and C. McArthur. 1950. The strontium content of human bones. *Journal of Biological Chemistry* **185**:519–524

Hopkins, D. M., J. V. Matthews, Jr., C. E. Schweger, and S. B. Young (Eds.). 1982. *Paleoecology of Beringia* (New York: Academic Press)

Huss-Ashmore, R., A. H. Goodman, and G. J. Armelagos. 1982. Nutritional inference from paleopathology. In *Advances in Archaeological Method and Theory*, vol. 5, ed. M. B. Schiffer (New York: Academic Press)

Isaacs, W. A., K. Little, J. A. Currey, and L. B. H. Tarlo. 1963. Collagen and a cellulose-like substance in fossil dentine and bone. *Nature* **197**:192

Ives, D. J. 1975. Trace element analysis of archaeological materials. *American Antiquity* **40**:235–236

Iyengar, G. V., W. E. Kollmer, and H. J. M. Bowen. 1978. The *Elemental Composition of Human Tissues and Body Fluids* (New York: Verlag Chemie)

Jackson, S. A., A. G. Cartwright, and D. Lewis. 1978. The morphology of bone mineral crystals. *Calcified Tissue Research* **25**:217–222

Jansen, H. S. 1962. Depletion of carbon-13 in a young Kauri tree. *Nature* **196**:84–85

Jenkins, G. N. 1978. Chemical composition of teeth. In *The Physiology and Biochemistry of the Mouth*, 4th edn. (Oxford: Blackwell)

Jochim, M. 1976. *Hunter-Gatherer Subsistence and Settlement. A Predictive Model* (New York: Academic Press)

Jowsey, J. 1973. Audiradiographic and microscopic studies of bone. In *Biology and Mineralogy*, ed. I. Zipkin (New York: Wiley)

1977. *The Bone Biopsy* (New York: Plenum)
Julien, D. G. 1979. Maritime adaptation in prehistoric coastal Peru. Paper presented at the Annual Meeting of Cibola Anthropological Association, Brownsville, Texas
Kadar, A. 1984. Pathobiology and ageing. In *Ultrastructure of Connective Tissue Matrix*, ed. A. Ruggeri and P. M. Motta (Boston: Martinus Nijhoff)
Katz, S. H., M. L. Hediger, and L. A. Vallery. 1974. Traditional maize processing techniques in the new world. *Science* **184**:765–773
Katzenberg, M. A. 1984. Chemical analysis of prehistoric human bone from five temporally distinct populations in southern Ontario. National Museum of Man, Mercury Series. Archaeological Survey of Canada, Paper 129
Katzenberg, M. A., and H. P. Schwarcz. 1984. Dietary change in southern Ontario prehistory: evidence from strontium and stable isotopes of carbon and nitrogen. *American Journal of Physical Anthropology* **63**:177
Keeley, H. M. C., G. E. Hudson, and J. Evans. 1977. Trace element contents of human bones in various states of preservation. I. The soil silhouette. *Journal of Archaeological Science* **4**:19–24
Keeling, C. D. 1961. The concentration and isotopic abundances of carbon dioxide in rural and marine air. *Geochimica et Cosmochimica Acta* **24**:277–279
Keeling, C. D., W. G. Mook, and P. P. Tans. 1978. Recent trends in the $^{12}C/^{13}C$ ratio of atmospheric carbon dioxide. *Nature* **277**:121–122
Kelley, D. H., and B. D. Bonavia. 1963. New evidence for pre-ceramic maize on the coast of Peru. *Nawpa Pacha* **1**:39–41
Kivirikko, K. I. 1970. Urinary excretions of hydroxyproline in health and disease. *International Review of Connective Tissue Research* **5**: 93–163
Klein, R. G. 1972. The Late Quaternary mammalian fauna of Nelson Bay Cave (Cape Province, South Africa): its implications for megafaunal extinctions and environmental and cultural change. *Quaternary Research* **2**:135–142
1976. The fossil history of *Rapicerus* H. Smith, 1927 (Bovidae, Mammalia) in the Cape biotic zone. *Annals of the South African Museum* **71**:161–191
Klepinger, L. L. 1983. Elemental analysis of archaeological bone: a cautionary tale. Paper presented at the XIth International Congress of Archaeological and Ethnological Sciences
1984. Nutritional assessment from bone. *Annual Reviews in Anthropology* **13**:75–96
Kroeber, A. 1930. Archaeological explorations in Peru, part II: the northern coast. Field Museum of Natural History Anthropological Memoirs 1, no. 2, Chicago
Krueger, H. W. 1985. Models for carbon and nitrogen isotopes in bone.

Poster paper presented at Biomineralization Conference, Airlie House, Warrenton, Va.
Krueger, H. W., and C. H. Sullivan. 1984. Models for carbon isotope fractionation between diet and bone. In *Stable Isotopes in Nutrition*, ed. J. R. Turnland and P. E. Johnson. American Chemical Society Symposium Series, no. 258
Kuhn, K. 1982. Chemical properties of collagen. In *Immunochemistry of the Extracellular Matrix*, vol. I, ed. H. Furthmayr (Boca Raton, Florida: CRC Press)
Kuhnlein, H. V. 1981. Dietary mineral ecology of the Hopi. *Journal of Ethnobiology* 1:84–94
Kuhnlein, H. V., and D. H. Calloway. 1979. Adventitious mineral elements in Hopi Indian diets. *Journal of Food Science* **44**:282–285
Kyle, J. H. 1986. Effect of post-burial contamination on the concentrations of major and minor elements in human bones and teeth: the implications for Palaeodietary research. *Journal of Archaeological Science* **13**:403–416
Lambert, J. B., C. B. Szpunar, and J. E. Buikstra. 1979. Chemical analysis of excavated human bone from Middle and Late Woodland sites. *Archaeometry* **21**:115–129
Lambert, J. B., S. M. Vlasak, A. C. Thometz, and J. E. Buikstra. 1982. A comparative study of the chemical analysis of ribs and femurs in Woodland populations. *American Journal of Physical Anthropology* **59**:289–294
Lambert, J. B., S. V. Simpson, J. E. Buikstra, and D. Hanson. 1983. Electron microprobe analysis of elemental distribution in excavated human femurs. *American Journal of Physical Anthropology* **62**:409–423
Lambert, J. B., S. V. Simpson, C. B. Szpunar, and J. E. Buikstra. 1984a. Analysis of soil associated with Woodland burials. In *Archaeological Chemistry III*, ed. J. B. Lambert (Washington, D.C.: American Chemical Society)
1984b. Copper and barium as dietary discriminants: the effects of diagenesis. *Archaeometry* **26**:131–138
1984c. Ancient human diet from inorganic analysis of bone. *Accounts of Chemical Research* 17:298–305
1985a. Bone diagenesis and dietary analysis. *Journal of Human Evolution* **14**:477–482
Lambert, J. B., S. V. Simpson, C. G. Weiner, and J. E. Buikstra. 1985b. Induced metal–ion exchange in excavated human bone. *Journal of Archaeological Science* **12**:85–92
Land, L. S., E. L. Lundelius, Jr., and S. Valastro. 1980. Isotope ecology of deer bones. *Paleogeography, Paleoclimatology, Paleoecology* **32**:143–151
Lanning, E. P. 1967. *Peru Before the Incas* (Englewood Cliffs, N.J.: Prentice-Hall)

Larco Hoyle, R. 1945. *La Cultura Viru* (Buenos Aires: Sociedad Geografica)

Larson, L. H. 1971. Archaeological implications of social stratification at the Etowah site, Georgia. In *Approaches to the Social Dimensions of Mortuary Practices*, ed. J. A. Brown. Memoirs of the Society for American Archaeology, no. 25

Larsson, L. 1983. The Skateholm Project – a Late Mesolithic settlement and cemetery complex at a southern Swedish bay. *Meddelanden från Lunds universitets historiska museum* 1983–84:5–38

Leavitt, S. W., and A. Long. 1986. Trends of $^{13}C/^{12}C$ ratios in pinyon tree rings of the American Southwest and the global carbon cycle. *Radiocarbon* **28**:376–382

Leblond, C. P., and M. Weinstock. 1976. A comparative study of dentin and bone formation. In *The Biochemistry and Physiology of Bone*, ed. G. H. Bourne (New York: Academic Press)

Lee Thorp, J., and N. J. van der Merwe. 1987. Carbon isotope analysis of fossil bone apatite. *South African Journal of Science* **83**:712–715

Legeros, R. Z. 1981. Consequences of fluoride incorporation on some properties of apatites. Chronicles of the 58th I.A.D.R. General Session, Osaka

Legeros, R. Z., and M. S. Tung. 1983. Chemical stability of the carbonate- and fluoride-containing apatites. *Caries Research* **17**:419–429

Lerman, J. C. 1975. How to interpret variation in the carbon isotope ratio of plants: biologic and environmental effects. In *Environment and Biological Control of Photosynthesis*, ed. R. Marcelle (The Hague: D. W. Junk Publishers)

Libby, W. F., R. Berger, J. F. Mead, G. V. Alexander, and J. F. Ross. 1964. Replacement rates for human tissue from atmospheric radiocarbon. *Science* **146**:1170–1172

Liebscher, K., and H. Smith. 1968. Essential and non-essential trace elements: determining whether an element is essential or non-essential in human tissue. *Archives of Environmental Health* **17**:881–890

Likins, R. C., H. G. McCann, A. S. Posner, and B. Scott. 1960. Comparative fixation of calcium and strontium by synthetic hydroxyapatite. *Journal of Biological Chemistry* **236**:2804–2806

Lindenbaum, A., and K. E. Kuettner. 1967. Mucopolysaccharides and mucoproteins of calf scapula. *Calcified Tissue Research* **1**:153–165

Lindsay, W. L. 1979. *Chemical Equilibria in Soils* (New York: Wiley)

Lindstedt, S., and D. J. Prockop. 1961. Isotopic studies on urinary hydroxyproline as evidence for rapidly catabolized forms of collagen in young rats. *Journal of Biological Chemistry* **236**:1399–1403

Lips, P., P. Courpron, and P. J. Meunier. 1978. Mean wall thickness of trabecular bone packets in the human iliac crest: changes with age. *Calcified Tissue Research* **26**:13–17

Livingstone, D. A., and W. D. Clayton. 1980. An altitudinal cline in tropical African grass floras and its paleoecological significance. *Quaternary Research* **13**:392–402

Long, S. B. 1980. The continuing debate over the use of ratio variables: facts and fiction. In *Sociological Methodology*, ed. K. F. Schuessler (San Francisco: Fossey-Bass)

Longin, R. 1971. New method of collagen extraction for radiocarbon dating. *Nature* **230**:241–242

Lovell, N. C., D. E. Nelson, and H. P. Schwarcz. 1986. Carbon isotope ratios in paleodiet: lack of age or sex effects. *Archaeometry* **28**: 51–55

Lovell, N. C., B. S. Chisholm, D. E. Nelson, and H. P. Schwarcz. n.d. Prehistoric salmon consumption in interior British Columbia. *Canadian Journal of Archaeology* (in press)

Lowden, J. A., and W. Dyck. 1974. Seasonal variations in the isotope ratios of carbon in maple leaves and other plants. *Canadian Journal of Earth Science* **11**:79–88

Lynott, M. J., T. W. Boutton, J. E. Price, and D. E. Nelson. 1986. Stable carbon isotopic evidence for maize agriculture in southeastern Missouri and northeastern Arkansas. *American Antiquity* **51**:51–65

Lyton, T. D. B., and M. S. Baxter. 1978. Stable carbon isotopes in human tissues. *Nature* **273**:750–751

Maat, G. J. R. 1981. Human remains at the Dutch whaling stations on Spitzbergen – a physical anthropology study. In *Proceedings of the International Symposium on Early European Exploitation of the Northern Atlantic 800–1700* (Groningen: Arctic Centre)

1984. Search for secular growth changes in the Netherlands preceding 1850. In *Human Growth and Development*, ed. J. Borms *et al.* (Brussels: Free University of Brussels)

McConnaughey, T., and C. P. McRoy. 1979. Food-web structure and the fractionation of carbon isotopes in the Bering Sea. *Marine Biology* **53**:257–262

McConnell, D. 1973. *Apatite: Its Crystal Chemistry, Mineralogy, Utilization, and Geological and Biologic Occurrences* (New York: Springer Verlag)

Macko, S. A., M. L. F. Estep, M. H. Engel, and P. E. Hare. 1982a. Stable nitrogen isotope effects in the transanimation of amino acids. Papers from the Geophysical Laboratory, Carnegie Institute, Washington, D.C.

Macko, S. A., M. L. F. Estep, P. E. Hare, and T. C. Hoering. 1982b. Stable nitrogen and carbon isotopic composition of individual amino acids isolated from cultured micro-organisms. *Carnegie Institute of Washington Yearbook* **82**:404–409

McLean, F. C., and M. R. Urist. 1968. *Bone: An Introduction to the Physiology of Skeletal Tissue*, 3rd edn. (Chicago: University of Chicago Press)

Maglio, V. J. 1978. Patterns of faunal evolution. In *Evolution of African*

Mammals, ed. V. J. Maglio and H. B. S. Cooke (Cambridge: Harvard University Press)

Mahler, H. R., and E. H. Cordes. 1966. *Basic Biological Chemistry* (New York: Harper and Row)

Mangelsdorf, P. C., R. F. MacNeish, and W. C. Galinat. 1967. Teosinte in the Tamalipas Caves. *Harvard University Botanical Museum Leaflets* no. 22:33–63

Mangrum, S. 1974. Salt and settlement in Viru valley. Paper presented to the Annual Meeting of the Southwestern Anthropological Association, Santa Monica, Calif.

Mann, W. B. 1982. An international reference material for radiocarbon dating. Paper presented at the 11th International Radiocarbon Conference, Seattle

Mechanic, G. 1979. Collagen cross-linking. In *Skeletal Research*, ed. D. J. Simmons and A. S. Kumin (New York: Academic Press)

Medina, E., and P. Minchin. 1980. Stratification of $\delta^{13}C$ values of leaves in Amazonian rain forests. *Oecologia* **45**:377–378

Meiklejohn, C., C. Schentag, A. Venema, and P. Key. 1984. Socioeconomic change and patterns of pathology and variation in the Mesolithic and Neolithic of Western Europe: some suggestions. In *Paleopathology at the Origins of Agriculture*, ed. M. N. Cohen and G. J. Armelagos (Orlando: Academic Press)

Meister, A. 1965. *Biochemistry of the Amino Acids* (New York: Academic Press)

Merimee, T. J., M. D. Siperstein, and J. D. Hall. 1970. Capillary basemembrane structure: a comparative study of diabetes and sexually ateliotic dwarfs. *Journal of Clinical Investigation* **49**:2161–2164

Mertz, W. 1981. The essential trace elements. *Science* **213**:1332–1338

Middleton, J. 1844. On fluorine in bones: its sources and its application to the determination of the geological age of fossil bones. *Proceedings of the Geological Society of London* **4**:431–433

Minagawa, M., and E. Wada. 1984. Stepwise enrichment of ^{15}N along food chains. *Geochimica et Cosmochimica Acta* **481**:1135–1140

Minson, D. J., M. M. Ludlow, and J. H. Troughton. 1975. Differences in natural carbon isotope ratios of milk and hair from cattle grazing in tropical and temperate pastures. *Nature* **256**:602

Miyake, Y. and E. Wada. 1967. The abundance ratios of $^{15}N/^{14}N$ in marine environments. *Record of Oceanographic Works of Japan* **9**:37–53

Møllgaard, H., K. Lorenzen, I. G. Hansen, and P. R. Christensen. 1946. On phytic acid, its importance in metabolism and its enzymic cleavage in bread supplemented with calcium. *Biochemistry Journal* **40**:589–601

Mooney, H. A., J. H. Troughton, and J. A. Berry. 1977. Carbon isotope ratio measurements of succulent plants in southern Africa. *Oecologia* **3**:295–305

Moore, C. V. 1968. Iron. In *Modern Nutrition in Health and Disease*, ed. M. G. Wohl and R. S. Goodhart (Philadelphia: Lea and Febiger)

Moreno, E., M. Kresak, and R. G. Zahadnick. 1977. Physiochemical aspects of fluoride–apatite systems relevant to the study of dental caries. *Caries Research* **11**:141–171

Morgenthaler, P. W., and C. A. Baud. 1957. Sur une cause d'alteration des structures dans l'os humain fossile. *Schweizerische Gesellschaft für anthropologie und ethnologie* (Bern) **33**:9–10

Morris, V. C., and A. O. Levander. 1970. Selenium content of foods. *Journal of Nutrition* **100**:1383–1388

Moseley, M. E. 1975. *The Maritime Foundations of Andean Civilization* (Menlo Park, Calif.: Cummings Publishing Company)

Nancollas, G. H., and M. S. Mohan. 1970. The growth of hydroxyapatite crystals. *Archives of Oral Biology* **15**:731–745

Neftel, A., H. Oeschger, J. Schwander, B. Stauffer, and R. Zumbrunn. 1982. Ice core sample measurements give atmospheric CO_2 content during the past 40,000 yr. *Nature* **295**:220–223

Nelson, B., M. J. DeNiro, M. J. Schoeninger, and D. J. DePaolo. 1983a. Strontium isotope evidence for diagenetic alteration of bone: consequences for diet reconstruction. *Geological Society of America Bulletin* **15**:652

Nelson, D. G. A., J. D. B. Featherstone, J. F. Duncan, and T. W. Cutress. 1983b. Effect of carbonate and fluoride on the dissolution behavior of synthetic apatites. *Caries Research* **17**:200–221

Nelson, D., and N. J. Sauer. 1984. An evaluation of post-depositional changes in the trace element content of human bone. *American Antiquity* **49**:141–147

Nelson, D. E., B. Chisholm, N. C. Lovell, K. Hobson, and H. P. Schwarcz. n.d. Paleodiet determination by stable carbon isotope analysis. *Proceedings of the International Archaeometry Conference, Washington D.C., May 1984* (in press)

Neuman, W. F., and B. J. Mulryan. 1967. Synthetic hydroxyapatite crystals, III: the carbonate system. *Calcified Tissue Research* **1**:94–104

Neuman, W. F., and M. W. Neuman. 1958. *The Chemical Dynamics of Bone Material* (Chicago: University of Chicago Press)

Nie, N. H., C. H. Hull, J. G. Jenkins, K. Steinbrenner and D. H. Bent. 1975. *SPSS: Statistical Package for the Social Sciences*, 2nd edn. (New York: McGraw Hill)

Norr, L. 1981. Prehistoric Costa Rican diet as determined from stable carbon isotope ratios in bone collagen. *American Journal of Physical Anthropology* **54**:258–259

Oakley, K. P. 1955. Analytical methods of dating bones. *Advancement of Science*, London **11**:3–8

1964. The problem of man's antiquity. *Bulletin of the British Museum (Natural History)* **9**(5)

O'Dell, B. L. 1985. Bioavailability of and interaction among trace

elements. In *Trace Elements in Nutrition of Children*, ed. R. K. Chandra (New York: Raven Press)
O'Dell, B. L., and J. E. Savage. 1960. Effect of phytic acid on zinc availability. *Proceedings of the Society for Experimental Biology and Medicine* **103**:304–306
Odum, H. T. 1951. The stability of the world strontium cycle. *Science* **114**:407–411
Okazaki, M., Y. Moriwaki, T. Aoga, Y. Doi, and J. Takahashi. 1982a. Solubility behavior of CO_3 apatites in relation to crystallinity. *Caries Research* **15**:477–483
Okazaki, M., J. Takahashi, and H. Kimura. 1982b. Crystallinity, solubility, and dissolution rate behavior of fluoridated CO_3 apatites. *Journal of Biomedical Materials Research* **16**:851–860
O'Leary, M. H. 1981. Carbon isotope fractionation in plants. *Phytochemistry* **20**(4):553–567
Ortner, D. J., D. W. von Endt, and M. S. Robinson. 1972. The effect of temperature on protein decay in bone: its significance in nitrogen dating of archaeological specimens. *American Antiquity* **37**:514–520
Park, R., and S. Epstein. 1960. Carbon isotope fractionation during photosynthesis. *Geochimica et Cosmochimica Acta* **21**:110–126
1961. Metabolic fractionation of C^{13} and C^{12} in plants. *Plant Physiology* **36**:133–138
Parker, P. L. 1964. The biogeochemistry of the stable isotopes of carbon in a marine bay. *Geochimica et Cosmochimica Acta* **28**:1155–1164
Parker, R. B. 1965. Electron microprobe analysis of fossil bones and teeth. In *Abstracts for 1966*. Geological Society of America, Special Paper 101:415–416
Parker, R. B., and H. Toots. 1970. Minor elements in fossil bones. *Geological Society of America Bulletin* **81**:925–932
1974a. Minor elements in fossil bone: application to Quaternary samples. *Geological Survey of Wyoming, Report of Investigations* **10**:74–77
1974b. A final kick at the fluorine dating method. *Arizona Academy of Sciences Journal Proceedings* **11**:9–10
1980. Trace elements in bones as paleobiological indicators. In *Fossils in the Making*, ed. A. K. Behrensmeyer and A. P. Hill (Chicago: University of Chicago Press)
Parker, R. B., H. Toots, and J. W. Murphy. 1974. Leaching of sodium from skeletal parts during fossilization. *Geochimica et Cosmochimica Acta* **38**:1317–1321
Pate, D., and K. A. Brown. 1985. The stability of bone strontium in the geochemical environment. *Journal of Human Evolution* **14**:483–492
Pellegrino, E. D., and R. M. Biltz. 1972. Mineralization in the chick embryo, I: monohydrogen phosphate and carbonate relationships during the maturation of the bone crystal complex. *Calcified Tissue Research* **10**:128–135

Perinet, G. 1957. Etude par diffraction des rayons X de la structure des ossements fossiles (Ph.D. dissertation, Université d'Aix-Marseille: Paris, Librarie Masson et Cie)
1975. The mineral of bone. *Clinical Orthopaedics and Related Research* **200**:87–99
Persson, O., and E. Persson. 1984. Anthropological report on the Mesolithic graves from Skateholm, southern Sweden, I. *University of Lund Institute of Archaeology Report Series* 21
Phillips, J. L., and J. A. Brown (Eds.). 1983. *Archaic Hunters and Gatherers in the American Midwest* (New York: Academic Press)
Polach, H. A., M. J. Head, and J. D. Goyer. 1978. A.N.U. radiocarbon date list 6. *Radiocarbon* **20**(3):360–385
Posner, A. S. 1967. Relationship between diet and bone mineral ultrastructure. *Federation Proceedings* **26**(6):1717–1722
1969. The crystal chemistry of bone mineral. *Physiological Reviews* **49**:760–792
1985. The mineral of bone. *Clinical Orthopaedics and Related Research* **200**:87–99
Posner, A. S., R. A. Eanes, R. A. Harper, and I. Zipkin. 1963. X-ray diffraction analysis of the effect of fluoride on human bone apatite. *Archives of Oral Biology* 8:549–570
Price, T. D. 1985. Late Archaic subsistence in the midwestern United States. *Journal of Human Evolution* **14**:449–460
1986. The reconstruction of Mesolithic diets. In *The Mesolithic in Europe, IIIrd International Congress*, ed. C. Bonsall (Edinburgh: Edinburgh University Press)
Price, T. D., and M. Kavanagh. 1982. Bone composition and the reconstruction of diet: examples from the midwestern United States. *Mid-Continent Journal of Archaeology* 7:61–79
Price, T. D., M. Connor, and J. D. Parsen. 1985a. Bone strontium analysis and the reconstruction of diet: strontium discrimination in white-tailed deer. *Journal of Archaeological Science* **12**:419–442
Price, T. D., M. M. Schoeninger, and G. J. Armelagos. 1985b. Bone chemistry and past behavior: an overview. *Journal of Human Evolution* **14**:419–447
Price, T. D., R. W. Swick, and E. P. Chase. 1986. Bone chemistry and prehistoric diet: strontium studies of laboratory rats. *American Journal of Physical Anthropology* 70:365–375
Prockop, D. J., K. I. Kivirikko, L. Tuderman, and N. Guzman. 1979. The biosynthesis of collagen and its disorders. *New England Journal of Medicine* **301**:13–24, 77–85
Raisz, L. G. 1979. Factors influencing bone collagen synthesis and their possible role in osteoporosis. In *Osteoporosis II*, ed. V. S. Barzel (Grune and Straton)
1982. Osteoporosis. *Journal of the American Geriatric Society* **30**:127–138

1983. Regulation of bone formation. *New England Journal of Medicine* **314**:1676–1686

Rau, G. H., R. E. Sweeney, I. R. Kaplan, A. J. Mearns and D. R. Young. 1981. Differences in animal ^{13}C, ^{15}N and D abundance between a polluted and an unpolluted coastal site: likely indicators of sewage uptake by a marine food web. *Estuarine, Coastal and Shelf Science* **13**:701–707

Reinhold, J., B. Faradji, P. Abadi, and I. Faramarz. 1976. Binding of zinc to fiber and other solids of wholemeal bread. In *Trace Elements in Human Health and Disease*, vol. I: Copper and Zinc, ed. A. S. Prasad and D. Oberleas (New York: Academic Press)

Reitz, E. 1979. Faunal materials from Viru 434: an early Intermediate period site from coastal Peru. *Florida Journal of Anthropology* **4**(2):76–92

Rheingold, A. L., S. Hues, and M. N. Cohen. 1983. Strontium and zinc content in bones as an indication of diet. *Journal of Chemical Education* **60**:233–234

Rindos, D. 1984. *The Origin of Agriculture: An Evolutionary Perspective* (Orlando: Academic Press)

Rose, J. C., B. A. Burnett, M. S. Nassaney, and M. W. Blaener. 1984. Paleopathology and the origins of maize agriculture in the lower Mississippi valley and Caddoan culture areas. In *Paleopathology at the Origins of Agriculture*, ed. M. N. Cohen and G. J. Armelagos (Orlando, Florida: Academic Press)

Rosenthal, H. L. 1963. Uptake, turnover and transport of bone-seeking elements in fishes. *Annals of the New York Academy of Science* **109**:278–293

Rottländer, R. C. A. 1976. Variation in the chemical composition of bone as an indicator of climatic change. *Journal of Archaeological Science* **3**:83–88

Rubey, W. W. 1952. Geology and mineral resources of the Hardin and Brussels quadrangle (in Illinois). *U.S. Geological Survey, Professional Papers*, no. 218

Sackett, W. M., W. R. Eckelmann, M. L. Bender, and A. W. H. Bé. 1965. Temperature dependence of carbon isotope composition in marine plankton and sediments. *Science* **148**:235–237

Salomon, C. D., and N. Haas. 1967. Histological and histochemical observations on undecalcified sections of ancient bones from excavations in Israel. *Israel Journal of Medical Science* **3**:747–754

Schiffman, E., B. A. Corcoran, and G. R. Martin. 1966. The role of complex metals in initiating the mineralization of "elastin" and the precipitation of mineral from solution. *Archives of Biochemistry and Biophysics* **115**:87–92

Schneider, K. M. 1986. Dental caries, enamel composition, and subsistence among prehistoric Amerindians of Ohio. *American Journal of Physical Anthropology* **71**:95–102

Schoeninger, M. J. 1979a. Dietary reconstruction at Chalcatzingo, a Formative period site in Morelos, Mexico. *University of Michigan Museum of Anthropology Technical Report* 9. Contributions to Human Biology 2. Ann Arbor.

1979b. Diet and status at Chalcatzingo: some empirical and technical aspects of strontium analysis. *American Journal of Physical Anthropology* **51**:295–310

1981. The agricultural "revolution": its effect on human diet in prehistoric Iran and Israel. *Paleorient* 7:73–92

1982. Diet and the evolution of modern human form in the Middle East. *American Journal of Physical Anthropology* **58**:37–52

1985. Trophic level effects on $^{15}N/^{14}N$ and $^{13}C/^{12}C$ ratios in bone collagen and strontium levels in bone mineral. *Journal of Human Evolution* **14**:515–526

Schoeninger, M.J., and M. J. DeNiro. 1982. Carbon isotope ratios of apatite from fossil bone cannot be used to reconstruct diets of animals. *Nature* **297**:577–578

1984. Nitrogen and carbon isotopic composition of bone collagen in terrestrial and marine and vertebrates. *Geochimica et Cosmochimica Acta* **48**:625–639

Schoeninger, M. J., and C. S. Peebles. 1981. Effect of mollusc eating on human bone strontium levels. *Journal of Archaeological Science* 8:391–397

Schoeninger, M. J., and K. Spielmann. 1986. Stability of human diet at Pecos pueblo during a period of exchange with plains hunter–gatherers. *American Journal of Physical Anthropology* **69**:263

Schoeninger, M. J., M. J. DeNiro and H. Tauber. 1983. $^{15}N/^{14}N$ ratios of bone collagen reflect marine and terrestrial components of prehistoric human diet. *Science* **220**:1381–1383

Schoeninger, M. J., B.K. Nelson and M.J. DeNiro. 1984. Bone strontium levels in modern animals and strontium isotopic evidence for diagenetic alteration of bone: consequences for diet reconstruction. Paper presented at the Annual Meeting of the American Association of Physical Anthropologists, Philadelphia

Schroeder, H. A. 1973. *The Trace Elements and Man* (Old Greenwich, Connecticut: Devin-Adair Co.)

Schroeder, H. A., J. J. Balassa, and I. H. Tipton. 1963. Abnormal trace metals in man: vanadium. *Journal of Chronic Diseases* **16**:1047–1071

1966a. Essential trace metals in man: manganese. *Journal of Chronic Diseases* **19**:545–571

Schroeder, H. A., A. P. Nason, I. H. Tipton, and J. J. Balassa. 1966b. Essential trace metals in man: copper. *Journal of Chronic Diseases* **19**:1007–1034

1967. Essential trace metals in man: zinc. *Journal of Chronic Diseases* **20**:179–210

Schroeder, H. A., A. P. Nason, and I. H. Tipton. 1969. Essential trace

metals in man: magnesium. *Journal of Chronic Diseases* **21**: 815–841
Schroder, H. A., I. H. Tipton, and A. P. Nason. 1972. Trace metals in man: strontium and barium. *Journal of Chronic Diseases* **25**:491–517
Schwarcz, H. P., J. Melbye, M. A. Katzenberg, and M. Knyf. 1985. Stable isotopes in human skeletons of southern Ontario: reconstructing paleodiet. *Journal of Archaeological Science* **12**:187–206
Sciulli, P. W., B. W. Aument, and L. R. Piotrowski. 1982. The Williams (33Wo7A) Red Ochre cemetery: preliminary description and comparative analysis of acquired dental pathology. *Pennsylvania Archaeologist* **52**:17–24
Sealy, J. C. 1984. Stable carbon isotopic assessment of prehistoric diets in the southwestern Cape, South Africa (M.Sc. thesis, University of Cape Town)
Sealy, J. C., and N. J. van der Merwe. 1985. Isotope assessment of Holocene human diets in the southwestern Cape, South Africa. *Nature* **315**:138–140
1986. Isotopic assessment of Holocene human diets in the southwestern Cape, South Africa. *Current Anthropology* **27**:135–150
Shipman, P. 1981. *Life History of a Fossil* (Cambridge: Harvard University Press)
Shipman, P., A. Walker, and D. Bichell. 1985. *The Human Skeleton* (Cambridge, Harvard University Press)
Silberbauer, F. B. 1979. Stable carbon isotopes and prehistoric diets in the eastern Cape Province, South Africa (M.A. thesis, University of Cape Town)
Sillen, A. 1981a. Strontium and diet at Hayonim cave. *American Journal of Physical Anthropology* **56**:131–137
1981b. Strontium and diet at Hayonim Cave, Israel: an evaluation of the strontium/calcium technique for investigating prehistoric diets (Ph.D. dissertation, Department of Anthropology, University of Pennsylvania)
1981c. Post-depositional changes in Natufian and Aurignacian bones from Hayonim Cave. *Paleorient* 7(2):81–85
1986. Biogenic and diagenetic Sr/Ca in Plio-Pleistocene fossils of the Omo Shungura formation. *Paleobiology* **12**:311–323
Sillen, A., and M. Kavanagh. 1982. Strontium and paleodietary research: a review. *Yearbook of Physical Anthropology* **25**:67–90
Sillen, A., and P. Smith. 1984. Sr/Ca ratios in juvenile skeletons portray weaning practices in a medieval Arab population. *Journal of Archaeological Science* **11**:237–245
Simpson, D. R. 1972. Problems of the composition and structure of the bone minerals. *Clinical Orthopaedics and Related Research* **86**:260–286
Sinex, F. M., and B. Faris. 1959. Isolation of gelatin from ancient bones. *Science* **129**:969

Singer, C. 1976. Puerto Moorin lithics: analysis and implications. Paper presented to the 75th Annual Meeting of the American Anthropological Association, Washington, D.C.

1977. A possible Early Horizon ceremonial complex in the Viru valley, Peru. Paper presented to the 17th Annual Meeting of the Institute of Andean Studies, Berkeley, Calif.

1978. Early metallurgical materials from the Viru valley, Peru. Paper presented to the 18th Annual Meeting of the Institute of Andean Studies, Berkeley, Calif.

Sinkins, K., and C. Taylor. 1958. Reactions between egg-shell matrix and metallic cations. *Quarterly Journal of Microscopical Science* 99:55–62

Siperstein, M. D., R. H. Unger, and L. L. Madison. 1970. Studies on muscle capillary basement membrane in normal subjects, diabetics and prediabetic patients. *Journal of Clinical Investigation* 49:2161–2164

Smith, B. N., and T. W. Boutton. 1981. Environmental influences on $^{13}C/^{12}C$ ratios and C_4 photosynthesis. In *Photosynthesis, IV. Photosynthesis and Productivity, Photosynthesis and Environment*, ed. G. Alcoynnoglon (Philadelphia: Balaban International Science Services)

Smith, B. N., and W. V. Brown. 1973. The Kranz syndrome in the Graminae as indicated by carbon isotope ratios. *American Journal of Botany* 6:505–513

Smith, B. N., and S. Epstein. 1971. Two categories of $^{13}C/^{12}C$ ratios for higher plants. *Plant Physiology* 47:380–384

Snyder, W. S., C. Feldman, I. H. Tipton, M. J. Cook, F. S. Jones, J. J. Shafer, and P. L. Stewart. 1964. Stable element metabolism. In *Health Physics Division Annual Progress Report*. Oak Ridge National Laboratory, Publication 3697, pp. 178–188

Snyder, W. S., M. J. Cook, L. R. Karhausen, E. S. Nasset, G. P. Howells, and I. H. Tipton. 1975. Report of the task group on Reference Man: ICRP Publication 23 (Oxford: Pergamon)

Sofer, Zvi. 1980. A simplified method for the preparation of CO_2 for stable carbon isotope analysis of petroleum fractions. *Analytical Chemistry* 52:1389–1391

Sokal, R. R., and F. J. Rohlf. 1969. *Biometry* (San Francisco: W. H. Freeman)

Sokolov, R. 1986. The good seed. *Natural History*, April: 102–105

Sowden, E. M., and S. R. Stitch. 1957. Trace elements in human tissue. *Biochemistry Journal* 67:104–109

Spadaro, J. A. 1969. Trace metal ions in bone and collagen (Ph.D. dissertation, Syracuse University)

Spadaro, J. A., R. O. Becker, and C. H. Bachman. 1970. Size-specific metal complexing sites in native collagen. *Nature* 225:1134–1136

Spielmann, K. A. 1982. Inter-societal food acquisition among egalitarian societies: an ecological analysis of plains/pueblo interaction in the

American Southwest (Ph.D. dissertation, University of Michigan, Ann Arbor)
Stenhouse, M. J., and M. S. Baxter. 1979. The uptake of bomb ^{14}C in humans. In *Radiocarbon Dating*, ed. R. Berger and H. E. Suess (Berkeley: University of California Press)
Stevenson, F. J. 1982. *Humus Chemistry* (New York: Wiley)
Stoltman, J. B. 1978. Temporal models in prehistory: an example from the eastern United States. *Current Anthropology* 19:703–746
Strong, W. D., and Evans, C. 1952. *Cultural Stratigraphy in the Viru Valley, Northern Peru: The Formative and Florescent Epochs* (New York: Columbia University Press)
Stuiver, M. 1978. Atmospheric carbon dioxide and carbon reservoir changes. *Science* 199:253–258
1983. Comment following B. S. Chisholm, D. E. Nelson and H. P. Schwarcz. Dietary information from $\delta^{13}C$ and $\delta^{15}N$ measurements on bone collagen. Presented to symposium held at Groningen, August 1981. *PACT 8 (^{14}C and Archaeology)*, p. 397
Stuiver, M., R. L. Burk, and P. D. Quay. 1984. $^{13}C/^{12}C$ ratios in tree rings and the transfer of biospheric carbon to the atmosphere. *Journal of Geophysical Research* 89(D7):11731–11748
Stump, R. K., and J. W. Fraser. 1973. Simultaneous determination of carbon, hydrogen, and nitrogen in organic compounds. *Nuclear Science Abstracts* 28:746
Styles, R. 1986. Faunal exploitation and resource selection. Scientific Papers, no. 3: Archaeological Program, Northwestern University, Evanston, Ill.
Styles, T. R. 1985. Holocene and late Pleistocene geology of the Napoleon Hollow site in the lower Illinois valley. Center for American Archaeology, Kampsville Archaeological Center, Research Series, vol. 5, Kampsville, Ill.
Sullivan, C. H., and H. W. Krueger. 1981. Carbon isotope analysis of separate chemical phases in modern and fossil bone. *Nature* 292:333–335
Suttles, W. P. 1968. Coping with abundance: subsistence on the northwest coast. In *Man the Hunter*, ed. R. B. Lee and I. DeVore (New York: Aldine)
Szpunar, C. 1977. Atomic absorption of archaeological remains: human ribs from Woodland mortuary sites (Ph.D. dissertation, Northwestern University)
Szpunar, C. B., J. B. Lambert, and J. E. Buikstra. 1978. Analysis of excavated bone by atomic absorption. *American Journal of Physical Anthropology* 48:199–202
Tanaka, G. I., H. Kawamura, and E. Nomura. 1981. Reference Japanese Man, II: distribution of strontium in the skeleton and in the mass of mineralized bone. *Health Physics* 40:601–614
Tanzer, M. L. 1982. Collagen biosynthesis and degradation. In *Disorders*

of Mineral Metabolism, vol. II: *Calcium Physiology*, ed. F. Bonner and J. W. Coburn (New York: Academic Press)

Tauber, H. 1979. C-14 activity of Arctic marine mammals. In *Radiocarbon Dating*, ed. R. Berger and H. E. Suess (Berkeley: University of California Press)

1981. $\delta^{13}C$ evidence for dietary habits of prehistoric man in Denmark. *Nature* **292**:332–333

Taylor, R. E., and R. Berger. 1967. Radiocarbon content of marine shells from the Pacific coasts of Central and South America. *Science* **158**:1180–1182

Termine, J. D., and D. R. Lundy. 1973. Hydroxide and carbonate in rat bone mineral and its synthetic analogues. *Calcified Tissue Research* **13**:73–82

Termine, J. D., A. B. Belcourt, K. M. Conn, and H. K. Kleinman. 1981a. Mineral and collagen-binding proteins of fetal calf bone. *Journal of Biological Chemistry* **256**:10403–10408

Termine, J. D., H. K. Kleinman, S. W. Whitson, K. M. Conn, M. L. McGarvey, and G. R. Martin. 1981b. Osteonectin, a bone-specific protein linking mineral to collagen. *Cell* **26**:99

Terri, J. A., and D. A. Schoeller. 1979. $\delta^{13}C$ values of an herbivore and the ratio of C_3 to C_4 plant carbon in its diet. *Oecologia* **39**:197–200

Terri, J. A., and L. G. Stowe. 1976. Climatic patterns and distribution of C_4 grasses in North America. *Oecologia* **23**:1–12

Terri, J. A., L. G. Stowe, and D. A. Livingstone. 1980. The distribution of C_4 species of the Cyperaceae in North America in relation to climate. *Oecologia* **47**:307–310

Tieszen, L. L. 1978. Carbon isotope fractionation in biological materials. *Nature* **276**:97–98

1984. Personal communication to M. Schoeninger. Gordon Conference, Oxnard, Calif.

Tieszen, L., and S. K. Imbamba. 1979. Photosynthetic systems, carbon isotope discrimination, and herbivore selectivity in Kenya, East Africa. Manuscript, Augustana College, Sioux Falls, South Dakota

Tieszen, L. L., M. M. Senyimba, S. K. Imbamba, and J. H. Troughton. 1979a. The distribution of C_3 and C_4 grasses and carbon isotope discrimination along an altitudinal and moisture gradient in Kenya. *Oecologia* **37**:337–350

Tieszen, L. L., D. Hein, S. A. Qvortrup, J. H. Troughton, and S. K. Imbamba. 1979b. Use of $\delta^{13}C$ values to determine vegetation selectivity in East African herbivores. *Oecologia* **37**:351–359

Tieszen, L. L., T. W. Boutton, K. G. Terdahl, and N. A. Slade. 1983. Fractionation and turnover of stable carbon isotopes in animal tissues: implications for $\delta^{13}C$ analysis of diet. *Oecologia* **57**:32–37

Toots, H., and M. R. Voorhies. 1965. Strontium in fossil bones and the reconstruction of food chains. *Science* **149**:854–855

Tosi, J. 1960. Zonas de vida natural en el Peru. *Instituto Interamericano de Ciencias Agricolas Boletin*, Tecnico No. 5, Lima

Treagan, L. 1984. Metals and immunity. In *Metal Ions in Biological Systems*, vol. 16, ed. H. Sigel (New York: Marcel Dekker)

Troughton, J. H. 1971. Aspects of the evolution of the photosynthetic carboxylation reaction in plants. In *Photosynthesis and Photorespiration*, ed. M. D. Hatch, E. B. Osmond, and R. O. Slayter (New York: Wiley Interscience)

Turekian, K. K., and J. L. Kulp. 1956. Strontium content of human bone. *Science* **124**:405–407

Tuross, N., D. R. Eyre, M. E. Holtrop, M. Glimcher, and P. E. Hare. 1980. Collagen in fossil bone. In *Biogeochemistry of Amino Acids*, ed. P. E. Hare, T. C. Hoering, and J. K. King (New York: Wiley)

Underwood, E. J. 1977. *Trace Elements in Human and Animal Nutrition* (New York: Academic Press)

Urist, M. R., and J. L. Abermethy. 1967. Effects of calcium ion upon structure and calcifiability of tendon: observation on xenogeneic transplants in the anterior chamber of the rat's eye. *Clinical Orthopaedics and Related Research* **51**:255–261

Van der Merwe, N. J. 1978. Carbon 12 vs. carbon 13. *Early Man* **2**:11–13

1982. Carbon isotopes, photosynthesis and archaeology. *American Scientist* **70**:596–606

1986. Carbon isotope ecology of herbivores and carnivores. In *Paleoecology of Africa*, vol. 17, ed. E. M. van Zinderen Bakker, J. A. Coetzee, and L. Scott (Rotterdam: A. A. Balkema)

Van der Merwe, N. J., and J. C. Vogel. 1978. ^{13}C content of human collagen as a measure of prehistoric diet in Woodland North America. *Nature* **276**:815–816

1983. Recent carbon isotope research and its implications for African archaeology. *African Archaeological Review* **1**:33–56

Van der Merwe, N. J., A. C. Roosevelt, and J. C. Vogel. 1981. Isotopic evidence for prehistoric subsistence change at Parmana, Venezuela. *Nature* **292**:536–538

Van der Merwe, N. J., J. Lee Thorp, and R. H. V. Bell. 1986. Carbon isotopes as indications of elephant diets and African environments. In *Paleoecology of Africa*, vol. 17, ed. E. M. van Zinderen Bakker, J. A. Coetzee, and L. Scott (Rotterdam: A. A. Balkema)

van Wijngaarden-Bakker, L., and J. P. Pals. 1981. Life and work in Smeerenburg: the bio-archaeological aspects. Paper presented at the International Symposium of the Arctic Center, Early European Exploitation of the Northern Atlantic 800–1700 A.D.

Veis, A. 1964. *The Macromolecular Chemistry of Gelatin* (New York: Academic Press)

Veis, A. 1967. *Treatise on Collagen* (New York: Academic Press)

Virginia, R. A., and C. C. Delwiche. 1982. Natural ^{15}N abundance of presumed N_2-fixing and non- N_2-fixing plants from selected ecosystems. *Oecologia* **54**:317–325

Vlasak, S. M. 1983. Elemental analysis of excavated human bone: a study of post-mortem deterioration (Ph.D. dissertation, Northwestern University)

Vogel, J. C. 1978. Isotopic assessment of the dietary habits of ungulates. *South African Journal of Science* **74**:298–301

1980. *Fractionation of the Carbon Isotopes During Photosynthesis* (New York: Springer)

1982. Koolstofisotoopsamestelling van plantproteine. *Die Suid-Afrikaanse Tydskrif vir Natguurwetenskap en Tegnologie* **1**:7–8

1983. Isotopic evidence for the past climates and vegetation of South Africa. *Bothalia* **14**:391–394

Vogel, J. C., and N. J. van der Merwe. 1977. Isotopic evidence for early maize cultivation in New York State. *American Antiquity* **42**:238–242

Vogel, J. C., A. Fuls, and R. P. Ellis. 1978. The geographical distribution of Kranz grass in South Africa. *South African Journal of Science* **74**:209–215

Von Endt, D. W., and D. J. Ortner. 1984. Experimental effects of bone size and temperature on bone diagenesis. *Journal of Archaeological Science* **11**:247–253

Von Schirnding, Y., N. J. van der Merwe, and J. C. Vogel. 1982. Influence of diet and age on carbon isotope ratios in ostrich eggshells. *Archaeometry* **24**:3–20

Wada, E. 1980. Nitrogen isotope fractionation and its significance in biogeochemical processes occurring in marine environments. In *Geochemical Journal* (Nagoya)

Wada, E. T., T. Kadonaga, and S. Matsuo. 1975. ^{15}N abundance in nitrogen of naturally occurring substances and global assessment of dentrification, the isotopic viewpoint. *Geochemistry Journal* **9**:139–148

Wadkins, C. L. 1968. Experimental factors that influence collagen calcification in-vitro. *Calcified Tissue Research* **2**:214–221

Waldron, H. A. 1981. Post-mortem absorption of lead by the skeleton. *American Journal of Physical Anthropology* **55**:395–398

Waldron, T., and C. Wells. 1979. Exposure to lead in ancient populations. *Transactions and Studies of the College of Physicians of Philadelphia* **1**(2):102–115

Walker, P. W., and M. J. DeNiro. 1986. Stable carbon and nitrogen isotope ratios in bone collagen as indices of prehistoric dietary dependence on marine and terrestrial resources in southern California. *American Journal of Physical Anthropology* **71**:51–61

Watt, B. K., and A. L. Merrill. 1975. *Handbook of the Nutritional Contents of Foods* (New York: Dover)

Weatherell, J. A., and C. Robinson. 1973. The inorganic composition of teeth. In *Biological Mineralization*, ed. I. Zipkin (New York: Wiley)

West, M. 1970. Prehistoric environment in Viru valley, Peru, and its implications for culture change. Paper presented to the 10th Annual Meeting of the Institute of Andean Studies, Berkeley, Calif.

1971a. Prehistoric human ecology in Viru valley, Peru. *California Anthropologist* 1(1):47–56

1971b. Prehistoric human ecology in Viru valley, Peru. *California Anthropologist* 1(2):22–32

1974. Prehistoric irrigation and society in Viru valley, Peru. Paper presented to the Annual Meeting of the Southwestern Anthropological Association, Santa Monica, Calif.

1976. Prehistoric environment and cultivation in the Viru valley, Peru. Paper presented to the 75th Annual Meeting of the American Anthropological Association, Washington, D.C.

1977. The Viru valley culture–historical model: a reassessment. Paper presented to the 76th Annual Meeting of the American Anthropological Association, Washington, D.C.

1979. Early water table farming on the north coast of Peru. *American Antiquity* 44:138–144

1980a. Prehistoric resource exploitation in the Viru valley, Peru. In *Catchment Analysis: Essays on Prehistoric Resource Base*, ed. F. Findlow and J. Ericson. Anthropology U.C.L.A., vols. 10–11. Department of Anthropology, University of California, Los Angeles

1980b. Nutritional stress and prehistoric population control in the Viru valley, Peru. Paper presented at the Annual Meeting of the Southwestern Anthropological Association, San Diego, Calif.

1981. Agricultural resource use in an Andean coastal ecosystem. *Human Ecology* 9:47–78

West, M., and T. Whitaker. 1979. Prehistoric cultivated cucurbits from the Viru valley, Peru. *Journal of Economic Botany* 33:275–279

Wetterstrom, W. 1986. *Food, Diet, and Population at Prehistoric Arroyo Hondo Pueblo, New Mexico*. Arroyo Hondo Archaeological Series (Santa Fe: School of American Research)

White, A., P. Handler, E. L. Smith, R. L. Hill, and I. R. Lehman. 1978. *Principles of Biochemistry*, 6th edn. (New York: McGraw Hill)

White, C. D. 1986. Paleodiet and nutrition of the ancient Maya at Lananai, Belize: as indicated by trace elements, stable isotopes, nutritional and dental pathologies (M.A. thesis, Department of Anthropology, Trent University)

White, E. M., and Hannus, L. A. 1983. Chemical weathering of bone in archaeological sites. *American Antiquity* 48:316–322

Willey, G. 1946. The Viru valley program in northern Peru. *Acta Americana* 4:224–238

1953. Prehistoric settlement patterns in the Viru valley, Peru. *Bureau of American Ethnology Bulletin* no. 155 (Washington, D.C.: Smithsonian Institution)

Willman, H. B., and J. C. Frye. 1970. Pleistocene stratigraphy of Illinois. *Illinois State Geological Survey, Bulletin*, no. 94, Urbana, Ill.
Wilson, D. J. 1981. Of maize and men: a critique of the maritime hypothesis of state origins on the coast of Peru. *American Anthropologist* 83:93–120
Wing, E., and A. B. Brown. 1979. *Paleonutrition* (New York: Academic Press)
Winter, K., J. H. Troughton, and K. A. Card. 1976. $\delta^{13}C$ values of grass species collected in the northern Sahara desert. *Oecologia* 25:115–123
Winterhalder, B. 1986. Diet choice, risk, and food sharing in a stochastic environment. *Journal of Anthropological Archaeology* 5:369–392
Wong, W. W. and W. M. Sackett. 1978. Fractionation of stable carbon isotopes by marine phytoplankton. *Geochimica et Cosmochimica Acta* 42:1809–1815
Woodhead-Galloway, J. 1982. *Collagen: The Anatomy of a Protein* (London: Edward Arnold)
Wyckoff, R. W. G. 1972. *The Biochemistry of Animal Fossils* (Bristol: Scientechnics)
Yablonskii, M. F. 1971. Use of differences in bone mineral content for identification of corpses. Sbornik Nauchngkh Trudor Vinnitskogo Gosudarstvennogo Meditsinskgogo Instituta. Collection of Scientific Works of the Vinnitsa State Medical Institute 14:368–374
1973. Identificational significance of major and trace elements of human long tubular bones. Sudebno-Meditsinskaya Ekspertiza, Ministerstvo Zdravookhraneniya SSSR. Forensic-Medical Arbitration, Ministry of Public Health of the USSR 16:16–18
Yutani, K., K. Ogasahara, and Y. Sugino. 1985. Effect of amino acid substitutions on conformational stability of a protein. *Advances in Biophysics* 20:13–29

Index

Page numbers in italics refer to figures and tables

Index

Index

Index

Index